HOSPITALITY
MANAGEMENT

An Introduction to the Industry

Robert A. Brymer

Florida State University

Seventh Edition

KENDALL/HUNT PUBLISHING COMPANY
Dubuque, Iowa

——Dedication————————————

The seventh edition of this book is dedicated to my family, the most important people in the world to me.

Becky, Renee, Ryan, and Rhett; Ann and Andy; Sandi, Billy, Corey, and Kristen; Patti, Jim, Ross, Reed, and Nicole; Jane, Shannon, and Brent.

Grandmother Myrtle and Grandfather Otto; Lorraine and Wayne; Chris, Tommy, Tyler, and Wesley; Lisa, Jimmy, and Drew; Myrtle and Otto; Vic; Dorthy and Art; Diana, Artie, Kevin, and Lacey; Leigh Ann, Mark, and Kaitlyn; Kim, Donnie, Derek, and Kristi; Toni, Timmy, Ben, Trent, Brad, and Renee; Ruth Ann and Stub; Rick; Joni; Laurie, Bryan, and Kari; Sandy and Dick; Nancy, Bill, and Steven; Wendy, John, Ryan, Nicole, and Johnny; Susie, Tom, Tommy, and Shannon; Audrey; Pam, Jennette, and Jennifer; Claudette and John; Aunt Mable; Virginia and Bob; Karen, Jack, Abby, and Sarah; Nancy, Wendy, and Bryan.

Grandmother Alma and Grandfather Andrew; Bubbles and Bill; Chris, Tom, Julianne, and Tommy; Barb and Bob; Katherine; Marie Louise and Greg; Karen; Ruthie and George; Vickie and Georgie; Linda, Warren, Lauren, and Cyndi; Janet, Trisha, and Corie; Eunice and John; Julie, Ed, Sarah, Nick, Callie, Matthew, and Cynda; Melody, Rod, Julie, and Wendy; Bob; Alice and Howard; Kathy, Tim, Andy, Scott, and Doug; Tom, Jeff and Wendy; and Jim.

Grace and Victor; Jean, George, Evan, Dee Dee, and Rebecca; Vicki and Ryan; Rhonda and Dan.

────Contents────

III Hospitality Organizations

IV Hospitality Operations

VI Hospitality Industry Career Menu

Acknowledgments

The seventh edition of this book is a compilation of readings from 62 different authors, representing 36 colleges and universities across the United States and Canada. These authors have written readings specifically for this book, and without their generous contributions the publication of this outstanding edition would have been impossible. I am very grateful to each and every author for the special role they played in creating this edition of the book, now in its seventeenth year of print.

The following is an alphabetized list of these authors.

John C. Baker, Assistant Professor
Department of Hotel, Restaurant, and
  Institutional Management
Indiana University of Pennsylvania
Indiana, PA 15705

Melissa Dallas Bandy, Director
Hospitality Management Program
Bowling Green State University
Bowling Green, OH 43403

Melvin N. Barrington, Chairman
Hotel, Restaurant, and Tourism
  Administration
University of South Carolina
Columbia, SC 29208

Clayton W. Barrows, Assistant Professor
School of Hotel, Restaurant, and Tourism
  Administration
University of New Orleans
New Orleans, LA 70148

Robert H. Bosselman, Associate Professor
Department of Hotel, Restaurant,
  and Travel Administration
University of Massachusetts
Amherst, MA 01003

Deborah Breiter, Assistant Professor
Harrah College of Hotel Administration
University of Nevada, Las Vegas
Las Vegas, NV 89154

Richard L. Brush, Chairman, Lodging
The Hospitality College
Johnson and Wales University
Providence, RI 02903

Robert A. Brymer, Professor
Department of Hospitality Administration
Florida State University
Tallahassee, Florida 32306

Polly Buchanan, Associate Professor
Hospitality Management Program
Eastern Michigan University
Ypsilanti, MI 48197

Ronald F. Cichy, Director
School of Hotel, Restaurant, and
    Institutional Management
Michigan State University
East Lansing, MI 48824–1121

Caroline A. Cooper, Assistant Dean
The Hospitality College
Johnson and Wales University
Providence, RI 02903

David A. Cranage, Instructor
School of Hotel, Restaurant, and
    Recreational Management
Pennsylvania State University
University Park, PA 16802

Linsley T. DeVeau, Dean
School of Hotel, Restaurant, and
    Tourism Administration
Lynn University
Boca Raton, FL 33431

Patricia E. Diaz, Administrative
    Coordinator
Department of Hotel and Restaurant
    Administration
Washington State University
Pullman, WA 99164

Duncan R. Dickson, Director of Casting
Walt Disney World Company
P.O. Box 10,000
Lake Buena Vista, FL 32830

Frédéric Dimanche, Assistant Professor
School of Hotel, Restaurant, and
    Tourism Administration
University of New Orleans
New Orleans, LA 70148

H. A. Divine, Director
School of Hotel, Restaurant, and Tourism
    Management
University of Denver
Denver, CO 80208

Vincent H. Eade, Associate Professor
Harrah College of Hotel Administration
University of Nevada, Las Vegas
Las Vegas, NV 89154

Taylor Ellis, Associate Professor
Department of Hospitality Management
University of Central Florida
Orlando, FL 32816

Stevenson W. Fletcher, III, Professor
Department of Hotel, Restaurant, and
    Travel Administration
University of Massachusetts
Amherst, MA 01003

Sheryl Fried, Associate Professor
School of Hotel and Restaurant
    Management
Widener University
Chester, PA 19013–5792

Jenene G. Garey, Associate Professor
Nutrition, Food, and Hotel Management
New York University
New York, NY 10003

Chuck Y. Gee, Dean
School of Travel Industry Management
University of Hawaii
Honolulu, HA 96822

R. Thomas George, Associate Professor
Hospitality Management Program
Ohio State University
Columbus, OH 43210

Gary A. Hamilton, Professor
School of Hotel and Restaurant
    Management
California State Polytechnic University
Pomona, CA 91768

Lynn M. Huffman, Chairperson
Education, Nutrition, Restaurant and
    Hotel Management
Texas Tech University
Lubbock, TX 79409–1162

William F. Jaffé, Assistant Professor
Department of Restaurant, Hotel, and
    Institutional Managementl
Purdue University
West Lafayette, IN 47907

Michael Kaile, General Manager
Waterfront Centre Hotel
900 Canada Place Way
Vancouver, BC V6C 3K2

Michael L. Kasavana, Professor
School of Hotel, Restaurant, and
    Institutional Management
Michigan State University
East Lansing, MI 48824

William E. Kent, Director
Hotel and Restaurant Management Program
Auburn University
Auburn, AL 36849

Ray D. Langbehn, Assistant Professor
Department of Hospitality, Meeting,
    and Travel Administration
Metropolitan State College of Denver
Denver, CO 80217–3362

Michael M. Lefever, Head
Department of Hotel, Restaurant,
    and Travel Administration
University of Massachusetts
Amherst, MA 01003

William F. Lougheed, Professor
School of Hospitality and Tourism
    Management
Ryerson Polytechnic Institute
Toronto, Ontario
Canada M5B 2K3

Jeannine L. Ludwick
1173 Montgomery St.
W. Lafayette, IN 47906

Ken W. McCleary, Professor
Department of Hotel, Restaurant,
    and Institutional Management
Virginia Polytechnic Institute and
    State University
Blacksburg, VA 24061

Audrey C. McCool, Chairperson
Department of Food and Beverage
    Management
Harrah College of Hotel Administration
University of Nevada, Las Vegas
Las Vegas, NV 89154–6022

William E. Miller, Director
Isbell Ethics Center
School of Hotel and Restaurant
    Management
Northern Arizona University
Flagstaff, AZ 86011

Leland L. Nicholls, Director
Center for Hospitality and Tourism
    Research and Services
Department of Hospitality and Tourism
University of Wisconsin–Stout
Menomonie, WI 54751

Jane Boyd Ohlin, Associate Professor
Department of Hospitality Administration
Florida State University
Tallahassee, FL 32306

Gary S. Page, Associate Professor
Hospitality and Tourism Management
    Program
Grand Valley State University
Allendale, MI 49401

Alan Paret, Assistant Professor
School of Hospitality Administration
Boston University
Boston, MA 02215

David V. Pavesic, Director
Cecil B. Day School of Hospitality
    Administration
Georgia State University
Atlanta, GA 30302

Larry Joe Perdue, Director
Business Management Institute Programs
Cecil B. Day School of Hospitality
    Administration
Georgia State University
Atlanta, GA 30303

Boyce W. Phillips, Associate Professor
Harrah College of Hotel Administration
University of Nevada, Las Vegas
Las Vegas, NV 89154

Lalia C. Rach, Dean
School of Hotel, Restaurant, and
    Tourism Administration
University of New Haven
West Haven, CT 06516

Robert D. Reid, Department Head
Department of Marketing and Hotel
    and Restaurant Management
James Madison University
Harrisonburg, VA 22801

Raymond S. Schmidgall, Professor
School of Hotel, Restaurant, and
    Institutional Management
Michigan State University
East Lansing, MI 48824

Teresa M. Schulz, Professor
Department of Hospitality and Tourism
University of Wisconsin–Stout
Menomonie, WI 54751

Michael Sciarini, Assistant Professor
School of Hotel, Restaurant, and
    Institutional Management
Michigan State University
East Lansing, MI 48824–1121

Gary M. Shingler, Assistant Professor
Department of Restaurant, Hotel,
    and Institutional Management
Purdue University
West Lafayette, IN 47907

Donald I. Smith, Professor
Department of Hotel and Restaurant
    Administration
Washington State University
Pullman, WA 99164

Yvonne L. Spaulding, Assistant Professor
Department of Hospitality, Meeting,
    and Travel Administration
Metropolitan State College of Denver
Denver, CO 80217–3362

John M. Stefanelli, Professor
Harrah College of Hotel Administration
University of Nevada, Las Vegas
Las Vegas, NV 89154

David L. Tucker, Associate Professor
School of Hotel and Restaurant
    Management
Widener University
Chester, PA 19013–5792

Hubert B. VanHoof, Assistant Professor
School of Hotel and Restaurant
    Management
Northern Arizona University
Flagstaff, AZ 86011–5638

Andrew N. Vladimir, Assistant Professor
School of Hospitality Management
Florida International University
North Miami, FL 33181

Thomas E. Walsh, Department Head
Department of Hotel, Restaurant,
    and Institutional Management
Iowa State University
Ames, IA 50011

Pamela A. Weaver, Professor
Department of Hotel, Restaurant,
    and Institutional Management
Virginia Polytechnic Institute and
    State University
Blacksburg, VA 24061

Leslie Stevens Weinberg, Professor
School of Hotel and Restaurant
    Management
California State Polytechnic University
Pomona, CA 91768

Richard A. Wentzel, Associate Professor
The Hospitality College
Johnson and Wales University
Providence, RI 02903

Lawrence Yu, Assistant Professor
School of Hotel and Restaurant
    Management
Northern Arizona University
Flagstaff, AZ 86011–5638

Hospitality Industry

Part I

1

Overview of the Hospitality Industry

Robert A. Brymer, *Florida State University*
Lynn M. Huffman, *Texas Tech University*

Introduction

What is the hospitality industry? To those who are relatively unfamiliar with the industry, the term can be vague and imprecise. It may seem hard to be really sure what should be considered part of the hospitality industry. *Webster's Ninth New Collegiate Dictionary* characterizes it as "those businesses which practice the act of being hospitable; those businesses which are characterized by generosity and friendliness to guests." *Hospitality industry* is an umbrella term used to encompass the many and varied businesses that cater to guests.

Because the hospitality industry includes so many different types of activities, this chapter examines the specific businesses most commonly associated with the industry. There is no definitive list of the businesses that make up the hospitality industry. However, for the purposes of this chapter and the scope of this book, the focus will be on four large areas that comprise the major segments of the industry: food service, lodging, travel and tourism, and meeting and convention planning (Figure 1). These huge national and international businesses are unquestionably part of the hospitality industry. The concept of hospitality is the common bond among these businesses.

When attempting to develop an outline that includes all parts of these four large segments of the hospitality industry, it is difficult to know where to start. It is virtually impossible to identify every single type of business in the food service, lodging, travel and tourism, and meeting and convention planning segments, but Figure 2 provides a starting point. Each of the four segments has several subdivisions. These smaller components within each segment are closely related but uniquely different. Each provides guests with varying types of hospitality services.

Further exploring each of these four major areas of the hospitality industry will provide a better foundation from which to understand this complex field. The next few pages briefly examine the various types and characteristics of food service, lodging, travel and tourism, and meeting and convention planning.

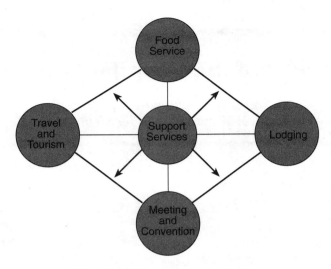

Figure 1. Hospitality Industry

Segments of the Hospitality Industry

Food Service

The food service business is the most expansive and diverse segment of the hospitality industry. It is the largest component of the hospitality industry and one of the largest industries in the United States and in the world. Even with its tremendous size, diversity, and integral relationship with the economy, food service operations still have a common thread—they all provide food prepared away from home for guests. Whether on an airplane, in a gourmet restaurant, or in an employee cafeteria, food service operations provide an essential and enjoyable part of life. The impact is so large that nearly one-half of all meals eaten in the United States today are provided by food service operations. The percentage of meals eaten away from home is increasing annually. The term *food service establishment* may also include operations that serve alcoholic beverages. It is not within the scope of this chapter to cover the varied beverage service operations, but be aware that any of the operations described in Table 1 may also serve alcoholic beverages.

Table 1 offers a general look at the most common types and characteristics of food service establishments and identifies some basic traits that exist in different types of operations. These should not be interpreted as the only characteristics found in food service operations

Food Service

Restaurants
Full Service
Theme
Coffee Shop
Cafeteria
Buffet
Quick Service

Lodging
Dining Room
Coffee Shop
Banquet
Room Service

Institutional
College
School
Hospital
Nursing Home
Military
Penal

Industrial
Centralized Employee Dining
Remote Employee Dining
Executive Dining
Vending

Clubs
Country Club
City Club

Catering
On Premise
Off Premise

Lodging

Luxury/Upscale Hotel
Hotel (Business/Convention Hotel)
All-Suite Hotel
Motor Hotels (Mid-Priced Hotels)
Bed and Breakfast Inns
Economy/Budget Motel
Resort/Gaming
Institutional Housing

Travel and Tourism

Travel
Transportation
Travel Agency
Tour Company
Recreation
Attractions/Destinations
Clubs
Parks

Meeting and Convention Planning

Meeting Planning
Convention Services

Support Services

Accounting
Human Resource Management
Marketing

Figure 2. Segments of the Hospitality Industry

Table 1. Types and Characteristics of Food Service Establishments

Restaurant	Size (in seats)	Location	Service
Full Service	75–200	Urban and suburban with high-traffic locations	Sit-down table service; often French service
Theme	100–400	Moderate traffic and shopping centers	Table service and beverage service
Coffee Shop	35–300	Moderate to heavy traffic areas	Service to table, booth, or counter
Cafeteria	100–400	Moderate traffic and shopping centers	Line service with limited beverage table service
Buffet	100–400	Free-standing near high traffic	Self-serve from buffet line
Quick Service	0–100	High-traffic locations with good accessibility	Inside counter service and drive-thru
Lodging Dining Room	75–200	In first-class hotels, resorts; on main floor or rooftop	Sit-down table service, often French service
Lodging Coffee Shop	100–300	In hotels, motor hotels, resorts	Casual table service; informal
Lodging Banquet	10–200	In hotels, motor hotels, resorts	Entire room served at one time—sit-down buffet service
Room Service	N/A	Food and beverage delivered to guest room	Convenience; food stored in warmer box; extended hours of service
Institutional/Contract	10–500	Integral part of larger organization	Very limited; self-service predominates; cafeteria or buffet
Industrial/Contract	Highly dependent on facility	Integral part of larger organization	Cafeterias, table service, vending, and snack bars
Clubs	50–300	Part of larger facility	Formal dining room, banquet services, beverage and snack bars
Catering	N/A	Food and beverage served on and off premises	Varied meals and functions

Price	Consumer	Menu	Management
High average check	Special occasion dinner crowd and business luncheons	Full range of items from appetizers to elaborate desserts	Independent or chain affiliated
Higher to moderate average check due to service and menu	Leisure dinner crowd and business luncheons and singles	Steaks, seafood, and ethnic specialties	Chain operation or franchise
Moderate average check varies due to location, service, and menu	Casual breakfast, luncheon, and dinner crowds	Wide range of items from appetizers to desserts	Chain operation or franchise
Moderate average check due to lesser services; a la carte pricing	Family; convenient; price-conscious consumer shoppers	Wide range of items on serving line	Chain operation
One price for entire meal, all you can eat	Price conscious	More limited than cafeteria but similar layout	Individual ownership or partnership
Lower average check because of limited service	Convenient and quick service with broad appeal	Limited to a few specialty items	Chain operation or franchise
High average check	In-house and local clientele	Limited to finely prepared items; often French cuisine	Under supervision of hotel food and beverage director
Moderate average check	In-house guests— breakfast and lunch	Wide range of items prepared for quick service	Under supervision of hotel food and beverage director
Moderate price on a per-person basis	Group functions and special occasions	Wide range of items— selected in advance	Under supervision of food and beverage director
Higher average check; 10-20% higher than the hotel restaurant	Weary traveler or those seeking privacy and convenience of room	Full range of items prepared for delivery	Under supervision of hotel food and beverage director
Often prepaid; daily, weekly and monthly prices available	Captive, consumer has limited or no choice	Limited to a few items per meal, cycle menu	Professional management, contract company, or government
Moderate average check	Captive, consumer has limited or no choice	Limited to a few items per serving	Professional management, contract company
Highly variable, good value for money	Members and other guests who expect high quality	Full range	Professional manager, hired by club members; or club management company
High average check; depends on menu and services	Serves special function needs of client	Full range—items selected in advance of meal	Individual proprietor or management company

as there is considerable overlap among the different categories. Many operations may fit into more than one category and some may not exactly fit into any category. However, it is useful in an overview to concentrate on the traits most often found. Despite the lack of absolutes the basic relationships and characteristics of many food service establishments can be set forth.

When you review Table 1, try to relate each type of food service operation to one with which you are personally familiar. Compare and contrast the characteristics, and notice how the establishments you are thinking of might match those described here.

Lodging

What is the first thing that comes to mind when thinking about the lodging business? For most people, the lodging industry is best represented by the large downtown luxury hotel or convention hotel or the lavish resort hotel. Such establishments account for most of the rooms in the lodging business but are only a small part of the actual number of lodging establishments in the country. The lodging industry is much more diverse than most people realize, and it seems that each year brings more diversity and specialization. For example, a hundred years ago travelers had little choice in lodging, with basically two types of establishments available: exclusive hotels for the upper class and modest rooming houses for everyone else. Today, travelers are faced with a myriad of choices ranging from luxury hotels, to bed and breakfast inns, to economy motels.

All lodging establishments have a single basic purpose—to serve the public by providing overnight accommodations away from home. Whether a high-priced secluded resort hotel or a college dormitory on a small campus, each provides temporary lodging away from a permanent residence.

Lodging establishments, though exhibiting differences in a variety of characteristics, are similar in many ways. Consequently, it is difficult to clearly distinguish among them at times, or to identify every type of facility available in one listing. Table 2 points out the characteristics of several types of lodging operations in a general way. Of course, there are exceptions and overlapping characteristics among the many types of lodging operations. However, this listing provides fundamental guidelines for categorizing various types of operations and gives the beginning student a basis for further learning and understanding.

Table 2 compares nine types of facilities in seven different ways. When reviewing the different types of establishments, try to envision an operation familiar to you and how the characteristics given might be similar to the one of which you are thinking.

Travel and Tourism

The travel and tourism industry is the largest in the world, generating the equivalent of more than $2 trillion U.S. annually. There is some dispute as to the correct definition of the travel and tourism industry. Some experts consider that travel and tourism is the umbrella term that covers the entire hospitality industry and thus includes all segments such as food service and lodging. Others feel that travel and tourism is merely a part of the hospitality industry, and is of equal importance with the other segments. For the purposes of this chapter the term *travel and tourism* is considered a part of the hospitality industry. Because travel and tourism is such a large and complex field, it is often divided into two areas: travel and recreation.

Travel

The travel segment of the hospitality industry involves the physical movement of people from one place to another. This includes transit to and from work each day, a short drive to a nearby resort, or a round-the-world trip requiring several weeks. The travel segment is composed of all businesses that cater to travelers' needs. For the purpose of this chapter, a traveler is considered one who leaves his residence usually for more than one day for business, pleasure, or some other personal or professional purpose. The travel industry is massive and multifaceted.

Transportation. Automobiles are the largest source of transportation for business or pleasure travel. The extensive interstate highway system and the network of state roadways make it possible to conveniently reach almost any location in the United States. Automobile travel has a widespread service infrastructure, which includes fueling stations, convenient lodging, gift shops, restaurants, state-supported rest areas, travel associations (i.e., the American Automobile Association), and other forms of service designed to meet the needs of the automobile traveler.

Airline travel has become the most convenient form of long distance travel in the world today. No longer does it take weeks to travel to another continent or days to reach a distant city in the United States. These trips are now taken in hours with relative comfort. As with automobile travel, air travel has spawned a large group of related service industries. Airline travelers have access to fast, efficient, safe, and comfortable aircraft; comfortable and efficient airports containing various food service operations, gift shops, and personal service activities as well as information and rest areas. Air travelers also count on extensive related travel services such as rental cars, shuttle vans, secure parking, etc.

Bus lines provide transportation for those who choose not to drive themselves or to fly. Buses are often the only source of public transportation to smaller cities and towns that airlines do not serve. In addition, many bus companies are in the charter and tour business. They provide transportation for groups on special trips and offer tours to unique tourist attractions in many parts of the world.

Railroads were the major source of long-distance travel in the United States before 1940. However, the automobile and airplane have appropriated a large share of the travel market, and railroads have become much less prominent in the overall passenger travel picture. Amtrak (the trade name for the National Railroad Passenger Corporation) is the major passenger railway system in the country. In parts of the country, particularly the East Coast,

Table 2. Types and Characteristics of Lodging Establishments

Type	Size	Location	Service
Luxury/Hotel Upscale	Small to midsize; 100–400 rooms	Large city with strong economic base	Extensive and very high quality; well-trained staff cater to all needs
Hotel/Convention Hotel Business/ Convention	Larger; 400 rooms and more, up to 2,000 rooms	Urban; downtown in large cities	Wide range of services available; doorman, room service, concierge and more; full-service staff
All-Suite Hotel	Small to midsize; 100–400 suites	Large city with transient population	Mid-range level of services; used by some guests as temporary housing
Motor Hotel— Mid-Priced	Midsized; 150–400 rooms	Suburban; in and near large cities; often at major interstate exits	Mid-range service available; fewer staff required
Economy/Budget	Smaller; 10–150 rooms	Rural and suburban, or near major highways or interstate roads	Limited range of service available; limited staff required
Bed and Breakfast Inn	Smaller; 10–150 rooms	Suburban and rural locations	Continental breakfast and early evening appetizers served in a casual central location
Resort/Gaming	100–500 rooms (can vary a great deal)	Isolated location; usually near geographical highlight (mountains, ocean, or lake)	Full range of services available; more than hotel because of isolated locations
Condominium Hotel/Time-Sharing	50–250 rooms (can vary a great deal); units often in smaller 4–5 unit clusters	Similar to resorts; rely on geographical highlight	Similar to resorts; optional housekeeping and other services
Institutional Housing	Larger; no normal range in number of rooms	Integral part of larger organization—military, college, or hospital	Very limited services available, self-serve predominates

Price	Consumer	Menu	Management
Very high room rate to cover additional services offered	Corporate officers, professionals, and upscale small meetings	Formal and very expensive decor, emphasis on tasteful appointments, quiet and sophisticated atmosphere	Professional management company
Higher average room rate; due in part to location, service, and facilities offered	Individual transient business traveler; group meetings and conventions; expense account business and meeting travelers	Elaborate and highly priced furniture and fixtures; large and attractive lobby; fine restaurants; extensive meeting space	Professional management company
Nightly, weekly, or monthly rates available	Business and family travelers; temporary residents	Similar to an apartment and nicely decorated	Professional management company
Mid-priced average room rate; between hotel and economy/ budget motel	Same as hotel except less affluent, also some leisure travel	Nicely appointed but not as elaborate or expensive as hotel; smaller lobby; coffee shop and dining room	Professional contract company, individual proprietor, or franchise
Lower average room rate, this is often primary attraction for customer	Overnight leisure travelers, en route to other destinations	Modest appointments to serve guest quickly and with no frills; little or no lobby; coffee shop or no food service	Individual proprietor or franchise
Mid-range price includes breakfast and appetizers	Business and leisure travelers seeking a more personal environment	Nicely appointed, often a converted plantation or new facility designed specifically for this market	Individual proprietor or chain affiliation
Higher average room rate due in part to location, service, and facilities; package prices available (American Plan) Casino hotels may have lower than average rates	Individual and family leisure destination point; group meetings and conventions	Elaborate and extensive development of recreation facilities; larger and attractive lobby; fine restaurants and meeting facilities may have casino	Independent or professional management company
Units are sold to individual owners— who live in and/or rent out; transient guests' prices similar to resorts	Individuals who purchase seek investment and vacation housing; transient guests seek as primary guest destination	Recreation facilities similar to resorts; smaller lobby; restaurant and meeting facilities; rooms are apartmentlike	Same as resort
Package price usually includes meals, often prepaid	Captive; individuals using other services of the organization; convenience and price conscious	Very modest, necessities provided for basic accommodations in a comfortable environment	Federal, state, local government; professional management company

it offers convenient service among several metropolitan centers. In other parts of the country service is more limited and infrequent. In recent years Amtrak has made a concerted effort to improve its travel network. However, the rail network probably will not be expanded unless the government supports the development of a high-speed train system (currently in use in Japan and Europe).

Passenger ships or cruise ships are popular with many travelers. These ships originally were designed to serve as transportation between distant cities in the world, and were the only transportation available until the development of airlines. Some ships still serve this purpose, but most now are considered floating resorts. They provide many of the amenities, services, and activities of fine resort hotels, with the added feature of touring different parts of the world (i.e., the Caribbean, Alaskan coast, or the Mediterranean). Many types and lengths of cruises are available. These range from the basic "barefoot" cruise on sailing ships, where passengers do part of the work in a rather spartan atmosphere, to the most luxurious environment where passengers are pampered and entertained, to educational and theme cruises. Cruise ships have enjoyed a resurgence in popularity in the past several years and serve as a unique traveling experience for many people.

Sightseeing companies serve the local transportation needs of arriving travelers by offering bus or taxi service from terminals to hotels or other accommodations. They also provide sightseeing tours to local points of interest at the destination.

Travel Agencies (Retail). The suppliers of travel products such as public transportation and accommodations need local sales outlets in every community that provides a market. Because it is not practical to have thousands of sales offices, the most effective means is to have an agent represent the various companies at the retail level. Such a business is called a travel agency. The travel agency provides two major types of services: making travel arrangements for their clients (customers), and giving advice as to the types of experiences and arrangements that would be most satisfying. This last service is very important if the traveler is going to a distant, unfamiliar destination or using an unfamiliar mode of travel.

Travel agencies do not charge clients for information or for making travel arrangements. Consequently, the traveler can obtain unbiased advice on all components of the trip at one place at one time. The travel agency is compensated by the travel product suppliers (e.g., airlines and hotels) in the form of commission based on sales.

Tour Companies (Wholesale). Tour companies are firms that organize and arrange the components of a group travel experience. The company may offer tours to a range of destinations or may specialize in one particular place. Tours may be for different lengths of time, different times of year, and different price levels to serve the needs of most travelers. An example would be a company that contracts with all necessary travel suppliers for a group wishing to visit the major capitals of Europe. Included would be the services for international transportation, hotels in various cities, meals, local transportation, and sightseeing.

Tour group members pay a fixed price. The tour brochure lists the travel services included for the price, so the prospective customers can determine the approximate cost in advance. Tour groups may be composed entirely of people acquainted with each other (friends, club members, or church groups) or may be individuals or very small groups interested in travel to the tour destination. Group members typically assemble at a predetermined point such as an airline counter at the airport and meet the escort accompanying them on the trip. The convenience of one-price travel along with the companionship and safety of a group have made tours quite popular.

Tour companies are often called wholesalers because they don't usually sell their tours directly to clients. Instead, they usually sell their tours through travel agents, who are paid a commission for tours sold.

Recreation

Recreation is another huge and complex segment of the hospitality industry. Visiting a local city playground, spending an evening at an amusement park, or playing golf at a luxurious country club are all part of the recreation business. Recreation is defined by one source as "any play, amusement, etc. used for refreshment of body and mind." The very nature of the recreation business is to provide many forms of recreation and relaxation to the public to use and enjoy. Recreation is closely intertwined with other areas of the hospitality industry. Food service, lodging, and travel are often an integral part of the recreation experience. The recreation business has three major components—attractions, clubs, and public parks—which are discussed in the next sections.

Attractions. Theme parks are an outgrowth of local amusement parks, still thriving in many areas of the country, with thrilling rides, cotton candy, and a carnival-like atmosphere. Theme parks differ considerably from the traditional amusement park in that they provide a wide array of entertainment for their guests. The entertainment is built around a particular theme or specialty created specifically for the park. Some of the best-known theme parks are Disneyland/Disney World, Sea World, Six Flags, Kings Island, Cedar Point, and Universal Studios. These parks normally have an extensive range of rides, food and beverage operations, gift shops, hotels, campgrounds, and shows for their audiences. Such parks are fun and enjoyable for people of all ages and often provide days of ongoing entertainment.

Sporting events are often the theme for popular, usually seasonal, attractions. Baseball parks, football stadiums, race tracks, and arenas for hockey and basketball are all popular locations for recreation. These facilities have food and beverage operations, retail operations for souvenirs, and occasionally hotels and campgroups associated with the facility. Both tourists and local residents often take advantage of these opportunities for an enjoyable afternoon or evening of entertainment and relaxation.

Scenic attractions are also a large part of the recreation business. Whether it be the local fishing hole, the beach, or a mountaintop ski resort, all offer recreational opportunities. These activities require many support services, including food service, lodging, equipment rental, and service, transportation.

Some attractions relate to special activities in a region or city that happen infrequently, perhaps annually, but are very meaningful to the area. Local historical pageants, parades, festivals, and fairs fall into this category. A good example is Mardi Gras in New Orleans or perhaps the Olympic games. These attractions require a wide range of sophisticated but temporary services, provided by local residents when possible. National and international events require much more elaborate planning and extensive outside assistance. All of these are important activities that offer local residents and tourists the chance for relaxation and entertainment.

Clubs. Clubs are another very popular form of recreation. There are many different types of clubs, some of which are not necessarily recreational. Civic clubs, fraternal clubs, university clubs, and retirement clubs are more social or service oriented. They are part of the hospitality industry in the broadest sense because they serve their guests or members in a special way. Clubs that provide recreational services to their clientele are becoming increasingly popular. These athletic clubs, country clubs, health spas, tennis clubs, and others provide a much-needed and desired outlet in a society increasingly concerned with physical exercise and good health. Such clubs are an important component of the recreation business, and their numbers increase every year.

Public Parks. A wide range of activities are provided in public parks. People may be jogging, enjoying a family picnic, playing volleyball, mountain climbing, or simply observing the natural beauty of a park. The activities offered by a public park facility vary tremendously depending upon size and location. For example, a local city park may provide recreation facilities for an afternoon of fun, whereas a large national park offers days of excitement and adventure for a camping trip. Whether the park be city, state, or federally managed and protected, the public park systems in the United States are an important aspect of our lifestyle.

The first park was developed in New York City and is known as Central Park. Since that time many parks have been established and are changing from the concept for which parks were first known. There seems to be a new set of standards for recreational opportunities. Today's parks combine both beauty and function into a single unit, making all types of recreation seekers feel that their needs can be met.

Meeting and Convention Planning

Industries, companies, and professional associations organize annual trade shows, meetings, and conventions. More than fifty-six hundred trade shows take place every year, with attendance ranging from a very few people to well over a hundred thousand attendees. Vendors come to educate others in the field about their products. Participants come to discover what is in the marketplace and to gain professional knowledge from their peers. Meeting and convention planning is indeed a very large business. More than $56 billion is spent annually in the United States alone on meetings and conventions, making it one of the top industries in the country. Trade show preparation and participation is an area in which professional management plays a large role in the success of the operation.

Meeting planners manage a variety of meetings, from intimate seminars and conferences requiring a room, lunch, and a slide show to massive conventions, trade shows, and symposia. Convention service managers usually work with the meeting or convention group to coordinate the needs of the visiting organization with the facilities available at the convention site. Convention service personnel may work directly for the convention center or may be employed by the city's chamber of commerce or visitors and convention bureau.

Meeting planners interact closely with all areas of the hospitality industry. They book rooms and arrange for meeting space at hotels, arrange for meals for meeting participants, and contract for large amounts of travel. A meeting planner must be well acquainted with all areas of the hospitality industry.

Support Areas

Because all segments of the hospitality industry are businesses, they must be supported by a business infrastructure that includes accounting services, human resource management, and marketing. These support areas also offer attractive career opportunities for hospitality graduates. While all businesses need this expertise, it takes a different form in the hospitality field. Hospitality by definition deals with services and thus has different needs from a manufacturing operation. There is a different accounting system for restaurants and hotels, employees need different skills, and marketing deals with services rather than things. Consequently, it is important for individuals who choose to work in the support areas of hospitality also to be familiar with the operations segment of the industry.

Conclusion

This chapter has provided a broad overview of the hospitality industry. The term *hospitality industry* has been defined and the major segments of the industry have been briefly discussed. Each of these areas—food service, lodging, travel and tourism, and meeting and convention planning—comprises tremendously large forces within the economy. These businesses and others make up a dynamic and growing industry that influences virtually billions of people in all nations of the world every day.

This overview also sets the stage for many of the readings to follow in this book. As the reader progresses there will be more information provided on specific areas of the hospitality industry. This information is organized in a way that will be easy to follow and comprehensive enough to give a solid foundation on which to build.

——References——

Kotler, P. (1991) *Marketing Management.* Englewood Cliffs, N.J.: Prentice-Hall.
Morgan, B. J. (1993) *Travel and Hospitality.* Detroit: Visible Ink.
Webster's Ninth New Collegiate Dictionary. (1990) Springfield, Mass.: Merriam-Webster, Inc.

2

Past, Present, and Future of the Hospitality Industry

Deborah Breiter, *University of Nevada, Las Vegas*
Vincent H. Eade, *University of Nevada, Las Vegas*
Boyce W. Phillips, *University of Nevada, Las Vegas*

Introduction

Today's hospitality industry exists in a different world from the one encountered by Ellsworth Statler and the Delmonico brothers years ago and will evolve even more distinctively in the future.* The technological and information-processing changes we are now witnessing would astound our forefathers, and future changes will make today's technology seem quite primitive by comparison. Despite the outward appearance of change, one common thread runs throughout the years—service. We have been, are, and will continue to be in the business of providing courteous, professional, caring service to our guests and customers. This is the key tenet hoteliers and restaurateurs must *never* forget. This being noted, let's take a look at the past, present, and future of the hospitality industry, remembering to focus not only on the tangible changes but also the reason these changes occur: to provide better service and live up to the definition of the term, the hospitality industry.

Past

A writer on modern hotel management, Gerald Lattin, tells us that to write a complete history of the hospitality industry we must go back in time about twelve thousand years, but certainly anything concerning the hospitality industry twelve thousand years ago would be short on fact and long on fancy.

However, for trade and travel to flourish even on a small scale, there first had to be an acceptable medium of exchange across great distances. Precious metals and stones did emerge as a medium of exchange as far back as the sixth century B.C. However, this was a cumbersome beginning and soon coins were being stamped out with their value established and standardized over larger trading areas.

---

*Statler's career is described in Chapter 3 of this book. The Delmonicos it is generally believed, opened the first restaurant in the United States, in New York City in 1832.

Exactly where, when, and how the business of renting room space began is open to speculation. An inn about 2,500 years old still stands just outside the ruined city of Pompeii, Italy. Some of the earliest inns were nothing more than overnight stopping places for camels and travelers along the trading routes between Baghdad and Babylon. Located along the trade routes traveled by the caravans were some fortresslike places built around an oasis where traveler and beast could rest after a day's journey.

Certain scholars think that inns originated in Egypt. Records from the tombs of the pharaohs show pictures of dining and cooking as far back as 1500 B.C.—almost 3,500 years ago. The first recorded 100% occupancy was 2,000 years ago when there was no room at the inn and Christ was born in a manger: from this we conclude that inns were well established and doing a good business at the time of Christ. Of course the concept of lodging was soon borrowed by the Romans and Greeks from the Egyptians. With Roman and Greek refinements, inns soon became extremely popular as more and more people traveled to and from national festivals and athletic games that the Greeks and Romans were wont to sponsor. Governing the far-flung Roman empire also required a lot of official travel: all of this added to the popularity of inns.

During what we refer to as the Dark Ages, from around 500 A.D., several hundred years passed during which the inn was largely lost to civilization. There was little need for inns or innkeepers because travel and trade were at a standstill. During those years the Roman Catholic Church was the dominant and only recognized authority from one country to another. Monasteries and religious houses accommodated what few travelers there were, with payment being in the form of donations on departure.

Shortly after the crusades the first inns began to appear in England. At first, these were mostly alehouses where men gathered to drink and discuss politics. Meals were an individual matter and most guests brought their own. As early as 1400 a few alehouses provided a main room with mattresses along the walls where guests could spend the night.

By the year 1500 stagecoaches had become common in England, travel was widespread, and some inns had expanded to 20 or 30 rooms to accommodate stagecoach guests overnight. Most people could not read, so inns were identified with signs picturing animals, such as the "Blue Bull," "Black Swan," "Boars," "Dolphin," or "Red Fox." These visual symbols enabled guests to say, "Meet me at the sign of the `Dolphin'," or "Meet me at the sign of the `Bull'." Most residents of a county, though illiterate, did recognize the coat of arms of important local families. By the late 1700s many of the animal signs had been replaced with coats of arms, which meant that the inn was in the territory of a particular noble family and under its protection.

Without much intending to, Henry VIII encouraged the growth of inns by suppressing the monasteries in 1530. Church lands were confiscated by the king, given away, and the church's function as host to the traveler disappeared. Another factor dating from the same period favored the development of the inn: certain innkeepers were forced by the crown to enlarge their property and in some cases build new properties to retain stables and horses to meet the demands of the royal post.

It was only natural that the founding fathers would bring the inn concept to America. Inns in America were usually called taverns, ordinaries, or commons. The first inn in Boston and probably the first in the colonies was opened by Samuel Coles in 1634 and was known as the Coles Ordinary. Many college dining halls today are still called dining commons; however, in early America food was served almost exclusively at an "ordinary." As was true in England, the early American taverns adopted the English custom of using visual symbols rather than names to identify themselves.

History records the intregal part that inns, taverns, and ordinaries played in the cause of liberty both in England and in America. In America, Patrick Henry called the taverns of colonial America the "cradles of liberty." In Boston, the Green Dragon and Bunch of Grapes were meeting places of the Sons of Liberty during the Revolution. The Boston Tea Party was planned at the Green Dragon Inn. William Penn spent long hours in the Blue Anchor Inn, planning his colony at what is now Philadelphia. The history of the American Revolution is filled with instances of taverns used as military headquarters, bivouacs, and hospitals. General George Washington bade farewell to his top-ranking military officers on December 4, 1783, at the Fraunces Tavern at the corner of Pearl and Broadstreet in old New York City. (Too, academicians remember that the Raleigh Tavern in Williamsburg, Virginia, was the scene of the formation of the Phi Beta Kappa fraternity by the students of William and Mary College in 1693.)

Hȏtel is a French word and was first used to identify the city residence of wealthy or prominent Parisians. The transition from tavern to hotel came about simply by changing the name from "tavern" to "hotel." The world *hotel* was first used in America by Joseph Corre when he opened Corre's Hotel in 1790 at 24th and Broadway in New York City. The name spread quite rapidly, and city directories of the 1790s show that many taverns had become hotels.

With no fanfare and probably little or no mention in print, an event occurred in the year 1794 that forever changed the economy of the hotel industry. It was in that year—1794—that the City Hotel in New York City opened for business. The City Hotel was not the first hotel ever built in New York, nor was it the biggest hotel ever built, or the most lavish. However, it was the first to be constructed by a stock company. Why was that significant? It tells us that hotels had become an established fact of life, selling a service that people were willing to pay for and others were willing to pool their funds to provide. Hotels had become a business rather than the family operation that they had been for hundreds of years.

The coming of the railroad in the mid-1800s signaled the decline of the roadside inn, at least for the time being. The train covered greater distances; made travel easier, faster, and more comfortable; and also gave impetus to the hotel railroad boom. The roadside inn had all but disappeared before its resurrection with the coming of the automobile. As soon as the automobile ceased to be a curiosity, it became the toy of the young sports-minded crowd. Weekend rallies and races were the fad of the day. Good camping spots and tents were set up for a weekend in the country. Farmers in the countryside got into the act by renting out shower facilities and outdoor toilets for the weekenders. Soon the farmers constructed rough shacks, put in a cot and a lamp, and rented them out, so the campers did not have to bother with a tent. The toilet and bathing facilities were finally moved inside, completing the circle to today's motel.

Automobile technology was spurred on by the often impassable roads that were being blazed across America's countryside. The impassable roads became highways, and Americans fell in love with the automobile. This, of course, resulted in more travel and the roadside inn was resurrected from near death. Not only was it resurrected, but it received a name and much-needed respectability. The new name of these roadside inns was *motel,* a term first used by Arthur Heineman in San Luis Obispo, California, in 1925. At first the hotel operators were a bit suspicious of these motels, thinking perhaps they were nothing more than a fad and would soon fall out of favor, with hotels reinstated as the accepted mode of overnight rest for the traveler. But this was not to be, and with the coming of Holiday Inns in 1952 hotel operators accepted the fact that motels were a legitimate part of the hospitality industry. The name of the American Hotel Association was changed to the American Hotel and Motel Association, and motel operators are now considered equals and enjoy all the rights and privileges previously offered to hotel operators only.

Present

The travel and tourism industry now generates more than $300 billion in revenues and employs more than 6 million Americans. Hotels, resorts, restaurants, conventions, travel agencies, and tour and transportation companies are very big business. They will continue to grow throughout the 1990s because travel and dining out have become ways of life, not just for Americans, but for many international visitors to the United States as well.

Even though the hospitality industry is growing, managers are facing some very exciting challenges and opportunities. With rapid changes in technology, continued government regulation, a multicultural workforce, an aging customer base, and the economy in question, hotel and restaurant managers are working smarter than ever to keep pace with the demands of the 1990s.

The Lodging Industry

The lodging industry changed tremendously during the 1980s. By the early 1990s there were too many hotel rooms (oversupply) and too few travelers (demand). The nationwide average occupancy rate (number of rooms sold ÷ number of rooms available for sale) in 1993 is just a little above 60%. This means that of the approximately 3 million hotel rooms across the country, four of ten rooms are vacant every evening. Competition is fierce and hotels are discounting their rates in order to attract guests. The average daily rate (ADR) is between $55.00 and $60.00.

Hotel companies are not just competing with other companies but sometimes with themselves. In the 1990s it is very common for one hotel company to own many different types of hotels. Marriott, for example, has Marriott Hotels and Resorts, Courtyard by Marriott, Fairfield Inn, Residence Inn by Marriott, and Marriott Suites. This product development strategy is called segmentation, marketing to specific groups of travelers who have similar wants and needs.

At the same time that hotel companies have developed different types of hotels, there has been consolidation of hotel ownership. In other words, many hotel companies have bought other hotel companies. It is becoming less and less common for a hotel to be completely independent, although there will always be a market for the privately owned hotel.

Another major change in hotel ownership has also taken place. There are now many international hotel companies that have properties in the United States. We now have British (Bass and Forte), Japanese (Nikko and Aoki), French (Accor and Meridien), and German (Novotel) corporations owning and operating hotels throughout the United States. American-owned hotel companies continue to expand overseas as well, with opportunities arising in the Pacific Rim and Eastern Europe.

In the United States, hotels are getting bigger (the 5,000 room MGM Grand in Las Vegas becoming the world's largest) and more creative in design. Theme hotels, especially those attached to casinos, offer guests the choice of a tropical paradise (the Mirage in Las Vegas or the Taj Mahal in Atlantic City) and everything in between. Fantasy is no longer the exclusive domaine of theme parks.

The Food Service Industry

One of every three meals is now eaten outside the home. Dining out is truly a way of life for Americans. We spend more than $200 billion a year eating out. Competition is fierce in the food service industry. Nontraditional operations like supermarkets and convenience stores are offering meals that were once only found in restaurants.

Food service companies continue to introduce new concepts as well. It doesn't matter whether it's a free-standing restaurant, part of a chain, or a food service contract feeder, food service operations are working hard to keep up with the changing tastes of the public. Even hospitals offer their patients a range of menus and service options. School food service operators are very often going into business with quick service restaurants (what we used to call fast food) to keep the students from leaving the cafeteria. Quick service restaurants are offering table service in order to compete with family restaurants. Take-out food, whether from the drive-through or delivered by a gourmet restaurant, is also becoming more popular. And everybody, it seems, is offering value meals, sometimes in the form of an early bird special and sometimes as combination meals found in quick service restaurants.

You can also find all kinds of ethnic foods that people could barely pronounce a few years ago. Traditionally American restaurants are including ethnic foods on their menus. In any major city you are likely to find Thai, Korean, Vietnamese, Salvadoran, and Moroccan restaurants along with the familiar Italian, Chinese, Japanese, and Mexican establishments. People going out to eat are looking for a change of pace. They are more willing to experiment with food.

Another big change in the restaurant business has been the proliferation of coffee bars. These go hand in hand with the increased consumption of sweets. Americans claim they are eating healthier foods but the sales of gourmet ice cream, cookies, and pastries keep going up. On the other hand, consumption of beef is down while consumption of chicken and turkey is on the rise.

People are also altering their drinking habits. Wine is becoming more popular, as is reduced-alcohol (lite) beer. There is an increased awareness of the problems associated with drinking alcoholic beverages. The food service industry is definitely making an attempt to educate employees on serving alcohol responsibly.

Theme Parks

Theme parks, led by Disney, are expanding at home as well as abroad. Other types of parks are also proliferating as families look for ways to spend their leisure time together. Water parks are more popular than ever, and there is now a water park in Las Vegas that is completely enclosed.

Gaming

Gaming has become a viable option for many towns, counties, and states looking for ways to increase revenues. In addition, many Native Americans have seen gaming as a means of economic development. Gaming on reservations can be found from Connecticut to California, from Wisconsin to Mississippi. Riverboat gaming is becoming very popular in Illinois, Iowa, and Louisiana. Land-based casinos can now be found outside of Nevada and New Jersey. Almost 40 states now have some form of legalized gaming.

Service: The Bottom Line

Value is something that is very important to all of our guests and customers. They want to believe they got their money's worth. Hotels, restaurants, theme parks, and other hospitality businesses are working very hard to provide memorable experiences to keep guests coming back. Service is still the key to this industry.

Providing quality service is a major focus for hospitality in the 1990s. Total quality management, quality assurance, quality circles, and quality teams are the buzzwords. These ideas have been around for a long time, but managers are beginning to understand that it is the front-line employees who are most critical to the success of the hospitality industry. Employee empowerment and employee involvement are two important aspects of the quality movement that managers are implementing in the never-ending quest for service excellence.

Future

Predicting the future of the hospitality industry is rather like predicting the weather. One takes a look at current conditions and trends and attempts to project the most likely scenario, always keeping in mind unforeseen variables that can dramatically alter the forecast. With this in mind, let's take a look at the future of the hospitality industry by focusing on current trends that will probably continue into the future as well as *new* innovations and challenges to be met by industry leaders with the understanding that, like the weather, nothing is guaranteed.

Perhaps the safest projection is the continuation of computerization and technological advances in *all* aspects of the industry. The high-touch–high-tech phenomenon witnessed during the 1970s through 1990s will increase as the affordability of technology enables even smaller operators to modernize their operations. Computerization has resulted not only in faster data assimilation and information, but also in the reduction of personnel. Computer functionality has eliminated such positions as rack clerk and status board operator from the hotel industry. A number of hotels are experimenting with computerized check-ins vis-à-vis the automated check-out process now used by most hotel chains. Although this sounds like an expeditious service concept, the industry must determine at what point it immolates humanization in favor of computerization. One can readily understand the introduction of robotics into a restaurant kitchen to achieve maximum efficiency and consistent production; however, is there a computerized substitute for a friendly front desk clerk who can show genuine concern for the travel-weary guest? Does the industry want Star-Trekian food service where, with the push of a button, the customer's order is systemically read by a computer and magically appears on the table with a programmed, monotoned "Thank you and have a nice day" message heard through a voice simulator speaker system? As the hospitality industry continues down the path to increased megabytes, it should be careful not to eliminate the soul and essence of our industry: *service,* person-to-person service.

Hotel and restaurant chains will continue to grow, and U.S. operators will seek nontraditional new markets. Conversely, foreign investors will look to the United States for investment opportunities much the same as Accor, Seibu Saison, Aoki, Bass PLC, and Forte did in recent decades. These investments will include continued expansion into the fast service restaurant industry. Again, worldwide economic and political conditions remain *the* variable. The independent operator will maintain a niche based on the owner/operator, hands-on success formula. In fact, many independents that did not fall prey to the overexpansion and marginal financing of chains will outlive their chain counterparts. The emphasis on health in the hospitality industry will take on increased importance as menus expand with health-related offerings, employee wellness programs emerge, and legislation virtually bans smoking in public accommodation facilities.

The extensive diversification trend witnessed recently by the lodging industry will dissipate in favor of selective expansion and/or product-line development. Thus, rather than a chain trying to develop an economy brand, *and* an extended-stay brand, *and* resorts, *and* mid-priced properties, *and* luxury hotels, it will focus on what it does best or where the most viable markets are. Hotels will continue the metamorphosis from simple lodging facility to self-contained attraction. Hotels will create themes, theme parks, and visitor fantasies that will draw tourists, putting these hotels in a must-see category.

Much to the chagrin of some industry analysts, casino and casino/hotel operations will flourish in the future. Today, the United States is witnessing a spectacular interest and growth in riverboat and Native American gaming ventures. Economics will continue to fuel this interest because many states are looking for ways to ease the financial burden that has virtually bankrupted several state governments. The casino industry represents an economic exigency solution. Operators, who had traditionally shunned this component of the business, will take the plunge. As a result, the operation of casinos will be elevated to new levels of respectability and eventually, educational institutions now offering degrees in hotel management will expand their course offerings to include casino management.

The workplace will witness subtle and dramatic changes. In the United States, the Americans with Disabilities Act will result in the main streaming of many physically and mentally challenged workers. Consequently, employers will introduce numerous types of assistive technology, enabling even the most severely disabled individuals to become productive citizens and to achieve virtual reality. The Fair Labor Standards Act will be amended, resulting in an increase in the minimum wage; higher salary guarantees for administrative, professional, and executive overtime exemptions; and a restriction on the hours that 16- and 17-year-olds can work. Additional federal legislation will likely require that employers provide child-care facilities accompanied by a tax incentive as well as the elimination of the employment-at-will status of employees by requiring employers to discharge only for just cause. National health care will become a reality and all employers will be required to provide some form of health insurance for their employees. The Family Leave and Medical Act will result in the need for more part-time/temporary workers, and these workers will see federal legislation enacted providing them with worker benefits comparable to those of full-time workers.

Federal and state regulators will place a greater emphasis on food and beverage storage, preparation, and sanitation safety standards based on the 1993 Jack-in-the-Box tragedy.

Larger employers will have on-site medical facilities for workers and employee wellness programs will be visible throughout the industry. Preemployment and posthire drug tests will become ordinary practice in the lodging and food service industry. Training will become computerized with individual touch-screen, modular sessions being state of the art.

Finally, what is the future for hospitality education programs? More doctoral programs are likely to emerge. Traditional degree programs eventually will offer minors or concentrations in emerging fields. Tomorrow's graduates may have a major in hotel administration with a minor in human resources management or culinary arts. If the current trend continues, fewer recruiters will visit campus, opting instead for student internships. Undergraduates may find the key to future employment is an internship with a prospective employer. Thus, educational institutes probably will focus attention on internships, co-ops, and field-based work experiences.

——References——

Brymer, Robert. *Introduction to Hotel and Restaurant Management, a Book of Readings.* Fifth edition. Dubuque, IA.: Kendall/Hunt Publishing Company.

Lattin, Gerald. (1958) *Modern Hotel and Motel Management.* Second edition. San Francisco, Calif.: W. H. Freeman and Company.

Lattin, Gerald. (1977) *Modern Hotel and Motel Management.* Third edition. San Francisco, Calif.: W. H. Freeman and Company.

Lattin, Gerald. (1958) *Modern Hotel Management.* San Francisco, Calif.: W. H. Freeman and Company.

Lundberg, Donald E. (1956) *Inside Innkeeping.* Dubuque, IA.: Wm. C. Brown Company.

3

Pioneers and Leaders of the Hospitality Industry

Richard L. Brush, *Johnson and Wales University*
Teresa M. Schulz, *University of Wisconsin-Stout*

Men

Over the past century, the hospitality industry has undergone tremendous growth and change. The development and innovations were due to changing consumer demands, shifts in the economic climate, and advances in technology. No analysis of the industry would be complete without an examination of industry leaders who had the foresight to respond to their customers' changing needs, adapt to fluctuations in the business climate, and take advantage of technological innovations.

Although these men worked in different times, they had several things in common. First, they understood that successful hospitality operations require organization, planning, and leadership. Each of these men, in his own way, was an excellent leader. Second, they understood the need to apply sound business principles in building their hospitality empires; a successful manager must know all aspects of the business from accounting to marketing to operations to finance. Most importantly, they knew that to be successful, hospitality operations must meet customer expectations. Those expectations change over time, and the successful manager responds to customers' varying wants and needs.

Cesar Ritz

Ritz began his hotel career in 1865, as an apprentice hotelkeeper at age 15. At 19, he became manager of a Parisian restaurant. He learned quickly what pleased and displeased the clientele. He became so proficient that the patrons began to insist that he alone serve them.

At 25, he became the manager of the Grand National Hotel in Lucerne, Switzerland. When the Grand National opened, it was touted as the most luxurious hotel in the world. However, it lost money until Ritz, using all the imagination and contacts he could muster, turned the situation around. He continued to manage the Grand National for the next 11 seasons, as it became a popular place for the social elite of the world.

Ritz' next opportunity occurred in London when he was asked to consult at the Savoy Hotel, which was not as profitable as expected after six months of operation. At age 38, he became the manager of the Savoy with a free hand to operate it on his own terms. Ritz made the Savoy a center of cultural activity. He introduced orchestras to the dining room and extended the dining period. Further, he made evening dress compulsory and restricted unescorted women. He understood men and women and their need for beautiful things and for romance. He went to great lengths to achieve the atmosphere he desired and to please his guests. Once he even had the lower dining room of the Savoy converted into a Venetian waterway complete with gondolas and gondoliers singing Italian love songs.

The stage was now set for the Paris Ritz, the first hotel to bear his name. During the final three months of construction of the Paris Ritz, he lived in the hotel so that he could personally supervise the outfitting of the property. He ensured that there would be king-sized closets and ample drawer space to accommodate the rich and fashionable men and women who would stay at the Ritz.

After the Paris Ritz became successful, he returned to London to supervise the renovation of Carlton House. Carlton House was the first hotel in London to have a bath in every room. It became an immediate success, opening just one year after the Paris Ritz.

For Ritz, guest service was the key to success. To that end, he established high standards of service that exist even now. In 1907, the Ritz Development Company franchised the Ritz name to the Ritz Carlton of New York and later to other hotels in Lisbon, Montreal, and Boston. Today many of these "Ritz" hotels continue to be counted among the great hotels of the world.

Statler, Hilton, and Henderson

Three names stand out from all others when one discusses the modern hotel chain: **Ellsworth M. Statler, Conrad Hilton** and **Ernest Henderson.** Each contributed significantly to the development of the hotel chain, and each has a special place in the history of the hospitality business.

Statler

In 1878, 15-year-old **Ellsworth Milton Statler** became head bellman in one of the leading hotels in Wheeling, West Virginia. Some fifty years later, he would have a hotel chain named after him and be considered one of the premier hotel men of all time.

As a youth, Statler moved from West Virginia to Buffalo, New York, where he opened a basement restaurant. The restaurant was unsuccessful, largely because, as Statler found out, Buffalo was a town in which almost everyone ate at home. The situation called for drastic action. He began to advertise all-you-can-eat specials, six meals for the price of four, and other promotions to attract customers. He controlled every aspect of his operation and ran it at peak efficiency. In three years the restaurant was out of the red and Statler was ready for his next opportunity.

In 1901, he opened a temporary 2,100-room hotel, the Outside Inn, to house visitors to the Pan American Exposition in Buffalo. The Exposition was a failure, but Statler was a success. He had his second opportunity to operate a temporary hotel, the 2,257-room Inside Inn, at the St. Louis World's Fair. This too was a success. By the end of the World's Fair, Statler had achieved national recognition.

Then, in 1908, Statler opened the first hotel to bear his name, a 300-room hotel in Buffalo. It was here that Statler's true genius became apparent. Before Statler, private baths were available only to the wealthy traveler who could afford a luxury hotel. Statler put a bath in every room in a hotel designed for the common traveler. His slogan "A Room with a Bath for a Dollar and a Half" changed the hotel industry for all time.

In 1912, he opened the Cleveland Statler. The Detroit Statler was built in 1915 and the St. Louis Statler in 1918, with many more to follow. As Statler expanded his company, he instituted many other innovative ideas such as telephone and writing supplies in every room, reading lamps, radios, and medical service. His design of back-to-back rooms used common shafts for plumbing and electrical conduits to keep building costs down. His guest rooms were decorated in such a way that draperies and bedspreads were interchangeable from room to room throughout the hotel. Most importantly, he gave all his hotels a common name—Statler—so that each hotel helped to market the other hotels.

Like Ritz, Statler continually emphasized the theme of service to the public. The Statler Service Code was a formal company policy. Each employee was required to memorize the policy and carry a copy while on duty. "Life is service. The one who progresses is the one who gives his fellow human being a little more, a little better service." This philosophy is as much a tenet of the hospitality industry today as it was eighty years ago.

Hilton

In 1914, when **Conrad Hilton** bought his first hotel at age 32, he had already been elected to the New Mexico Legislature, tried his hand at banking, and served briefly in the Army. He purchased the Mobley Hotel in Cisco, Texas, for $5,000. The Mobley was the first of a chain of seven Texas hotels that Hilton had put together by 1929, when the stock market crashed.

During the Depression, Hilton was hard hit and at one point was a half million dollars in debt. However, by doing everything possible to cut costs and increase revenue, he was able to hold on to five of his hotels. By 1937, he was able to resume acquiring hotels.

He purchased the Sir Francis Drake in 1938, and for the first time attracted national attention. Then, in 1946, the Hilton Hotel Corporation was formed. In 1949, he acquired controlling interest in the famed Waldorf-Astoria Hotel in New York City and in 1954, master-minded the purchase of all the Statler Hotels for $111 million.

Hilton was, arguably, the first American hotel operator to see the advantages of internationalization. In 1949, he obtained a management contract to operate the Caribe Hilton Hotel in Havana, Cuba, one of the most successful hotels of all time. In 1960, The Hilton International Hotel opened in Istanbul, Turkey. Hilton's overseas operations were very successful due largely to the company's international referral and promotion system. At last count, Hilton International, now a separate company, had more than seventy hotels outside the United States.

Henderson

Unlike Ritz and Statler, **Ernest Henderson** did not get started as a hotelier until he was in his forties. Henderson founded the Sheraton hotel chain in 1942. When he died 26 years later, Sheraton, with 154 hotels, was the largest hotel chain in the world.

Henderson, like the pioneers before him, was a master of organization and had great self-discipline and a strong sense of duty. He was a financier of the first order. The measure of each hotel deal was made against the tax base and depreciation that could be taken. These were the most important considerations in building the Sheraton chain. Henderson would not hesitate to buy and sell the same hotel repeatedly if the deals were right. He believed that operating a hotel chain called for as much attention to real estate matters as it did to lodging and food service. However, this should not be taken to mean that he was not concerned with the operation. Just the opposite was true. He wanted hotel managers to make decisions based on facts and information rather than on feelings.

Kemmons Wilson

During the 1950s, a major initiative of the Eisenhower administration was the building of what we now know as the interstate highway system. **Kemmons Wilson,** the founder of the Holiday Inn chain, saw that the older downtown hotels, many of which had been built in the 1920s, were poorly equipped to handle the needs of an increasingly mobile traveling public. He was determined to build motels on the highways where people were going to travel. Like his predecessors, Wilson knew that to be successful he needed to have more than just a better location. He needed to meet travelers' changing needs: informality, lower prices, and family-oriented services like air-conditioning, color televisions, swimming pools, and free parking.

Wilson also knew that to build a truly great chain, he needed to build brand-name recognition. He wanted the Holiday Inn name to be synonymous with value-oriented travel, and he wanted to establish a Holiday Inn at every convenient travel stop throughout America. Although not the first chain to use franchising as a technique for growth, Holiday Inn certainly popularized and perfected it. Today, the vast majority of Holiday Inns are owned by independent operators and smaller franchise companies, all taking advantage of the Holiday Inn name recognition and reservation system and meeting Holiday Inn's standards of service.

As Holiday Inn grew, Wilson, the consummate entrepreneur, saw a need to standardize the supplies used in the motels. He also saw an opportunity to make money. To that end, he developed several subsidiary companies to supply company-owned and franchised Holiday Inns. Innkeepers Supply Company, the Institutional Mart of America, and Holiday Press are a few of the companies.

Ray Kroc

Ray Kroc did not become a restaurateur until age 52. In 1954, he met the McDonald brothers, who had opened a fast-food hamburger restaurant in San Bernadino, California. Kroc immediately saw that the brothers were on to something and, since the brothers did not want to expand, purchased the exclusive rights for the name and the system they used. McDonald's has become, possibly, the most successful company in the hospitality industry.

Kroc did not know a lot about restaurants, but he did know what people wanted: fast, consistent food served in a clean, friendly atmosphere. Kroc insisted from the beginning that his new venture was to be a family-oriented restaurant. He would not permit jukeboxes, vending machines, or pay telephones in any McDonald's restaurant. He believed these things encouraged loitering, something he did not want at McDonald's.

Kroc, like Wilson, also understood that if his restaurant chain was to grow he would need to become an expert franchiser. Today, of the 12,000 McDonald stores, approximately 8,000 are franchised.

You can learn a great deal from these and other leaders of the hospitality industry in the twentieth century. As you study their careers, ask yourself the questions: How and why were customer needs changing during each era? What economic shifts and technological advances were taking place? How did the leaders respond to those changes and advances?

And as you move into your own hospitality career in the twenty-first century, learn to ask those same questions of yourself: Who are my customers and how are their needs changing? How can I best respond to those changing needs? What kind of a business climate am I operating in? How can I maximize profits in this climate? What new technology can I use to help meet my customers' changing needs and current business conditions?

Women

One of the biggest changes in American society in the twentieth century is the number of women employed outside the home. However, statistics show that the movement of women into the work force dates from the 1890s. In 1970, only half of women between ages 25 and 44 were in the work force; by 1995, more than 80% are expected to be working (Schuster, 1986).

These statistics reflect some changing trends in the contemporary job market and in societal expectations for women. It is not just that women have to work; they want to work (Schuster, 1986). Many women work out of necessity, but others pursue a career because of the personal satisfaction received from the job. The career opportunities in the 1980s were considerably more interesting than the traditional pink-collar and blue-collar jobs of a generation ago. Today, 30% of working women are professionals or managers (Nasar, 1990).

The movement of women into the hospitality industry reflects the overall movement of women within the work force. Thirty years ago women entered the industry as part-time workers, mainly as waitresses or maids. For many it was a way to earn money and remain at home during part of the day. Because of industry needs, flexible hours including day or night were available. That too has changed. Slowly, women are entering the hospitality industry as professionals. The number of female graduates from hotel and restaurant schools and culinary schools once was negligible. Now women constitute 50% or more of the current enrollments in hospitality programs in many colleges and universities (Weinstein, 1987).

As women enter the work force with more education and motivation, their expectations and aspirations also have increased. Some few women have achieved executive status and titles in the industry, but the gains have been slow in coming. The time has come to identify the women who have had an impact on the industry and the women who have just begun that long climb up the career ladder. As the years pass, no doubt the number of women identified as pioneers and leaders in the hospitality industry will increase.

Pioneers

Mahala Stouffer

The Stouffer restaurant chain began as a family-owned lunch counter in 1924 in Cleveland, Ohio (Lundberg, 1989). Mahala Stouffer was an important part of that business. She was known for her home style desserts, especially her Dutch apple and lemon meringue pie. Her recipes were the backbone of the menu and the reason many people returned day after day. When her sons Vernon and Gordon completed their studies at the Wharton School of Finance they introduced changes to the restaurant and placed their mother in charge of the kitchen. She supervised and trained others to carry out the "new idea" of a recipe-controlled kitchen. Working with her sons she developed standardized recipes, organized the kitchen areas and helped develop a system that would operate in an efficient and cost-effective manner (Powers, 1992). The use of standardized recipes, departmentalization, and human resource management continue to be an important part of every Stouffer establishment.

Alice (Allie) Marriott

Alice Marriott appears in all accounts of the Marriott corporation. She was involved in the success of the first root-beer stand in Washington, D.C., in 1927 (Lundberg, 1989). When the change to Hot Shoppes occurred Alice was instrumental in getting recipes for chili can carne, tamales, and other needed menu items from the chef at the Mexican Embassy. (She spoke fluent Spanish.) When it became apparent that it would be difficult to obtain many of the ingredients needed for the menu items, Alice was able to convince the chef to give her the names of his suppliers (O'Brian, 1987).

Alice also became the bookkeeper for the business, a simple task in the early years. She continued this interest and served as treasurer of the company for many years (Lundberg, 1989). Alice, as described by J. W. Marriott (O'Brian, 1987) "is undoubtly the most important asset in my life." Alice Marriott was a wife, mother, and business partner for her entire life.

Helen Corbitt

Helen Corbitt was a noted author, lecturer, food writer, newspaper columnist, and teacher. She felt strongly that one of the responsibilities of the restaurateur was to teach people to eat. Stanley Marcus, president of Neiman Marcus, described Helen Corbitt as "my wild Irish genius" in his book *Minding the Store*. She served as food service director in the Zodiac Room of the Dallas department store from 1955 until her retirement in 1970 ("Ten Pioneers," 1976).

During that time she changed the eating habits of many Texans. In an article in *Institutions/Volume Feeding* (1976) Corbitt stated, "When I first came to Texas, everyone ate beans, ate their meat well done, ate very little salad and no fruit. Well, I changed that" (p. 30).

Helen Corbitt not only raised the standards of retail food service, she struggled to overcome the obstacles put in her way by a male-dominated industry. **She Won!** ("Ten Pioneers," 1976).

Katherine Manchester

In 1940, Katherine Manchester began one of the many steps in her career, one that spanned 31 years, brought hospital food service out of the dark ages, and turned the position of dietitian into a profession ("Ten Pioneers," 1976).

Katherine Manchester, the first civilian dietitian taken into the army, began her first assignment at Walter Reed Army Medical Center. During a later assignment at Brooke General Hospital, Ft. Sam Houston Texas, she adapted centralized tray service and airline hot-and-cold cart system to the hospital's delivery system. She found that when she needed new equipment she would often have to pressure companies to design and develop the equipment she required. In some cases she would sketch out what she needed and the company would then produce it ("Ten Pioneers," 1976).

In 1965, as chief of food service at Walter Reed, she implemented computer programming that resulted in standardized recipes, computerized production and delivery charts, and computerized ingredient control ("Ten Pioneers," 1976).

As noted in *Institutions/Volume Feeding* (1976), Manchester's other achievements included: first Army dietitian promoted to full colonel, first military winner of IFMA's Silver Plate, and first military dietitian to head the American Dietetic Association. (p. 41).

Julia Child

Teacher, author, and television chef are just of few of the roles Julia Child has played. Born and raised in Pasadena, California, she graduated from Smith College, joined the OSS, and was sent to Asia during World War II. It was here she met her husband, whom she credits with piquing her interest in food (Child, 1968).

Child began her first television series in 1943. As the years went by, she authored several cookbooks, took part in another television series, and became known as America's favorite chef. Her series made Francophiles of millions of viewers. Not only were people educated about French cooking, they were able to produce some of the dishes right in their own kitchens (Burros, 1993).

She is a cofounder of the American Institute of Wine and Food. Her goal, through education, is to make the culinary arts a true profession. Through the Institute, experienced, established chefs network with young-and-up coming chefs, giving them advice and help and occasionally a position as an apprentice or assistant (Burros, 1993).

Julia Child recently celebrated her eightieth birthday. Has she been resting on her laurels the past few years? Certainly not! Her new cookbook, _The Way to Cook,_ is a success. It is considered a teaching book and this time provides a number of low-fat dishes. In an interview for _Newsweek,_ Child noted that it took five years of working 10 to 12 hours every day, sometimes six days a week, to complete the book. Now she is ready to have a little fun (Starr, 1991) ("The latest recipe," 1990).

Leaders

Elaine Grossinger Estes

Elaine Grossinger Estes grew up in the hotel business, a family-owned resort in the Catskills. Although she had no intention of returning to the industry after becoming a wife and mother, this was not to be. She returned to work in the family-owned resort and held the title of executive vice-president until the sale of the business in 1986 ("Women in the Industry," 1988).

This did not end her involvement in the hospitality industry. She has always felt that professional association membership is important, so in 1980 she chaired the New York State Hotel & Motel Association. At that time she was also a member of the AH & MA Board of Directors—the only female member ("Women in the Industry," 1988). In 1989, Grossinger Estes became the first female president of the AH & MA. In an article in _Restaurants and Institutions_ (1988) she stated "It was 76 years before they elected one woman. If I muck it up, it will be 176 years before they elect another one." (p. 118)

Estes continued her work in the hospitality industry by owning and operating her own consulting firm in Boca Raton, Florida, and as an executive assistant to the president of American Inns Management Company of Tucson, Arizona (Women in the Industry," 1988).

Alice Waters

Alice Waters has been called the mother of California cuisine and has become a role model for women chefs throughout the nation. Although she downplays the fact that she is a successful woman, she is often mentioned as someone who, in the past 20 years, has definitely opened doors for many women (Messick, 1992).

Although she had no formal culinary training, she did spend a year of study abroad eating in the best French restaurants. Waters returned to the United States and opened her restaurant, Chez Panisse, in 1971, vowing to serve food as good as she had eaten in France (Messick, 1992). Food served at Chez Panisse is the freshest, best, in-season, organically grown food that can be found. Waters has been instrumental in developing a French-style farmers market in Oakland and finding local growers and distributors willing to produce the special products she demands (Patterson, 1988).

Waters has written several successful cookbooks. Her most recent, *Fanny at Chez Panisse* (Harper & Collins) views the family restaurant business from the eyes of a young girl—her daughter, Fanny (Plummer & Fernandez, 1992). Waters has continually educated and trained other young chefs, sending them out to continue the practice of cooking with only the freshest and the best (Ross, 1988).

In May 1992, at the second annual James Beard Awards, Alice Waters was named Chef of the Year and Chez Panisse was named Best Restaurant of the Year. This great honor seemed most appropriate as the year's theme was "A Salute to Women Chefs in America" (Keegan, 1992).

Ruth U. Fertel

The headline in *Nation's Restaurant News* (Sept. 21, 1992) declared: "Ruth Fertel: Tireless Entrepreneur." Fertel had been named one of the winners of the 1992 Golden Chain award selected by the Multi-Unit Foodservice Operators (MUFSO). Ralph J. Giardina, president of Ruth U. Fertel Inc., stated that her enthusiasm is real and tireless. He went on to describe how much she enjoys helping a franchisee start a business and become successful (Allen, 1992).

Fertel graduated from Louisiana State University with a degree in chemistry. After teaching for a short time she married, and became the mother of two sons. A divorce forced her back into the work force as a lab technician. She soon realized that it would be difficult to put her sons through college on the salary she earned (Ross, 1988).

In 1965, she found an advertisement in the paper offering a steak house for sale in New Orleans. She viewed the property, mortgaged her house, and bought the business all in the same day. That $18,000 investment has grown into an $80-million business (Allen, 1992).

In 1977 the first Ruth's Chris Steak House was franchised. There are now 13 company-owned restaurants and 25 franchised establishments throughout the nation. Plans are in progress to open units in Cancun, Mexico, and possibly Taipei (13 in fashion, 1993). Business associates describe Fertel as hard-working, honest and decisive, willing to take a risk, down to earth, and knowledgeable (Allen, 1992). That does describe a tireless entrepreneur.

When asked about her success (Allen, 1992), Fertel stated that "failure never entered my mind. I've always had a lot of confidence in my ability to do anything that I set my mind to." . . . Fertel considers herself semiretired at age 66. This means seven- or eight-hour workdays instead of 18- or 20-hour ones. Will she ever really retire? Probably not.

Joan Sills

In 1991, Joan Sills was appointed president of Colony Hotels and Resorts, a division of Carlson Companies. She is the only women president of a major international hotel company. Sills, a 16-year veteran of the hospitality industry, was employed by the Marriott Corporation in sales and marketing positions for several years. She also held the title of vice president of operations for Radisson Hotels International and executive vice president of Colony (Del Sesto, 1993; Ricciardi, 1992; Bartlett, 1992).

Sills feels that as more women remain in the hospitality industry for longer periods, more women will hold higher positions (Ricciardi, 1992). In an article in *Lodging* (1993), Sills stated that "the more business experience women can get, the better opportunities they will have for advancement." (p. 31).

Does this listing include all successful women in the hospitality industry? Of course not! This is just a sample. To profile every successful women a book would have to be written, and perhaps that is the next step. The examples chosen were women who have made a difference and in some cases will continue to make a difference. A variety of words were used to describe the traits of the women in the reading. Are there special traits a woman must have to be successful? Of course not, although persistence seems to be essential.

The women were chosen from a variety of fields. As you begin to sort through the opportunities available to you, become aware of women who have paved the way. Review the reference list. Choose several and begin to identify other women who were not included in this reading. Become involved in professional student organizations. Develop the habit of doing some informational interviews every semester. Don't be afraid to ask "How did you get to where you are today?" Students need role models and mentors and they are out there.

Many articles begin, end, or include the phrase, "You've come a long way, baby." This reading concludes with the phrase, "We've only just begun."

——References——

Allen, R. L. Ruth Fertel: Tireless Entrepreneur. *Nations Restaurant News.* September 21, 1922, p. 81.

Bartlett, T. Colony Resorts Refocuses Its Energies on Expansion in Hawaii. *Travel Weekly.* April 20, 1992; p. 81.

Boas, Max and Chain, Steven. (1976) *Big Mac, The Unauthorized Story of McDonald's.* New York: E. P. Dutton.

Bolton, Whitney. *Silver Spade: The Conrad Hilton Story.* Plainview, N.Y.: Books for Libraries.

Brymer, Robert A. (1981) *Introduction to Hotel and Restaurant Management: A Book of Readings.* Third edition. Dubuque, Ia.: Kendall/Hunt Publishing Company.

Burros, M. For Julia Child, An Intimate Dinner for 500 Guests. *New York Times.* February 10, 1993; pp. B3, C1.

Child, Julia. (1968) *The French Chef Cookbook.* New York: Alfred A. Knopf, Inc.

Dabney, Thomas E. *The Man Who Bought the Waldorf* Duell, Sloan, & Pearce. 1950.

Del Sesto, C. Women in Lodging: How Far Have They Come? *Lodging.* May, 1993; pp. 26–32.

Fitzerald et al. *Holiday Inns, Inc.* Department of Business Administration, University of Northern Florida. 1983.

Henderson, Ernest. (1960) *The World of "Mr. Sheraton,"* New York: D. McKay Publishers.

Hilton, Conrad N. (1957) *Be My Guest.* Englewood Cliffs, N.J.: Prentice-Hall.

Institutions/Volume Feeding. Reprint. September 1972.

Keegan, P. O. Waters, Chez Panisse Grab Top Beard Awards. *Nations Restaurant News.* May 25, 1992; p. 7.

Kroc, Ray and Anderson, Robert. (1976). *Grinding It Out, The Making of McDonald's.* Chicago: Regnery Co.

Lundberg, D. E. (1989) *The Hotel and Restaurant Business.* Fifth edition. New York: Van Nostrand Reinhold.

Lundberg, Donald E. (1979) *The Hotel and Restaurant Business.* Third edition. Boston: CBI Publishing Co. Most of the data on Ritz, Statler, Hilton, Henderson, and Johnson were taken from this source.

Messick, R. Silver Spoon Award, Alice Waters. September 1992; *Food Arts.* p. 88.

Nasar, S. Women's Gains Will Keep Coming. *U.S. News and World Report.* April 2, 1990; p. 45.

O'Brian, R. (1987) *Marriott: The J. Willard Marriott Story.* Salt Lake City, Utah: Desert Book Company.

Patterson, P. Alice Waters' Chez Panisse Chefs Pick Their Own Fresh Vegetables. *Nation's Restaurant News.* November 7, 1988; p. 75.

Plummer, W. Radical Chef: Chez Panisse's Alice Waters Foments Another Revolution: Turning Cooing into Child's Play. *People Weekly.* November 23, 1992; pp. 184–186.

Powers, T. (1992) *Introduction to Management in the Hospitality Industry.* Fourth edition. New York: John Wiley & Sons, Inc.

Ricciardi, Al. L. Colony Chief: Bright Prospects for '92. *Travel Weekly.* February 3, 1992; p. 19.

Ritz, Marie Louise. (1938) *Cesar Ritz Host to the World.* Philadelphia: Lippincott.

Ross, N. R. Wonder Women! *Restaurants and Institutions.* September 16, 1988; pp. 115, 116, 122, 126.

Schuster, K. The High Cost of Success. *Food Management.* September 1986; pp. 72–76, 142, 144, 146, 148.

Starr, M. Eat, Drink and Be Sensible: Is Life Worth Living Without a Bit of Butter? *Newsweek.* May 27, 1991; p. 52.

Ten Pioneers Who Shaped Modern American Foodservice. *Institutional/Volume Feeding.* July 1, 1976; pp. 27–32.

The Latest Recipe from Julia Child: Start Enjoying Your Food. *Newsweek.* August 6, 1990; p. S2.

Thirteen Are in Fashion. *Working Women.* May 1993; p. 62.

Weinstein, J. Slowly But Surely, Women Gaining Stature. *Restaurants and Institutions.* February 18, 1987; pp. 18–19.

Wilson, Kemmons. (1972) The Holiday Inn Story. Second Edition. In Sapienza et al. (1977) *Readings on Managing Hotels, Restaurants and Institutions.* Rochelle Park, N.J.: Hayden.

Women in the Industry *Lodging.* November 1988; pp. 44, 46, 48.

4

Hospitality Industry Associations

David L. Tucker
Widener University

The hospitality industry has numerous professional associations, whose abundance and variety reflects the magnitude and diversity of the industry itself. The field of hospitality runs the gamut from vending machines; in-flight food service; and hotel, prison, school, hospital and military feeding to the more commonly known anchors of the industry: restaurants. Students of hospitality management have a noteworthy advantage at graduation, because the food service industry presents many opportunities as it grows and changes to accommodate a society increasingly dependent on it. Students can explore any one of many segments in the hospitality industry. Each provides distinct levels of growth, challenge, and creativity, as well as career directions that students seek.

Graduating from college is only the beginning of the learning process and development of one's personal life and career. Active participation in industry associations is an excellent method of continuing to learn different aspects of one's chosen field as well as gleaning insights into oneself and discovering how the two fit together. It behooves industry professionals and faculty to show students the advantages, if not the necessity, of joining groups and becoming involved.

The wisest students are those who realize that, as students, they have three objectives to accomplish before graduation to become prime hire candidates. Their first objective should be the achievement of good grades. Second, during their college careers students must acquire industry experience. Few companies, if any, will seriously consider HRI students for management positions or fast tracks if they have not worked in the industry. A third objective should be to get involved in activities on campus whether they be social, academic, or industry related. Doing so indicates interest, ability to be committed, and willingness to work for a cause. Hotel, Restaurant, and Institutional (HRI) students have many opportunities to become involved and active, as the organizations listed below have student chapters. If not, organize one on campus.

Professional organizations with student chapters are great vehicles for win/win relationships. Students win by becoming involved with associations, for this is one of the three qualifications most recruiters look for. Associations win by establishing relationships with various colleges and universities whose students are prospective employees.

All too often, students do not realize the benefits and importance of participation in student branches of professional and industry organizations. As well as providing an opportunity to meet and get to know other people, such organizations give students a valuable chance to network. Meeting industry professionals, traveling on field trips, and participating in social functions helps round out a student's experience. In addition, student organizations on campus provide situations for acquiring leadership skills, which can boost confidence when it comes to crucial job interviews. A student who has held offices such as president, vice president, secretary, or treasurer, stands out in a crowd and is the kind of person the hospitality industry seeks to hire.

It is often difficult to get students to join and participate in such groups because they have other commitments such as part-time work, sports activities, studying, and social life.

At this point, it is up to faculty to encourage, wheedle, cajole, and challenge students to join students organizations. Having a number of professional clubs on campus may be reason enough to attract students and enhance the curriculum. Results will justify the effort invested in these organizations; everybody will benefit.

Industry Associations

What follows is a list of hospitality industry associations. Most are directly involved with the industry, although some fall into the category of being indirectly allied with the industry. The list will show students the great diversity of organizations available, which may better enable them to develop careers in the hospitality industry. Whichever segment of the industry the student chooses, there is a group to join and participate in.

National Restaurant Association (NRA)[1]

This association is the leading national trade group for the food service industry, founded in 1919. Today the NRA has more than 20,000 members who represent more than 150,000 food service outlets. The association works to promote the ideals and interests of its members. It also provides education, research, communications, conventions, and government affairs services.

The NRA operates through a staff of more than 100 located in Washington, D.C., and Chicago, Illinois. The association has state and local level chapters as well as those at the national level.

Some of the greatest benefits to NRA members are access to information and library resources. The NRA's toll-free number, (800) 522–7578, is frequently used. Another helpful service is the education courses that the NRA offers in various cities throughout the nation. These seminars cover labor issues, cost controls, and dining room, server training, nine in total. An annual schedule details the courses.

---

[1]NRA has offices at 1200 Seventeenth St., NW, Washington, DC, (202) 331–5900, (800) 424–5156; and 150 N. Michigan Ave., Suite 2000, Chicago, IL 60601, (312) 853–2525.

Various memberships are available to people working in and associated with the industry. There are also not-for-profit memberships, foreign memberships, allied members, education/faculty, and education/student memberships.

American Hotel and Motel Association (AH & MA)[2]

The American Hotel and Motel Association is a combination of more than seventy lodging groups in the United States and approximately thirty countries. Its membership consists of managers of lodging facilities around the world, and represents 1.3 million hotel rooms. Importantly, these rooms generated 82.6% of total revenue in 1985. In addition to all the lodging facilities represented, more than 675 allied companies are members of AH & MA. Students of hospitality education, faculty, and military personnel can obtain AH & MA memberships at special lower rates.

AH & MA was founded in 1910. Its prime objectives are to provide education programs, information on legislative changes, and conduct conferences and seminars. The AH & MA works very closely with various state organizations and complements their programs.

One of the major services provided by AH & MA is its Educational Institute (EI). This nonprofit educational division offers textbooks, seminars, tapes, industry experts, and more for industry use. The Educational Institute also offers many courses that lead to certificates, including Certified Hotel Administration (CHA).

AH & MA publishes several periodicals for benefit of the industry, including *Lodging Magazine* and *Hotel and Motel Red Book,* which contains names, addresses, phone numbers, and other pertinent information for member hotels throughout the country. AH & MA helps sponsor the International Hotel/Motel and Restaurant show held annually in New York City.

Hotel Sales and Marketing Association International (HSMAI)[3]

The Hotel Sales and Marketing Association International has more than 6,500 members, who represent 43 countries. HSMAI was founded 62 years ago, and it is one of the hospitality industry's largest and oldest organizations. The group is composed mostly of members whose expertise is sales and marketing in hotels, motels, and other lodging establishments.

HSMAI has many student chapters and holds an annual national student conference. These conferences are well attended. Each year students compete for the honor of hosting the succeeding year's convention. Consequently, HSMAI gives students valuable experience in marketing their clubs and moves the conference to different locales each year.

---

[2]American Hotel and Motel Association, 888 Seventh Ave., New York, NY 10019, (212) 265–4506. Education Institute, 1407 South Harrison Rd., East Lansing, MI 48823, (517) 353–5503.

[3]Hotel Sales and Marketing Associations International, 1300 L Street, NW, Suite 800, Washington, DC, 20005.

Like many of the other associations, HSMAI offers professional certification as a Certified Hotel Sales Executive (CHSE). Other services include national and international conferences, monthly chapter meetings, several publications, and education and research resources.

American Dietetic Association (ADA)[4]

The American Dietetic Association is the nation's largest professional association for dietitians, dietetic technicians, and dietetic professionals. The ADA was founded in 1917 and has more than 59,000 members.

The main purpose of the ADA is to promote good health and nutrition throughout the nation by means of sound dietetic practice, advocacy, and research.

With their extensive scientific backgrounds, ADA members apply knowledge of food, nutrition, biochemistry, physiology, management, and behavior and social sciences to promote health, prevent disease, and assist recovery from illness.

Dietitians work in many positions for numerous organizations, including schools, health care facilities, U.S. government installations, and community agencies as well as in business and industry. In addition, many dietitians consult in nursing homes, restaurants, and doctor's offices.

Management ADA members are registered dietitians (RD) who have completed a bachelor's degree, an internship, and an examination. Continuing education credits are offered, and are required to keep RD status up to date.

Membership benefits include legislative representation, maintenance of educational and practice standards, continuing education programs and materials, professional publications, member discounts, and annual meetings and conferences.

The ADA is divided into seven areas across the country. Each state provides at least one delegate. The number of delegates depends on the number of voting members who belong to the ADA from the particular state. Within some states, district associations have been organized for activity at the local level.

American Culinary Foundation (ACF)[5]

The American Culinary Foundation is the largest organization of its kind, with more than 18,000 members organized in 200 chapters throughout the United States and the Caribbean. The ACF was founded in 1929 in New York City.

The primary goal of ACF is upgrading the profession through education. This is accomplished through the American Culinary Federation Education Institute (ACFEI), a subsidiary of ACF. The ACFEI organizes and sponsors training programs for culinary students.

---

[4]The American Dietetic Association, 216 W. Jackson Blvd., Suite 800, Chicago, IL 60606-6995, (800) 877–1600.

[5]The American Culinary Foundation, Inc., P.O. Box 3466, St. Augustine, FL 32084, (904) 824–4468.

With this ACFEI training, chefs may be certified as skilled and knowledgeable professionals meeting the qualifications of experience, education, and ACF activity. Currently the institute oversees 96 culinary apprenticeship programs with 2,600 apprentices.

Another subsidiary of ACF is American Academy of Chefs (AAC). The Academy was organized in 1952 and gives recognition to fellow culinarians who meet the highest standards. A Hall of Fame was established recently to honor those chefs who excel in skill and leadership.

The ACF elects officers every two years, including president, secretary, and treasurer. The ACF is divided into four national regions, each with a regional vice president. Each region has a spring conference, followed by a national conference in July.

American Correctional Food Service Association (ACFSA)[6]

The American Correctional Food Service Association was formed to represent food service managers who work in correctional facilities throughout the country. ACFSA was founded in 1969. The Association is divided into eight regions. There is a national conference annually.

The ACFSA has over 1,000 members. Nearly 600 people attended the most recent national conference in Phoenix, in 1989.

Services offered to their members include certification, certified food service professional (CFP), bimonthly newsletters, regional seminars, and employment referral services, among others.

This organization does not have high visibility among college students but is striving to change that situation.

American School Food Service Association (ASFSA)[7]

The American School Food Service Association represents those food service managers who work in school food service across the nation. This is one of the faster-growing segments of food service management serving children in grades K through 12. This organization has nearly 65,000 members.

---

[6]American Correctional Food Service Association, McCann-Cannard and Associates, 20–40 Chestnut St., Harrisburg, PA 17104, (717) 233–2301.

[7]American School Food Service Association, 1600 Duke St., 7th floor, Alexandria, VA 22314, (800) 877–8822.

National Association of Catering Executives[8]

The National Association of Catering Executives is an organization especially for those people interested in catering and catering functions. The organization has more than 2,600 members in the United States and Canada. The goals of NACE are to foster networking and professionalism as well as to provide continuing education to the professional caterer.

National Society for Healthcare Food Service Management (HFM)[9]

The National Society for Healthcare Food Service Management (HRM) is an organization for those independent managers who have an interest in food service in the health care field. There are more than 533 members across the country. The main purpose of HFM is to provide members with the knowledge and tools to be on the cutting edge in hospital food service management.

Council of Hotel, Restaurant and Institutional Educators (CHRIE)[10]

The Council of Hotel, Restaurant, and Institutional Educators was formed in 1949 by several hospitality educators. Today the organization has more than 1,000 members. Educators comprise the greatest percent of the membership; however, there are also industry members as well as a conglomeration of allied members from such diverse areas as food surveying to textbook publishing. This group is greatly varied, with almost every area and interest of the hospitality industry represented.

CHRIE has a national annual meeting, usually in August. The national organization is divided into regional chapters, which meet more frequently—usually every month or two.

CHRIE is valuable for its members when it comes to sharing knowledge and research that is done in the hospitality industry. It is also a great resource network for industry and graduate students in many research areas.

---

[8]National Association of Catering Executives, 304 W. Liberty St., Suite 201, Louisville, KY 40202, (502) 581–9786.

[9]National Society for Healthcare Food Service Management, 204 E St., NE, Washington, DC 20002, (292) 546–7236.

[10]CHRIE 1200 Seventeenth St., NW, Washington, DC 20036, (202) 331–5990.

Club Managers Association of America (CMAA)[11]

Club Managers Association of America is the professional association that represents more than 4,000 members in yacht, athletic, faculty, corporate, city, and military clubs. The objectives of the association are to promote good relations among managers, to encourage education and advancement, and to help club officers and members, through their managers, to have the most efficient and successful club operations possible. There are 53 chapters in the United States and abroad.

CMAA conducts more than 30 national education programs each year. On the local level, more than 200 professional development programs are offered. The CMAA awards a Certified Club Manager (CCM) designation to those managers who prove themselves through rigorous course work and a personal development program.

CMAA offers other services to its members, including the Executive Search Career Service, government and public affairs information, and the in-house resource library.

CMAA represents more than 265,000 employees, who account for more than $2 billion in payroll. In addition, member clubs raised more than $183 million for charity in 1988.

What may be most important for the student to know is that CMAA provided more than $5 million in scholarships in 1988 and that 33% of the clubs sponsor student internship programs. CMAA has proven to be a very popular industry organization among students and educators.

Eta Sigma Delta (EDS)[12]

Eta Sigma Delta is the honor fraternity for hospitality students. The organization has chapters on more than 35 college campuses around the country. Since members must have a minimum GPA of 3.5, this fraternity surely represents some of the best hospitality management students.

ESD members are usually very active and visible on campus. They hold fund raisers, give VIP's guided tours, and provide tutoring services for other students.

Eta Sigma Delta representatives usually meet twice a year, at the New York Hotel Show and the NRA Show in Chicago. ESD has also started meeting annually at the national CHRIE conference.

Inflight Food Service Association (IFSA)[13]

The Inflight Food Service Association is composed of airline companies, airline caterers, allied members, and all interested in serving quality food in airplanes. It was formed about 25

---

[11]Club Managers Association of America, 7615 Winterberry Pl., Bethesda, MD 20817, (301) 229–3600.

[12]Eta Sigma Delta can be contacted through Donna McHugh, CHRIE, 1200 Seventeenth St., NW, Washington, DC 20036-3097, (202) 331–5990.

[13]Inflight Food Service Association, 304 West Liberty St., Suite 301, Louisville, KY 40202, (502) 583–3783.

years ago and now has more than 1,200 members. Inflight Food Service Association has an annual convention and regional meetings. This group also sponsors culinary competitions internationally.

Airlines and airline caterers face some unique problems in their food service environments due to very limited space in carriers. The annual and regional meetings help these managers face some of these challenges and solve the problems.

International Food Service Executives Association (IFSEA)[14]

The International Food Service Executives Association was established in 1901 and now has more than 5,000 members in 25 states and 10 countries. IFSEA is an organization that draws members from many segments of the hospitality industry. Members come from all aspects of food service management, including restaurants, clubs, hospitals, contract food service, and airlines among others.

The IFSEA offers many services to its members, including national and local conferences and seminars, networking, certification as a food expert, and travel around the world with a military team.

This association is among the largest of the industry's professional associations, and is probably the most widespread. One characteristic of IFSEA is its steadfast commitment to education. This group offers financial assistance and many scholarships to students studying hospitality management.

International Association of Hospitality Accountants (IAHA)[15]

The International Association of Hospitality Accountants represents hotel accountants and controllers in more than 50 countries. IAHA has more than 35 chapters in North America, with membership about three thousand. The primary objectives of this organization are development, education, and support for the professional members in accounting and financial management.

IAHA's official publications, *The Bottomline* and *The President's Log,* help keep members up to date on recent industry events. Members may also apply to Certified Hospitality Accountant Executive Program (CHAEP). Other services include a referral service, annual convention, and membership rosters. IAHA provides scholarships to students in hospitality accounting at accredited universities.

---

[14]International Food Service Executives Association, 1100 State Road 7, Suite 103, Margate, FL 33068, (305) 977–0767.

[15]International Association of Hospitality Accountants, P.O. Box 27649, Austin, TX 78755-2649.

National Association of College and University Food Services (NACUFS)[16]

The National Association of College and University Food Services was formed in 1958 and represents those professionals who manage food services on college and university campuses. NACUFS is divided into nine regions, including Canada, Puerto Rico, the Virgin Islands, Hong Kong, and Australia.

Like other industry associations, NACUFS offers varied services to its members, such as newsletters, referral services, networking, and national and local conferences. NACUFS is very active in helping to develop managers and future managers by providing scholarships and seminars through its Leadership Institute.

NACUFS has been very responsive to college students' needs and each year offers extensive internships at member colleges and universities around the country. Over fifty college and university sites are offered for this internship experience.

Society for Foodservice Management (SFM)[17]

The Society for Foodservice Management is composed of professionals who manage food service facilities for business and industry. The Society for Foodservice Management was founded ten years ago and has a membership of more than 1,100. SFM is organized into six regions throughout the United States. The organization has both client (corporate) and contract company members. In addition to these two groups, many allied members such as purveyors, consultants, and educators belong to SFM.

SFM provides many services to its membership, including national and local conferences, a networking directory, membership lists, and educational meetings. SFM has been active on a few college campuses promoting business and industry food service through its student chapters. The organization also is currently setting up an education foundation to help industry, students, and educators promote an increased awareness of business and industry food service.

The foundation provides funds and/or resources to individuals to further research, education, and other activities, on request and verification of needs.

---

[16]National Association of College and University Food Services, 7 Olds Hall, Michigan State University, East Lansing, MI 48824.

[17]Society for Foodservice Management, 304 West Liberty St., Suite 301, Louisville, KY 40202, (502) 583–3783.

Summary

After examining the above list of hospitality industry associations, it's clear that there is something for almost everybody. As mentioned earlier, associations are an important and useful part of any industry. They bring together people with common interests and talents, providing the atmosphere for necessary networking and communication.

Students and academic communities alike who use and become involved with these industry associations generally are at a greater disadvantage than those who choose not to use associations. Any of these associations can provide benefits for the student in the form of contact with industry professionals, national and regional conferences, networking, scholarships and awards, and a place to demonstrate and prove leadership skills. Only the foolish will not see the value of industry associations.

——References——

American Correctional Food Service Association. *Newsletter.* Fall 1989.

The American Culinary Federation. *ACF News.*

American Dietetic Association. Chicago, Ill.

American Hotel and Motel Association. *Programs and Services.* New York, N.Y.

The Bottomline, The Journal of the International Association of Hospitality Accountants. December/January 1990; Volume 4, Number 6.

Club Managers Association of America. *Who We Are.*

Eta Sigma Delta. *Newsletter.* Fall 1989.

Hotel Sales and Marketing Association International. *Marketing Review.* Fall 1989; Volume 8, Number 1.

IFSA Report. Fall 1989.

Inflight Food Service Association. *Membership Invitation.*

International Association of Hospitality Accountants. *Ready to Go Places with Your Career?*

International Food Service Executives Association. *Hotline.* Fall 1989.

NACUFS. *News Wave.* November/December 1989; Volume 23.

National Restaurant Association. *A List of Member Services.*

An Organization That's for You and About You Shouldn't Be Without—Your NACUFS. East Lansing, Mich. 1986.

SFM. *Annual Report.* Louisville, Ky. 1988.

5

Hospitality Industry Rating Services

Melvin N. Barrington
University of South Carolina

Finding a place to sleep or eat is relatively easy for the traveling public, but finding one that meets individual needs and tastes is a little more difficult. Fortunately, the contemporary American traveler's task of choosing quality accommodations is simplified tremendously by the proliferation of referral groups, chains, and franchise operations. Through their extensive quality assurance programs and inspection systems, they all but guarantee consistency and excellence no matter where the lodging or restaurant is located.

Before the existence of chains and franchises, with their consistent standards and predictable product, the public had to rely on other methods to rate hospitality businesses. Initially, ratings were informal—mostly by word of mouth—especially in the cities. For rural or roadside areas the watchword was to stop where the truckers ate, presumably they were familiar with all the good spots because they were experienced travelers. Yet, eating or sleeping at an establishment with a lot of trucks parked out front left a lot to be desired, so more formal systems of rating services came into vogue.

Triple A

Established in 1902, the grandaddy and probably the best known of all rating services is the American Automobile Association (AAA), better known as Triple A. Motel and restaurant operators have strived to earn a rating from the Triple A in order to proudly hang the blue-and-silver oval disk from their sign, thereby beckoning the weary traveler to a nice, clean place to eat, sleep, or both. In addition to the instant recognition of the sign, which may attract random travelers, each approved property is listed in a directory supplied to members. Since rating properties is not as necessary as it once was, Triple A has expanded its services to include emergency road service, bail bonds, trip information, and maps, as well as advisories on road construction, speed traps, and unsafe highways—any on which motorists have been shot at or stoned.

Each lodging establishment listed in AAA tour books and travel guides is assigned a rating of one to five diamonds, which reflects the overall quality of a property within its classification. Diamond ratings are determined through annual inspections by full-time field representatives, who submit detailed reports on each property concerning the following aspects: exterior, public areas, guest room decor, guest room equipment, bathrooms, housekeeping, maintenance, management, and guest services. These reports are assessed by a committee on accommodations and assigned ratings based on their review. Each property is inspected and rated individually. Therefore, a rating of a member property of a chain operation does not constitute a blanket approval of an entire chain.

Mobil

The Mobil Oil Corporation has been rating restaurants and lodging establishments since 1958 and publishing the rating in their *Mobil Travel Guide*. They use a system of categorizing properties from one to five stars. For lodging establishments rating criteria cover the number and quality of facilities, furnishings, maintenance, housekeeping, food service, guest services, quality of appointments, and the attitude and professionalism of both staff and management. Restaurant evaluations include the quality of food preparation, presentation, freshness of ingredients, and quality of service as well as the attitudes and professionalism of staff and management. Also, for both lodging and restaurants, distinctive historic, cultural, and regional attractions are major factors in each rating. The ratings are determined in two ways, through inspections by anonymous company representatives who submit detailed reports and through an extensive review of guest comments received by the editors of the *Mobil Travel Guide*.

Classifications

Both Triple A and Mobil also base their ratings on a property classification system that takes into account architectural style and services offered. In other words, the more luxurious the physical structure and the more services offered by the property the higher the rating. However, a lower-rated property with fewer services and amenities may be just as clean and the employees as attentive as a higher-rated property. The difference lies in the extras being offered. The American Automobile Association classifies its properties based on architectural style and services as follows:

> **Hotel**—A multistory building which can be in a downtown, suburban, or resort location. Amenities include coffee shop, dining room, lounge, room service, convenience shops, valet, laundry, and banquet and meeting facilities. Parking is generally limited in downtown areas, while ample parking is usually provided in suburban locations. Full-service expectations.

> **Motor Inn**—Generally two to three stories but may be a multistory high-rise building. Usually offers recreation facilities and food and beverage service. May have limited banquet and meeting facilities. Ample on-premises parking. Moderate service expectations.

Motel—Usually one to two stories. Food service, if any, consists of a limited facility or snack bar. Often has some recreational facilities, such as a swimming pool and playground. Ample, convenient parking, often at the door. Limited service expectations.

Country Inn—Many have a historic background. Rooms reflect the ambience of yesteryear but may lack some modern amenities and have shared baths. Usually are owner operated and provide food and beverage service. On-premises parking is usually available. Moderate service expectations.

Historical—Provides accommodations in restored structures, generally built before 1930. Establishments reflect the ambience of yesteryear and the surrounding region, with many playing roles in the history of the area. Rooms may not offer all of the modern amenities, and a few may have shared baths; usually are owner operated. Food and beverage service is often available. On-premises parking is usually available. Moderate service expectations.

Lodge—Typically two or more stories with all facilities in one building. Located in vacation, ski, or fishing areas. Usually has food and beverage service. Adequate on-premises parking. Moderate service expectations.

Cottages—Individual buildings (bungalows, cabins, or villas) usually containing one rental unit equipped for housekeeping. May have a separate living room and bedroom(s), occasionally have more than one rental unit per building as in duplex cottages. Parking usually located at each unit. Limited service expectations.

Ranch—Features outdoor, Western-type recreational facilities. Moderate service expectations.

Apartment—At least 50% of rental units are equipped for housekeeping. Usually located in a vacation destination area. Units typically provide a fully equipped kitchen and generally have a living room and one or more bedrooms, although they may be studio-type rooms with kitchen equipment in an alcove that can be closed off from living/sleeping areas. May require minimum stay and/or offer lower rates for longer stays.

Suites—All units consist of one or more bedrooms and a living room which may not be completely closed off from the bedrooms.

Resort—Has a vacation atmosphere and often is far removed from metropolitan areas. Offers extensive recreational facilities on the premises; may cater to specific interests such as golf, tennis, or fishing. Rates may include meals under American or modified American plans.

AH & MA

Using a slight variation of the above, the American Hotel and Motel Association (AH & MA) rates properties according to services, physical amenities, and price. For example:

Budget Motels—Usually have no bellman, room service, telephone, nor television in the room without extra charge. Most are priced in the lower range of rates.

Economy Motels—Usually include a restaurant, pool, and private bath at a rate slightly higher than budget motels.

Full Service—Midpriced hotels have more attractive design, round-the-clock front desk operation, choice of restaurants, bar, room service, dry cleaning, and convention facilities. Moderately priced room rates.

Full Service—Upscale hotels. Same range of services as midpriced but have more luxurious design and surroundings at room rates in the higher range.

Luxury Hotels—Boast more lavish surroundings with additional amenities such as health club, in-room minibars, haute cuisine restaurants, and a concierge. Normally the highest priced of all the lodging properties.

Resort Hotels—Always include several restaurants and offer a wide variety of activities and charge in the higher price ranges.

All-suite Hotels—Offer a separate living and sleeping area and kitchen facilities. Most have large lobbies, restaurants, and bars. Prices range from moderate to high.

Others

In addition to Mobil, at least two other major oil companies (Amoco and Exxon) offer travel clubs to their credit card customers. They often team up with other companies such as Allstate (Sears) or campground franchisers such as Kampgrounds of America (KOA) and for an annual or monthly fee offer a multitude of services similar to Triple A, such as trip kits, maps, road hazard service, and bail bonds.

Mobil, Exxon, Fodor's, Baedeker's, Fielding's, Michelin, and Rand McNally publish travel guides, which are sold in most bookstores. These tour guides provide extensive travel information through the description and rating of geographic locations, provision of maps, and in general listing the important points of interest as well as recommendations for hotels and restaurants. For the special traveler who tows or carries accommodations in the form of a tent or recreation vehicle (RV), several publications list and rate campgrounds. One of the more extensive RV publishers is Woodall's, which annually publishes several campground directories, one for North America and several regional editions. Woodall's diamond rating system is based on quantity of facilities and services provided rather than quality.

Finally, numerous free booklets and rating guides promote cities, states, regions, and other travel destinations, and are distributed in welcome centers, airports, hotel lobbies, and restaurants. Although these publications provide valuable information on tourist attractions as well as places to eat and sleep, their ratings of such facilities must be taken with a grain of salt because they usually only include those businesses who subscribe to advertising space.

Governments

In foreign countries ratings of hotels and restaurants are established by individual governments.[*] Since there are no unified rating criteria, a five-star or luxury-rated property in one country may differ significantly from a similar level in another country. In Europe with the evolvement of the European Common Community (ECC) there is a push for standardized rating levels of hotels in all countries. As with many other standardization problems confronting the ECC, this one is also meeting with resistance because individual governments wish to retain their rating authority. A possible solution to this dilemma is being proposed by a consortium (HOTREC) made up of hotel and restaurant owners throughout Europe. They propose the use of international symbols to simply denote amenities and services: for example, whether a property is family oriented or primarily for seminars and conferences. They feel the traveling public is sophisticated enough to judge quality without a formal star rating system.

The only rating system carried out by governments in the United States centers around those issued by health inspectors representing the various state and county agencies. These letter ratings are placed in a prominent location in each establishment to be seen by the public in order for them to judge if they wish to patronize an establishment with less than an "A" sanitation rating.

The Future

With the implementation of the Americans with Disabilities Act (ADA), the current legislation for the rights of nonsmokers, and the increasing concerns for environmental illness (sick building syndrome), it's foreseeable that there will eventually be rating systems for the degree of handicapped accessibility as well as the level of toxins in public and private enclosures.

It appears that in spite of the tremendous job accomplished by chains and franchises to ensure quality, rating services will continue to play an important role in tourism and travel. The traveling public tends to be adventuresome and the more frequently they travel the more they tend to avoid the chains in order to experience local hospitality. The caveat, however, is that they will want to do some research beforehand and obtain advanced knowledge in order not to be taken completely by surprise.

_____

*For an extensive discussion of China's hotel rating system see Yu, Lawrence. Seeing Stars: China's Hotel-Rating System. *The Cornell Hotel and Restaurant Administration Quarterly.* Volume 33, Number 5: October 1992; pp. 24–27.

Hospitality Industry Career Development

Part II

6

Planning for a Hospitality Management Career

Michael Sciarini
Michigan State University

The mass of men lead lives of quiet desperation.

Henry David Thoreau

The happiest people in the world get paid for doing what they would do anyway on their summer vacation.

Mark Twain

As you ponder your future and specifically the potential for a career in the hospitality business, it is my hope that this brief chapter will be of some benefit to you. Perhaps the words that follow may help you avoid the sort of life Thoreau ascribed to most people. If you have not already realized it, I hope that after reading this chapter you will know that it is up to you to discover and create the sort of career that will allow you to join the happiest of people, as described by Mark Twain.

To help you plan for and get started on a fulfilling hospitality management *career* (and not just a series of jobs), I recommend that you make use of this process: first, self-assessment—take a good, long and hard look at yourself; second, explore your options—determine the paths you might create and follow; and third, market yourself—develop and use employment opportunity search skills. This should become an ongoing process, one that will remain valuable at any stage of your career.

Self-Assessment

Since the career under consideration here is YOUR hospitality management career, self-knowledge and understanding are critical. If you haven't really thought about who you are and what you want, then your plan for a hospitality career may have a flawed starting point. Spending the time to learn and truly understand your values, interests, skills, and motivations is time well invested.

There are many ways to go about this. Beyond contemplating these issues and discussing them with friends and family, take advantage of the many resources that may be available to you through the school you now attend. I'm referring specifically to career counselors and the batteries of self-exploration profiles at their disposal as well as the computerized assessment and information tools that may also be available. In addition to people and computers, there are a number of good books that you may find helpful. The resource list at the end of this chapter includes some recently published examples.

Explore Your Options

Having developed an understanding of yourself and your priorities provides the context for asking questions about the hospitality management career opportunities that exist or might be created. How does one become more familiar with the many and varied hospitality management career opportunities? One obvious answer is to read books like this one.

Additionally, keep in touch with the career information center and the career counselor you may have visited during your self-assessment activities. Career fairs and open houses sponsored by hospitality organizations that recruit at your school also provide information about career opportunities. Consider the source at events like these. In other words, be cognizant of the motivation of those who are describing the opportunities. It is not my intention to suggest that recruiters will be dishonest. However, it is important for you to remember that in any recruiting situation, the recruiter will usually attempt to position their organization in the most favorable light. Listen carefully and with an open mind. Don't hesitate to ask questions.

Your hospitality coursework, your school's faculty, and any "guest lecturers" invited into class are additional resources. Contacting alumni of your school may prove especially helpful. Previous graduates of your program often provide excellent opportunities for research and information interviews. This is a networking technique whereby you "interview" the individuals employed within the industry/field you are interested in to gather career information and advice (e.g., what's it really like? what should I do to prepare for a career in this field? what do you wish you had known more about when you were getting started?). This is often a great way to learn about positions you might otherwise have never become aware of. Certainly you need not limit your resource and information interviews only to alumni of your school. Networking opportunities with those of a similar background to your own are often the most fruitful.

I remind you again that it is *your* career under consideration. While it is common (as noted earlier) to seek the advice of family and friends when exploring career options, BEWARE. A career decision should be what *you* want, not necessarily what your parents, friends, counselors, or anyone else wants or suggests for you. In fact, if you can't find anyone (especially among your family) who disagrees with your choice, then you may not be doing enough independent thinking.

Avoid becoming what some have called a "job snob." In other words, be careful not to get caught up in the imagined glamour of certain hospitality segments such as luxury resorts or fine dining restaurants. In the process you may overlook opportunities in areas such as noncommercial food service, quick service/fast food restaurants, or senior care. This is not to suggest that any one of these segments of the hospitality industry is the best or right one for you. Take time now to learn about all of these segments (and more) so that you choose wisely as you continue on your hospitality career journey.

The time and other resources you invest in research now will yield considerable dividends over the course of your career. The stories of those who have not chosen wisely or allowed others to make career decisions for them are too common. In her book, *Information Interviewing—What It Is and How to Use It in Your Career,* Martha Stoodley relates the story of a frustrated individual who had become "successful" in a career that he found unfulfilling. He finally had guts enough to change careers and move on to a more personally satisfying situation. His comment as he left the job he had come to loathe was, "don't get too good at something you hate—they'll make you do it the rest of your life." A telling commentary, and a good example to demonstrate that no matter what stage of our career we are in, we all have *choices.* The phrase "I had no choice" is often used to rationalize a lack of faith or confidence, sometimes laziness or unwillingness to take risks. The fact is, almost all of us retain our opportunity to choose throughout our lives, yet sometimes we hide behind words like "I had no choice." In the process, we may become too good at things we dislike and then feel stuck in jobs we come to detest. This need not happen to you and, in fact, you owe it to yourself not to allow it to happen.

Market Yourself

As you solidify your perceptions of who you are and what matters to you *and* what paths are out there in the field of hospitality management, you will discover (though I suspect you already know) that you are not likely to advance in your career by sitting on your hands. Most career opportunities will not fall in your lap. You must position yourself to create opportunities, to identify your options, and market yourself so that others perceive you as an attractive employment candidate.

A proven method for securing meaningful employment on graduation from college is through the completion of internships. Most, if not all, hospitality management schools require their students to complete a significant number of hours of professional work experience, often referred to as internships. Use these experiences to explore the segments of industry that interest you. The outcomes of the internship are usually mutually beneficial for you and your employer. You have the opportunity to learn and gain experience, and the employer sees you in the workplace and is able to make a better assessment as to your long-term potential. Each party can take a closer look at the other to determine if the relationship should continue. Even if you determine (after completing an internship) that a particular hospitality segment or situation is *not* for you, you have still expanded your knowledge base and are able to move on to examine other choices.

The next portion of this chapter presents a brief overview of a few fundamentals of the employment search process, especially relating to resumé development and interviewing. These topics were selected based on input from hospitality recruiters as well as from my experiences in working with hospitality management students over the past three years. As noted earlier, the conclusion of this chapter includes additional resources to assist you in some of the more specific components of the employment search process.

Tom Jackson, noted career counselor and author of *Guerilla Tactics in the New Job Market,* believes that there is a "Universal Hiring Rule" which follows:

> Any employer will hire any applicant as long as they believe the applicant's value exceeds his/her cost.

The point is, when you are targeting organizations that you would like to join, look to add value to that organization. The question you must be prepared to answer and answer well is, "Why should they hire me?" If your answer is "because *I* want a new car, new clothes, and minimally some way to pay the rent and feed myself" then you obviously aren't adding much value. But, if you are able to demonstrate to the employer your ability to enhance guest satisfaction and increase revenues and/or reduce expenses (increase profits) then you are solving problems and adding value that will exceed the cost of employing you.

In general, employers look for intelligence, integrity, relevant experience, and a positive attitude. It is important for you to learn what specific attributes are sought by the organizations you have targeted for employment.

We recently surveyed hospitality recruiters and asked them what matters most when they are deciding which candidates to interview. On average, a candidate's willingness to relocate, his/her work experiences, and extracurricular involvement were most important. However, the range of opinion across the sample of 51 recruiters we asked was fairly broad. For example, most of the recruiters did not attach much importance to a candidate's grade point average. However, there were a few recruiters who put significant importance on grades. The message for you is, research not only the organization but also try to find out about the specific individual with whom you'll interview. Like any other sales situation, learn as much as you can about anything else involved before you begin. Ask your faculty, use information interviews, and even ask recruiters directly (at career fairs or open houses for example) to learn about what matters to them. This will allow you to prepare appropriately.

If you learn what employers want to buy, you can be certain that you have it for sale. You may also learn that what certain employers want to *buy* as well as *sell* doesn't fit with what is important to you. This sort of information is better learned *before* you invest any more time and effort in the process, so that you may search elsewhere. Obviously, not all choices will be the right ones for you, but again, *you* must make and live with your choices.

A brief note on resumé development. Remember that a resumé is a tool you use *to get interviews.* It is not unlike an advertisement for a hospitality business intended to generate interest and inquiries. The resumé is not likely to get you an offer of employment in and of itself. It can, though, prevent you from getting interviewed. Be careful to make it neat and free of grammatical and punctuation errors. I agree with those who say that there is no one perfect resumé format or style. The consensus among hospitality recruiters I have asked seems to be that *the best resumés are those that they receive from people they know.* Think about that, and ask yourself, how much attention do you pay to junk mail that appears out of nowhere in your mailbox? Compare that to the amount of attention you pay to a personal letter from a familiar return address, say from a good friend. Think about the whole employment search process and put the importance of the resumé in perspective. Don't overemphasize its value but do create a document that is the best paper representation possible. Remember, your resumé is a valuable tool, one you use to obtain interviews. The time you invest in networking will help you get the resumé to the right person at the right time. Hospitality recruiters and managers are busy people . . . don't allow your resumé to come floating across their desks like junk mail (bound for the recycling heap).

Entire books and lengthy seminars are available on interviewing skills. Read the books, go to the seminars, and remember: *interviews are two-way streets.* You'll want every person who interviews you to think of you as a preferred candidate—one they want to hire. But, you are shopping too. You must call upon all of your research of that organization and the specific recruiter you are interviewing with and relate all of this to who you are and what you want so that you find the best fit in terms of a career opportunity.

Conclusion

If you will invest time in understanding yourself and the options available to you, I am optimistic that you will shape a fulfilling hospitality management career. In fact, if you effectively work through the process of self-assessment, exploring options, and marketing yourself, you may find yourself with several options for your first job out of school. As you get to that point and make your choice, consider the following, from Victor Frankl, a noted psychiatrist:

> Don't aim at success—the more you aim at it and make it a target, the more you are going to miss it. For success, like happiness, cannot be pursued; it must ensue and it only does so as the unintended side-effect of one's personal dedication to a cause greater than oneself or as the by-product of one's surrender to a person other than oneself.

My sincere wish is that you will find the causes and people to which you are able and willing to devote yourself. I believe that when you do, you will be able to enjoy a hospitality management career well balanced in terms of success and happiness. To a very great degree, it is up to you to position yourself among Mark Twain's "happiest people."

——Recommended Career Planning Resources——

Bolles, Richard N. (1993). *The 1993 What Color Is Your Parachute?* Berkeley, Calif.: Ten Speed Press.

Covey, Stephen R. (1989). *The 7 Habits of Highly Effective People.* New York: Simon and Schuster.

Frankl, Victor E. (1984). *Man's Search for Meaning.* New York: Washington Square Press.

Fry, Ron. (1991). *101 Great Answers to the Toughest Interview Questions.* Hawthorne, N.J.: The Career Press.

Jackson, Tom. (1991). *Guerrilla Tactics in the New Job Market.* Second edition. New York: Bantam Books.

Jackson, Tom. (1990). *The Perfect Resumé.* New York: Doubleday.

Lindquist, Carolyn and Diane Miller, ed. (1991). *Where to Start Career Planning.* Eighth edition. Ithaca, N.Y.: Cornell University Press.

Marino, Kim. (1992). *The College Student's Resumé Guide.* Berkeley, Calif.: Ten Speed Press.

McWilliams, John-Roger and Peter. (1991). *Life 101.* Los Angeles, Calif.: Prelude Press.

Medley, H. Anthony. (1992). *Sweaty Palms: The Neglected Art of Being Interviewed.* Berkeley, Calif.: Ten Speed Press.

Morgan, Bradley J. (1993). *Travel and Hospitality Career Directory.* Second edition. Detroit, Mich.: Visible Ink Press.

Shingleton, John D. (1992). *Career Planning for the 1990's: A Guide for Today's Graduates.* Garrett Park, Md.: Garrett Park Press.

Stoodley, Martha. (1990). *Information Interviewing.* Garrett Park, Md.: Garrett Park Press.

Yate, Marvin. (1993). *Knock 'em Dead: The Ultimate Job Seekers Handbook.* Holbrook, Mass.: Bob Adams, Inc.

7

Careers in the Hospitality Industry

Caroline A. Cooper
Johnson and Wales University

If one is to look at careers in the hospitality industry, it becomes necessary to define the industry. To most educators, the hospitality industry divides naturally into six major areas: lodging, food service, tourism, recreation, meeting and entertainment management, and retirement living management. The hospitality industry, of course, is a major part of the economy, and one of the service industries. John Naisbitt, the trend analyst, dates 1956 as the beginning of a predominantly service economy in the United States, "because for the first time in American history, white collar workers in technical, managerial and clerical positions outnumbered blue collar workers; Industrial America was giving way to a new society."

Naisbitt has called this phenomenon the "information society" while others, like Harvard's Daniel Bell, have labeled it the "postindustrial society." The U.S. Department of Commerce predicts that there will be continued fast growth in service jobs, with hospitality being one of leaders.

George Wills, a *Newsweek* columnist, observed that McDonald's has more employees than U.S. Steel and that the "Golden Arches" are now a truer symbol of the American economy than are blast furnaces.

As the service industries and the hospitality industry in particular grow, it becomes necessary to look at the number of positions that are projected to open in the future. At the conference of the Council of Hotel, Restaurant and Institutional Educators (CHRIE) held in 1992 in Orlando, Florida, industry speakers noted the continued need for graduates from the hotel/restaurant institutional and hospitality programs who understood the needs of customers. Although the recent worldwide recession has decreased the number of job offers per graduate, there will still be more positions available than graduates through the year 2000. This picture is compounded by the decreasing number of college graduates through the year 1996. By the year 2000, 90% of the United States labor force is expected to be employed in the service industries. At the same time it is imperative that students who want to enter these fields not only be competent in the technical aspects of their career, but also be people oriented. Students entering these fields must realize that one's work performance, unlike school, can't be just an average of highs and lows, but must be consistently good from the very beginning. Newly hired college graduates must assume total responsibility at once.

Employers are now emphasizing a college education as the best preparation for entrance into the hospitality industry. Vocation certificates, diplomas, and two- and four-year degrees provide particularly strong preparation for entry-level positions. There is a continued demand for more technically skilled employees as well as competent, mature, thoughtful employees, capable of handling what Jan Carlzon, president of SAS airlines, called the moment of truth: moments when those front-line employees have continued contact with customers. The ability to manage this situation and respond appropriately to customer needs that makes the difference as to which companies the customer continues to patronize.

An M.S. or an M.B.A. degree in hospitality or a closely related field has also become desirable for advancement in large chains or corporations. During the recent worldwide recession a larger than usual number of undergraduates entered master's degree programs as an alternative to the work force. This group of students will just now be available for positions within the industry, and it will be interesting to see whether their advancement is accelerated. Starting positions generally would not be affected by a degree.

The doctorate degree is in demand for those who want to teach in this field. As of 1987, there were approximately six doctoral candidates graduating in the hospitality field per year, with approximately 300 openings in higher education for them. This means that related areas of business, economics, and tourism, have become acceptable areas for doctoral education emphasis. Those who choose to continue on this path have numerous job options. Let us now explore the opportunities open in each of the six major areas.

The Food Service Industry

Food service employees are generally broken down into two categories: general workers can be subdivided into "front of the house" and "back of the house" employees. The front of the house includes waiters, waitresses, counter people who serve food, bartenders who create and serve drinks, and dining room attendants who clean tables, remove soiled dishes, and set up for future use. Back of the house jobs range from dishwashers who wash dishes and pots and clean the production areas to pantry personnel who prepare salads, sandwiches, and other cold food items that may be needed. Janitors and porters are other necessary positions within this group and their job is to keep the operation, floor, and equipment clean and in good working condition. Back of the house positions may also include the producers of hot food, who are generally termed cooks and chefs. There is a continuous hierarchy of these employees, and sometimes the terms get confused in a small operation. In general the term *cook* refers to those employees who produce the food, particularly the "hot items." In some kitchens, positions include first cook and head cook; sometimes the term *chef* refers to the head person in the area.

The second group of workers in the food service area can be classified as administration. This encompasses all employees who manage the employees who process and serve the food product. The chef (or the executive chef in many operations) is the manager of the back of the house, with a maitre'd or hostess managing the front of the house. Such functions also can be handled by a production manager, service manager, banquet manager, or service supervisors. Management layers may include assistant food and beverage directors, food and beverage director, and district manager, for chains and conglomerates. In some cases the owner becomes the chief executive officer (CEO) and may simultaneously be manager and chef.

In many institutional and industrial operations the allied profession of dietetics will be able to place dietitians both as management personnel and as menu writers.

Other personnel often are needed to help maintain food service operations. Sometimes they can be "in house" (on the premises) or "out of the house" (independent companies) such as accounting, public relations, advertising, stenography, personnel, music, and entertainment groups.

According to the federal government and forecasters of industrial trends, food service positions should continue to grow at a faster pace than other occupations. According to the National Institute, the food service industry will need 25,000 new employees each year to keep up with the growing demand for service. The National Restaurant Association has reported a modest increase in 1992 in every aspect of the industry from institutional to commercial fields. Growth in the number of eating and drinking establishments will result in faster than average growth in employment. As reported in spring 1992, Department of Labor Occupational Outlook book restaurant and food service manager's positions should increase by 32% by the year 2005.

There will be 1.035 million positions added to the cook, chef, and other back-of-the-house positions. Additionally, 1.223 million positions will be added to the front of the house. There are more than 710,000 food service operations in the United States with 43¢ of every consumer food dollar going for food and snacks away from home. The consumer now eats close to two meals per day away from home. A growing trend to eat convenience foods that were prepared at a commercial food service operation, then home-delivered or carried home, is a rapidly rising segment of this field. There is a continued need in the industry for entry-level employees to handle such convenience foods.

Earnings of food service workers vary depending on the size, locale, and region of the country. Entry-level workers' hourly wages vary from $2.87 an hour for service personnel who also collect tips to $4.45 per hour for some of the positions. Hourly wages will increase with the increase in the federal minimum wage. However for many regions, because of the scarce labor market, workers in these same positions are being paid up to $7.00 an hour.

Managerial positions, where college students start obtaining entry-level jobs, continue to show salary increases. Most associate-level positions start in the upper teens ($18,000), and positions for employees who have a bachelor's degree show approximately a $4,000 increase ($22,000). Although these rates have been stable through the recession, increases of 4% to 6% per year in starting salaries are projected for the future. In hard-to-attract segments, such as fast food and airline catering, starting positions in the middle twenties are not unusual. Many experienced managers make between $28,000 to $80,000 and eventually enter the six-digit category. This is not unusual for experience corporate managers.

Employee working conditions vary by segment. Although commercial operations usually allow for free meals, they have numerous disadvantages such as long hours, split shifts, and night and weekend work. Industrial operations usually work a forty-hour week, Monday through Friday. Institutions ordinarily provide excellent benefits, such as medical, dental, and life insurance, vacation, and sick pay.

The Hotel Business

The lodging industry has become more complex, and the demand for highly trained personnel is constantly increasing. The increased demand for service requires employees to have some training from either vocational schools or colleges. Most lodging companies also include programs to familiarize the employee with the specifics of that company's concepts, goals, and services.

In order to provide increasingly varied services, the lodging industry hires employees for a variety of occupational categories. Top management, middle management, service, and craft positions must be filled. The top management classification refers to corporate managers who direct the operations of chain hotels.

Middle management refers to the positions of assistant manager and shift manager in each of the different departments within a hotel. Such departments include front desk, food and beverage, banquet, sales and marketing, housekeeping, security, engineering, maintenance, purchasing, accounting and the controller's office, and personnel. These positions usually require considerable education, formal training, job experience, or all three.

Service positions such as front desk clerks, bartenders, bellhops, and maids generally require less training while positions in vocational areas such as carpenters and electricians require more training.

Such a variety of positions under one roof necessitates support personnel such as secretaries, typists, clerks, cashiers, bookkeepers, and telephone operators. Still other people may work in a hotel and be considered employees, including barbers, gardeners, detectives, cosmetologists, and fashion retailers.

In accordance with past trends, the lodging industry is expected to grow but at a slower pace than other segments of the hospitality industry. Because it takes almost five years to build a hotel, the recession caught the lodging industry with an excess of hotel rooms on line and more that came on line during these down years. This growth bottomed out in 1991, with room occupancies at a 60% level. Early 1993 showed some recovery due to the slowing of supply growth and an increase in demand: occupancy levels rose to 63%. In the mid- to late 1990s, expect a continual increase in occupancy and room rate. This puts a burden on hotels to be extremely competitive in their pricing and offerings to customers.

Industry seeks entry-level candidates who are people oriented and who share the goal of "100% guest satisfaction and 0% deficits." Such conditions may mean slower upward mobility in the immediate future for those entering the lodging field. However, most line personnel will find much decision making and teamwork needed within new, leaner organizations. The U.S. Department of Labor expects to see a 44% increase in the number of managers in the next 12 years, with the best opportunities for those people with college degrees in the hotel or restaurant management.

Entry-level wages for workers in comparable positions will vary with the size, location, and region of the lodging facility. In general, large luxury hotels pay their employees more than budget motels. Workers in some areas receive tips, which supplement their incomes.

Salaries of hotel workers vary with training, experience, and education. Those graduating from college with a bachelor's degree sometimes enter a formal year-long management training program. However, many of these programs are now being shortened to 6 months or discontinued due to the recession. Students entering these programs will usually start at slightly lower wages—the upper teens ($19,000) rather than the lower twenties—but will generally find their long-term careers more satisfying and higher management levels more accessible. Most college graduates should research the type of company they wish to work for and uncover which entry-level position has upward mobility within that company. Other entry-level positions carry compensation of $14,000 for vocational trained graduates, and up to $22,000 for bachelor's degree graduates. Although these levels stabilized during the recession, a 4% to 6% annual increase is expected to return by the end of the decade. It is the perks and fringe benefits that become quite attractive as you advance in the field. Those entering lodging must be flexible and willing to meet the needs for a nationally and internationally growing chain. According to the 1994 U.S. hospitality industry salary outlook of the Educational Institute of the American Hotel and Motel Association (AH & MA), management positions generally quickly jump from the mid-twenties to the eighties for different levels of middle managers, and six figures are attainable in corporate positions. Often salary levels at the upper levels are accompanied by bonus programs worth an additional 30%.

The central fact of the lodging industry is that each lodging becomes a home away from home, open 24 hours a day, 7 days a week, 365 days a year. Such demands translate into long hours for most managers climbing the corporate ladder. And such demands may also require that young managers continue to relocate in order to advance within their firms. (Many managers and companies try to keep this down to only once every two years, but in a fast-growing operation where advancement and experience may be more rapid, more frequent changes often are seen.)

The Travel and Tourism Industry

Travel and tourism is the fastest-growing segment within the hospitality industry. We would be remiss if we did not discuss the people who help travelers get to their destinations, and help create the desire to travel in the first place.

The travel business for many years was thought to be nothing more than another retail outlet in a block of stores. However, for one who studies this field, a wider horizon awaits you than just work in a travel agency. Many positions in travel and tourism can be filled with good clerical help, for example, ticket agent, reservationist, tour leader, tour operator, program specialist, interpreter, translator, and assistant to convention center and civic center managers. However, those with a bachelor's degree in the area of tourism, hospitality marketing, meeting management, or entrepreneurism with a travel minor can anticipate more challenging careers as meeting and conference planner, business travel specialist, tour wholesaler, tour bureau manager, or destination development specialist.

Such positions are available from a wide variety of employers, including convention bureaus, travel agencies, travel wholesalers, chambers of commerce, cruise ship lines, airlines, car rental companies, bus companies, resort associations, colleges, government agencies, tour operators, parks, corporations, civic centers, and hotels.

Positions can be found in both public and private sectors. In the international arena, tourism is a powerful economic force that can be used by the developing nations to generate wealth necessary to compete in today's international arena. This development of tourism means that there will be greater and greater use of the "tripartite plus one" formula: government, the private sector (hotels and restaurants), the people, and the "plus one" of education must work together to create a stable economy and an environment that will attract tourism and economic development. All participants must be aware of cultural gaps and sacred cows, coping with them is the central task for the country's best economists, environmentalists, educators, and politicians. Tourism in developing nations affords some of best challenges for the future and represents areas in which the hospitality industry will find its best growth.

The earning and working conditions in the travel and tourism segment of the hospitality industry vary with the diverse areas that the student chooses to explore. The associate's degree graduate has earnings starting at approximately $14,000 (1992), with bachelor's degree students hovering in the range of $16,000 to $21,000 annually. These wages seem low in comparison with other positions in the different segments of the hospitality industry, but many entry-level positions involve sales and marketing tasks that allow commission to be added to the entry-level salary. For many, the idea of travel is an attractive benefit. However, this benefit has a down side: continually living out of a suitcase can get very old. Upper-level management salaries in this segment run easily into the upper five digits.

The travel industry is expected to see continued growth through the end of the century. Tourism is now the largest industry in the world, 15 years in advance of Herman Kahn's predictions. Travel and tourism shows no signs of a significant slowdown. Estimates indicate that tourism now employs, directly or indirectly, 60% of the labor force in the world. Throughout the 1990s, Americans are expected to satisfy their yen for travel, so related positions in the service industry are expected to grow. According to the U.S. Department of Labor, a 34% increase is predicted in the positions within the travel-related industries over the next 12 years in the United States.

The travel and tourism industry is the nation's third-largest retailing or service industry. It generates billions of dollars in revenue and one job for every 15 working Americans, according to the Travel Industry Association of America.

The Recreation and Leisure Management Industry

Probably one of the newest segments of the hospitality industry to become recognized on its own is recreation and leisure management. The rise in such fantastic theme parks as

Disneyland, Disney World, and Busch Gardens has led to the development of this end of the industry, with its accompanying hotel and food service operations. A second major trend is the increased use of recreational facilities during leisure time, particularly by Americans. People attend such facilities either for pleasure or the combination of pleasure and physical fitness. Such trends will become more important as the baby boom generation moves into their late forties and fifties and have more disposable income.

The recreation business has been developing in a number of arenas such as municipal parks, recreation agencies, commercial recreational facilities, state and federal agencies, industrial recreational facilities, armed forces, outdoor recreation, colleges, and universities, and youth service agencies.

These different areas hire superintendents, community center directors, playground supervisors, public relations officers, resort managers, directors of programs or specific sport facilities such as golf courses, wildlife managers, Red Cross area directors, campus recreation directors, 4-H directors, managers for youth services (such as YMCA, Girl Scouts, Boys Club), and senior citizen centers.

At entry level, most of these services have assistants or shift supervisors with whom a student can begin to develop skills and obtain experience. Currently, the tremendous need for managers in this field is being met by other areas of the hospitality field and/or business majors. At present, a few schools offer a major in recreation development. Earnings for these majors are in line with the rest of the hospitality industry: around the mid-teens ($17,500) and upper teens ($18,500) for bachelor's degree graduates.

The increase in business in this area can be documented by National Restaurant Association (NRA) statistics, which put overall growth at a rate of 8%. Projections for overall recreation demands made in 1962 for the year 2000 were surpassed in 1980. In a recent study called "Participation in Outdoor Recreation Among American Adults and the Motivation Which Drives Participation," the United States was described as an outdoor-oriented country. Of American adults, 75% visit local, state, and national parks annually. Week-long vacations are taken by 75% of U.S. citizens, and 85% took mini-vacations with three of ten taking six or more such mini-vacations.

Attendance at national parks is up, while marine manufacturers report 100% growth since 1980 in sales of marine goods. Continued growth at very close to that rate is expected through the year 2000. The fishing industry is expected to continue to flourish, and sales of recreational vehicles (RV's) continue to climb. Gallup's 1985 leisure activities audits cite camping as the fourth most popular recreational activity in the United States, while swimming remains the number one recreational activity. Water parks are increasing in popularity, with an estimated 25% annual growth rate.

A survey of recreation sports and leisure taken in July and August 1986 calculates that 10% to 20% of recreation managers have some college education, with 24% to 30% having attained a bachelor's degree. Graduate degrees were completed by 19% to 24%, while another 2% to 6% have earned a doctoral degree. The Department of Labor expects a 24% increase in recreational workers, with programs for special groups and greater interest in fitness and health leading the expansion. Additionally, there should be a 39% increase in recreational therapist positions over the next 12 years. These positions will be created because of the anticipated growth in the long-term care field and for rehabilitation and services for the developmentally disabled.

The salaries in this field increase with education, but experience seems to be an overriding factor. Other factors are region of the country, with the Pacific West leading the way, and job type, with city administrator, board member, or private sector CEO positions paying the highest.

Meeting and Entertainment Management

Management of meetings and entertainment has become an increasingly attractive segment of the hospitality industry. The segment includes management of civic centers, sport arenas, convention centers, and performing arts centers. Many of these organizations need employees in three distinct areas.

First, managers are needed for the civic centers, sport arenas, convention centers, and performing art centers themselves. Positions range from box office management, concession management, and safety and security to crowd control.

The second area includes meeting planners for associations and industries. There is an increased need for this particular expertise because association management has evolved into a field of its own. Work with convention centers and hotels while handling the internal politics of different associations offers diverse yet exciting jobs.

The third area affecting the meeting and entertainment segment is sales. Sales has come into its own as individuals carry out the marketing plan for their respective companies: hotels, resorts, attractions, food and beverage operations, associations, or trade centers.

Salary expectations vary but are comparable to other areas of the industry. Total wages become very attractive when you attach commission to base salary.

Retirement Living Management

As the greying of America takes place, opportunities will expand for many managers in the health care field. Many of the same skills needed for hotels and restaurant management are used in retirement living management and assisted care management. Those venturing into these fields will need some specialized courses in science and finance. All states maintain their individual license requirements for nursing home administrators. The need for staff in these areas is great and will continue to increase for the next 40 years. The Department of Labor is forecasting a 42% increase in health services managers, with the establishment of 108,000 positions in the next 12 years. Employment in home health care services and nursing care facilities will grow most quickly.

Management Information Systems

In all of these industry segments, people with solid business skills are needed. It is noteworthy that the other major division within the service industries is management information systems (MIS). An outgrowth of data processing, MIS is becoming an integral part of each of these segments of the hospitality industry. The computer has applications in each of these areas, and students of both hospitality and data processing fields should have bright futures. MIS job opportunities exist not only in the hospitality industry proper, but also with the hardware and software companies seeking to do business with the hospitality industry.

8

Realities of a Career in the Hospitality Industry

Ken W. McCleary, *Virginia Polytechnic Institute and State University*
Pamela A. Weaver, *Virginia Polytechnic Institute and State University*

The hospitality industry offers some of the most exciting and challenging careers that you can find. The potential rewards are unlimited and advancement can be rapid. But like most things in life, excitement and reward do not come without a price. The price in the hospitality industry comes primarily in the form of hard work and varying degrees of sacrifice in your personal life.

Work Hard, Play Hard

Long work weeks tend to be the norm in the hospitality industry. While many firms are moving toward a five-day work week, which of course may entail 10- to 12-hour days, it is not uncommon for managers to work six days a week and more than 60 hours. During these long work weeks, managers are bombarded with problems and expected to perform a variety of tasks from budgeting to settling disputes between customers and employees. This is the "work hard" part of the industry.

Because of the long hours and stress often encountered on the job, hospitality industry people tend to play hard as well. The "hospitality attitude," which is so important for success on the job, carries over to time away from work for many people. During leisure time, hospitality people tend to enjoy life to its fullest. As discussed later, this can be both good and bad.

Is the Hospitality Industry Really Different from Other Fields?

The hospitality industry is different from other industries, especially those that produce tangible products, in several ways. Hospitality is people dealing with people. This results in a less-standardized product and a less-controlled environment. Whereas a manufacturing operation can stop the assembly line or deal with product defects at a later time, the hospitality industry is constantly making and delivering products. Products are produced and consumed at virtually the same time, allowing little margin for error. This causes stress for managers and employees alike.

Another difference is that hospitality operations are open long hours to serve the customer. Most lodging operations are open 365 days a year, 24 hours a day. While some smaller motel operations may close the office at night, and seasonal operations close during the off season, these are exceptions rather than the rule. Some restaurants may be open 24 hours a day, seven days a week, and most others are open until at least nine or ten o'clock at night. In total, 78% of the American people do not work "regular hours," 8:00 A.M. to 5:00 P.M. weekdays.[1] The percent for the hospitality industry would be even higher.

In the hospitality industry, you will most likely be working when your friends are having fun. Weekends and special days, such as Mother's Day, are busy times in restaurants. While others are celebrating New Year's Eve, you will be serving them. And someone has to manage the hotel on Christmas Day. More than in any other industry, with the exception perhaps of emergency services such as fire, medical, and police, hospitality managers are likely to work the less desirable hours.

In defense of the working conditions in the hospitality industry, it is fair to say that working with hotel and restaurant guests is seldom boring. Every new customer is a new challenge, and you certainly are not chained to a desk. Furthermore, there are some real advantages to shopping, banking, and enjoying a movie on your day off during the week when crowds are slight.

We should note here that, although we keep stressing the long hours worked in the industry, you cannot really work a 40-hour week in most fields if you expect to get ahead. General retailing has notoriously long hours, as does medicine. Managers, in any field, will not receive rapid promotions by doing only the minimum that is required of them. Even schoolteachers, at least the good ones, put in many more hours than are perceived by the general public. In other words, it is not so much the number of hours put in as *when* the hours are worked that makes hospitality different from other fields.

Your First "Real" Job

Okay, so you decide to stick with this hospitality business and find a job. If you picked up industry-related work experience while you were in college and did reasonably well with your studies, the chances are good that you will have several job offers to choose from. There are a number of things to keep in mind when choosing which job to take and how to proceed after you have taken it.

Moving

The more flexible you are in your willingness to relocate, the more attractive you are to most companies. Taking that first job and moving to an unfamiliar geographical location is exciting. But be prepared for some lonely times.

When selecting the company you are going to work for, check to see if they will pay any of your moving expenses. Some companies do, some don't. Although you probably won't have many possessions when you graduate, long-distance moves can still be very expensive.

Be sure that you have saved some money for the expenses associated with moving. Utility companies want deposits, you may want to subscribe to cable television, and apartment owners usually want a month's rent plus a damage deposit. If you move out of state you will also have to pay new driver's license fees and purchase new automobile license plates if you have a car. So try to have at least $1,000 ready for just these kinds of items. In other words, if you receive some cash for graduation, don't spend it. You are going to need it.

Finding an Apartment

Do you picture yourself living in a luxury apartment building that has a health club on the roof and a secure parking garage for your new Trans Am? Does this apartment just happen to be located on Lake Shore Drive just blocks from the downtown Chicago hotel at which you work? If this is your picture, erase it and start over unless you have someone who wants to subsidize your salary to the tune of $10,000 per year. Living in large cities is expensive.

When you look for an apartment, use your head. Initially, look for something that is close to your work. Whether you drive to work or take public transportation, this will cut down on costs and save time. Consider finding a roommate to share expenses. You may be tired of living with someone after college, but you can always move out later. It is also nice to have the moral support of a roommate when you are in a strange place. Don't feel as though you have to have the most luxurious apartment around. You probably won't be spending much time there anyway and it is nice to have some money to do things on your day off.

You may not think it is possible, but there are people in this country who do not own cars. If you live in a city such as New York or Chicago, you will rapidly find out why. Parking is expensive if you can even find a space, insurance is outrageous—especially if you are young and single—traffic is horrendous, and mass transit is usually quicker. So when selecting a place to live, check how close you are to mass transit stops.

Making New Friends

Be prepared for some periods of depression and loneliness. It is hard for anyone to leave the security of college and dozens of friends and acquaintances. Don't sit around your apartment and mope. There are at least a million other people in the same boat as you are, so get out and find them!

The most natural way to make friends is through work. You will do this, but do it with care. Becoming close friends with people who work under you or above you in the organization can cause problems. Try to limit your job-related friends to other managers and trainees who are at the same level as you. These people can also introduce you to their own roommates and acquaintances. Follow up on these introductions to ensure that you have friends outside of the workplace. It is unfortunate, but because of working hours and the nature of the industry, most relationships tend to be with people from your place of business.

There are other ways to meet people. Get involved with a church if you are so inclined. Sign up for dance lessons, scuba lessons, or ski clubs. Get involved with local politics or volunteer organizations like JayCees, Big Brothers/Big Sisters, the historical preservation group, or the Sierra Club. These organizations are usually listed in the phone book and will welcome your help. It will take some time, but remember, you *will* make new friends if you try.

On the Job

Hours

Sitting in class and hearing your professors talk about working long hours is one thing: the reality of it is another. While most hospitality students don't seem to be overly concerned about the length of their future work week before graduation,[2] working long hours is one of the biggest complaints related by graduates who have been out of college for a year or two. Even though you may have worked summers, your job was probably not much more than 40 hours a week. Besides, you knew that it would end in August and you would go back to college. To add to your security you probably lived at home, or had housing secured for you if you worked in a resort area during your internship.

Back at college, you may have worked part time and learned how to balance classes, work, and social life. But you usually had flexibility to blow off a class here and there, and your responsibility at work was probably not too taxing. And, of course, no matter how bad calculus was or how much work that darn hotel and restaurant prof piled on, it would be over in 10 to 15 weeks and you would have a break.

Like it or not, you have been living an unrealistic existence.[3] On your first job, after training, you are likely to be working 50 to 60 hours a week or more. If part of your job is to make up the work schedule for your restaurant and you don't have it finished on time, you can't hand it in late and hope that your boss is "nice" like your college professor might have been. In fact, you won't just get a lower grade, you'll be fired if you can't do the job. No matter how many hours you have worked, you stay until you are done.

Some of the biggest complaints about hours which former students express include the difficulty of doing things like laundry and picking up dry cleaning. Getting blocks of time to go home and see your parents, or to spend time with your spouse and/or children if you are married, is also a problem. Having a steady relationship with someone of the opposite sex becomes a problem if you work late in the evening and on weekends. And remember, you no longer have spring break, Christmas break, summer, and Thanksgiving break like you did in college. You have, perhaps, two weeks vacation.

Understanding Corporate Culture

Every organization has its own personality. This is called the corporate culture and consists of the rules, personalities, and environment of the organization. Corporate culture dictates how you act, dress, and respond to both superiors and subordinates. The corporate culture is usually set at the top of the corporation and filters down to all levels, although it is possible that the culture in individual units of a chain may be different from at headquarters.

An example of one type of corporate culture can be seen at the headquarters of Red Roof Inns near Columbus, Ohio. The culture here includes an emphasis on the person, with time off during work hours to visit the fitness center housed in the building. Attire is informal, and the comfort of easy interactions in the lunch room is obvious. Another corporation, however, may have a strict dress code, rigid procedures for seeing superiors (by appointment only), and have a high-pressure ambience. Things such as dress code may never appear in writing, but nonetheless they are there, and the person who wants to succeed must follow them carefully. When interviewing for a job, it is important to find out what the corporate culture is so that you can see whether there is a match between you and the environment in which you will be spending most of your waking hours.

Managing People

Your job is to manage. The choice of whom you must manage usually is not up to you. So you must be flexible in your ability to deal with all types of people. One of the greatest challenges in any job is to manage people who are older than you. In the hospitality industry, you will have direct responsibility for people who may in fact be twice your age. Give some serious thought to how you will interact with these people. It may be true that technically you have the authority to simply order people around, but be assured that employees, especially those who have been with your employer a long time, can make your life miserable if you don't treat them right. A little respect goes a long way with older workers, particularly if it is mixed with a sincere desire to learn from them. Don't be afraid that your employees may know more about some things than you. Rest assured that someone will *always* know more about something than you do. Accept help and guidance thankfully.

Be ready for some good-natured hazing on your first job and also when you change jobs. Show people that you have a sense of humor. At a hotel where one of the authors worked, it was a favorite trick to put new management trainees at the 20-line switchboard with little instruction. While one employee would divert the trainee's attention, another employee would engage all the lines from a companion switchboard unit (PBX) at the front desk. The trainee would turn back to the PBX unit and see all the lines flashing at once. As the "rookie" furiously tried to answer all 20 lines, the rest of the staff would gleefully watch through the open door of the front office. Those trainees who laughed along were instantly accepted, those who didn't often had problems.

The hospitality industry attracts an unbelievable variety of people as employees. In large cities, it is not uncommon for a portion of your staff to speak little or no English. Levels of hygiene, dedication to work, and mental abilities are likely to differ considerably from your own. Today's work force also includes both mentally and physically challenged people. Therefore, it is important that you be familiar with the Americans with Disabilities Act, which was passed in 1990.

How can you manage a group like this? It is difficult, challenging, and fun. Sameness is boring. Variety is the spice of life, and the first step to managing a diverse work force is to embrace the differences among workers. A good helping of respect and understanding is critical. Remember the Golden Rule: Do unto others as you would have them do unto you. This will go a long way toward helping you be a successful manager. A recent graduate, who was working as an assistant housekeeper in Atlanta, came back to visit campus moaning about his problems. "What is wrong with these people?" he said. "They don't show up for work half the time and even though I threaten to fire them I know I won't be able to find replacements if I follow through on my threats." Well golly gee, it is really hard to understand why those employees are often absent from an exciting job like making the same beds day after day. Or, maybe they are just tired of having a wet-behind-the-ears kid for a boss who thinks that the answer to employee problems is to threaten to fire them. And all that for a whopping 50¢ more than minimum wage.

Good managers obtain a personal loyalty from their employees. This loyalty in part comes from developing a mutual respect with your employees by taking a sincere interest in them as people. Take a language in college (Spanish is helpful for many areas of the country) or learn a few words of several languages. Use this knowledge to show your employees that you respect their cultures and individual backgrounds. Let them know that you understand that they have personal problems too.

Unfortunately, there are times that employees have to be dismissed. If you enjoy firing people, you don't belong in the hospitality industry. When you must fire someone, do it quickly, have well-documented reasons, and do it in private. One particularly difficult problem to deal with is illegal aliens. Some areas of the country have relied on illegal aliens as a cheap source of labor. You must check to see if foreign nationals have a permit to work in this country, the "green card." If you have a doubt as to a person's eligibility to hold a job, call the government immigration office. This is a hard problem because illegal aliens are often good workers and very nice people.

Major Issues in Today's Workplace

It is more difficult to be a manager today than it used to be. Expectations for managers become higher every year. There are more forms to file and more rules to follow. By the way, some of these rules are long overdue.

One particularly difficult area surrounds the interactions between men and women on the job. Sexual harassment has recently become a major issue and has forced managers to carefully analyze their interactions with the opposite sex. One of the difficulties with trying to avoid sexual harassment is that it is not clearly defined. There are some obvious things that you would have to be stupid to do, like tying sexual favors to promotion. Less obvious actions like telling jokes that are degrading or even unflattering to one sex can be considered sexual harassment. This is something that you have to deal with. A rule of thumb that also goes along with avoiding racial and religious slurs is, if something is questionable, don't do it, say it, or encourage others who are doing or saying it.

Another very difficult problem you may encounter is falling in love with a coworker. To suggest that it shouldn't happen is unrealistic. As mentioned earlier, most of your interactions are on the job, and there is a natural tendency to get romantically involved with someone at work. However, you should avoid social relationships with employees. It will cause problems. If the person is another manager, you better see what the corporate culture dictates. Enlightened companies realize that it is possible for a husband and wife to work at the same company. If your company is not enlightened, be prepared for one of you to seek employment elsewhere.

Alcoholism has always plagued the hospitality industry. Managers of many operations are constantly exposed to alcohol and may use it extensively to relieve stress. It is odd that, although we sell alcohol, our industry is slow to recognize its responsibility for alcohol-related problems. More recently, other types of drugs have become commonplace among managers and hourly employees alike. Drugs in the workplace cannot be tolerated. Progressive firms have drug rehabilitation services. Whenever possible, try to help employees who have drug-related problems. Drug problems must be dealt with when they occur.

Pay

The hospitality industry provides great opportunities for rapid advancement and rapid pay increases. While starting salaries for managers are often less than in other industries, advancement opportunities often allow hospitality managers to catch up with and pass their counterparts in other fields. There is still a significant "pay your dues" attitude in the hospitality industry. This means that you are expected to prove yourself before you begin to reap greater rewards. Whether you agree with this philosophy or not is beside the point. You simply have to recognize that the attitude exists and deal with it.

One complaint that new managers often have is with salaries related to hours worked. Many times even if starting salaries are similar to other fields, breaking pay down on an hourly basis becomes shocking, particularly considering the amount of evening, weekend, and holiday hours worked. This is a reality of the industry. If you want to work steady hours and have a standard work week, choose another occupation. Of course, with some jobs you may have to sit at a desk all day.

If pay is a major issue, and it probably is, be sure to check out all segments of the industry. Compare starting salaries, hours, rates of advancement, and ambience of various opportunities. Know what you are getting into. For example, institutional feeding tends to require fewer and more stable hours. Quick service restaurants may not have the luxurious surroundings of an upscale hotel, but may pay better. The Council on Hotel, Restaurant, and Institutional Education publishes salary data for positions in the hospitality industry.[4]

You should be aware that there seems to be some salary discrimination in the hospitality industry based on gender. Salaries for men and women with similar backgrounds should be the same, but sometimes are not. For example, _Restaurants and Institutions_ reported that a 1992 study found pay raises for men averaged 5.5% and 4.46% for women. If a promotion was involved, increases averaged 10.6% for men and 9.23% for women.[5] It is a difficult task to make sure that you are treated fairly when it comes to promotion and pay increases, so be prepared to stand up for your rights.

Promotion

One complaint that is often levied against new managers is that their expectations for promotion are unrealistic. It is natural for you to be eager for advancement, but you also need to understand that although you may think you are ready for promotion, it takes a while to learn a job thoroughly. When you interview for a job, be sure to ask about how quickly you would be eligible for promotion and then ask how long it takes the average manager to be promoted. Recruiters are often optimistic and may be giving you the shortest time span possible. This is particularly true if there is a shortage of entry-level managers, and recruiters are under pressure to fill positions.

Getting Along with Your Immediate Supervisor and Other Superiors

Students often form conflicting perceptions about hospitality firms in terms of their desirability as an employer. You may hear from one person that XYZ Hotel Company is terrible to work for, and hear from another that they are great. How can this happen? Well, the fact of the matter is that your happiness on your first job is going to depend mostly on the people you work with at that particular unit, especially your immediate supervisor.

The implications of the relationship with your supervisor are twofold. First, you need to know that if things aren't going well you can request a transfer. Unless the problem is you, the environment is likely to be different elsewhere. Second, regardless of your opinion of your supervisor, it is up to you to get along with him. This may seem unfair because you may see upper management doing some pretty bizarre things. Unfortunately, their seeming incompetence is only your opinion. The person who is your boss will have a great impact on your future with the company. If the person is really as bad as you think, sooner or later it will be discovered by her boss. You may ask the question: shouldn't my boss have to follow good management principles just like I was taught? In the best of all possible worlds, the answer is yes. Unfortunately, we don't live in a perfect world. Besides, you may not understand everything your boss has to do and the reasons behind some of his or her actions. Try to discuss your problems with him or her before you do anything drastic. Then when you get promoted you can run the show however you think best.

Personal Issues

Today's world is complex, much more so than when your parents were your age. You will be under pressure to do a lot of self-destructive things like consuming drugs, especially alcohol, but also cocaine and "designer" drugs. You probably have already been exposed to most of these in high school and college. The difference is that you probably will have more money to purchase drugs than in the past and may feel that you need drugs to provide an outlet from the stress of your job. You do need an outlet, but it needn't be drugs. Select a positive outlet like a physical fitness program, working for social causes, or studying for your master's degree.

Values

Research has shown variation in the personal values that are considered most important from one generation to the next.[6] Many people in the older generations only dreamed of some of the things that many young people are able to take for granted. Twenty or thirty years ago, it was a rare college student who had visited Europe. But for many students today, the economic situation of parents has provided all kinds of opportunities for travel and to accumulate material goods. Many students own CD players, VCRs, and new cars before they even graduate from college. These were the types of things that older generations saved for and acquired on a long-term basis.

Even if you have not had the advantages just described, you need to be aware that many young people have. The stereotype of the college graduate who has had everything can cause resentment among older workers and managers who know that they themselves had to work for what they got while younger people had it handed to them.

Differences in values between generations provide a certain amount of frustration for managers. Recruiters often complain that it is hard to motivate some young managers because they don't see the relation between hours worked and rewards. As a manager yourself, you are likely to be in a situation where you are supervising high school students whose weekly allowance may be more than they are making working at your restaurant. Add to this the fact that you may also have workers over the age of 60 who still remember the Great Depression, and you have a real challenge in setting up reward systems that motivate the entire crew.

Relationships

As mentioned earlier, some people have trouble developing a serious personal relationship because of the nature of the industry. It takes a special individual to tolerate a person who works long, erratic hours. While it is true that the divorce rate in the hospitality industry is relatively high, there are many successful relationships. It is just as much your responsibility to consider your significant other whenever you can as it is his or her responsibility to understand the requirements of your job. Be honest about the job requirements. You may want to go out for a drink with the gang after a long day, but is it really necessary? The temptations in the industry are great. You are surrounded by energetic, fun-loving, often attractive people. Add the ready access of alcohol to the picture and the formula for failed relationships is at hand.

Finishing School

Just because you have a degree in hotel and restaurant management doesn't mean that you know everything you need to know to excel in the hospitality industry. It is important that you continue educating yourself. Knowing the proper etiquette in social situations is important, and developing knowledge in areas such as wines, the arts, and world events makes you a much more exciting person and probably a better candidate for promotion. You should also work hard to develop the ability to empathize with others. Working on your vocabulary and public speaking abilities is also a way to further your career and make you a well-rounded individual. In the old days, young women were sent to a finishing school to learn social graces. In a similar vein, time spent improving yourself as a human being will be much more productive than time spent guzzling beer. Even the conservative University of Chicago business school is placing more emphasis on what are often called "touchy-feely" aspects of managing a business and living successfully.[7]

Finally, perhaps the best formula for having a successful career and leading a happy life is to achieve balance. The traditional work-hard, play-hard hospitality industry model needs to be mixed with a portion of self-fulfillment and the feeling that comes from doing something beneficial for society. The hospitality industry is a dynamic, exciting, and wonderful place to work. There is a new challenge every day. A career in hotel and restaurant management can provide a lifetime of pleasure as long as you control your job and not let it control you.

——References——

1. Associated Press. America Today: Random glances. *Roanoke Times and World News.* February 1, 1990.
2. McCleary, Ken W. and Pamela A. Weaver. Expectations of Hospitality Students Regarding Entry Level Positions in the Hospitality Industry. *Hospitality Education and Research Journal.* 1988; Volume 12, Number 2: pp. 163–174.
3. McCleary, Ken W. The New Generation of Managers. *Restaurant Business.* February 1, 1980; pp. 119–123.
4. The Council on Hotel, Restaurant and Institutional Education. (1991) *A Guide to College Programs in Hospitality and Tourism 1991/=n/92.* New York: John Wiley & Sons, Inc.
5. Weinstein, Jeff, Susie Stephenson, and Brenda McCarthy. Jobs '92. *Restaurants and Institutions.* December 23, 1992; pp. 56–76.
6. McCleary, Ken W. and Richard M. Vosburgh. Towards a Better Understanding of the Value Systems of Food Service Managers and Hospitality Students. *International Journal of Hospitality Management.* 1990; Volume 9, Number 2: pp. 111–123.
7. Chicago's B-School Goes Touchy-Feely. *Business Week.* November 27, 1989; p. 140.

9

Hospitality Periodicals and the Library

Michael M. Lefever
University of Massachusetts

Libraries

Whether the libraries you have encountered are dusty, dimly lit, storagelike facilities or high-tech, state-of-the-art, computerized operations, a world of information, entertainment, and enlightenment truly resides beyond those bronze doors. So, fasten your seatbelt and join me on a whirlwind journey into the wonders of education through library science.

If you're like me, it is possible to like college and enjoy learning without the help of libraries. Be that as it may, going to college without understanding and using the vast benefits of a library is like watching your neighbor win the state lottery. In other words, libraries provide one of the quickest routes to experiencing the thrill of learning for yourself.

For me, today, knowing the location of libraries is as essential as knowing the location of the closest restroom and snack bar. I still go to libraries to browse and to write, even to peek through the stacks. But libraries also give me the opportunity to visit faraway places—as if I were really there—and see the world through the eyes of others—as if I had really lived their lives. Best of all, walking into a library instantly releases me from the stress and worry of everyday life and lets me choose from the many dreams and imaginary friends patiently waiting on the shelves.

So, what does this mean for you? It's easy. Use the library only for pleasant tasks or when you just want to exist somewhere for awhile. If you have to study something unpleasant—and you will—go somewhere unpleasant like a bus depot, a vacant classroom, or a closet (not your dorm room or apartment, these should be pleasant places, too). Finally, you'll know the library is a friend when you walk inside and the smell of old books acts instantly like a mild narcotic. Yes, it's addictive.

Hospitality Periodicals

Since I spent a considerable amount of energy avoiding anything that was remotely related to libraries during my freshman year of college, it comes as no surprise that I really wasn't sure what the term *periodicals* meant. In fact, I was suffering from a common form of freshman brain drain whereby all I knew for sure was that I didn't know anything for sure. Then in my sophomore year, I accidentally wandered into a place called a *periodicals room* in the university library. It had something to do with magazines and newspapers. As I grew personally and professionally, I gained a needed dose of confidence when it came to intimidating concepts like libraries, periodicals, and life in general. So, I began spending more and more time in the periodicals reading room (a place where recent magazines, among other things, were shelved for easy browsing). No, I wasn't there to study. I wasn't even there to do any serious reading. Instead, I found that the periodicals reading room, among other things, was the best newsstand around, and it was free.

Another reason I never went for the serious stuff in the periodicals reading room was because I could find more than enough serious information for my term papers from plain old books without having to dig very hard. Needless to say, it was much easier and quicker to do my term paper research up in the stacks where I had access to thousands of dusty old books that were more comprehensive and easier to understand. Unfortunately, there were a thousand other students up in the stacks with the same idea.

Then in my senior year, I got hopelessly hooked on education and was even getting serious about it. Incidentally, it took a momentous occasion for me to get serious about anything in those days. Overnight I changed from a slightly above average student into a "wannabe expert" in my major field of study (I suggest that you attempt this transformation somewhat earlier in your academic career). The problem was that in order to be an expert in any field of study, I would have to get out of the crowded book stacks, away from the other slightly-above-average students, and move back into the periodicals room. You see, books are more or less containers of *old* information (of course, some of which never really gets old) whereas all the current, cutting-edge stuff is found in periodicals. It was amazing what information I found in all those *serious* journals, quarterlies, and reviews. Even more amazing, I found that one of the quickest ways to change slightly-above-average grades into excellent grades is to get acquainted with and use the periodicals in your field of study.

So, what are periodicals? It's a rather broad term encompassing any publication that comes out regularly (daily, weekly, or monthly) and is published on a continuing basis. Interestingly, periodicals cover everything from tabloids (you know, those small newspapers at the supermarket check-out lanes with headlines such as *Distinguished professor was a Nazi youth*) to scholarly research journals such as the *Journal of Morphogenesis, Physiogenesis and the Common Dust Mite.* But between these two extremes are three different kinds of periodicals. First, there are newspapers and magazines written for the general public (e.g., *Fitness Tomorrow*). Second, there are trade journals or periodicals aimed at the practical side of business (e.g., *Bankruptcy Today*). Finally, there are scholarly research journals like the one mentioned above that focus in detail on a particular subtopic or specialty area of research interest.

The word *magazine* implies that the periodical is oriented toward the general public whereas the words *journal, quarterly* (a journal published four times a year), and *review* (another name for *journal*), are aimed at the practitioner (e.g., hotel general manager) or professional (your professor). It's almost worth reading the latter, heavier stuff just so you can call yourself a professional, isn't it? Even if you can't understand what you are reading, at least it's good to be seen in the periodicals reading room with one in front of you.

You, a professional student of hospitality administration, should become familiar with all three kinds of periodicals, especially the trade and scholarly research journals, when it comes to writing papers or researching a topic for a class project. Hospitality trade journals look very much like popular magazines since they frequently have full-cover photographs and extensive advertising. However, they differ from magazines in that most of the articles will be of interest to hospitality professionals like yourself. Specifically, trade journals provide a rich and unending flow of current information on almost every issue in the hospitality industry. What this means for you is that trade journals can be your ticket to an "A" paper or project.

To get you started, Table 1 lists many of the general paper or project topics in hospitality administration, along with three related trade journals for each topic. All you have to do is find your topic (or choose one) from the list and then locate the corresponding trade journals in your library. The result will be a wealth of information that will surely impress your professors and even yourself. If you can't find these exact journals for your topic area, then look for related or similar titles. Luckily for you, there tends to be a generous amount of topic overlap among hospitality trade journals. If all else fails, change your topic to something that matches the available journals.

Now, scholarly journals are a different story. Their articles tend to use indecipherable scientific jargon and spout highfalutin theories that confuse the best of us. Just like taking classes in sequence, you'll be able to understand these higher-level publications as you gain knowledge and experience in your chosen field and in researching and writing more complex

Table 1. Hospitality Topics and Related Trade Journals

Topic	Trade Journals
Accounting and Finance	*Bottom Line* *Hospitality Investment Survey* *Wall Street Journal*
Club Management	*Club and Restaurant* *Club Management* *CMAA Club Manager Association of America*
Culinary Arts	*Bon Appetit* *Cooking for Profit* *Culinary Trends*
Food and Beverage Operations	*Nation's Restaurant News* *Restaurant Business* *Restaurants and Institutions*

Table 1.—*Continued.*

Topic	Trade Journals
Hotel Operations	*Hotel and Motel Management* *Lodging* *Lodging Hospitality*
Human Resource Management	*Hospitality Management* *Protection and Safety* *Training and Development Journal*
Information Systems	*Computer Currents* *Random Access* *PC Magazine*
Legal Aspects	*Hospitality Law* *Hotel and Casino Law Letter*
Hotel Motel Security and Safety Marketing	*Advertising Age* *Marketing News* *HSMAI Marketing Review*
Meetings and Conventions	*Business Meetings* *Convention Preview* *Meetings and Conventions*
Multicultural International	*Tourism Management* *Travel Industry Monitor* *International Tourism Reports*
Property Management	*Building Operating Management* *Facility Manager* *Energy Conservation*
Service Management	*Hotel Resort Industry* *Restaurant Hospitality* *Service Industry*
Travel and Tourism	*Tour and Travel News* *Travel Age* *Travel Weekly*
Wine and Beverages	*American Institute of Wine and Food* *Bar Management* *Food and Wine*

Note: The journals listed in Tables 1 and 2 serve only as a starting point for your information search. Many other quality journals are available in most libraries.

Table 2. Scholarly Journals Related to Hospitality Research

Comprehensive journals targeting educators and practitioners	*Cornell Hotel & Restaurant Administration Quarterly* *FIU Hospitality Review* *Hospitality & Tourism Educator* *Internal Journal of Hospitality Management*
Traditional academic journals targeting educators and researchers	*Annals of Tourism Research* *Hospitality Research Journal* *Journal of Hospitality & Leisure Marketing* *Journal of Travel Research*

materials. For your convenience, Table 2 lists the scholarly journals in which most hospitality professors (including yours) publish their articles. Yes, they have to write papers, too. The "Comprehensive" journal is considered moderately heavy stuff (maybe a cross between a trade and scholarly journal). On the other hand, the "traditional" journal is strictly heavy-duty stuff. I would suggest starting with the "comprehensive" journals and then gradually worming your way into the "traditional" ones!

Now let's do some advanced study in the field of periodicals. Let's say you have a topic but don't have the time or inclination to leaf through the hundreds of past issues of journals listed in Tables 1 and 2. (Hey, get real, it's almost the weekend.) In this case, you can save dozens of precious hours by using the periodical indexes. Indexes are thick, heavy volumes located in the periodicals room that list references by topic area, author, or journal. Better yet, you can save a dozen hours of effort by asking a friendly librarian to show you their exact location and how to read them. In particular, you are looking for the following hospitality-related indexes:

- Business Periodicals Index (trade and scholarly)
- Leisure, Recreation & Tourism Abstracts (mostly scholarly)
- Lodging and Restaurant Index (trade and scholarly)
- Hospitality Index (trade and scholarly)

In short, these indexes will pinpoint hundreds of articles on a given topic and steer you toward the exact issues of the journals in which they are located. Just make sure you know which journals are available in your library before you start plowing through the indexes. Be aware, too, that professors often have large journal collections in their offices.

Now, if you'd like to pinpoint the same articles but bypass all the hassle of the indexes, then you are a candidate for CD-ROM. CD-ROM stands for _Compact Disk—Read Only Memory._ This handy gadget makes it possible for a massive amount of information to be stored on five-inch plastic disks, similar to what goes into your CD player at home. These disks operate in conjunction with a computer terminal, so you'll probably be an expert after a few minutes of self-instruction. The CD-ROM database is similar to the long shelves of thick, heavy index volumes. But the big difference is that you can search and locate hundreds of specific trade and scholarly articles in a matter of seconds. Even better, some of the databases include a brief summary or abstract of each article (a real time-saver in the hectic life of a professional student like you). Finally, CD-ROM not only allows you to locate certain articles, it also allows you to print out their locations and abstracts at the touch of the _print_ key. Totally awesome, huh? Ask the librarian to help you find the following hospitality-related CD-ROM databases:

- _ABI/Inform_ (mostly scholarly)
- _Lexis_ (full-text trade)
- _ERIC_ (mostly scholarly)

Well, that's it. You now have what took me almost eight years in college to figure out: the awesome power of periodicals, and the attraction of libraries. So, put down those picture magazines and engage your brain in some down and dirty research.

Hospitality Organizations

Part III

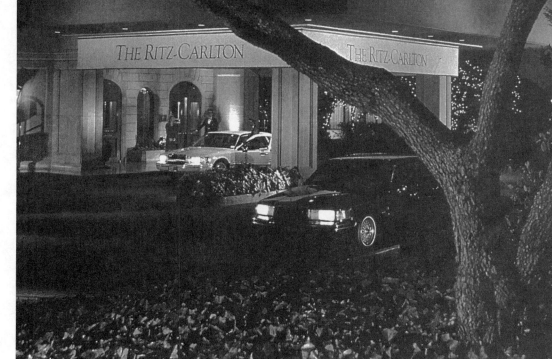

10

Independent/Entrepreneurial Perspective on Hospitality Operations

Leslie Stevens Weinberg
California State Polytechnic University

This chapter explains the role of independent hotels and food service organizations in the hospitality industry today. Historically, an independent operation was considered to be one that was independently owned and operated. In other words, it was not affiliated with any chain or multisite service firm.

Today, however, the definition of an independent has become rather fuzzy. Take, for example, the Huntington Hotel, a small luxury hotel located on San Francisco's Nob Hill. The Huntington is considered to be an independent hotel. However, it realized that it needed the support of a national and international reservation system and an international marketing support system in order to perform well during the intensely competitive late 1980s and early 1990s. Therefore, it teamed up with many other independent luxury properties and became a member of Small Luxury Hotels and Resorts, a collection of luxury properties throughout the world. Groups of independents working together can afford international reservation systems and sales and marketing programs that could not be supported by just one hotel.

As you can see, the definition of an independent is not as clear-cut as it might seem. For our purposes, we can consider an independent to be any hotel or food service organization that is not owned, operated, or franchised by a chain but may be part of a network of other independent operations. In many cases, the independent may be family owned and operated.

Our discussion will begin with the lodging industry. Independent hotels account for more than half of the hotel rooms in developed countries in the world.[1] However, there has been a definite trend toward consolidation and chain affiliation over the past decade. For example, in 1990, 39,883 rooms went from independent status to chain status; however, 29,305 went from a chain to an independent identity![2] Clearly, independent hotels are not the dinosaurs some would claim.

The food service industry has followed similar trends over the past two decades; much of the growth in food service has come from franchise chains, which account for roughly

25% of U.S. restaurant outlets and about 43% of sales, compared with just 15% of sales in 1970.[3] However, there is certainly plenty of opportunity for independent restaurants, which account for approximately 49% of all eating places in the United States.[3,4]

Reasons for the Trend Toward Chain Affiliation

Let us now examine the reasons for the trend toward chain affiliation in lodging and food service. First, hotel and restaurant franchise opportunities continue to abound. Many entrepreneurs, individuals starting their own businesses, found that it was easier to obtain financing for new projects if they were affiliated with a national franchise brand name.

Second, many existing independents realized that they needed national and international marketing and brand recognition. Hotels also needed international reservation systems in order to compete effectively. Such systems were cost prohibitive unless the independents teamed up with nationally recognized chains.

Third, other economies of scale could also be gained by affiliating with a nationally recognized chain. For example, many of the chains provide purchasing services, training, or other corporate services resulting in lower costs to participants.

Fourth, many independent hotel operators realized the need for a critical mass of hotels in order to assure customer loyalty. For example, customers might "defect" to hotel chains offering more visibility via more locations or incentives such as frequent guest stay programs.

Fifth, the introduction and growing popularity of management contracts represents another cause of the increase in chain-operated hotel properties. Management contracts are an agreement between a hotel operating company (such as Marriott or Hilton) and a hotel owner (such as an insurance company or pension fund). The management contractor receives a fee from the owner for managing the hotel. Thus, it became easy for an independently owned hotel to team up with a national chain and secure their lodging expertise.

Sixth, many believe that chain-operated properties are more successful than independents. As a general rule, in 1992, chain-affiliated full-service hotels outperformed independent properties by a substantial margin.[5] Chain-affiliated limited-service hotels achieved higher occupancy rates than independent properties and were more profitable than independent properties.[5] However, independent limited-service hotels achieved higher revenues per available room.[5]

For all of these reasons, many independent hotels and restaurants decided to affiliate with chains over the past decade. There are, however, many good reasons to remain independent!

Reasons to Remain Independent

First, independence means freedom and control. Independent operators are not constrained by rules and regulations issued by a corporate office perhaps thousands of miles away. Independents do not have to deal with red tape and the bureaucracy often encountered by chain properties. This is a critical consideration, as many independent operators cherish the freedom to make business decisions that may reflect adventure, risk, or experimentation.[6] These decisions might be viewed as unacceptable to shareholders if they were part of a publicly held national chain. In an independent environment, policies can be created and implemented in the same day!

Independence means the ability to realize entrepreneurial dreams. An entrepreneur may be defined as one who starts his own business or one who buys a small business with the intention of growing or changing it significantly.[7] An entrepreneur may also be one who owns a portion of a business and is active in its daily management, or it may be a small team of business founders.[7] Entrepreneurship is a path to self-realization; it allows one to take control of her life and provides an opportunity to improve one's economic standing.[8] The restaurant industry in particular provides many opportunities for entrepreneurship as it requires relatively small amounts of capital and provides services that are relatively technologically unsophisticated.

Independence means the ability to offer the guest a truly unique experience. Because independents are not part of a group, they are free to offer unusual, daring, or distinctive products or services. Many guests _do_ want pleasant surprises or unique environments, which are sadly lacking in closely controlled, monitored, and sanitized chain environments. Ron Callari, president of INNovations, a sales and marketing organization that represents 80 independent inns, reports that even business travelers, who have traditionally opted for chain standardization, are now looking for a home away from home, old-world ambience, intimacy, and, most importantly, service.[9] Independents are ideally poised to offer these amenities. Callari's inns have continued to prosper despite the recession.

Independence means the ability to react swiftly to changing consumer tastes and preferences on a local basis. As customer needs and wants change, chains may spend excessive time "analyzing" these changes and test-marketing new products. They may miss many local trends. An independent can change menus or operating procedures daily without seeking corporate approval three or four layers up the organization.

Independents are not subject to the "bad apple" effect.[10] In other words, a negative guest experience at one chain property reflects poorly on all units in the chain. For example, the recent Jack in the Box food crisis has had a detrimental impact on all of their restaurants, not just those in the Pacific Northwest where the tragedy occurred.

Independent hotels can now achieve many of the benefits of affiliation by joining reservation and representation service groups such as Leading Hotels of the World or Preferred Hotels. These services provide independents many of the services a chain would normally provide, such as advertising, marketing, and reservations.

Finally, independence means no costly franchise fees or royalties to be paid monthly. Nor do independents have to contribute funds to advertising pools each month.

Pros and Cons of Working for an Independent

What does this all mean to you? On graduation from your hotel and restaurant management program, you will have to decide whether a chain-affiliated or independent property is right for you. We will now discuss some of the pros and cons of choosing an independent versus chain-affiliated property to work for.

Structured Management Training Program

If you are looking for a structured management training program that essentially continues your hospitality management education, then a chain-affiliated property is more appropriate for you. Because independents generally have less-formal organizations and are smaller, they are unlikely to offer structured management training opportunities. They are more likely to hire people to fill existing needs. They are often anxious to hire individuals who have already been trained by the chains so that these individuals can bring their knowledge and skills with them. Because of respected training by the majors, it is often easier to move from a position at a chain-operated property to an independent rather than begin your career at an independent.

Immediate Placement into Jobs of Responsibility

If you feel that after four years in college, you have had enough formal training and are ready to go immediately into a position of responsibility, then an independent operation is generally a good choice. Certainly, chains also have direct hire positions. However, you are likely to be given a position with greater responsibility in an independent because there are usually fewer layers of management in an independent.

Salary

Smaller properties generally pay managers less than larger properties, and independents do tend to be smaller than chain-affiliated properties. However, independents sometimes pay better than chains in order to be able to attract high-caliber individuals.

Job Security

Generalizations about job security are difficult to make. An established chain-operated property will certainly offer more job security than a new entrepreneurial venture. However, even major corporations such as Marriott and Hyatt experience severe economic downturns corresponding to recessions in the economy as a whole. Downsizing and across-the-board cutbacks at many chains were prevalent during the early 1990s. Hence, a position at an established independent was probably more secure in this environment.

Promotion Opportunities

Both independents and chain-operated properties offer excellent promotion opportunities. Due to the greater number of units within a chain, promotion opportunities are generally more frequent in a chain environment. However, many times these promotions require relocation, possibly thousands of miles away. Thus, specific geographic preferences are often not accommodated.

Two Independent Success Stories

If this discussion so far has left you uncertain as to whether an independent or chain is best for you, perhaps the following success stories will help to sway your opinion.

Micarl Hill (Mica) is the youthful general manager of the prestigious, 140-room Huntington Hotel, atop San Francisco's Nob Hill. He has worked for independents and chain hotels. Mica is a 1985 graduate of the School of Hotel and Restaurant Management at California State Polytechnic University.

From a general manager's perspective, Mica summarizes the advantages of working for independents as the following:

- You can be a big fish in a little pond.
- Decisions can be made and implemented more quickly.
- There is little or no chain of command.
- You can establish personal relationships with owners.
- Job security is greater—there is no one coming up the corporate ladder from another hotel within the chain to compete for your job.
- There is no fear of job transfer.
- There is less paperwork and fewer systems and procedures.

However, according to Mica, the disadvantages consist of the following:

- Owners tend to operate the property on a smaller staff scale (i.e., a manager may also perform human resources and marketing functions.
- Money is much tighter.
- It is more difficult to attract talented upper management because you can't recruit from other hotels within the chain.
- There is no real opportunity for growth without leaving the individual property.

Mica's advice to students beginning a career in the hospitality industry:

Begin in a chain-affiliated training program. Learn all you can about all departments and acquire as much management experience, expertise, and knowledge as possible. Then, after you are tired of relocating, look to an independent hotel!

Our second interview is with Mark Peel, entrepreneurial co-owner of the highly acclaimed Los Angeles restaurant, Campanile and La Brea Bakery. Campanile was rated the city's fourth most popular restaurant in the *1993 Zagat Restaurant Survey.* Mark attended The School of Hotel and Restaurant Management at California State Polytechnic University from 1975 to 1977.

Mark and Nancy Silverton, his wife and an internationally renowned pastry chef, fulfilled their entrepreneurial dreams when Campanile and La Brea Bakery opened in 1989. Mark started in the restaurant business at age 17 as a dishwasher and cook's helper and is now one of the most influential executive chefs in the United States.

Mark believes that luxury restaurants must be independents to succeed. For example, his menu changes daily to reflect the unique availability of ingredients that are highly seasonal or difficult to obtain. Chain restaurants must be consistent; this standardization reduces their flexibility and ability to take advantage of special opportunities. Chains, however, do have great corporate support and have proven programs to solve most operational problems. Independents are often operated by the seat of the pants, and they must often reinvent the wheel. Hence, Mark would advise graduating students to get some good chain training first, which they can apply and implement at an independent operation. Then, when ready to move to a more creative, independent environment, they should have a flexible attitude and be willing to be untrained a little!

For future entrepreneurs, Mark cautions that it is a lot easier to work for someone else! However, he just didn't want to work for someone else any more. He feels that it is crucial to put together a team for a successful venture. He, Nancy, and general manager, Manfred Krankl have all been crucial to Campanile's success.

The Outlook for Independents

The 1990s represent significant opportunities for well-conceived and -executed independent lodging and food service operations. With the excess capacity of the 1990s, many low-cost opportunities will be available for those who would like to start their own business and be their own boss. Existing and new entrepreneurial ventures should flourish once the U.S. and global economies pick up as expected by 1994.

——References——

1. Selwitz, Robert. Loews, Covia Bring CLAS On-Line. Hotel and Motel Management. August 20, 1990; Volume 205: p. 3.
2. Overbuilt Hotel Industry in Slump. *Standard and Poor's Industry Surveys.* March 12, 1992; p. L34.
3. Spending Holds Up in Week Economy. *Standard and Poor's Industry Surveys.* March 12, 1992; p. L45.
4. Chain Restaurant Companies. *Directory of Chain Restaurant Operators.* 1992–1993; p. XXIX.
5. Arthur Andersen and Smith Travel Research. *The Host Report.* (Midyear Report for the Year 1992).
6. Michaelides. Independents: The Way We Are. *Restaurant Hospitality.* January 1989; Volume 73: p. 16.
7. The Center for Venture Management. *Proceedings of Project ISEED, Summer 1975.* Milwaukee, Wis.: p. 46.
8. Small, R. W. (1987) A Discriminant Analysis of Restaurant Entrepreneur Types and Restaurant Classifications. Ph.D dissertation. The Claremont Graduate School.
9. Berman, Judy and Pamela Lanier. Bed-and-Breakfast Inns Come of Age. *The Cornell Hotel and Restaurant Administration Quarterly.* April 1993; Volume 34: p. 20.
10. J. R. Wells. (1984) In Search of Synergy. Ph.D. dissertation. Harvard University. p. 457.

11

Chain Operations in the Hospitality Industry

William F. Jaffé
Purdue University

. . . All-suite hotels . . . $2.99 extra value meal . . . Big foot pizza . . . Caribbean sports resorts . . . Happy meals . . . Everyday is a fiesta . . . Have it your way, right away . . .

The above examples are an unmistakable part of the hospitality industry as it draws closer to the twenty-first century. All of these are a product of one of the most American of institutions—the chain restaurant or hotel. Whether it's a burger chain, hotel, resort, or yogurt chain, the chain food service or lodging enterprise has been a driving force in the hospitality industry in the last quarter of the twentieth century. As our society approaches the next millennium, the chain operation will play an even larger part in everyday life.

In the past it was the independent hospitality operation that broke new ground and pushed for innovation. But this began to change in the 1970s, as the leading food service and lodging chains began their phenomenal growth. While growth continued into the 1980s, it was the downturn of the economy, in the mid- to late 1980s, that forced the chain operation to re-examine how it would do business in the future. Chain companies, both food service and lodging, began searching for the specific niche in which they could do what they did better than any other company. These chains found that by targeting a specific customer group, called a market segment, they could continue to grow and prosper. The lessons learned through these lean years have taught chain hospitality companies to utilize segmentation as the vehicle to drive them into the next century.

Types of Chain Operations in the Hospitality Industry

A chain-operated hospitality unit can be simply defined as two or more units that operate under the same name and that follow the same standard operating procedures. The chain operation in the food service industry will most likely operate under one of the following three ownership/management relationships:

1. Totally owned and operated under the direct control of the chain's management. An example of this is Pizza Hut. All Pizza Hut restaurants are owned and operated by Pizza Hut, Inc., which in turn is owned by the parent company, PepsiCo.
2. A combination of corporate-owned units and franchised units. KFC is an example of this type of chain operation. About 40% of KFC restaurants are franchised operations, with the remainder being corporate-owned and -operated restaurants.
3. All units of the chain are owned and operated as franchised units (see Chapter 12, "The Franchising Industry"). Subway restaurants are an example of this type of chain. All units are operated as a franchise, meaning the name, recipes, and operating procedures are leased to a franchisee for a specific fee and a percentage of the profits. The franchisee can then identify their restaurant as one of the chain and reap the benefits of the chain's name recognition plus national advertising and promotion.

Chain operations in the lodging industry also operate under the above arrangements but with some distinct differences. Examples of these include the following:

1. Marriott Courtyard hotels are an example of a chain that is totally owned and operated by the chain company. In this example the Courtyards are a division of Marriott Corporation.
2. Hyatt Hotels operate some of their hotels under a management contract (see Chapter 13, "Management Companies in the Hospitality Industry."). The chain corporation (Hyatt) provides management for the hotel under an agreement with the hotel owners. The management firm also has no legal claim to the physical property. In addition, the firm normally has limited financial responsibility if there is an operating loss and reaps limited benefit if there is a profit. Many luxury hotels now operate under this type of arrangement.[1]
3. Best Western hotels operate within a referral group (see "Referral Associations in the Hospitality Industry" and Chapter 5, "Hospitality Industry Associations"). Privileges in the Hospitality Industry and Chapter 5, "Hospitality Industry Associations" connected with this group are similar to those available to members of a club. That is, each member hotel pays a fee to belong to the referral group and must conform to group standards. Each individual hotel is owned and operated separately from the rest of the referral group (through one owner often owns and operates more than one hotel). Each referral group member derives the benefits of a centralized reservation service and regional or national name recognition. However, each member maintain its own identity and style. In fact, the products, services, prices, and decor of each member hotel may vary from property to property.[1]

Chain Operations and Segmentation

As mentioned earlier, market segmentation is changing the face of chains in American society. *Segmentation* is a marketing term that assumes heterogeneity in the marketplace and divergent demand. Implicit in this assumption is the conclusion that perceived differences are inadequate for product definition. Instead, the product must be defined for specific market segments based on basic differences in users' needs and wants.[2] Thus each segment is targeted at a particular part of the population that is similar in its motivation.

An example of this is Taco Bell, which in the early 1990s developed a strategy to distinguish itself from other fast food chains. Taco bell's price-tiered menu items were clearly aimed, or targeted, at that part of the market which was looking for quick, tasty food at a price considered a good value. This segment could be labeled a price/value segment because price is the key purchase motivation.

Other types of market segments may include geographic segments, demographic segments, behavioristic segments, and psychographic segments, as well as needs and benefits segments (for more on segmentation see Chapter 25, "Hospitality Marketing Management"). A chain of sports resorts is an example of a needs and benefits segmentation. The hospitality chain identifies a market segment that is differentiated by the desire to participate in sports as a vacation motivation. The chain then molds its product specifically to meet the needs of this segment and sets itself apart from other resorts by providing unique benefits. If done correctly, the chain can thrive by marketing only to this small niche of the market. While this description may over simplify the concept, the key to successful segmentation meeting a customers' need or want better than any competitor.

It is important to understand why segmentation is so desirable and can be so rewarding. If all products and services can be designed to meet a specific need or want, then all resources can be targeted toward this aim, thus better utilizing the resources of the company. The trick to success is to accurately identify the market segment to target and to provide those customers with the right product/service mix that satisfies their needs and wants. A look at the leading lodging and food service chains illustrates how the leaders have targeted their products and services to specific segments of the market.

The Leading Lodging Chains

The lodging industry is generally segmented by price type. The major segments are luxury hotels, all-suite hotels, mid-market hotels, and economy hotels. As seen in Table 1, four industry giants dominate the top 25 brands of lodging chains in the United States. These five companies represent over 54% of all hotel rooms of the top 25 leading hotels.[3]

Each of these industry leaders has lodging brands that are targeted at more than one segment of the travel market. Holiday Inn is number one with its flagship brand (mid-market segment) and has the twenty-fourth brand with its Holiday Inn Crowne Plaza (luxury segment). Its product portfolio also includes Holiday Inn Express (economy segment), and Holiday Inn SunSpree Resorts.[4] Choice International targets the economy and mid-price segments with Comfort Inns, Quality Inns, and Econo Lodge brands. Hospitality Franchise Systems is a lodging chain with the brands Days Inn (economy), Ramada (mid-market), and Howard Johnson (both mid-market and economy). Marriott is also a top-five lodging chain with its multiple-segment brands Marriott Hotels, Marriott Suites, Marriott Resorts, Courtyard Hotels, Fairfield Inn, and Residence Inn.

Table 1. Top 25 Commercial Lodging Chains

	Company	Properties	Rooms	Rooms Added*
1	Holiday Inn	1,535	296,691	14,689
2	Best Western	3,338	276,797	17,100
3	Days Inn of America	1,330	139,990	17,100
4	ITT Sheraton	421	130,859	7,682
5	Marriott	205	103,000	2,417
6	Ramada Inns, Hotels	565	94,436	7,634
7	Hilton Hotels Corp.	236	92,348	5,097
8	Comfort	1,010	87,390	8,621
9	Motel 6	754	84,637	12,565
10	Quality	608	74,762	8,975
11	Radisson	269	66,392	NA**
12	Econo Lodge	818	58,868	4,619
13	Super 8 Motels	941	57,595	4,259
14	Hyatt	105	55,573	NA**
15	Howard Johnson	388	50,484	3,966
16	Hampton Inns	327	40,206	3,446
17	Travelodge	433	35,904	5,715
18	Westin	64	33,697	1,433
19	Courtyard by Marriott	202	29,911	598
20	La Quinta	209	26,464	55
21	Embassy Suites	103	24,000	732
22	Red Roof Inns	209	23,261	0
23	Residence Inn (Marriott)	178	22,277	300
24	Holiday Inn Crowne Plaza	64	21,664	NA**
25	Knights Lodging	193	19,500	2,560

* 1991–1992
**Information not available
Source: *Lodging*

While segments of the lodging industry are classified by price type, true segmentation is by service level. Customers' service expectations are different for a luxury hotel versus an economy hotel, and the chain hotel must be able to clearly understand customer needs in order to provide the expected benefits for each distinct segment. The problem that the chain hotel must solve is that within each segment the target customer usually represents more than one distinct group. A resort hotel may choose middle- to upper-class families as its target customer and build its service packet to meet the needs of this group. But in order to sustain a high occupancy rate (and acceptable profits), the hotel may also need to target convention and conference groups. In order to be successful, the hotel must satisfy both segments simultaneously with limited or declining resources.

The Luxury Hotel

Chain hotels in the luxury segment attempt to create an environment approaching opulence, with an atmosphere that is comfortable. The key chains in this segment are Ritz-Carlton, Four Seasons, Marriott, Inter-Continental, and Hilton Hotels.[5] The challenge for this segment is to meet high customer expectations while streamlining costs. What the successful chains have done is to redefine what is best in service and amenities, redesigning delivery systems to meet guests' expectations for less money. The cost/value expectation is high for this segment, and it is the successful chain that learns how to satisfy the customer.

Ritz-Carlton uses an information handling system to track customers' needs, including the type of pillow they prefer or the brand of soft drink they usually drink. Four Seasons researched the needs of its business customers and found that most preferred an in-room fax machine to a hair dryer. Hilton Hotels utilizes an in-room interactive video entertainment and service system to provide customers with pay-per-view movies and games, plus room service, messages, and express checkout.[5] Chains in this segment continue to seek the right balance between luxury and efficiency to satisfy the needs and wants to their target customer.

The All-Suite Hotel

This segment is better identified as the extended-stay segment. The motivating force for this segment is the desire of the business traveler to have a place to live and work while at a destination for more than five days. This segment of the hotel industry is still relatively new and is continuing to grow. A recent study indicated that almost 35% of travelers stay at least five consecutive days at a location. However, extended-stay properties account for less than 1% of the nation's hotel rooms.[6] The leading chain hotels in this segment are Embassy Suites, Guest Quarters Suite Hotels, Residence Inn (Marriott), and Homewood Suites.

Research has shown that most long-stay business travelers use their hotel rooms as a place to live and to work. Extended-stay hotels feature apartment-style suites that provide a separate bedroom and living area, fully equipped kitchens, and a separate vanity area and bathroom. Many hotels in this segment also provide conveniences such as business centers equipped with personal computers, fax machines, photocopiers, grocery shopping, and laundry services for guests. Since an extended stay means many travelers are away from friends and families, these hotels are laid out as a community concept, clustered around a "neighborhood center" with landscaped gardens, bridged walkways, and recreation areas. The extended-stay chain hotel seeks to provide a familarity with the hotel from destination to destination. Thus, guests who are away from home for long periods of time can feel they are in a home away from home when they stay at the extended-stay chain hotel in whatever city they visit. With the combination of homelike amenities and a staff dedicated to making guests feel welcome in a new setting, the extended-stay chain hotel can help minimize traveler stress.[6]

The Mid-Market Hotel

The key chains in this segment are Holiday Inn, Best Western, Ramada Inns, and Marriott with Marriott Hotels and Courtyard Hotels. Once the core of the chain hotel industry, the mid-market has been steadily losing ground to the luxury and economy segments of the hotel industry. In 1970 the traditional mid-market represented more than 90% of room night demand in the United States. Twenty years later, this percentage had fallen to 41%. However, by defining their segment as the customer does (something between the luxury and the economy segments), the mid-market segment has rallied to a 65% market share and is continuing to grow.[7] In 1991, mid-market chains were reported to have sold more than 270 million room nights—40% more than the luxury and economy segments combined. Experts agree that the mid-market segment will continue to grow if these chains are able to do the following:

1. Distinguish themselves from obsolete hotels
2. Deliver the technology and training that will be essential in capturing the more sophisticated traveler
3. Raise product quality[7]

The continued success and growth of this segment depends on chain hotels properly positioning, furnishing, staffing, and maintaining their properties in this core segment of the hotel industry.

The Economy Hotel

The economy segment is probably better defined as the limited-services segment. Many of the leading hotel chains are this segment's major players. Hampton Inns, Days Inn of America, Marriott Fairfield Inn, Super 8, Travelodge, and Choice Hotels are all key chains in this growing segment. Also, traditional mid-market hotel chains are entering this market. Examples of this are Holiday Inn's economy segment entry called Holiday Inn Express and Howard Johnson's HoJo Inns.[8]

The 1990s continue to be good for this segment, as room sales and occupancy rates continue to grow. Room supply is also increasing as the major chains continue to grow. Unlike other segments of the hotel industry, though, the growth of the economy segment is mainly through the sale of franchises. Quality control is a significant factor in this segment: some franchisees may be difficult to control property by property to maintain the image of the chain. Segment leaders agree on a key issue of the 1990s: chains need to find a way to assist franchisees with finding financing to improve their facilities, thus maintaining the quality image of the chain.[9]

The Leading Food Service Chains

Categories of food service chains are generally identified by menu type. These categories, as labeled by *Restaurants and Institutions (R&I)* magazine, are burgers, cafeterias and buffets, chicken, dinner houses, family dining, Mexican, pizza, sandwiches, seafood, steak houses, and sweets.

R&I annually ranks chain food service companies as to sales volume (categorized by menu type). *R&I* also annually polls 2,500 American households to find which food service chains deliver the best value, service, convenience, atmosphere, cleanliness, and best variety of food.[10]

When looking at each category it is important to see how the chain performs in regard to both sales and their success in meeting the needs and wants of their target market. A comparative look at these rankings illustrates how the leading food service chains successfully utilize market segmentation strategy.

Burger Chains

The top ten burger chains are ranked by sales volume in Table 2. McDonald's continues to be the leader in this category. McDonald's, however, continues to look for new ways to bolster sagging customer counts. McDonald's has expanded to airline food service, providing its Friendly Sky Meals to United Airlines. Burger King, the number two chain in this category, seeks to expand by placing kiosks in nontraditional outlets, expanding the number of in-line restaurants in shopping malls, and increasing its sales volume while decreasing labor costs with more double-drive thru restaurants.[11]

Table 2. Food Service Operatons by Category: Burgers*

Rank	Organization	Sales in Millions $
1	McDonald's	19,928.2
2	Burger King	6,200.0
3	Hardee's	3,431.0
4	Wendy's	3,223.6
5	Jack in the Box	978.0
6	Carl's Jr.	614.0
7	Sonic Drive-Ins	518.0
8	Whataburger	318.4
9	White Castle	300.0
10	Rally's Hamburgers	221.0

*Source: *Restaurants and Institutions'* Top 400 Foodservices

The real leader in this category appears to be Wendy's. With founder Dave Thomas back in control, Wendy's has increased sales and continues to deliver to its customers the right mix of menu variety, atmosphere, and cleanliness. For 1992, Wendy's was voted the most popular (*R&I* annual poll) in the burger category.[10] Wendy's was chosen number one because it consistently met customers' needs by providing the right mix of benefits. Another big winner in this category is Rally's Hamburgers. The Rally's chain, ranked tenth in sales volume, was the overall second in the burger category.

While both Wendy's and Rally's are classified as burger chains, Wendy's can be better described as part of the needs and benefits segment and Rally's as part of the price/value segment. Wendy's needs to continue providing the benefits (menu variety, cleanliness, and atmosphere) their customers identify as their basic needs. On the other hand, while atmosphere, menu variety, and cleanliness may concern Rally's customers, their primary motivation is price/value. Thus, to best reach its market niche, Rally's needs to aim their service and product mix to fulfill the primary expectation of price/value (in fact, Rally's was rated number one in best value among burger chains).[10]

Pizza/Italian Food Chains

Pizza Hut continues to dominate this category over rivals Little Caesar's, Godfather's, and Domino's (Table 3). Trends in this segment include alternative delivery concepts such as kiosks, take-out and delivery-only units, and breakfast pizza and dessert pizzas including in-house bakeries and dessert promotions. Little Caesar's joint venture with retail giant Kmart will allow this pizza chain to grow rapidly and expand its menu to include breakfast pizza and other breakfast items.[12]

Table 3. Food Service Operatons by Segment: Pizza/Italian*

Rank	Organization	Sales in Millions $
1	Pizza Hut	5,300.0
2	Domino's Pizza	2400.0
3	Little Caesars	1725.0
5	Round Table Pizza	320.0
6	Sbarro	273.3
7	Godfather's Pizza	233.5
8	Shakey's Pizza	225.0
9	Pizza Inns	176.0
10	Chuck E. Cheese	155.0

*Source: *Restaurants and Institutions'* Top 400 Foodservices

Pizza Hut was the preferred chain in this category as to food quality, atmosphere, and cleanliness. The leading pizza chain in the price/value segment was Little Caesar's. Domino's, while slipping in sales volume, was the preferred pizza chain in regards to good service and convenience.[10]

Cafeterias/Buffets

Cafeterias (Table 4) continue to be caught between two segments. At one end is the price-sensitive, casual-dining segment and at the other is the value-driven quick service segment. While leader Luby's cafeterias continues to increase sales, most of the others in this category see sales volumes decreasing. The bright spot in this category is clearly Old Country Buffet. While only ranked fifth in sales volume, Old Country Buffet was chosen tops in value with its one price, all-you-can-eat format. Customers also rated this chain tops as to menu variety and food quality.

Family Dining Chains

Sales leaders Denny's, Shoney's, Big Boy, and Friendly's continue their dominance of this category (Table 5).[13] But it is Cracker Barrel that is the major star among family dining chains. Though its sales volume only ranks it eleventh, it is ranked first in the 1992 *R&I* Most Popular Chain for this category. In fact it was rated number one in the categories of food quality, menu variety, good service and value, atmosphere, and cleanliness. Cracker Barrel also was the top-rated chain, for all categories, in providing good service. Cracker Barrel appears to have a firm grasp of the needs and wants of its segment.[10]

Table 4. Food Service Operatons by Segment: Cafeterias*

Rank	Organization	Sales in Millions $
1	Luby's Cafeterias	330.4
2	Morrison's Cafeterias	306.4
3	Piccadilly Cafeterias	275.0
4	Furr's Cafeterias	216.0
5	Old Country Buffet	207.0
6	Wyatt's Cafeterias	166.0
7	King's Table Buffets	84.2
8	K & W Cafeterias	75.0
9	Homestyle Family Buffet	49.4
10	MCL Cafeterias	46.8

*Source: *Restaurants and Institutions'* Top 400 Foodservices

Chicken Chains

While KFC continues to dominate this category with sales volume more than ten times greater than its nearest rival, (Table 6) it is the small Chick-fil-A that rates high marks from its customers.[14] According to the *R&I* 1992 poll, Chick-fil-A was rated highest in the categories of food quality, service, atmosphere, and cleanliness. KFC was rated highest for convenience.[10]

Table 5. Food Service Operatons by Segment: Family Dining*

Rank	Organization	Sales in Millions $
1	Denny's	1,591.3
2	Shoney's	1,099.0
3	Big Boy	1,076.4
4	Friendly's	530.0
5	Perkin's Family Restaurants	505.0
6	International House of Pancakes	413.6
7	Bob Evans Restaurants	381.5
8	Waffle House	312.7
9	Bakers Square	312.7
10	Village Inn	245.7
11	Cracker Barrel Old Country Store	242.6
12	Marie Callendar Pie Shops	240.8

*Source: *Restaurants and Institutions'* Top 400 Foodservices

Table 6. Food Service Operatons by Segment: Chicken*

Rank	Organization	Sales in Millions $
1	KFC	6,200.0
2	Popeye's Famous Fried	540.2
3	Church's Chicken	506.6
4	Chick-fil-A	324.6
5	El Pollo Loco	185.9

*Source: *Restaurants and Institutions'* Top 400 Foodservices

Dinner House Chains

Dinner house chains (Table 7) have seen customers change over the past few years. Conspicuous consumption is gone, value is in.[15] The key to customers' perceptions as to value is the caliber of service and the food quality.[15] Olive Garden is the chain that customers perceive as providing those two ingredients for satisfaction. Customers in the *R&I* poll rated Olive Garden highest for value, service, atmosphere, and cleanliness as compared to other dinner houses. Further, Olive Garden was rated highest for all chains in all categories for atmosphere, cleanliness and overall restaurant preference.[10]

Sweet Chains

Sweets chains' signature items, whether cookies, frozen yogurt, or ice cream, aren't enough for today's customer (Table 8). These customers' desire a break from the monotony of "the same old thing." Chains in this market segment have begun to expand product lines to increase sales. TCBY sells Mrs. Field's cookies, brownies, and muffins in some of their stores, while Baskin-Robbins is testing bakery items to add to its selections.[16] Dairy Queen, this segment's leader, has added a line of gourmet frozen cakes. Customers chose Baskin-Robbins, as best in this segment, followed by TCBY and Dunkin' Donuts.

Table 7. Food Service Operatons by Segment: Dinner Houses*

Rank	Organization	Sales in Millions $
1	The Olive Garden	808.0
2	T.G.I. Friday's	570.0
3	Chili's Grill & Bar	531.9
4	Bennigan's	463.0
5	Applebee's Neighorhood Grill & Bar	289.6
6	The Ground Round	288.6
7	Stuart Anderson's Restaurants	258.0
8	Ruby Tuesday	241.5
9	Houlihan's	198.2
10	Red Robin	173.2
11	Hard Rock Cafe	157.8
12	Chart House	150.0
13	Specialty Restaurants	141.0
14	J.B.'s Restaurants	127.3
15	Black-eyed Pea	117.7
16	Houston's Restaurants	102.9
17	Hooter's Restaurants	100.0

*Source: *Restaurants and Institutions'* Top 400 Foodservices

Steak House Chains

While Americans' consumption of beef is down in homes, beef, and the steak houses that feature it, remain fairly steady in away-from-home consumption. The key players in this segment (Table 9) have upgraded their menus to include upscale entrees such as New York strip, filet mignon, and lobster at Ponderosa; prime rib at Sizzler, and marinated and grilled sirloin at Golden Corral.[17] Customer choice in this segment is clearly Golden Corral. This chain was highest rated for food quality, service, atmosphere, cleanliness, and convenience. Ryan's Steakhouses were best in class for menu variety and value.

Table 8. Food Service Operatons by Segment: Sweets*

Rank	Organization	Sales in Millions $
1	Dairy Queen	2,352.4
2	Dunkin' Donuts	990.8
3	Baskin-Robbins	829.7
4	TCBY	321.0

*Source: _Restaurants and Institutions'_ Top 400 Foodservices

Table 9. Food Service Operatons by Segment: Steak Houses*

Rank	Organization	Sales in Millions $
1	Sizzler	983.6
2	Ponderosa	744.1
3	Golden Corral	449.0
4	Western Sizzlin'	400.0
5	Bonanza	389.2
6	Ryan's Family Steak Houses	355.1
7	Quincy's Family Steakhouses	283.3
8	Stuart Anderson's Restaurants	258.0
9	Tony Roma's—APlace for Ribs	241.0

*Source: _Restaurants and Institutions'_ Top 400 Foodservices

Mexican Chains

Price/value is the main customer motivation in this segment. Thus the major players (see Table 10) are changing and supplementing menus to feature lower-priced entrees. Taco Bell continues to be the leader in this segment. Its price-tiered menu has resulted in larger increases in sales and profit. Taco Bell continues to seek new ways to expand their sales base by offering price-tiered breakfast items and nontraditional delivery methods including, small less labor-intensive sites in malls and kiosks on high school and college campuses.[10] Chi-Chi's continues to be the customer preferred chain in this segment. Consumers in the *R&I* poll ranked Chi-Chi's highest in food quality, menu variety, service, atmosphere, and cleanliness.[18]

Sandwich Chains

This segment of the food service industry attracts one of two types of customers. One group is willing to pay a slightly higher price for what they perceive to be a high quality product. The other group is attracted to the low price, similar to the Taco Bell customer. Sandwich chains (Table 11) target either one group or the other. The top trends in this category include value-priced sandwiches and marketing geared toward customers willing to spend more for higher quality products. Other trends see the major players (Arby's, Subway, and Rax) seeking to expand into nontraditional markets including colleges, hospitals, and sports facilities.[18]

The leaders in customer satisfaction in this category are Rax Restaurants and Subway. Rax was rated highest in the 1992 *R&I* poll for the categories of menu variety, atmosphere, and cleanliness. Subway leads the category, in food quality, value, good service, and convenience.[10]

Table 10. Food Service Operatons by Segment: Mexican*

Rank	Organization	Sales in Millions $
1	Taco Bell	2,800.0
2	Chi-Chi's	456.3
3	El Torito	375.0
4	Del Taco	177.0
5	Taco John's	137.0

*Source: *Restaurants and Institutions'* Top 400 Foodservices

Seafood Chains

The key trend in this category is value. Value menus are designed to attract the customer to the seafood chain with the lure of complete meals. Fish and chicken combo platters are also hooking customers on the seafood chains. After value, health is the next most common theme. The leading seafood chains (Table 12) are expanding baked, grilled, and broiled seafood lines, with some offering chicken as an alternative to fried fish.[19]

Value, service, and expansion into smaller markets are key components of Red Lobster's continued success. This chain is also the preferred one in the seafood category. Customers rated Red Lobster number one in food quality, menu variety, good service, atmosphere, and cleanliness. Long John Silver's (the number two chain in sales volume) was ranked tops as to value and convenience.

As the United States enters the twenty-first century, the one thing that will remain constant, when speaking of chains in the hospitality industry, will be change. Chain hospitality companies, whether lodging or food service, will continue to change as the needs and wants of their target customers change.

Table 11. Food Service Operatons by Segment: Sandwiches*

Rank	Organization	Sales in Millions $
1	Arby's	1,450.0
2	Subway	1,400.0
3	Roy Rodgers	236.6
4	Rax	202.8
5	A & W Restaurants	217.0

*Source: _Restaurants and Institutions'_ Top 400 Foodservices

Table 12. Food Service Operatons by Segment: Seafood*

Rank	Organization	Sales in Millions $
1	Red Lobster	1,600.0
2	Long John Silver's Seafood Shoppes	555.0
3	Captain D's	420.0
4	Skipper's	100.5

*Source: _Restaurants and Institutions'_ Top 400 Foodservices

——References——

1. Rousselle, J. R. and H. Adler. (1989) Chain Operations in the Hospitality Industry. In R. Brymer (ed.), *Hospitality Management: An Introduction to the Industry*. Dubuque, Ia.: Kendall/Hunt, p. 48.
2. Lewis, R. C. and R. E. Chambers. (1989) *Marketing Leadership in Hospitality: Foundations and Practices*. New York: Van Nostrand Reinhold, p. 204.
3. The Top 25 (Hotel) Brands. *Lodging*. 1993; Volume 18, Number 6: pp. 14–18.
4. O'Dwyer, C. Chains: Who Won in 1991? *Lodging*. 1992; Volume 17, Number 6: pp. 29–38.
5. Bruns, R. A Touch of Class. *Lodging*. 1993; Volume 18, Number 8: pp. 18, 20.
6. Schultz, R. Just Like Home. *Lodging*. 1992; Volume 17, Number 9: pp. 62–66.
7. Kinsell, K. High Hopes for the Mid-Market. *Lodging*. 1992; Volume 18, Number 1: pp. 102–105.
8. Achorn, E. Unlimited Prospects. *Lodging*. 1993; Volume 18, Number 7: pp. 24–30.
9. Hayward, P. Small Gains, Great Hopes. *Lodging*. 1992; Volume 18, Number 4: pp. 12–18.
10. Chanudhry, R. American Rates the Chains. *Restaurants and Institutions*. February 1993; Volume 103, Number 3. 23–27.
11. Bertagnoli, L. and K. Cheney. Burger Chains Sizzle with Activity. *Restaurants and Institutions*. July 1992; Volume 102, Number 16: pp. 62–65.
12. Weinstein, J. Pizza/Italian Shows Strong Growth Curve. *Restaurants and Institutions*. July 1992; Volume 102, Number 16: pp. 78–80.
13. Cheney K. Cater to Kids: Please Parents. *Restaurants and Institutions*. July 1992; Volume 102, Number 16: pp. 93–97.
14. McCarthy, B. Chicken Chains Leave the Skin Off. *Restaurants and Institutions*. July 1992; Volume 102, Number 16: pp. 101–106.
15. Dawson, B. M. Service, Value Top Dinner Houses' List. *Restaurants and Institutions*. July 1992; Volume 102, Number 16: pp. 116–120.
16. Bertagnoli, L. Not by Yogurt Alone. *Restaurants and Institutions*. July 1992; Volume 102, Number 16: pp. 111–115.
17. Dawson, B. M. Away-from-home Beefeaters Keep Steakhouses in Shape. *Restaurants and Institutions*. July 1992; Volume 102, Number 16: pp. 125–128.
18. Lorenzi, B. Sandwich Chains Target Budget Buyers and Quality Seekers. *Restaurants and Institutions*. July 1993; Volume 102, Number 16: p. 145.
19. Straus, K. Seafood Chains Lure Customers with Value and Health. *Restaurants and Institutions*, July 1992; Volume 102, Number 16: pp. 151–153.

12

Franchising and the Hospitality Industry

R. Thomas George
Ohio State University

Personal achievement and control over one's employment have been two of the major influences for many individuals to enter into business ownership. The desire to own one's own business has caused many to initiate an activity for what is hoped will be the road to independence. While the potential for success may be great, so are the risks. The U.S. Department of Commerce reports that 38% of all new businesses fail within the first year of operation and 77% fail within the first five years of operation.[1] Two often-named reasons for new business failure are attempting to provide a product for which there is no market and a poor location. However, the most frequently named reason for failure is the combination of a lack of sound business control system and poor management skills.

One approach to reduce the risk is to become part of a business venture that has demonstrated success in the marketplace. By joining an established firm that has refined the delivery of an accepted product or service and has formulated a sound system of financial control and operating procedures, the new operator increases the opportunity for success. Franchising is an approach to business ownership in which an individual is able to affiliate with an established chain while retaining some degree of independence. The International Franchise Association has defined franchising as ". . . a continuing relationship in which the franchisor provides a licensed privilege to do business, plus assistance in organizing, merchandising and management in return for a consideration from the franchisee."[2] The franchisor is able to achieve greater market penetration with a minimum investment, while the franchisee is able to establish a business with a reduced degree of risk. While research on the failure rate for franchise businesses is incomplete, Bond has suggested that between 4.4% and 5% of all franchise businesses fail within the first year.[1] The franchise company, through experimentation and experience, has worked to eliminate many of the causes of new business failure.

Franchising in the Hospitality Industry

There are two primary categories of franchising. The first, known as product and trade name franchising, is a product distribution system. This category accounts for the largest total dollar sales of all franchised businesses. Auto and truck dealers, gasoline service stations, and

Table 1. Restaurant Franchising

Restaurants All Types	Company-Owned Number	Sales	Franchisee-Owned Number	Sales	Totals Number	Sales
1991	30,533	30.5	72,780	55.0	103,313	85.5
1990	29,152	27.9	70,188	50.0	99,340	77.9
1989	27,596	25.5	64,359	44.6	91,955	70.1

Note: Sales are in $ billion.

Table 2. Hotel, Motel, and Campground Franchising

Units All Types	Company-Owned Number	Sales	Franchisee-Owned Number	Sales	Totals Number	Sales
1991	1,307	7.1	10,091	18.9	103,313	26.0
1990	1,261	6.5	9,785	18.4	11,046	24.8
1989	1,232	6.2	8.880	15.3	10,112	21.6

Note: Sales are in $ billion.

soft drink bottlers are examples of this type. The hospitality industry is most often identified with the second category, known as business format franchising. Examples of hospitality business format franchises include Pizza Hut, Country Kitchen Restaurants, Sheraton Inns, and Embassy Suites Hotels. In each of these, the franchisee has been granted the right to use the name, image, products, procedures, and systems of the franchiser. Participation in the marketing strategy is usually required. The franchise company has developed a complete business format, or method of operating, and a franchisee purchases the right to put this format to use.

Growth of the Industry

Franchising in the hospitality industry is primarily concentrated in the food service and lodging areas. However, resorts, campgrounds, and amusement parks may also be franchised. Table 1 indicates a breakdown of restaurants, franchisor-operated and franchisee-operated, by a number of units and sales for the years 1989, 1990, and 1991.

The sales and number of hotels, motels, and campgrounds, franchise-company operated and franchisee-operated, for the years 1989, 1990, and 1991, are indicated in Table 2.

From the data in Tables 1 and 2, it can be seen that franchising in the hospitality industry has been a growing industry.[1]

While there has been growth in the franchising of hospitality establishments, the Naisbitt Group, in a study entitled "The Future of Franchising" prepared for the International Franchise Association, has predicted a leveling of sales growth in the franchising of restaurants, hotels, and motels.[3]

With this leveling in the United States, many franchise companies will be increasing their international operations. In 1988, 13% of all restaurant franchisors and 36.5% of all lodging franchisors were involved in international operations. An additional 1.5% of the restaurant franchisors and 3.0% of the lodging franchisors were planning to locate outside the United States.[4] Many of these firms will offer master franchises or enter into joint ventures to develop the expanding international markets. This development will not come easily, as there are concerns over the political environment, economics, culture, and traditions and resources of each host country. (5–7)

Development of the Franchise

The business begins with an entrepreneur developing a product or service that is expected to meet the needs of the buying public. Ideally, the developer tests the product or service and refines the system in an operating unit. To demonstrate greater success, several operations may be developed, thus giving the new concept an expanded test.

Expansion Methods

To achieve an increase in market expansion and penetration, the entrepreneur may elect to either build and manage new establishments or sell to others the opportunity of participating in the venture. By selling franchises, the franchisor will expand the business and access an additional source of operating funds. The franchisees will share in the expense of advertising and promotion of the product or service and will benefit by being part of a larger and proven system.

To facilitate the growth of the franchise, the franchisor may elect any one or a combination of expansion plans. The franchisor may sell master franchises that encompass a specific geographic area. The master franchisee will in turn sell franchises in that area. Once the initial training and support are developed, the franchisor will then develop and continue the relationship with the franchisees. However, the master franchisee may continue to receive a percentage of the royalty paid to the franchisor. A second form of development agreement is known as subfranchising. In this approach the subfranchisor is responsible for the selling of franchises in a set geographic area and acts in place of the franchisor. This subfranchisor sells the franchise and develops the ongoing franchisor–franchisee relationship. The area developer method is a third approach to expansion. With this method an area developer, usually a group of investors, pays a fee to the franchisor for the opportunity to develop a defined geographic area. The area developer retains a partial ownership of the franchises developed and receives a share of the profits of those franchises. The franchisee's ongoing relationship is with the franchisor.

These approaches are helpful to a new franchisor in initiating a quicker expansion of the franchise opportunity. Once the new franchise company is established, the franchisor may prefer to sell individual franchises for specific sites rather than large geographic areas.

Franchisor Disclosure

The Federal Trade Commission has adopted Rule 436, "Disclosure Requirements and Prohibitions Concerning Franchising and Business Ventures," that requires companies wishing to franchise their business disclose certain information to prospective franchisees. The purpose of the franchise offering circular is to have the prospective franchisee become more fully informed about the franchise company and the business requirements and restrictions involved in being a franchisee. It seeks to protect the prospective franchisee from any unsubstantiated claims or promises of future sales or profits by the franchisor. While the franchiser is not prohibited from making statements regarding future sales, information must be given to substantiate those claims. This disclosure must be made prior to the signing of any agreements, contracts, or the exchange of money.

The disclosure document contains 23 sections, prepared under the basic guidelines of the Uniform Franchise Offering Circular (UFOC). These sections detail the background of the franchise company and the nature of the franchise offering. Some organizations will use the term "Licensee" in place of "Franchisee." Table 3 lists these sections.

Table 3. The Sections of the Uniform Franchise Offering Circular

1. Identifying franchisor information
2. Identity and business experience of persons affiliated with the franchisor
3. Litigation history
4. Bankruptcy history
5. Franchisee's initial franchise fee
6. Other fees to be paid by the franchisee
7. Franchisee's initial investment
8. Obligations of franchisee to purchase or lease from designated sources
9. Obligations of franchisee to purchase or lease in accordance with specifications designated by franchisor
10. Financing arrangements
11. Obligations of the franchisor; other supervision, assistance, or services
12. Territorial rights and obligations
13. Trademarks, service marks, trade names, logotypes, and commercial symbols
14. Patents and copyrights
15. Obligation of the franchisee to participate in the actual operation of the business
16. Restrictions on goods and services offered by franchisee
17. Renewal, termination, repurchase, modification, and assignment of the franchise agreement and related information
18. Arrangements with public figures
19. Actual, average, projected, or forecasted franchisee's sales, profits, or earnings
20. Information regarding franchisees of the franchisor
21. Financial statements
22. Contracts
23. Acknowledgment of receipt by prospective franchisee

Franchising and the practices of franchisors are undergoing examination at both the state and federal levels. As a result of this study, many states have initiated their own versions of the Uniform Franchise Offering Circular. Additional disclosure information and registration requirements of the franchising organization are being mandated. The disclosure document must conform to the laws of the state in which the franchise is being sold.

The License Agreement

Once an offer is made by the franchisor and accepted by the prospective franchisee, a franchise agreement is signed. This contract, more specific than the franchise offering circular, becomes the legal document that binds the franchising company and franchisee in a business relationship. Table 4 outlines the general provisions covered in the license agreement, although terminology and order may differ among contracts. These sections will include the details of the agreement and will be made specific to the signing franchisee.

Duration and Termination of the Franchise

The contract will define the length of the franchise agreement and outline the reasons for possible termination of the agreement. The usual initial term of the contract ranges from

Table 4. Representative Sections of the License Agreement

1. Grant of license
2. License fee
3. Royalty payments
4. Operating standards and conditions
5. Building and equipment
6. Construction of the hotel
7. Expansion of the hotel
8. Personnel and management
9. Product and service standards
10. Variation of terms
11. Right of inspection
12. Advertising and marketing
13. Reservations
14. Trademarks
15. Licensee's financial responsibilities
16. Licensee covenants
17. Duration of the license agreement
18. Default and termination
19. Sale of business or transfer of license agreement
20. Miscellaneous

5 to 20 years and may be renewed at the pleasure of both parties. The franchisee may be required to pay a franchise fee upon renewal. Terms and conditions of the franchise agreement may be renegotiated.

Although the number of terminations is low, it is important that the reasons for termination be well defined. Potential causes for ending the agreement include failure to maintain franchisor standards of operation, nonpayment of franchisee fees, or other just cause. The violation of quality control standards is a leading cause of lodging agreement termination. It is becoming increasingly difficult for a franchise company to arbitrarily end a contract. Sound reasons for the termination with supporting evidence must be given. The franchisee must have an opportunity to correct the deficiencies. If the changes are not made within a reasonable time, the franchisor may file to terminate the agreement. The franchise contract will also explain the conditions under which the franchisor may repurchase the contract, or the franchisee may terminate or sell to another investor. The nature of the "protected" territory will be defined.

Financial Requirements in Franchising

There are a variety of costs involved in becoming and remaining a part of a franchise system. These include the franchise fee, development costs, the royalty, and advertising fees.

The Franchise Fee

The franchise fee of a restaurant may range from $7,500 to $50,000, depending on the type of establishment. Most of the franchisee fees tend to be in the range of $20,000 to $30,000.

For lodging establishments, the franchise fee may be either a set amount, be based on the number of rooms to be constructed, or a combination of the two. The defined minimum initial fee generally ranges between $10,000 and $35,000 with an additional per room cost of $100 to $500. The more elaborate the rooms and expensive the property to be developed, the higher the costs of the franchise. This payment is due at the time of the signing of the contract.

For this franchise fee the new franchisee is entitled to receive a standard set of blueprints, complete operating manuals, management training for the franchisee at an operating unit and training for employees before, and usually during the opening of the new unit. Some franchise companies will aid in the identification of a site and provide assistance in the selection of suppliers. Others leave this to the discretion of the new franchisee, providing minimum standards are met.

Development Costs

The cost of land, building, equipment, and furnishings most often are the responsibility of the franchisee. These will vary in cost according to the location, design of the facility, and the interior decor package required by the franchisor. A sandwich shop may cost between $30,000 and $50,000, while a full-service restaurant may exceed $2,000,000 in facility development expenses. A rooms-only motel construction cost may be between $2 million and $4 million, while a full-service hotel of one hundred rooms, with a restaurant, may cost between $7 million and $10 million. General supplies, employee costs, and miscellaneous opening expenses will add several thousand dollars more.

The Royalty Paid to the Franchisor

In addition to the initial cost of the franchise, the operator is required to pay a "royalty fee" to the franchisor based on sales. However, for some ice cream shops the franchisee purchases the ice cream from the franchisor rather than pay a royalty fee, or may pay a very low royalty fee. Royalty fees generally range from 3% to 6% of gross sales for food service establishments. Hotels may charge a 3% to 5% royalty based on gross room sales. In addition, hotel franchising companies may offer a reservation service. The fee for participation in this system may be included in the royalty or advertising fee or may be a separate assessment based on use. The amount of the payment and payment date, usually weekly or monthly, are stated in the franchise agreement.

For this royalty fee, the franchisor provides routine visits by company field operations personnel who review the operation, make suggestions for improvement, and assist in solving operating problems. The franchise company may also maintain a research and development program to initiate new products or services designed to increase sales. Equipment evaluation and productivity improvement studies may also be carried out by the franchisor. To maintain a current image, the franchisor may suggest changes in decor and furnishings. These costs may be borne by the franchisee or shared with the franchisor.

Advertising Programs

In addition to the royalty fee, an advertising fee is paid to the franchise company or to a franchisee advertising association. For restaurants, this fee ranges from 1% to 5% of gross sales. Franchisors of lodging establishments most often base the advertising fee on gross rooms revenue rather than total establishment sales. The income is used to generate new advertising campaigns, promotions, and public relations programs to benefit all properties. It may also be used to support cooperative advertising programs at the local unit level. While the franchisor retains an influence in the advertising program, national and regional franchisee committees may be constituted to control the use of these advertising programs and funds.

Sources of Funds to Become a Franchisee

While it may appear the initial costs involved in becoming a franchisee are not high, it is only the beginning of a long list of expenses that the new franchisee will incur. While some franchise companies will offer either a financing package or assistance in securing financing, this is not always the case. The franchisor will require the franchisee to have a net worth sufficient as to not incur a large debt in the opening of the new enterprise. This may be from $100,000 to more than $1 million in liquid assets. It is for this reason that partnerships and corporations are often formed to finance the franchise. In many situations it is possible to lease the land, building, and equipment. Lease payments may be either fixed or variable, that is, dependent on the gross sales of the establishment. A franchisee may become involved in a sale and lease-back arrangement for land and building. Suppliers will often extend a line of credit to the new franchisee, especially if the franchise is well known.

Banks, savings associations, venture capitalists, and small business investment companies are additional sources of financing. All of these will cause the franchisee to incur additional debt and possibly give up some control of the business. The Small Business Administration may be of assistance in securing funds. There are many sources of funds and financing methods, each with its own advantages and disadvantages. All should be carefully investigated.

Franchisor–Franchisee Business Relationship

Franchising should be beneficial to both the franchisor and to the franchisee. It expands the business of one and gives an opportunity to the other. However, the franchisee must be willing to accept the franchisor as the parent company. While the franchisee is an independent businessperson, much independence and control may be relinquished to operate by the procedures and standards of the franchise company. Menu and services offered, style of employee uniform, operating hours, and procedures may have to be approved by the franchisor. The franchisee must be willing to pay a portion of the income of the business to the franchisor for services rendered, even if the services were not requested. The franchisee may also have to accept new products or services that may involve an increase in costs, but hopefully will result in additional sales.

Questions to Ask

Many questions should be asked of the franchise company when considering the purchase of a franchise. How long has the company been in the business of franchising, how many franchises have been sold, and where are they located? How many units does the franchisor own and manage and what are their sales in relation to franchisee sales? What are the plans of the franchisor for growth with respect to franchisor-owned units, and where will this growth take place? Will international growth efforts reduce the energy placed in domestic operations? How many units have been closed and for what reasons? If the franchise company wants to establish units in my territory, wants to purchase my establishment, or wants to terminate the franchise agreement, what are my legal rights? Under what conditions may another franchisee build near my establishment? While many of these questions are addressed in the Uniform Offering Circular and in the franchise agreement, it is important to understand fully the future intentions of the franchise company.

The continuing acquisition and merger activity in the hospitality industry may be a concern for many franchisees. The surviving organization may want to change the terms of the franchise agreement and seek to sell off or terminate "undesirable" properties. Royalty payments, territory assignments, and operating procedures may be changed by the new franchisor. On a more positive side, additional money and products or services may be available to enhance the development of the organization.

Dispute Resolution

Disagreements arising between the franchisor and franchisee may be settled in several ways. While court trials have been common in the past, the processes of negotiation, mediation, arbitration and minitrials are becoming more accepted.[8] Some franchise agreements will specify the method of dispute resolution to be used and the place of resolution. However, this is coming under examination by many state legislatures as they examine franchise programs. More freedom is being given to the franchisee in this matter especially when binding arbitration is to be used.[9] To assist in the process of dispute resolution, the National Franchise Mediation Program has been initiated by many of the leading hospitality firms and their suppliers.

Franchising Associations

A franchisee association may be formed by the members of a chain to promote their mutual concerns and interests with the franchisor. The association may seek to encourage the development of compatible products, services, and advertising programs in order to ". . . advance the competitive position of their members."[10] The American Franchisee Association, founded in 1993, seeks to represent the interests of franchisees from many different businesses. The franchisee associations also lobby for legislation favorable to their interests at all levels of government.

The International Franchise Association, founded in 1960, is an organization of franchise companies that seeks to raise the standards of franchisor conduct. It publishes a code of ethics and encourages members to maintain an ethical working relationship with the franchisees.

The International Franchise Association Educational Foundation conducts a variety of programs to help both potential franchise companies and potential franchisees to make more informed decisions regarding franchising.

In Canada, the Canadian Franchise Association performs many of the same functions for franchisors based in Canada. Many other countries have similar associations.

Franchising presents an opportunity to establish a business while reducing the risks involved in the start-up and operation of a new enterprise. Although no franchisor is able to guarantee success or a specific level of profitability, there is a history of similar businesses on which a prospective franchisee may draw. At yearly meetings and conventions, the franchise company and franchisees may share ideas and encourage each other in striving for success. The individual operator knows there are several sources of help in meeting operational problems. The success of one unit may have an impact on the success of others as they share the same name, image, and product or service. Persons traveling from one geographic region to another often seek out a particular franchise name because of previous experiences with that franchise. The abilities of the customer to recognize a familiar establishment and knowing what to expect are two of the strong points of affiliating with an established franchise system.

——References——

1. Bond, Robert E. and Jeffrey M. Bond. (1993) *The Source Book of Franchise Opportunities 1993*. Homewood, Ill.: Business One Irwin.
2. United States Department of Commerce. *Franchise Opportunities Handbook*. Washington, D.C.: USGPO. October 1985; p. xxvii.
3. Reynolds, John. Franchising Explodes into the '90s. *Franchising Opportunities*. February 1990; Volume 22, Number 1: p. 15.
4. International Franchise Association Educational Foundation, Inc. and Horwath, International. (1990) *Franchising in the Economy: 1988–1990*. Washington, D.C.: International Franchise Association. p. 101.
5. Khan, Mahmood A. When Foreign Markets Beckon. *Restaurants USA*. March 1990: Volume 10, Number 3: pp. 26–27.
6. Van Warner, Rick. Franchisors Plunge into Foreign Markets. *Nation's Restaurant News*. vol. 24, 8 February 19, 1990; pp. 1+.
7. Khan, Mahmood A. (1992) *Restaurant Franchising*. New York: Fan Nostrand Reinhold. pp. 171+.
8. Lambert, Kim A. Fundamentals of Alternative Dispute Resolution. *Franchise Law Journal*. Spring 1992; Volume 11, Number 4: pp. 99–103.
9. Dienelt, John F. and Jerome D. Penn. "State Efforts to Limit Arbitration," *Franchise Law Journal*. Spring 1993; Volume 11, Number 4: pp. 104–106.
10. Zwisher, Carl E., III. That Special Relationship. *Nation's Restaurant News*. January 20, 1986; p. F7.

13

Management Companies in the Hospitality Industry

Audrey C. McCool, *University of Nevada, Las Vegas*
Patricia E. Diaz, *Washington State University*

Introduction

The 1960s and the 1970s were decades of amazing growth for both the lodging and food service segments of the hospitality industry. Many large chains and corporate management companies became heavily involved in extensive growth. The rapid expansion, though, soon used up available capital. Franchising then became a popular way of financing growth, as did another form of expansion—contract management.

Management contracts allowed firms owning lodging properties to continue to grow with little capital investment or risk. Management contracts were also popular among developers who had no experience in operating a lodging property. Such contracts enabled the developers to still reap returns on their investments without having to assume the responsibilities of property management.

In the institutional setting, food service contractors have continued to grow once businesses, manufacturing plants, varied health care facilities, elementary and secondary schools, and colleges and universities saw subsidies vanish. Efficient management, able to manage costs and potentially generate profits, was instituted once subsidies were gone. Major growth in recreational facilities and increased travel demands have also significantly contributed to the extensive growth in food service management companies.

Definition of Contract Management

The management contract is a written agreement between the owners of lodging facilities or between the owners or managers of host facilities for institutional (noncommercial) food services and the management companies which specialize in operating such facilities. The owner or host firm manager, through lack of desire or because of inadequate management expertise, does not wish to manage the property or the food service facility. Therefore, an agreement is negotiated with a management firm to operate the property in accord with the specifications set by the owner or host firm management. Developers of lodging properties may often find that contracting with a professional management firm can ease the financing requirements for the property development.

Lodging Contract Management

There are four basic components of lodging management contracts. These components include the following:

1. The operator has the right to manage the property without owner interference.
2. The owner pays all the financing and operating expenses.
3. The owner assumes all financial and ownership risks.
4. The operator is indemnified, or protected, from his actions except for fraud or gross negligence.

The contract guarantees the operator a management fee while the remaining cash flow goes to the property owner to meet taxes, insurance, and debt load. In return, the owner delegates all operating responsibility to the operating firm and must not interfere with or influence the property's operations.

Equity Contributions

Owners now encourage operators to make an equity contribution in order to increase operator risk and incentive in managing a particular property. With increased competition for management contracts today, more operators are making equity contributions in order to obtain contracts. Operators may be particularly interested in making an equity contribution where a lodging property has strong potential and when they desire to have more say in the decision-making process regarding the disposition of that property. Some lodging management companies, though, prefer making fee waivers or concessions rather than having to produce money up front.

Similarly, food service management companies may be asked to finance renovations or expansions to food service facilities in exchange for longer contracts. However, the food service management companies expect to recover this investment, seeing the capital advance more as a loan to the host firm than as an equity investment, as is the case in the lodging industry.

Management Fees

Yearly management fees for lodging properties can vary from an agreed-on flat sum to variable arrangements related to the success of the operation. Such variable arrangements might include a fee based on the total revenue of the property, a fee based on the property's gross profit, or a combination of the two.

The method of fee calculation can be advantageous to either the owner or the management firm operating the property. If the fee is based solely on revenue produced, the operator can spend money freely for activities such as advertising to achieve a high revenue. However, since expenses will be high, there will be less profit for the owner from this high revenue. If the fee is based solely on gross profit, there is a strong obligation on the part of the operator to manage the hotel profitably. A combination of the two methods—consideration of total both revenues and gross profit—seems to be the approach to fee calculation that is most equitable to both the operator and the owner.

Length of the Contract

The length of the contract is a major concern for all parties involved: owner, operator, and lender. Operators desire long-term contracts in order to protect their investment in equipment, design, and other up-front costs, as well as the significant effort involved in beginning a contract with an owner. Long-term contracts, however, tend to be a disadvantage for the owner in terms of both flexibility and termination power because an early termination of a contract can lead to settlements, lawsuits, or both with the management firm. Lenders like to see contracts of a length equal to that of the property's financing. Major lodging operators like to negotiate contracts for eight to ten years. Because of their established recognition and expertise, large national management firms are more able to negotiate longer contracts than small individual operators are.

Contract Renewal and Termination

The renewal option is another important issue in contract management. For lodging facilities, most common renewal options still rest with the operator. An owner that has significant bargaining strength can sometimes gain the option to renew the contract or can negotiate new performance levels with the operator. A new set of problems is created when an owner wishes to sell the property before the expiration of the contract. When this problem arises, there are four major areas of negotiation to consider:

1. Whether the operator has the right to purchase the property
2. Whether the operator has a right to approve the purchaser
3. Whether the management contract continues after the sale
4. What operator compensation will be if the contract is terminated at the sale of the property.

There are three provisions for contract termination always available for either the operator or owner in management contracts. Contracts can be terminated in the following situations:

1. If either party fails to perform or observe agreements for 30 days following notice of default
2. If either party files for bankruptcy or assigns the property to creditors
3. If either party causes the property's licenses to be suspended or revoked.

Contracts can also be terminated by negotiation between the two parties.[1]

Many management contracts today have provisions for operator performance, generally in the form of a ten-year operating pro forma statement (a forecasted budget) that is jointly written by the owner and the operator.[1] This statement often becomes the basis for deciding the management fee structure.

Lodging Contract History

There seems to be some dispute as to when contract management actually entered the lodging industry. Some say that the Cesar Ritz Group was a management contract company in Europe around the turn of the century when Ritz and his famous chef, Escoffier, were paid a retainer to oversee hotels and call them the Ritz Hotels. Other say the first U.S. hotel management company was the Treadway Hotel Co., which began operating small college inns in the 1920s.[2] Another early company, the Western Hotels Group, now Westin, began operating hotels in the 1930s.[3]

U.S. companies, expanding internationally, adopted contract management in earnest in the 1950s. It was not until the early 1970s, however, that domestic management contracts gained importance. It was apparently Hyatt that was the earliest major player in lodging contract management.

There are now two kinds of lodging contract management companies. Most are chain operations that serve as management companies for hotels under their franchises. Examples of such companies are Hilton, Holiday Inn, and Sheraton. Independent management companies, such as The Hotel Group, operate properties under several franchises or different names. The independent companies usually offer owners more control over daily operations and more flexibility in terms and brand affiliations than do chain companies.[2]

Major Players in Lodging Management

Today, there are many major players in the lodging arena of contract management. Seven well-known U.S.-based hotel chains that operate using contract management will be discussed here. These firms operate both domestic and international management contracts. While hotel management is their main focus, they also work closely with outside development partners.[4]

Hilton Hotels Corporation

Headquartered in Beverly Hills, Hilton Hotels Corporation operates 262 hotels with nearly 97,000 rooms in more than 219 cities in the United States.[5] Hilton was started in Dallas, Texas, in 1929 by Conrad Hilton. The chain began operating internationally in 1949 as Hilton International. In 1967, it was acquired by TWA. Hilton Corp. is now headed by Barron Hilton. Hilton's lodging products are Hilton Hotels, Hilton Inns, Hilton Suites, Cresthil by Hilton, and Conrad International Hotels.[6]

Holiday Inn Worldwide

Holiday Inn Worldwide is the world's largest innkeeper, with headquarters in Atlanta, Georgia. It operates more than 1,600 hotels in the United States, Canada, Europe, Asia, and South America. The company was started by Kemmons Wilson in 1952 when he opened the first Holiday Inn near Memphis. In 1980 Holiday Corp. acquired Harrah's casino hotels and began developing new concepts to serve the changing market. In 1983, they developed Embassy Suites and Holiday Inn Crowne Plazas to serve the upscale market. The Hampton Inn concept was also introduced to target the high end of the economy lodging segment. In the late 1980s, a few selected Holiday Inns were sold to Bass PLC, a British firm, as the beginning of their effort to target the mid-range market in the United States. Bass subsequently purchased all of the Holiday Inns and the right to the Holiday Inn name in 1990. The remaining portions of the original Holiday Inn were reconfigured under the name of Promus Companies. Promus, based in Memphis, Tennessee, now operates the Embassy Suites, Hampton Inns, Homewood Suites, and the Harrah's Casino Hotels.

Hyatt Hotels Corporation

Hyatt Hotels Corporation, headquartered in Chicago, gained worldwide recognition in 1967 when it introduced the world's first atrium hotel in Atlanta—the Hyatt Regency Atlanta. Hyatt operates 110 hotels and resorts with a total of more than 66,000 rooms in 30 states, Canada, and the Caribbean. Hyatt International operates 61 hotels and resorts in more than 30 countries. The corporation, owned by the Pritzker family of Chicago, opened the first Hyatt hotel at the Los Angeles International Airport in 1957. Hyatt's lodging products are the Grand Hyatt Hotels, Hyatt Regency Hotels and Resorts, Park Hyatt Hotels, and Classic Residences by Hyatt (senior rental apartment housing complexes).

Marriott Corporation

Headquartered in Washington, D.C., Marriott Corporation entered the lodging business in 1957. Previously, the Marriott family had been in food service, operating Hot Shoppe restaurants in the Washington, D.C., area since 1927. Currently, Marriott operates 212 properties with over 93,000 rooms. They launched the Courtyard concert in 1983 and both the Marriott Suites and the Fairfield Inns concept (economy level properties) in 1987. They also acquired the Residence Inn suite hotels chain in 1987. Marriott Corporation has now become involved in the development of both life care communities and time-share condominiums. Their current properties include Marriott Suites, Residence Inns, Courtyard by Marriott, Fairfield Inns, Senior Living services, and Marriott Vacation Ownership Resorts.

Radisson Hotels International

Radisson Hotels International, located in Minneapolis, operates 170 properties in the United States, Canada, Europe, the Caribbean, Mexico, the Middle East, the Far East, and the Asia/Pacific Rim. Founded in 1962 as a subsidiary of Carlson Hospitality Group, Radisson seldom maintains an equity position in the hotels that bear the Radisson name.[4] The company has had an aggressive period of international expansion, and has entered into partnership agreements with several international companies, such as SAS Hotels in Scandinavia, European-based Moevenpick Hotels, Park Lane Hotels in the Asia/Pacific Rim area, Commonwealth Hospitality of Canada, and Paraiso Hotels of Mexico. Radisson's products are Pierre Radisson Inns and Colony Hotels and Resorts.

The Sheraton Corporation

The Sheraton Corporation, headquartered in Boston, was established in 1937 when Ernest Henderson and Robert Moore acquired the 200-room Stonehaven property in Springfield, Massachusetts. It was not until 1939, however, that they took the name of Sheraton when they acquired Boston's former Sheraton Hotel. The company expanded internationally in 1949 by acquiring two Canadian hotel chains. In 1956 they entered the Hawaiian market. In 1968, Sheraton became a wholly owned subsidiary of ITT Corporation. Sheraton operates 427 properties around the world. They manage, lease, and franchise their properties, maintaining up to 25% equity interest in some properties.[6]

Westin Hotels and Resorts

Westin Hotels and Resorts, based in Seattle, is the oldest of the lodging contract management operators. In 1930, a consortium of six hotel operators in the Pacific Northwest formed Western Hotels. In 1960, they changed the name to Western International Hotels. They were bought out by United Air Lines in 1970, and the name was changed to Westin in 1981. For a brief period in 1987, United Air Lines and Westin became part of the Allegia Corporation. In 1988, however, Westin was purchased by a subsidiary of Aoki Corporation. Today Westin manages 66 hotels, and the firm rarely maintains equity interest in the properties. Their lodging products are Westin Hotels and Resorts. Westin expects to double in size over the next few years with a goal of becoming an internationally recognized first-class hotel and resort company before the year 2000. New emphasis will be placed on quality assurance and regional operations.[6]

Trends in Lodging Contract Management

There has been a significant shift in the lodging segment of contract management over the past ten years. No longer do contracts favor operators. They are now shifting to favor the owners. Three factors seem to be responsible for this shift:

1. Increased competition among operators, mergers, and the entry of international chains into the United States
2. Increased sophistication of owners' knowledge regarding the industry and its contracts
3. Leaders' more active role in the negotiation process

For lodging operations, the biggest results from this shift are a greater sharing of financing risks by operators and an increase in joint decision making about hotel projects.[1]

Other trends will be more performance provisions written into contracts, more stress on incentive fees, and an overall increase in management contracts. Eyster believes that franchising and traditional ownership may increase due to increased operator dissatisfaction with owner influence.[1]

Food Service Management Companies

Food service management companies today are an integral part of the noncommercial (institutional) food service field, that comprises between 25% to 30% of the total food service industry (see Table 1). The feature distinguishing this part of the food service industry is that almost all of these noncommercial operations are housed in host organizations which do not have food services as their primary business. The food service is there only to support the host organization's overall primary goal or business. Other features that characterize these food services are that most of them do some or all of their food production in large quantities, and this food is served to their clientele in limited, fixed time periods.

These food services may be self-operated or managed internally by the host organization. However, many host organizations do not want to manage their own food services, so they contract these management responsibilities to a food service management company. When the contract negotiations are completed and a contract is signed, the host organization is referred to as the client of the food service contractor. The many environments in which food service management companies might be found are summarized in Table 2.

Table 1. Comparative Size of the Non-commercial Food Service Industry

Market Segment	Number of Units	1993 Sales Estimates ($ billion)	Percent of Total Food Service Industry
Health care	34,730	17.390	6.4
Educational Food Services	121,460	26.074	9.6
Business and Industry	16,255	17.913	6.6
Transportation	300	3.508	1.3
Recreation	31,075	4.475	1.7 ·
Miscellaneous	9,975	2.528	0.9
Total	213,795	71.888	26.5

*Data from '93 R&I Forecast. Restaurants and Institutions. January 1, 1993; Volume 103, Number 1: p. 22.

Table 2. Environments for Contract Food Service Operations

Business and Industry (employee food services)	Manufacturing plants Office buildings
Private clubs (city and country clubs)	
Institutional Environments	Elementary and secondary schools Colleges and universities Correctional facilities Hospitals Extended care facilities Life care facilities
Transportation Environments	Airlines and airports Toll-road rest stop facilities Bus and train stations
Recreational Environments	Convention centers Stadiums and sports arenas Amusement and theme parks Local, state, and national parks Zoos and aquariums Race tracks Ski areas Recreational centers Movie theaters Bowling alleys Special events (Olympics, golf tournaments) Miscellaneous tourist attractions

The Development of Food Service Management Companies

Contract food service management in the United States originated in industrial food service. In the late nineteenth century, Nicholas Cease quit his job in a locomotive plant in Richmond, Virginia, to sell ice-cold lemonade for a penny a dipper to his former fellow employees to keep them from patronizing the local bar during their lunch time. The plant management attributed a drop in their accident rate to the availability of the nonalcoholic cold drinks for the employees. By 1904, they had invited Cease to expand his operation to an indoor service. Other companies were soon developed that usually operated on a regional basis.

Over the years there have been many mergers of these food service management firms as markets have changed and expanded. For example, the original Cease company merged with a firm called Factory Stores to form United Food Management. By 1945 United was operating more than 300 separate accounts in 14 states. They were completely organized, with standard recipes, cost control systems, and management development methods that made them very competitive as a food service management company. In 1964, they merged with Interstate Vending to form Interstate United, a firm later purchased by Canteen Corporation, a large national food service management firm. Such acquisition and merger has been the way many of today's large national firms have dramatically expanded the size and scope of operations.

Where Food Service Management Companies Are Located

Food service management companies are located in almost every community throughout the United States. These contractors currently operate most business and industry and recreational food services. However, they are responsible for managing less than 50% of the food service operations in many of the other possible settings. The increasing recognition of the specialized expertise and efficiencies that food service management firms can provide to their clients is resulting in continual expansion of contract-managed food services throughout the noncommercial field. Their greatest opportunities are in the rapidly expanding health care food service market where contractors currently manage only about 25% of the food services.

Association with food service management companies could mean working with some of the largest corporations in the hospitality industry, or it could mean employment with smaller local or regional firms. Local companies may be quite small (with fewer than ten accounts) or they may service only a small geographical area (100-mile radius or less). However, all companies must start somewhere. Many small, local companies have been started by entrepreneurs or food service professionals who at one time or another worked for a large regional or national food service management firm.

Regional companies are many in number. While they vary in size, their operating area is usually limited to a particular region of the United States. Or companies such as these may focus on a very specific niche within the contract market.

Large National Food Service Management Companies

National companies are large firms that have accounts throughout the United States. Table 3 lists several of the largest national food service management companies. ARA Services and Marriott Management Services are the two largest food service management companies in the United States. They are both actively involved in the management of almost all types of food services. Along with their longstanding prominence in business and industry food services, ARA Services has acquired a dominant position in the management of correctional food services through their recent acquisition of Szabo. They are also very active in the recreational market, holding food service management contracts for major convention

Table 3. Major National Food Service Management Firms

• ARA Services	• Marriott Management Services
• Canteen	• Morrison's Hospitality Group
• CaterAir	• Service America
• Delaware North	• ServiceMaster
• Gardner Merchant	

centers, several national parks, and the total management contract for the Lake Powell National Recreational Area in Southern Utah. In addition to food service management, ARA Services also manages food and magazine distribution, uniform rental services, and child care centers as well as other types of services.

Marriott Management Services is the contract management arm of Marriott Corporation. Marriott experienced dramatic food service management growth throughout the 1980s as a result of extensive acquisitions. Companies such as Service System, Stouffer's Management Foodservices, Host International Corporation, and Saga Corporation were all acquired by Marriott. However, as the recessionary 1990s arrived, Marriott sold its in-flight food service operations to the senior management personnel of that division in a leveraged buyout. The new company that was formed, CaterAir, is now one of the largest in-flight food service contractors. Marriott Management Services is now working to penetrate the retirement community market through a recently formed division known as Senior Living Centers. They are also developing one-stop management services for clients, incorporating not only food service management, but also facilities management and the management of retail outlets, child care centers, and other services into a single overall service management contract.

Specialty areas of other leading food service management companies include Canteen's prominent position in sporting facilities and recreational facilities in parks across the country; Morrison's Hospitality Group's emphasis on health care, education, and business and industry; ServiceMaster's health care interests along with interests in lawn care, residential housekeeping services, and the management of child care centers; Service America's presence in health care, business and industry, college and university, and leisure and recreation food services; Delaware North's position in recreational facilities such as parks (including Yosemite Park), race tracks, arenas, and baseball complexes as well as in the management of airport food service operations throughout the United States under the name of their subsidiary firm—Concession Air.

Career Potential with Food Service Management Companies

Noncommercial food services are a high-growth area today, and the trend is toward increasing use of contract management companies. This growth means that there are many career options now available with food service management companies—or in the field of contract food services.

Persons working in contract food service help provide a variety of food services in a very diverse range of settings. Some of the services offered might include cafeteria and dining room management, vending, fast food, or fine dining services, and frequently a major emphasis on catering services. In some venues, concession management is an important service component while others may focus on nutritional care. Indeed, all types of services offered by restaurants or hotels are also offered by food service management companies in the noncommercial field.

Career Advantages

There are many advantages to a career in contract food service. Indeed, these career opportunities are often called the best-kept secret within the food service industry because of the working hours of these positions. Contract food service managers are often not required to work the late night hours or the regular weekend hours characteristic of careers in commercial food service. Many persons feel that the more regular hours associated with contract food services enhance their quality of life. However, the hours worked vary considerably with the type of contract. For example, working in a professional sports stadium may require many evening and weekend hours because the concession operations must match the events schedule. On the other hand, compensation for working to match the events schedule might consist of extra days off or vacations during periods when the events schedule is light. In comparison, the manager of a school food service account will rarely, if ever, work evenings or weekends and will enjoy many of the holidays and vacation periods scheduled on the school calendar as well.

The frequent opportunities for creativity offer another advantage. The clientele served in many of these contract managed food services eat many meals in the host firms' facilities, often for extended periods of time, with little option for alternative meal services. Many persons find it an exciting challenge to be able to manage with such creativity that these clientele remain pleased with their food service. Examples of such situations are food services for inmates of correctional institutions, patients in hospitals, residents of college dormitories, participants in school lunch programs, or employees of manufacturing plants.

Managers of contract food service operations often feel as though they are entrepreneurs in business for themselves. A most intriguing aspect of contract food service is that every client and every operation is different—different clientele, service needs, contract provisions, equipment, layout, and procurement and menu patterns. This uniqueness of each operation means that the manager assigned has no set rule book or policy manual to turn to for solutions to problems that may occur. The food service management company may have general operating guidelines available. But each operation is unique, so it is up to the on-site manager to determine what to do to meet the operation's service requirements. Each operation's uniqueness fosters the manager's feeling of entrepreneurial creativity, and managers realize the satisfaction that results from developing their own successful operation.

At the same time, the manager of a particular contract operation has the support of the management firm, which means that help is available when needed. It also means that

Entry Point

Assistant Manager	Manager	General Manager, Larger Operation	District Manager

Decision Point

Remain in operations or move into corporate structure or possible staff positions

Regional manager	Vice president of an area	Corporate vice President	Other Senior Corporate Officer

Possible staff positions include areas such as

Human Resource Recruitment and Training	Corporate Sales and Marketing	Purchasing	Product Research and Standards Development
Facilities Planning	Operations Analysis	Administration	

Figure 1. Sample Career Path in Contract Food Service Management

opportunities exist for growth and development, promotion, or relocation within one company. Since contract food service management is a growth industry today, opportunities for promotion and relocation are frequent. It also means that promotional opportunities are not limited just to operations. Career paths can extend beyond operations well into the corporate structure. Figure 1 illustrates career options within food service management firms.

Challenges Associated with Food Service Management Companies

There are some challenges associated with this field as well. Relocation is always a consideration in the hospitality industry. Relocation may actually be an advantage for those who enjoy new adventures. For others, especially if it occurs too frequently, it may be a significant disadvantage. Advancement may sometimes be contingent on relocation to another corporate account. Sometimes managers are not successful in transferring from one account to another, because each operation makes unique demands on the account manager. A highly successful manager in one environment simply may not fit the new environment to which she has relocated. This lack of fit may limit a manager's advancement opportunities.

Persons who like structure in their jobs may have difficulty adapting to the work of contract food service management. Generally this environment is quite unstructured because of the uniqueness of each operation. There may be limited support for the manager immediately available. Further, many operations, such as stadiums, are often peak operations where there are very busy, very high-demand times with little second chance to rectify any errors. Persons considering this career field should be flexible, adaptable, and have at least some entrepreneurial spirit. They should also be creative self-starters with good communication skills along with the ability to accept criticism. They must understand and believe in the service concept.

This facet of the industry feeds so many meals to so many different types of people on such a regular basis that is impossible to please everyone all the time. However, it is each manager's responsibility to maintain the best possible quality food service with a minimum of guidance. A self-motivated manager with strong communication and organizational skills can use constructive criticism to help ensure that the food service operation is truly servicing the needs of its clientele. Indeed, a career in contract food service management offers some of the most intriguing opportunities and interesting challenges of any career field in the hospitality industry.

——References——

1. Eyster, J. J. (1988) _The Negotiation and Administration of Hotel and Restaurant Management Contracts._ Third edition. Ithaca, N.Y.: Cornell University Press.
2. Powers, T. (1988) _Introduction to the Hospitality Industry._ New York: John Wiley & Sons.
3. Kleinfeld, S. (1989) _The Hotel. A Week in the Life of the Plaza._ New York: Simon and Schuster.
4. Profiles: Seven Major Hotel Chains. _Restaurant/Hotel Design International._ November 11, 1988; pp. 6, 8, 10.
5. Turner, R, editor. (1992) _1992 Directory of Hotel and Motel Companies._ 61st edition. New York: American Hotel and Motel Association.
6. Koepper, K. and C. O'Dwyer. Chains Poise for Development at the Dawn of a New Decade. _Lodging._ January, 1990; pp. 12–18.

14

Referral Associations in the Hospitality Industry

Lawrence Yu
Northern Arizona University

Referral associations are one of the many hospitality organizations in the hospitality industry. The original concept of the referral association was to get independent lodging operators to band together within a relatively small area to refer guests to each other for mutual support. The assumption was that when one general manager referred a valued guest to another establishment in the association, he was confident that the guest would receive the same excellent level of services and facilities. This form of hospitality organization was first developed by M. K. Guertin in 1946 in California. His group of Best Western Motels, the granddaddy of today's Best Western International, was then an informal referral system among member motels.

Today, many referral associations have developed into sophisticated hospitality organizations with global recognition. The intensified competition from hotel chains and franchise operations challenged the referral associations to improve their own brands, membership services, marketing strategies, reservation technology, and operational standards. These referral associations compete vigorously with hotel chain and franchise operations and play a very important role in the hospitality industry.

Difference Between Referral and Franchise Organizations

People are often confused by referral associations and franchise organizations and think that these two hospitality organizations operate lodging establishments in the same manner, only under two different labels. This is a misconception. A referral association consists of independent lodging operators who band together to gain the advantages associated with national or international promotion and a centralized reservation service while maintaining management autonomy. The membership promotion by Best Western International, the leading referral association in the United States, describes this concept more succinctly: the independent advantage.

This management autonomy is the key aspect that distinguishes the referral association from the franchise organization. Unlike franchise operations, the referral associations do not mandate their membership establishments to operate hotels in accordance with the policies of the association. As long as the membership establishments meet the minimum operational standards of the association, they are left alone to make decisions on property architectural style, decor, facility improvement, rate change, and menu modification. This is often described as non– "cookie-cutter" properties, as opposed to the uniform building and operation standards used by the franchise organizations.

The referral associations also allow flexible membership agreements. Many franchise organizations require 5-, 10-, or even 20-year commitments from the franchisees. This rigid agreement makes it very difficult for franchisees to terminate the agreement if they do not agree with the franchiser on certain policy issues. Early termination of an agreement can cause severe financial penalties and frequently incurs heavy legal costs. The referral associations usually offer flexible, and not long-term, locked-in memberships. The Phoenix-based Best Western International provides its members with a one-year renewable membership. Members are free to terminate the agreement with the association at any time, and they have the option to renew membership annually as long as they adhere to Best Western's standards.

Another major difference between referral associations and franchise organizations is that a referral association is managed by its members and does not own lodging establishments. Thus, the referral association has no shareholders or corporate investors to satisfy, no price/earnings ratio to be concerned with, and no dividends to generate. The objective of the referral association is to enhance the success and profitability of its members by offering the expertise of a professional headquarters staff and the latest technological developments. This explains why many referral associations are known as nonprofit associations, solely owned by the members.

This nonprofit characteristic of referral association further demonstrates the difference in affiliation costs between referral and franchise organization. Initial fees and other annual fees are typically lower in referral organizations. A current independent study on lodging affiliation costs by Hospitality Valuation Services identifies Best Western International as the hospitality organization with the lowest total affiliation cost for the midrate hotel category in the United States. Total annual fees and dues of Best Western are typically one-quarter to one-fifth of those of other major chain or franchise affiliations. This reflects the cost-recovery philosophy of the referral association: membership fees pay only for the services members receive.

Finally, the referral associations are very aggressive in appealing to smaller lodging operators who are left out of the franchise organizations because of a minimum-room entry requirement. Referral associations accept establishments of every type and size as long as they satisfy the association's minimum entry requirements. The referral associations thus offer an opportunity to the small independent hoteliers to be affiliated with a nationally or internationally recognized brand name. This development explains why Best Western International is the largest lodging organization in the United States in terms of total number of properties.

This section attempts to identify the major differences between the referral association and franchise organization. The referral association is distinguished from the franchise organization by offering its members independence in management decisions and choices, flexibility in membership agreement, low affiliation cost, and flexible entry requirement for minimum number of rooms. These factors, along with nationally or internationally recognized brand name, centralized reservation system and marketing, and other technical expertise, combine to develop the referral association into one of the most effective lodging management organizations in today's hospitality industry.

Referral Membership Services and Obligations

The 1980s witnessed the rapid growth of some globally known referral associations. Amid financial turmoil in the hospitality development market, these referral associations provided a twist to portfolio expansion through a simple membership agreement. At present, Best Western International has become one of the largest referral associations in the world. It grew from a small regional referral association into a globally recognized brand name with a worldwide reservation system, marketing services, mass buying and bargaining power, and legal and insurance services. There are many other well-known referral associations representing thousands of hotels and resorts around the world. Table 1 lists the ten major referral associations. The listing is ordered according to the total number of establishments that each association represents.

Though all referral associations share the same mission for development and excellence, each association has its own requirements for membership applications, membership fees and dues, and obligations. These aspects are discussed and illustrated by two examples: Preferred Hotels and Resorts Worldwide, and Best Western International.

Table 1. Major Referral Associations

Name	Number of Properties	Number of Rooms
Utell International	6,500	1,300,000
Best Western International	3,400	276,000
Golden Tulip Hotels International	230	47,929
Rescorp International, Inc.	222	11,300
Budget Host Inns	161	6,445
Independent Motels of America	128	5,046
Preferred Hotels & Resorts Worldwide	102	26,283
Small Luxury Hotels	72	4,694
The Grande Collection of Hotels	37	9,064
HSI Reservations	26	4,999

Sources: *Directory of Hotel and Motel Systems.* (1992) 61st edition. American Hotel and Motel Association; *Best Western International Corporate Fact Sheet.* Best Western International, Inc. March 1993; Frances Martin. Partnerships, Mergers Dominate in a Competitive Year. *Hotels.* 1992; pp. 56-59.

Membership Qualification

Preferred Hotels and Resorts Worldwide has a high standard for its members. Membership in this association is restricted to "independent luxury hotels and resorts." An applicant must have a reputation for excellence. To complete the membership application, prospective members are required to submit a detailed application. In addition, two unannounced inspections of the property are conducted. If an inspection is favorable, the application is reviewed by the Association's Board of Directors, at which time representatives of the property are asked to make a presentation. A two-thirds affirmative vote by the Board is required for the application to be approved for membership.

Membership Fees

Membership fees and dues vary among the referral associations. To illustrate the difference in amount and method of computation, samples of membership fees and dues required by Preferred Hotels and Resorts Worldwide and Best Western International are shown in Tables 2 and 3 respectively.

Membership Obligations

Although referral associations do not mandate management and operation policies, they do have mandatory identification policies and other membership obligations. Preferred Hotels and Resorts Worldwide mandates that its logo, in its registered form, must be prominently displayed on all advertising done by a member property. Its association directory

Table 2. Membership Fees by Preferred Hotels and Resorts Worldwide

Application fee	$4,000
Initiation fee (one time)	$50/room Minimum $10,000; maximum $20,000
Membership dues	$130/room/year Minimum $10,000; maximum $84,500
Reservation charges	7% of total room revenue
Annual evaluation fee	$995/property
North American sales council meeting (optional)	$1,000/year

Source: Membership Service Department, Preferred Hotels and Resorts Worldwide, 1991

Table 3. Membership Fees by Best Western International

No. of Rooms	Entrance Fee	Anmnual Dues	Monthly Fees		Total Annual Costs
			Membership Fees	Reservation Fees	
20	20,000	1,108	4,818	1,825	7,751
21	20,100	1,145	5,059	1,916	8,120
22	20,200	1,182	5,300	2,008	8,490
23	20,300	1,219	5,541	2,099	8,859
24	20,400	1,257	5,782	2,190	9,229
25	20,500	1,294	6,023	2,281	9,589
50	23,000	2,225	11,589	4,563	18,377
51	23,100	2,239	11,790	4,654	18,683
52	23,200	2,254	11,990	4,745	18,989
100	28,000	2,949	21,626	9,125	33,700
101	28,100	2,963	21,823	9,216	34,002
102	28,200	2,977	22,020	9,308	34,305
151	33,100	3,687	31,675	13,779	49,141
152	33,200	3,701	31,868	13,870	49,439

Source: Best Western International, December 1992

must be displayed in the lobby area of every member property and in each guest room. Brass plaques must be displayed on the building exterior and in the lobby of each property, identifying the property as a Preferred hotel or resort. Each member must display at least one framed Preferred Membership list in their lobby area. Members must accept the American Express card to guarantee reservations and as payment for guest charges. In addition, American Express charge card applications must be displayed in the lobby area of every member property and in each guest room.

Best Western International also has its own association rules and regulations. The Best Western golden crown logo must be incorporated into all signage that includes the individual property name and measures 40 square feet or larger. In areas where the allowable square footage is restricted by local ordinances, and the largest property name permitted is less than 40 square feet, the Best Western logo should be incorporated with the largest, most prominent property name sign. Regarding reservations, no member is allowed to refer Best Western guests to nonmember properties unless all available Best Western rooms in the area are filled.

Clearly, the referral associations formulated association rules and regulations for business promotion and property identification purposes. These policies and regulations are written by the members, who control the articles of incorporation and bylaws. Therefore, the referral associations are governed by the members for the members. These identification policies and promotion strategies represent the operational philosophy of all members in the association.

Globalized Referral Associations

International travel and tourism has become one of the largest industries in the world. With the increase of world travel, referral associations jockey for position aggressively in the foreign hospitality markets. Many referral associations are now truly global hospitality organizations. Best Western International has members in 46 foreign countries. Twenty-one Best Western affiliate organizations, structured in the same manner as Best Western International, operate in Europe, the Middle East, Mexico, South America, Southeast Asia, and the South Pacific. These overseas associations coordinate membership development within their respective regions and offer their members services similar to those in the United States. New agreements have already been signed with China and Laos. Long-range plans call for the establishment of the Best Western brand on the African continent.

Foreign referral associations, particularly European associations, are now turning their attention to North America. Golden Tulip Hotels International, a subsidiary of KLM (Dutch Royal Airline), is one of the most competitive foreign referral brands in North America. The London-based Small Luxury Hotels selects only members with small but quality hotel properties in North America. Another London-based referral association, Utell International, has recently established its membership service and reservation system in Omaha and Los Angeles. This rapid globalization of referral associations will add a new dimension to international hospitality operations.

Conclusion

In summary, referral associations offer independent hoteliers the alternative of being affiliated with a nationally or internationally known brand name. They can take advantage of the association's central reservation system, marketing promotion, market research, and various other services at relatively low costs, yet still maintain the freedom of management and operation choices. This form of organization appeals to hoteliers who want to keep their own identities in their own locale and do not want to be a cookie-cutter type of property. This hospitality development niche is well established by the referral association and such development will keep growing both nationally and internationally.

——References——

Best Western International Corporate Fact Sheet. Phoenix: International Headquarters, Best Western International, Inc. March 1993.

Best Western International: The Independent Advantage. Phoenix: Membership Development Department, Best Western International, Inc. 1993.

Directory of Hotel and Motel Systems, 61st edition. Washington, D.C.: American Hotel and Motel Association. 1992.

Dittmer, Paul R. and Gerald G. Griffin. (1993) *The Dimensions of the Hospitality Industry: An Introduction.* New York: Van Nostrand Reinhold.

Martin, Frances. Partnerships, Mergers Dominate in a Competitive Year. *Hotels.* July 1992; pp. 56–59.

Powers, Tom. (1988) *Introduction to Management in the Hospitality Industry.* Third edition. New York: John Wiley & Sons.

Preferred Hotels and Resorts Worldwide: Membership Information. Oakbrook Terrace, Ill.: Membership Service Department, Preferred Hotels Association, Inc. 1991.

Russo, Michelle S. (1993) *Hotel Franchise Fees Analysis Guide.* Mineola, N.Y.: Hospitality Valuation Services.

Hospitality Operations

Part IV

15

Food Service Operations and Management

David A. Cranage, *Pennsylvania State University*
Gary S. Page, *Grand Valley State University*

Introduction

There is a wide range of food service operations in the hospitality industry. Operations have usually been segmented by type of ownership; independent versus chain operations, and by the type of menu and service provided; fast food, sit-down dining, and upscale dining. Table 1 shows some examples for these segments. As can be seen, chains dominate the

Table 1. Segmentation of Commercial Food Establishments

		Independent	Affiliation
Fast Food			
	Quick Service Limited Menu Budget Pricing	Coffee Shop Donut Shop Burger and Hot Dog Stand	McDonald's Burger King KFC Taco Bell Subway Dairy Queen
Sit-Down Dining			
	Table Service Full Menu Moderate Pricing	Family Restaurant Theme Restaurant Cafeteria Pizza Shop Steak House	TGI Fridays Chi-Chi's Furrs Pizza Hut Chart House
Upscale Dining			
	Full Service Extensive Menu High-End Pricing	French Cuisine Northern Italian Cuisine Haute Cuisine	

Table 2. Segmentation of Institutional Food Service Establishments

Health Care	Hospitals Nursing homes Rehabilitation centers
Education	Elementary schools High schools College and Universities
Business Dining	Office buildings Factories Corporate headquarters

fast food (quick service) segment, and are well represented in the moderately priced table service operations. Independent food service operations dominate the upscale dining segment. Note that Table 1 only represents restaurant food service. There are very rewarding careers in institutional food service operations. Here, just as in restaurants, institutional food service covers a variety of food service operations (Table 2).

All of these food service operations differ in type of service, size of menu, price range, and style of preparation. As different and distinct as these operations seem, there are basic components to any food service operation that make these operations similar in many ways. This chapter will present components of a typical food service operation.

The Food Service Operation

The business of food service deals with the preparation and service of food for consumption by others, whether the food is made from scratch or is convenience food products that are finished in a microwave or deep fryer, whether the service is over the counter or at the table.

Operations in the lowest level (fast food/quick service) tend to focus on standardization and strict cost controls (food and labor) and tend to be characterized by huge volume at a low price. Operations in the uppermost tier focus on providing an overall dining experience. They are nonetheless concerned with quality standards and control, but tend to be more differentiated (unique) and are characterized by an extended stay and a higher price. However, all food service operations have the common objectives of providing a quality food product, a safe and sanitary environment, and guest service and satisfaction at a desired level of profit. To achieve these objectives, management needs to successfully manage the basic components of any food service operation.

Basic Components

Menu

All aspects of any food service operation start with the menu. The menu will determine the location of the operation, management and employees required, the layout and design of the building, the equipment needed, and ultimately the customer that is attracted. In some instances (especially institutional food service), the clientele is established and the menu is designed to meet their needs. But the menu still determines almost all other factors.

Purchasing

What is purchased (both quantity and product form) will be determined by the menu. The first step is to develop standardized recipes for each menu item. Standardized recipes are the key to quality and consistency.

From these recipes management can develop product specifications. These are written requirements identifying the characteristics (weight, count, grade, size, and color) of each food (and nonfood) product. These specifications are issued to the purveyors that management intends to buy from as well as to the receiving, storing, and preparation employees so that everyone knows exactly which products are to be purchased and used. Specifications allow the purchasing agent to set up a competitive bid system with purveyors. Since everyone is bidding on the exact items, comparing prices becomes simpler.

Another system that can improve purchasing, as well as receiving, storing, and issuing is a par stock system. Par stock is a predetermined amount in inventory for each item. For example, the par stock on ketchup may be ten bottles, and when the number of bottles falls below that number, a case of ketchup is ordered. This takes the guesswork out of purchasing. Par stock for each item can be established by looking at past usage figures and comparing that to delivery schedules of purveyors.

Receiving

After the items are purchased, they need to be properly stored. This may sound simple, but good internal controls must be used. Receiving may be of two types—invoice or blind receiving. With invoice receiving, items received are weighed, counted, and otherwise inspected against what is shown on the supplier's invoice. The items should also be checked against the purchase order and established specifications. Blind receiving is when no invoice or purchase order is made available (specifications should still be used) for comparison, and all weights, counts, and inspection results must be documented in a receiving report. The receiving reports are reconciled later with invoices and purchase orders. Blind receiving forces the receiving personnel to fully check in and inspect all orders received. It is, however, more costly.

Storage

Storage is usually an important part of receiving. Proper storage is required to ensure consistent quality and availability. Items must be properly labeled and rotated. The label should include the item name, date received, and any expiration date. When items are stacked on a shelf, they should be rotated from back to front, right to left, and bottom to top because people naturally take items first from the top, left, and front position.

Issuing

Issuing of items is often done on a causal basis, with little or no control. A system with only a few controls can greatly improve efficiency and effectiveness. Items to be issued should be placed on a requisition sheet by the department requiring those items. This requisition form is turned in to the storage or issuing clerk to receive those items. This form is used to keep a perpetual inventory, a running count that tells management what should be in inventory. A physical inventory should be taken periodically (usually monthly) to show what is actually in inventory.

Preparation

A preparation schedule should be made daily and weekly. The weekly schedule is used to balance the daily preparation workload. For example, minestrone soup might be made on Monday, Wednesday, and Friday. The daily schedule determines exact quantities to be made based on usage and predicted sales. Here again par stock can be useful. Two methods are common. One is when a predetermined level is reached, a set amount is made. For example, when we get down to one gallon of soup, we make three more gallons. The second is a predetermined level that the quantity on hand is brought up to. For instance, on Monday we need to have four gallons of soup on hand. If we only have two gallons, then we make two more. Guest check counts or item counts from the register or precheck machine (explained in section on Service, below) can help in establishing these par stocks.

All prepared items should be made from standardized recipes with exact measurements and specific procedures. This ensures consistency, which is a basic expectation shared by most customers. Your customers choose your establishment with certain expectations. If they have already eaten in your restaurant, then the reason they are coming back is to have the same great food again.

Service

We are a service industry. Quality food and all the systems previously mentioned mean nothing if the guest doesn't receive good service. Quality food can be purchased at a gourmet shop, delicatessen, grocery store, or any take-out establishment. It can be prepared at home. It is the service that makes us different. We are in the food _service_ industry.

Several types of services are available in food service—limited, moderate, and full service. Fast food is more accurately called quick service. The service offered the guest is limited: the order is taken, food is delivered, and the check rung up. Most sit-down and family-style restaurants offer additional service. The guests are seated. The order is taken and the food is delivered or served at the table (not at a counter). The guests have a waiter or waitress to cater to their needs. This type of service is often referred to as plate or American service.

Full service in upscale dining is of two types. The first is French or cart service. In French service, food is brought to the table in a raw or semiprepared state and finished in front of the guests in the dining room on a cart. This type of service is the most elaborate and offers the guests the greatest personal attention. However, this service requires more numerous and highly skilled personnel, which increases costs and raises menu prices.

The second type of service is Russian or platter service. With Russian service, the food is fully prepared in the kitchen and placed on platters to be served to the guest. The server brings the platter (usually ornate silver) to the dining room and serves the guests from the platter. This service also requires skilled personnel in the kitchen and dining room, increasing the menu price.

However, whatever the style of service, management must have a system to maintain control. This is usually accomplished with a guest check. The guest check is then used to requisition drinks, appetizers, entrees, and desserts from the different stations.

In an efficient guest check system, guest checks are prenumbered. A specific set of prenumbered guest checks is assigned to a server. The service personnel are then accountable for those checks assigned to them. They will either be turned in at the register by the guest or returned unused by the server at the end of the shift. A guest check usually has several parts or copies, so that each station can be given a separate copy for preparation. Lastly, a precheck machine is often used to assure that all items are counted and rung up. After a guest order is taken, the order is prechecked or rung into a precheck register. The register marks each item on the check, showing each station that the item has been accounted for. A station does not prepare an item for a guest until it has been prechecked. When the meal is completed and the guest pays the tab, the guest check is rerung at the front register, and the two totals should match.

Scheduling

One of the most frustrating jobs of management is scheduling employees for all the positions in the restaurant. Again, a system will make the job easier, more efficient, and effective.

First, develop *job descriptions* for every position. This allows both management and employees to know what is expected in each job. Second, *train* employees for their positions. A good, ongoing training program can eliminate many problems and mistakes. Such a program should also improve the quality and service of the food as well as reduce turnover. Lastly, *plan* out your schedule. A quality electronic spreadsheet program for the personal computer (e.g., Lotus or Excel) can organize the scheduling system and reduce labor costs. Each employee, wage rate, and proposed schedule can be entered into the spreadsheet. The proposed schedule for all employees can then be costed and compared to predicted sales for the same period. If a satisfactory labor cost is not projected, then adjustments can be made and new costs automatically calculated until an acceptable schedule is developed. At the end of the schedule period, actual labor costs and actual sales can be compared to the projected figures and adjustments made to future schedules.

Conclusion

Much of food service management must be complete *before* the fact. The food service manager must be able to visualize what people will want and be able to systematically put together the right things in the right order and in the right way, to accomplish the desired ends to everyone's satisfaction—guests', employees', and management's.

Food service requires a great deal of organization. Approaching it in a systematic way is important. The manager must have tangible, measurable operational standards—for the product, the process, the performance, and the programs—so it is clear what is supposed to happen and evaluation is easy. Standards are vital to control.

The system should not be demanding your time, but freeing you during operating hours to work the floor, to deal with the exceptions and unexpected and, above all, to interact with your people.

16

Quantity Food Preparation and Service

Alan Paret
Boston University

Introduction

Today, the dining public knows where the values are, but they still expect quality and professionalism. Such value expectations can choke profits. Therefore, operators must re-examine all functions of the food service process.

The explosive 1980s were a very exciting time for the food service industry. The economy was expanding along with rapid job growth. These good times brought on a change in American taste buds. Consumers were becoming more sophisticated. They were traveling more. Regional pride, as shown through the use of indigenous ingredients, was at the very core of this culinary renaissance. There was a new glamour associated with being a chef. The graduates of the Culinary Institute of America were making their mark as chef/owners in every major city.

The "go-slow" 1990s have produced a price-resistant customer. In 1992 restaurant prices rose an average of only 2% nationwide. This is the lowest increase reported by the Federal Bureau of Labor Statistics since 1964. The 1990s guest is forcing operators to look at their customers from a completely new perspective. In the past, operators made the assumption that if one used good ingredients and cooked a good meal, then the guest will come—the "Field of Dreams" marketing strategy.

Today, in order to be successful, you must be a customer-driven business. This "management from the front door" views the kitchen as an integral part of the customer satisfaction process. The number one reason why customers stop patronizing a business is due to an attitude of indifference by the service staff. It makes little sense (or dollars) to prepare food that customers don't want. Especially if the staff has not been trained to deliver quality service.

There are many new management ideas related to the functions involved in food production. Many of these ideas have had their origins with total quality management (TQM). TQM is a commitment to quality, applied to all aspects of a company's operation, including the products, marketing, customer service and, most importantly, human resources. TQM is designed to measure performance, then uses those measurements to improve efficiency. This works fairly well in manufacturing where there are products made within specifications.

With service, one can measure customer satisfaction by measuring customer retention.[1] TQM can be applied to the kitchen operation by looking at all the processes in order to become more efficient, cut any unnecessary costs and improve the quality.

In order to rework the kitchen process, TQM forces an operator to view customers as an integral part of the organization, not just an anonymous group you sell to. A well-run kitchen operation must constantly ask what the customer wants. This monitoring must be done not only by the customer service department but also by the chef, kitchen manager, and even the rounds cook. It requires getting the customer involved in areas such as menu development through customer focus groups or regular formal surveys.

TQM also believes in tapping the brainpower of every employee. Changes in quality can start today simply by leading and training people. The food service industry has been notoriously "immature" in its lack of training. This has resulted in industrywide high turnover rates. A maverick bucking this trend is Kevin Dunn, who runs the Ashville, North Carolina-based McGuffey's restaurant chain. He has a rule that managers must "catch an employee doing something right at least ten times a month." This certainly is contrary to the ongoing industry attitude of management indifference to employees.

In a sense, quantity food production should be renamed *quality* food production. In the kitchen, we deal with product quality. However, one can no longer view product quality in isolation from the whole process. It is the function of the service staff to make the customer happy. The data on customer service put out by the White House of Consumer Affairs has become quite well known:

- For every customer who bothers to complain, there are 26 others who remain silent.
- The average "wronged" customer will tell 8 to 16 people.
- Some 91% of unhappy customers will never buy from you again.
- It costs about five times as much money to get a new customer as it costs to keep a current one.[2]

On the other hand, companies that rated high on the quality of their customer service do the following:

- Keep customers longer—50% longer or more
- Have lower sales and marketing costs—20% to 40% lower
- Experience higher return on sales—7% to 12% higher
- Have better net profits—7% to 17% better[3]

It is important to view the kitchen with this customer quality background. The kitchen is just one of the functions involved in making customers happy. The final results of a successful food service operation can be measured in terms of employee and customer satisfaction and customer retention.

The best result that a kitchen's meal can have is to exceed the expectations of its customers. However, a person getting something to eat at a ballpark or a fast food restaurant will have a different set of expectations from someone dining at The Olive Garden or Le Cirque. Those expectations probably will change in the near future. Volume Services, a contract feeder, provides food and catering services at baseball stadiums around the country. At their five stadiums, fans will consume 8.5 million hot dogs. However, at Yankee Stadium in

New York, they just opened a cappuccino bar pouring flavored coffees, cappuccino cordials, and espresso. At Giants Stadium in San Francisco, they offer red and white clam chowder served in sourdough bread bowls, "veggie" burgers, and caesar salads.[4] TQM focuses an operation on exceeding customer expectations. The goal of an operator is to find out what a customer wants, find out how they want it, and give it to them just that way.

Issues Related to Quantity Food Production

Many areas are important in a quality food operation, including new purchasing and receiving concepts, safety and sanitation, nutrition, and present and future food trends. The importance of these issues has increased considerably during this new age of the consumer.

Purchasing

The art of purchasing is going through a revolution, with new strategies such as just in time, no stockpiling, partnering, global market availability, and development of solid relationships with suppliers. Today, operators must adapt to these new rules in order to remain competitive.

The following are some innovations going on within purchasing:

- Total partnership with suppliers. Today, operators need to rely on their suppliers. This means trusting them and asking for their input. In return, suppliers will have to customize their operations to suit specific needs. Omni Hotel's food and beverage director Peter Hothorn has enlisted 18 "supplier-partners" to create an annual promotions calendar. For example, he has arranged with Fetzer Wines to provide recipe and tent cards, a training outline for servers, and pricing guidelines during a monthly wine promotion.[5]

- In 1992 Chicago-based Northside Packing Co. was named Supplier of the Year by S. & A. Restaurant Corporation, parent of both the Steak & Ale and Bennigan's dinnerhouse chains. In order to be eligible, the vendor must have a progressive strategy with regard to new ideas, products, and technologies; be a community member, and exhibit a dedication to solid waste issues.[6]

- The increased use of cost-plus pricing with wholesalers. For example, Costa Produce of Boston and its customers will agree ahead of time on a certain margin of markup. In other words, Costa will contract with an operator for a certain price, enabling the customer to "lockin" for a period of time. This relationship can benefit both parties.

- One-stop purchasing versus the use of two or more suppliers. This challenges the old strategy of leveraging or playing suppliers off one another. Often times, getting daily quotes from suppliers and then placing only part of your order with each will force the supplier to become more price competitive. This strategy is still actively used in the food service industry.

Another strategy coming of age is to develop a loyalty with a full-line distributor in order to achieve volume discounts. This will also reduce the number of deliveries at your establishment, resulting in a less hectic kitchen, less paperwork, and fewer labor hours necessary for receiving and storage.

- As part of the regional cuisine movement, food service operators now deal directly with local farms and fishermen. Buying locally brings in fresher products that are sometimes less expensive because of the costs saved by dealing direct and not transporting the products. Two restaurants, Greens in San Francisco and Gordon in Chicago, are examples of operations that own farms where they grow their own organic products.
- Use of an independent purchasing group. In order to combat the cost advantage of multiunit chains, independent operators may want to hire a purchasing group to take advantage of volume purchasing.

Regarding selection of a supplier, the following questions might be helpful:

1. What do you, as the operator, need? This question asks you to prioritize the following areas: quality, quantity, price, service (in terms of frequency of sales calls and assistance in selling the products), and credit terms.
2. What does each vendor need from the operator? How much volume, minimum order, and lead time are required? In addition, what payment terms are offered?

Sanitation

Food safety is clearly an issue for the 1990s. It can be a relatively simple goal. On one hand, in the ideal situation, you purchase high quality food, and trained employees prepare it in a safe and sanitary process. But in reality, even with the best of intentions, your source of food can be questionable. In 1993 hamburgers from the Jack in the Box restaurant chain were tainted with *E. coli* 0157:H7 bacteria, allegedly resulting in at least two fatalities and at least 450 cases of severe food poisoning. This unfortunate situation has now put the spotlight on food safety and operator standards.

According to a Centers for Disease Control and Prevention study of foodborne illness, more than 6 million people become ill from food a year, though the cause of more than half of the reported illnesses can't be identified. The study findings pinpointed the following sources of foodborne illness:

Unknown	55%
Dairy	13%
Poultry	10%
Beef	9%
Seafood	5%
Pork	5%
Produce	2%
Eggs	1%

Examples of some foodborne illnesses include the following:

Illness-producing organism	Symptom	Prevention
-*Staphylococcus*	Nausea, vomiting, diarrhea	This toxin cannot be destroyed by heat; employees with illnesses shouldn't handle food
-*Salmonella*	Diarrhea, fever, vomiting	Avoid cross-contamination; reheat leftovers; *Salmonella* is killed at 165° F
-*Shigella*	Diarrhea, cramps	Good personal hygiene
-*Clostridium perfringens*	Diarrhea, nausea, cramps	Cool meats quickly; reheat to 165° F

Almost 80% of all foodborne illnesses occur at food service establishments. The following is a list of percentages of all outbreaks and the related cause. (Some illnesses have more than one cause.):

Improper holding temperature	43%
Inadequate cooking	20%
Poor personal hygiene	20%
Contaminated equipment	12%
Unsafe source	8%
Other	8%

On review of the causes, one can construct a sanitary checklist for a well-run and sanitary kitchen operation.

Some Safe Food Tips

- Buy pasteurized milk and milk products. However, contamination can occur after the milk has been pasteurized. In 1985 tainted pasteurized milk from a Chicago dairy caused 16 thousand confirmed cases of *Salmonella* food poisoning—and several deaths—in six states.[7]
- Avoid cross-contamination—from the cutting board, the knife, even juices from poultry. Wash everything that comes in contact with the birds with soap and hot water.
- Stuff raw poultry just before cooking. Remove the stuffing right after the bird comes out of the oven.
- Cook poultry thoroughly, until the juices run clear and there is no pink—a temperature of 165° F+.
- Be sure hamburgers are fully cooked to 160° F to kill *E. coli* bacteria.
- Buy your seafood from well-established and reputable sources.
- Store the seafood in the coldest part of the refrigerator and cook it within 24 hours of purchase.
- Hold foods in the danger zone (40°–140° F) for no more than two hours.
- If prepared in advance, hot foods should be brought to 140° F as quickly as possible.
- When reheating, foods must be brought to a minimum temperature of 165° F. Steam tables are *not* adequate for reheating.

Safety

In 1990 the food service industry reported 357,200 on-the-job accidents. On the average, 35 workdays are lost when a food service industry employee suffers a serious injury. The most common food service injuries are sprains and strains (30%), cuts (20%), and burns (13%).[8]

The goal of an excellent food service operation is to reduce the chance of accidents, which will result in lower insurance premiums. Loss prevention efforts work best when they involve all employees. This process can start by studying past accidents in order to see if there are any recurring problems. Call in your insurance company or the local fire department to do a safety audit and assist in setting up a safety training program.

Strains and sprains occur mostly from slips, falls, and improper lifting. A good guide to prevent such injuries would include the following:

- Set up a good housekeeping program and maintain it throughout the operation: spills should be cleaned up immediately with a proper cleaning method using fresh hot water and a strong detergent.
- Work areas and aisles should be free of obstructions.
- Employees should be instructed to always walk, not run; never to carry a load that obstructs their vision; and to always use a ladder to get items from higher shelves.
- To lift with the legs and not the back.

Employees should be instructed in the safe use and proper care of knives and other tools and equipment. Kitchen employees should have adequate mitts, potholders, and side towels for handling hot pots and pans. In order to prevent burns and strains, employees should ask for help when moving any heavy, hot items.

A safety program should have incentives to encourage employees to work safely. The Bakers Square chain of Matteson, Ill., gives out a $20 gift certificate to employees for every quarter a restaurant remains accident/claim–free.[9] The Medical City Dallas Hospital, which prepares more than 2,300 meals a day, was experiencing a high rate of injuries.[10] Thanks to a new team approach, a contest was started and small rewards now are given each month to teams that are injury free. This contest has raised safety awareness. In summary, for safety to be an issue, it needs to be incorporated into employee orientations, become part of the company mission, and be emphasized on a continuous and daily basis.

Nutrition

High fat intake has been associated with an increased risk for heart disease and some cancers. Low fat and no fat is the direction food is going. This was emphasized when the U.S. Department of Agriculture officially launched the new Food Guide Pyramid. Foods were categorized with the dual goal of keeping fat and cholesterol low and limiting the intake of sodium and sugar. The pyramid has the following structure:

1. At the base is the bread, cereal, rice, and pasta group (6–11 servings).
2. The next level is the fruit group (2–4 servings) and the vegetable group (3–5 servings).

3. Above that level is the milk, yogurt, and cheese group (2–3 servings) and the meat, poultry, fish, dry beans, eggs, and nut group (2–3 servings).
4. The top of the pyramid lists the general category of fats, oils, and sweets and states they should be used sparingly.

This new pyramid has been written to reduce the amount of calories from fat and sugar by almost two-thirds. Given these new food guidelines, a healthy diet consists of the following:

- A reduction in fat to 30% or less of daily calories and a reduction in saturated fat to 10% of those calories
- A reduction in cholesterol to less than 300 milligrams a day
- An increase in carbohydrates—primarily complex carbohydrates found in whole-grain foods and fruits and vegetables. A healthy diet will increase carbohydrates to 55% of total daily calories.

Along with reducing fat and cholesterol, one should increase consumption of foods high in fiber, vitamins, and minerals. To accomplish these recommendations, chefs need to use more of the healthier cooking methods such as baking, roasting, grilling, braising, steaming, and poaching. Seasoning with fresh herbs and spices and using citrus fruits and vinegars helps to bring out the fresh taste of food. Using low-fat versions of high-fat foods such as part-skim mozzarella cheese, nonfat yogurt, nonfat sour cream, and buttermilk also results in a lower-fat meal.

Food service operators find themselves in a quandary because Americans still prefer taste yet want a healthy diet. According to the latest Louis Harris and Associates poll, Americans are consuming excessive amounts of salt and fat and declining amounts of fruits, vegetables, and foods with fiber. It seems they are eating low-fat meals that aren't as tasty. They are making up for this tastelessness through eating high-fat desserts. Americans have traded saturated fat for butterfat! For example, Haagen-Dazs has a new higher-fat ice cream called Extraas, with flavors such as Carrot Cake Passion and Triple Brownie Overload. The company's market share has jumped from 5.9% to 7.9%.

Another development contrary to the health and fitness movement has been McDonald's testing of the new half-pound Mega Mac and an introduction of the Mickey D., a one-third pound hamburger. The challenge that has always existed for operators is to prepare healthy food that tastes good. This goal still exists.

Food Trends

Because customers are limiting meat consumption at home, they are more likely to order a steak when they dine out. Steakhouses such as Sizzler's new Buffalo Ranch Steakhouse in Mission Viejo, California already has lines out the door. Specialties include a thick-cut 12-ounce sirloin steak, smoked prime rib, and a 22-ounce "ranch house" porterhouse steak. Other popular players include the Outback Steakhouse and Lone Star Steakhouse chains.[11] This new trend runs counter to the previous decade when the beef industry had run into trouble. Beef consumption dropped from a high of 95 pounds per capita in 1976 to 70 pounds per capita in 1988. Meanwhile, the opposite trend characterized the poultry industry: poultry consumption increased from 55 pounds per capita in 1984 to 72 pounds per capita in 1990.

Many operations are now looking at purchasing beef and poultry that has been naturally raised. Broadly speaking, naturally raised is defined as raised without hormones (i.e., steroids). Antibiotics will only be administered to treat disease or in feed during infancy. In most cases, naturally raised also means that caging and close confinement is forbidden and the animals are fed wholesome food, including natural grains and grass. Free range indicates regular access to the outdoors.

Because many consumers would like to avoid seafood harvested from waters, some seafood is now raised using aquaculture. This is the practice of raising fish in tanks on farms or in controlled ocean beds. Another key issue facing operators is overfishing and the resulting dwindled supply of the common, well-known species, such as haddock, cod, and flounder. The stocks of these fish are at their lowest levels ever.[12] Tomorrow's catch of the day may be the name of a "trash fish" we hardly recognize today, such as pout, croaker, and parrotfish.

Another issue that needs to be addressed is the lack of seafood inspection in the United States. As FDA commissioner David Kessler states, "the current system of food-safety regulation is reactive. What is needed is a system that is built on preventing problems in the food supply. He goes on to state that the seafood industry is highly decentralized and made up of thousands of small businesses. There is an unacceptable number of deaths and illnesses from foodborne illnesses. The FDA is now looking at pilot studies using new quality-control regulations.[13]

Grains have become the pasta of the 1990s. Names such as spelt, amaranth, and quinoa are appearing on many restaurant menus. Grains are a good source of fiber and they have half the calories of fat. Pasta still retains its enormous popularity, fitting in nicely with the new food pyramids, which calls for an increase in consumption of complex carbohydrates. Organically grown fruits and vegetables, however, have been slow to catch on.

Ethnic cuisine continues to influence American palates. The big three are Chinese, Italian, and Mexican. Salsa, including picante, enchilada, taco, and similar chili-based sauces, toppled ketchup from the condiment throne in 1991.[14] Indian restaurants continue to grow in number as Americans become more comfortable with curry. Caribbean tastes also grow as its hot, peppery style resembles salsa. Even Pillsbury has a new retail product—Green Giant Black Beans.

Kitchen as a Factory

The kitchen is one of the most difficult areas in which to manufacture consistent products. There are several reasons for this difficulty.

Labor

The kitchen operation is a labor-intensive process. Standardizing kitchen output is quite difficult due to different and varying human input, techniques, and behaviors.

Technology

In general, technological advances in equipment have been slow in comparison with other manufacturing areas. There have been some recent changes in this area, such as McDonald's automatic ARCH Fry and Drink and Taco Bell's robotic taco maker. ARCH stands for *A*utomated *R*estaurant *C*rew *H*elper and is a robotlike system that speeds food preparation. The use of these "McRobots" produces less waste, offers improved service and quality, and allows McDonald's to focus more on customer service.[15]

Products

The square tomato has not yet been invented, although Calgene, a California company, has genetically altered a tomato in order to extend the time it takes to decompose. There have been many innovations with food products, such as ready-to-eat vegetables and *sous vide* meals. However, it is difficult to create a consistent finished product with inconsistent raw materials.

Given these limitations, there are three chains or restaurants that are making big strides in turning the kitchen into an efficient factory.

Taco Bell

Taco Bell has redesigned its restaurants, shrinking the kitchen space from 70% to 30% (the K-minus program). The dining space was expanded to 70% of total restaurant space. Many of the new menu items were designed for easy preparation in the new, smaller kitchens. The kitchen has become an assembly operation using just in time delivery, *sous vide,* and other outsourced products. Because of these changes, the food has become more consistent.

Much of what Taco Bell has achieved is because of its focus on value. Unlike other restaurants before it, Taco Bell found out its customer's definition of value through a sophisticated customer study. Customers said they wanted FACT: fast food *F*ast; fast food orders *A*ccurate; fast food in a restaurant that was *C*lean, and fast food at the appropriate *T*emperature.[16] In 1992 Taco Bell had systemwide sales of $3.28 billion from more than four thousand restaurants.

Olive Garden and Red Lobster

Minneapolis-based General Mills owns the Olive Garden and its sister, Red Lobster. With both restaurants, General Mills has created an efficient production system. A restaurant is the end of an assembly line. Like any factory, at the beginning of the line, raw material goes in. Red Lobster serves more than 60 million pounds of seafood a year. Seafood from all over the world arrives at warehouses and processing plants and then is shipped to the restaurants. Every night, each restaurant's computer tells the manager how many customers to expect based on historical data. This system has led to decreased food waste, and improved scheduling has cut down on labor costs.

In the kitchen, meals are prepared to precise timing specifications. Cooks place food on plates according to an illustrated diagram. Temperatures of food and beverage items are constantly monitored. Much like a factory, General Mills controls the input variables in order to create a consistent output for the customer.[17] General Mills operates about a thousand restaurants, which contributed about $2.34 billion in sales.

Gotham Bar and Grill

The Gotham Bar and Grill is a 170-seat upscale restaurant in New York City. Executive chef Alfred Portale oversees the daily production of more than 450 meals. At times, the kitchen receives up to 40 orders within five minutes. In order to assure consistency, Portale studies every minute detail of food preparation before he puts a dish on the menu. Realizing this is a high-volume three-star restaurant, Portale creates a menu that allows his chefs to prepare the food by themselves.

Gotham's cooks are highly trained culinary school graduates who know how to handle the products, thus avoiding waste. They are cross-trained for all the other kitchen stations. Timers are used all over the kitchen to ensure precise cooking times. All items, such as fish fillets, are cut to exact dimensions. Every leaf of lettuce must face up.[18]

The preceding three restaurants are examples of kitchens that use every available resource in an attempt to standardize output and deliver a consistent product to every customer.

Summary

In 1992 the James Beard Foundation awarded its Outstanding Service Award to the Union Square Cafe of New York City. In the cafe's summer 1992 newsletter, owner Danny Meyer wrote of his gratitude and honor on being chosen, and how proud he was of the whole Union Square Cafe team for displaying the essential pro-guest attitude that defines great service.

To summarize how the kitchen fits into this new customer service attitude, he writes,

If service is an attitude, then surely you can taste its excellence in the food. Every cook in our kitchen excels at sharing a real love of food and sincerely cares that the guest enjoyed it. When a diner sends back an undercooked steak in most restaurants, it is common to hear the chef grumble about having to cook it all over again. At the Union Square Cafe, the only grumbling you'll ever hear is from a cook who is honestly upset with himself that the guest wasn't satisfied.[19]

Guest satisfaction is the driving force. The kitchen, through the pursuit of excellence, high quality, and continuous improvement, has its role: to exceed the expectations and fully satisfy the customer.

——References——

1. Reichheld and Sasser. Zero Defections. *Harvard Business Review.* September–October 1990; p. 1.
2. Albrecht and Zemke. (1985) *Service America.* Homewood, Ill.: Dow Jones–Irwin. p. 6.
3. American Management Association. Bell and Zemke. (1992) *Knock Your Socks Off Service.*
4. *Foodservice Director.* May 15, 1993.
5. *Lodging Magazine.* April 1993; p. 34, 36.
6. *Nation's Restaurant News.* April 17, 1993.
7. *Nutrition Action Newsletter.* CSPI. July–August, 1991; p. 5.
8. *Restaurants and Institutions.* September 23, 1992; p. 103.
9. *Restaurants and Institutions.* September 23, 1992; p. 124.
10. *Foodservice Director.* May 15, 1993; p. 16.
11. *Wall Street Journal.* December 14, 1993.
12. *New York Times.* May 12, 1993.
13. *Wall Street Journal.* February 14, 1993.
14. *New York Times.* April 10, 1992.
15. *Prepared Foods.* May 1993; p. 82.
16. Harvard Case Study: Taco Bell. November 19, 1991.
17. *Forbes.* July 8, 1991; pp. 88, 89.
18. *Nation's Restaurant News.* January 4, 1993.
19. *Union Square Cafe Newsletter.* Summer 1992.

Hotel Operations and Organizational Structure

Gary A. Hamilton
California State Polytechnic University

Introduction

The experience of staying at a hotel can often be compared with going to the theater or the movies, or to watching television. We observe all the activity and sometimes wonder "How do they do that?" Whether it's providing dinner for 2,000 people at once or providing the guest a swim with a dolphin at a resort, the special effects that impress a hotel guest clearly do not happen by chance. A hotel staff is a cleverly crafted and tightly choreographed cast of employees, all working together to ensure that every aspect, every detail, every service which the hotel offers will be the best. What we are really seeing in these situations is not magic but rather the efforts of countless individuals, working both independently and collaboratively, to create a unique experience. In the end, it is the hope of every hotel employee that guests will find their hotel stay magical enough to prompt a return visit.

A number of companies, Walt Disney in particular, are famous for referring to both front of the house employees (those employees having direct guest interaction on a regular basis) and back of the house employees (those not having direct guest contact) as "cast members." These companies maintain that every employee plays a unique role in their operation. Cast members must not only know their own jobs but appreciate how their jobs serve as a foundation on which other cast members build in order to create a memorable guest experience.

Like any large organization, each hotel has specific departments. Each department is responsible for a particular set of functions in order to efficiently provide services to the guest. While the individual expertise of a department is important, the assembly and delivery of the final product is achieved only by the cooperation of all departments and employees. The end result for a hotel operation is a satisfied guest.

The purpose of our discussion in this chapter is to begin to identify the structure needed to organize hotel employees into effective and efficient teams or departments. This structure will then allow the hotel organization to efficiently serve the guest. As one might expect in any good theater, movie, or television production, the effort made among and between various departments and functional areas of a hotel may not be noticed by a guest when it is very good. But it will undoubtedly be remembered by the guest when it is bad.

The following sections outline the major functional departments of a hotel, illustrate a typical organizational chart, and briefly outline how differences in management structure shape and influence the reporting avenues for hotel personnel.

Overview of Hotel Operations

In recent years, there has been an explosion in the types and styles of hotel accommodations available to the public. The proliferation of these concepts has in large part been due to the impact of segmentation. Segmentation is the breaking down of a market into smaller sections as a means of capturing different portions of the traveling public. Take a close look at almost all the chain or brand-name hotels that you know, and you'll find that these companies have created a number of different concepts—budget hotels, extended-stay hotels, suite hotels, and luxury hotels. All these concepts carry the company's brand name yet are designed to appeal to a specific targeted customer or demographic segment.

In relation to organizational structure, each of the concepts developed by various hotel companies requires a different approach to the design and implementation of hotel operations. Additional factors that may also impact the organizational structure of a hotel are the form of actual ownership, the level of services provided the guest, labor costs, the type of hotel operation being created (e.g., casino or resort hotel), and the kind of operating and management arrangement(s) that may exist between the owner of the hotel and the management team.

In any industry, whether service or manufacturing based, one of the prime determinants of organizational structure is the size of the business endeavor. The possibilities available in creating a hotel's organizational structure based on size are truly limitless. We find, for example, that hotel concepts can range anywhere from a bed-and-breakfast operation having fewer than five rooms, to enormous mega-resorts like the MGM Grand Hotel and Casino in Las Vegas, which has more than five thousand rooms—to a budget hotel with fewer than 100 rooms that includes a drive-up window instead of a lobby, has no restaurants, and has no recreational amenities at all! In addition to the wide range of possibilities that organizational size presents, hotel operations must also take into consideration numerous other variables, specific functions, and its own unique characteristics when determining its organizational structure.

For example, the number of employees required to operate a 100 to 150-room limited-service hotel without food and beverage service is relatively small. Therefore, such a situation should lead to a relatively simple organizational structure. Let's see whether that statement is true.

Identifying the primary functional areas needed to serve guests in a 150-room limited service hotel, we find that we would need a front office operations department and a housekeeping department. These departments would most likely fall under the direction of a single manager. In theory, all other major areas, for example—maintenance, accounting services, and security—could be contracted to independent companies outside the hotel. Therefore none of these areas would appear on its organizational chart. These basic management functions for a property this size are illustrated in the organizational chart in Figure 1.

While the structure of a hotel can be as simple as the example above, it also can vary dramatically on almost a property-by-property basis. For the purposes of our analysis, we will focus our attention on an urban full-service hotel that offers both lodging and food and beverage operations and has 500 rooms.

Organizational Structure

The organizational chart in Figure 2 illustrates the pyramidal structure of job functions and positions within a 500-room full-service urban hotel. It also visually represents the relationships among various departments and their respective personnel. Organizational charts attempt to show the areas of specific responsibility and the authority that each department at

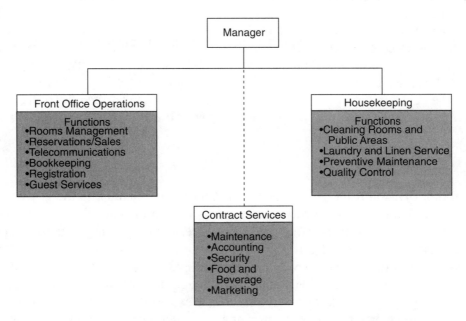

Figure 1. Organization and Primary Functions of a Limited-Services Hotel

least theoretically possesses. An organizational chart is intended to provide a framework from which each member of the organization can determine reporting relationships both horizontally and vertically throughout the hotel.

A point worth remembering when examining any organizational chart is that the chart represents a unique set of circumstances. Corporate culture and geographic uniqueness often influence the structure of an organization and may prompt changes to accommodate any, all, or none of the factors outlined in this discussion.

Classically, hotels (depending on the type and complexity of the services offered) are organized by their functions and the specific services that they provide the guest within the operation. An organizational chart identifies not only the primary departments but the senior managerial positions responsible for supervising and delegating each of the tasks within the department.

Continuing the classical definition, it is instructive to note that the important functional areas of a hotel are often designated as either revenue/profit centers or as support centers. Typically, any area of a hotel operation that sells a service or goods qualifies as a revenue/profit center. Usually, the front office and the food and beverage departments are identified as the principal centers of potential revenue for a hotel. More than 90% of all hotel revenue comes from these two areas. The rooms division generates the largest percentage of revenue, more than 60%, while food and beverage averages approximately 30%. All other areas, unless operated under an independent contract or lease, are defined as support centers. These usually include accounting, human resources, housekeeping, security, and engineering.

While the revenue versus nonrevenue characterization is used primarily for accounting purposes, the value, importance, and contribution to bottom-line profitability of traditionally non-revenue producing departments remains vital to an efficient hotel operation.

Rooms Division

The rooms division is the functional area of a hotel most familiar to the general public. With most guest transactions involving the rooms division occurring in the public area known as the lobby, it is also one of the primary areas from which guests form opinions about the quality of the hotel and its services. As a result of its location and function, it is also the single department most responsible for handling guest requests and complaints.

Normally, the rooms division is composed of three functional areas: front office operations, housekeeping, and uniformed services. In our example, we will include reservations and the telecommunications system as part of front office responsibilities but treat housekeeping as a separate function. Note, however, that this is one of the many areas in which organizational structure and design is fast changing depending on a hotel company's particular strategies and emphasis.

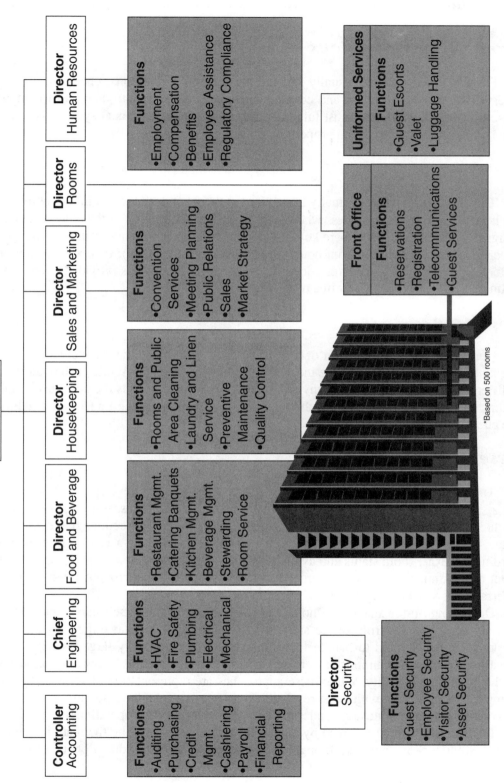

Figure 2. Organization and Primary Functions of a Full-Service Hotel*

General Manager

Controller Accounting
Chief Engineering
Director Food and Beverage
Director Housekeeping
Director Sales and Marketing
Director Rooms
Director Human Resources

Director Security

Functions
•Auditing
•Purchasing
•Credit Mgmt.
•Cashiering
•Payroll
•Financial Reporting

Functions
•HVAC
•Fire Safety
•Plumbing
•Electrical
•Mechanical

Functions
•Restaurant Mgmt.
•Catering Banquets
•Kitchen Mgmt.
•Beverage Mgmt.
•Stewarding
•Room Service

Functions
•Rooms and Public Area Cleaning
•Laundry and Linen Service
•Preventive Maintenance
•Quality Control

Functions
•Convention Services
•Meeting Planning
•Public Relations
•Sales
•Market Strategy

Functions
•Employment
•Compensation
•Benefits
•Employee Assistance
•Regulatory Compliance

Functions
•Guest Security
•Employee Security
•Visitor Security
•Asset Security

Uniformed Services
Functions
•Guest Escorts
•Valet
•Luggage Handling

Front Office
Functions
•Reservations
•Registration
•Telecommunications
•Guest Services

*Based on 500 rooms

Front Office Operations

Front office operations usually involve the following functions: check-in, check-out, reservations, and information and concierge services. With the introduction of computers, these functions have been almost fully automated. Reliance on manual systems is now limited in most cases to very small properties.

Check-in

The check-in function normally takes place at the front desk located in the lobby area of the hotel. Check-in is the process whereby people register as guests of the hotel, where room assignments are made, and where keys are assigned for guest accommodations. The specific check-in process can differ from hotel to hotel based on the type of computer system used, different policies and procedures adopted, and the level of services provided. However, the ultimate goal—to put the guest in a room—remains the same.

Check-out

Check-out is the termination of a guests's visit. It involves the reconciliation of guest accounts and their payment by the most efficient method possible. While each hotel may use a different procedure, the key to any successful check-out system is the accuracy of the accounts and efficient processing of the required paperwork avoiding unnecessary delays for the guest.

Reservations

The process whereby rooms, meeting space, and food and beverage facilities are held for a specific guest or group of guests for later use is called the reservation system. The introduction of computers to assist front office staff in this procedure has dramatically changed the way room nights are sold to the customer. Immediate access to information regarding the exact room status and availability of hotel facilities on any given day allows the hotel to maximize use of all resources within the property. This computerized approach is referred to as yield management.

Depending on the size of the hotel, the reservation function itself can be carried out in various ways: by the front office staff in addition to their regular duties, by reservation clerks specifically hired to handle future reservations—or (in very large hotels) the entire function is assigned to an independent department in which there is heavy emphasis on sales of the entire hotel facility. While these approaches are representative of some of the developing trends in dealing with guest reservations, in our example, the reservation function will be contained in a separate area, under the direction of front office operations.

Reservations can be received by a hotel in several ways. Among them are use of a toll-free, 1-800 telephone number, through travel agency bookings, by direct phone call, through the organized strategies of the sales department, or by phone, fax, mail or cable. With more than half of all guest night reservations made in advance, the tracking, maintenance, confirmation, and management of the reservation system is essential to a profitable and successful hotel operation.

Guest Information and Concierge Services

One of the primary functions of the front desk is to provide the guest information on the availability of hotel services and amenities. Front office personnel usually provide information regarding transportation, local areas of interest, and restaurants as well as handle special guest requests. The impressions generated by the front office staff play a major role in establishing and promoting a positive guest experience.

Uniformed Services

Front of the house employees who also have constant exposure to and interaction with guests include uniformed employees, who provide support in transporting guest luggage, providing valet parking and transportation, and executing major lobby functions such as unloading guests from cars, hailing taxis, and escorting guests to the registration area. The basic function of uniformed services is to meet, greet, and assist guests when arriving and departing the hotel. This area works closely with other operating departments in satisfying the needs of each guest.

In addition to guest responsibilities, the front desk serves as one of the nerve centers for information regarding the current status of the hotel in many areas. It can provide room status information (whether the room is occupied or unoccupied) to housekeeping, provide account status to both the customer and hotel accounting staff, and provide a database of information—on everything from guest nights sold to "no shows"—from which management decisions can be made.

Front office staff also perform many other tasks that can be classified primarily as clerical in nature but are nonetheless vital to the efficient functioning of the hotel. These tasks include posting charges to appropriate rooms or accounts, crediting payments by guests, and operating the telecommunications center.

Food and Beverage

Historically, food and beverage operations have always been part of a traditional hotel operation. Unfortunately, many of these food and beverage outlets proved unprofitable, but were nonetheless still considered indispensable to running a successful hotel.

Today the emphasis is on profitability and efficient operations. As a result, hotels have developed new approaches to food and beverage service. In the attempt to meet the public's wide range of tastes and needs, today's food and beverage operations range from traditional lavish dining rooms to sports bars and clubs, to fast food. It is no longer unusual to see a hotel include a limited service food operation, or the food service operation contracted to a well-known restaurant chain, or even fast food delivery from outside the hotel. In fact, many new hotel concepts have no food and beverage outlets at all! This shift in strategy recognizes that the food and beverage amenity may not be needed, or may be more efficiently and profitably provided by outside contractors.

If we use any of the hotel rating systems, AAA or Mobil for example, full-service hotels are required to have a full complement of food and beverage service available to their guests. Second only to the rooms division in terms of revenue generation, the food and beverage department of a full-service hotel occupies a major place in the organizational chart (Figure 2).

In addition to multiple food outlets (all of which are supported by one or more kitchens under the direction of an executive chef), beverage outlets, and room service, a full-service hotel includes catering and banquet operations, which provide additional revenue for the hotel. The catering and banquet operations also act as a valuable marketing tool to attract different kinds of business to the hotel, such as group business, weddings, conventions, associations, and trade shows.

Housekeeping

Often overlooked yet vital to all hotel operations, housekeeping performs the basic and essential job of cleaning guest rooms and the public areas. More than that, the role of the modern housekeeping department has been expanded to play a major role in preventive maintenance, energy conservation, and hotel security. Housekeeping is the single largest department within the hotel and has the largest number of employees.

One of the keys to a successful housekeeping department is a close working relationship between housekeeping and the front office. The wealth of information generated by the rooms division regarding arrivals, check-outs, and stayovers are critical to the housekeeping division and to the overall performance of the hotel. Close and frequent communication between these two departments ensures clean guest rooms on demand. Given the heavy emphasis that guests place on overall cleanliness as shown in numerous studies on guest satisfaction, housekeeping stands as one of the most important departments within a hotel organization.

Accounting

The internal finances of a hotel are monitored by the accounting department, whose functions generally include accounts receivable, accounts payable, payroll, food and beverage controls, cash management, and financial reporting. The extent of the functions that the accounting staff engages in is dependent principally on the size and complexity of the operation and the cost-effectiveness of retaining outside services. Smaller properties often rely on an internal office staff to handle tasks like payroll or have staff download the hotel data from their computers to be transmitted off site for processing. A hotel will contract outside accounting firms to generate more sophisticated reports like operating statements and operational analysis as well as provide traditional functions like periodic audits.

Daily functions like night audits, bank deposits, and credit checks are handled internally by the hotel's accounting department or in smaller properties by front office staff. Larger properties will have an entire accounting division designed to monitor the accounting systems, generate cost control reports, and conduct departmental audits.

Engineering and Maintenance

The mechanical, electrical, plumbing, fire safety systems, and HVAC (heating, ventilation, and air conditioning) functions of a hotel have obvious importance. While usually one of the most invisible of hotel departments, engineering goes to the head of the organizational chart when the hot water system fails on a Monday morning at 6:00 A.M. and you have 100% occupancy!

The role of the engineering department within a hotel is a combination of preventive maintenance, troubleshooting, and crisis management. The extent of the expertise that the engineering staff possesses will dictate the types of repairs which can be made by the engineering staff and those repairs which require additional expertise and will be handled by outside contractors.

In addition, depending on the hotel, many specialized maintenance functions will also be contracted out to other companies: landscaping, maintenance of interior plants, heavy duty kitchen cleaning, and window washing are a few examples. Once again, the team relationship and the degree of cooperation needed between the front office, housekeeping, and engineering and maintenance to provide a successful level of guest service is important. Guest complaints need to be carefully monitored and expeditiously handled to ensure excellence in guest services.

Security

The growing exposure of hotel operations to liability for injuries and damages sustained by their guests while on the premises dictates that hotels increase their awareness of guest security and safety. The security staff is charged with the primary responsibility of protecting not only hotel guests but hotel visitors, employees, and hotel assets. The security department may consist of contract personnel from a security service or may be made up of retired law enforcement officials hired by the hotel to implement policies and procedures for the protection of the hotel, its guests, and employees. The responsibility for protecting guests and employees extends to every department within the hotel. One way a department can assist the security staff is by complying with specific procedures and policies as set forth by the hotel. For instance, issuing room keys strictly according to hotel policy can substantially reduce the opportunity for crimes to be committed against guests and employees alike.

Human Resources

Sometimes referred to as the personnel office, human resources is the department within a hotel charged with providing a wide range of support services, including employee recruiting, benefits, compensation, labor relations, employee relations and assistance programs, and information on federal, state, and local regulatory issues.

While not a revenue/profit center in its own right, human resource departments are beginning to be recognized by management as a tool to assist in cost containment by reducing significant expenses like employee turnover. This can be accomplished, in part, by providing orientation and training sessions as well as career planning and staff development opportunities for all hotel employees. Using this approach, the human resources department can then be defined as generating revenue in an indirect but nonetheless tangible way that assists hotel operations and profitability.

Sales and Marketing

The sales, marketing, and public relations functions of a hotel can be located within the front office operations of a small hotel property or, as in large hotels, involve a director and staff who manage these functions in a comprehensive manner.

Hotel marketing is focused on developing strategies for reaching new customers. Each hotel, through the efforts of its marketing department, identifies the specific market segments to be targeted by the sales force. This is accomplished by researching hotel guest histories, current demographics, and market preferences. Once the determination of the market has been made, the guest mix—those guests who will most likely use the services, facilities, and amenities of the hotel—is then identified and solicited in different ways.

It becomes the primary role of the sales staff to try to reach these prospective customers and sell them rooms, food and beverages, services, and meeting facilities. The sales staff are responsible for making sales calls and contacting related businesses, conventions, and trade associations.

The public relations function focuses on the formulation of strategies designed to attract publicity to the hotel. Any number of devices can be used to accomplish this end ranging from sponsorship of local events to donating services to charities.

At its most effective, the sales, marketing, and public relations functions should involve all hotel staff in "selling" the hotel.

Hotel Management

In examining the organizational chart provided in Figure 2, it should become apparent that those positions sandwiched between the general manager's position and the various departments of the hotel hold a unique organizational status both in terms of authority and information. While membership may vary on a property-to-property basis, these individuals generally comprise what is commonly known as the executive committee of a hotel.

The executive committee is usually represented by the director from each of the major divisions. The role of the committee is to assist the general manager by providing communication in the areas of information, feedback, forecasting, strategy, and problem solving, using a team approach.

General Manager

The general manager is the primary decision maker for the hotel. It is the general manager's role to supervise the various department heads, delegate tasks as necessary, report the financial status of the hotel to the owner(s), and develop the appropriate strategies necessary to ensure the continued success of the operation. But perhaps most importantly, it is the general manager on whom the employees rely to provide leadership, vision, and a sense of purpose. It is the general manager's role to coordinate and facilitate the various projects that are the focus of the hotel. It has often been stated that excellence is a top-down phenomenon. In the instance of a hotel operation, the excellence and professionalism of a hotel staff is usually a reflection of the excellence and professionalism of its general manager.

Summary

Hotel operations and organizational structure can range from basic to the complex. The factors that influence organizational structure are numerous. In all cases, however, the fundamental functions required to provide a hotel "room night" for a guest are the same. Front office operations and housekeeping play a major role in any hotel organizational structure.

We also noted that most successful hotel operations are a collaborative effort requiring the participation and cooperation of all departments and employees within the hotel. Armed with this knowledge, the task and challenge for management is to bring these elements together to create the magic that will delight guests and ensure their return.

18

Rooms Division Management

Hubert B. VanHoof
Northern Arizona University

Introduction

Hotels are in the business of selling rooms. Many of them, the full-service hotels, also sell food and beverages, cater functions, and charge guests for such things as phone calls and dry cleaning. Yet, rooms generate the largest part of the revenue for a hotel. Two-thirds of all gross revenues in full-service hotels are generated by room sales, as compared to about one-fifth for food and beverage revenues (Figure 1).[1]

Besides the fact that the largest part of total revenue for hotels is generated through room sales, the cost that can be directly attributed to selling those rooms amounts to only 18% of a hotel's overall costs, as compared to a 23.4 cost percentage for food and beverage sales (Figure 1). Rooms generate a 73% departmental profit; the departmental profit for the food and beverage department is only 15%.[1]

For limited-service hotels, those that do not sell food and beverages, these numbers become even more striking: almost 95% of their revenue is generated through room sales. The direct costs associated with selling such rooms amount to 25.5%. These numbers imply that for every $1.00 a limited service hotel earns in room sales, 75 cents is departmental profit.[2] It is more profitable for a hotel to sell rooms than it is to sell anything else.

The department in charge of maintaining and selling rooms is, appropriately, the rooms division department. Its main function within the operation is to accommodate guests comfortably, safely, and efficiently. The activities of the rooms division can be separated into five basic departments:

- Front office
- Guest services
- Housekeeping
- Engineering/maintenance
- Security

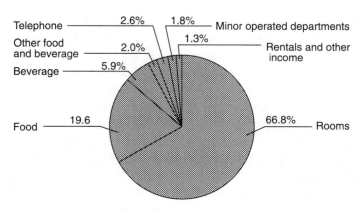

Figure 1. Full-Service Hotels Revenue Distribution—U.S. January–June 1992; Ratios to Total Revenue

This chapter will discuss each of these departments separately. We will look at how the rooms division functions within the overall hotel operation and how the departments within the division interact. The discussions of the individual departments will present an overview; greater detail will be left to future coursework.

Two things must be said as preface. First, all hotels are different. They cater to different markets, attract a different clientele, have different sizes and service levels, and have different locations. Some hotels do not have a separate rooms division department; this is primarily due to their size. A 25–room motel located in the suburbs of a rural town can be operated successfully by one manager/owner. An 800–room hotel in downtown New York, on the other hand, will probably have a rooms division and a rooms division manager.

Second, not all hotels include the security and engineering/maintenance departments in their rooms division. Some properties do include them in the responsibility of the rooms division manager though. They will also be included in this discussion.

Throughout this chapter, the importance of automation in the rooms division will be emphasized. Its role in the lodging industry will only increase as time goes by.

The Front Office

The front office is often called the "hub" or the "heart" of the hotel. Both qualifications are used to indicate that a hotel centers around its front office; all the departments in the hotel are connected to the front office, from engineering/maintenance to the accounting office and from the food and beverage department to housekeeping.

To enable the front office to know what is going on everywhere else, many hotel properties have installed computerized property management systems (PMS).

A PMS is a set of computer programs that is designed to allow departments to interact. When all departments in the hotel have the capacity to communicate with each other, it is often referred to as integration. Integration allows for fast and smooth communication, a much more efficient organization, and ultimately, improved guest service. Here are some ways in which an integrated system can simplify life for guests and for staff.

When a guest charges her dinner to her room by signing the check, the property management system will automatically and instantaneously update her account. A long-distance call made from a room will automatically be charged to the guest account. When keys are issued at the front desk, the system will keep track of their use, not only by guests, but also by housekeepers, management, security, and maintenance. And if the front office knows which rooms have been cleaned by the housekeeping department on a minute-to-minute basis, the assignment of rooms on check-in will be fast and accurate. The more advanced the integration, the better the front office can attend to the wants, needs, and safety of guests.

The front office in larger hotels consists of three departments: reservations, front desk, and PBX (public branch exchange, the telephone system).

Reservations

The main functions of the reservations department include the following:

1. Handling guest reservations and inquiries
2. Maintaining reservation records
3. Providing reports and updates on availability, room revenue, and expected arrivals

Although it is often said that the front desk has the first contact with the guest, this is only partly true. The reservations department handles the initial guest inquiry. Reservationists should therefore not only be familiar with the reservation system, they should also be well informed and enthusiastic about the property.

While it is true that the sales and marketing department is in charge of "selling" the property, a surprising amount of selling is also done at the reservations department, where good reservationists practice the art of "upselling." Upselling is encouraging and convincing a guest to make reservations for a more expensive room than he initially had intended. This will not only increase the hotel's average daily rate (ADR), but also its overall room revenue amount.

Requests for reservations reach the department in various ways: by fax, by letter, by means of a direct call to the property, through a referral from sales and marketing, or through the hotel's or chain's central reservation system (the 800 number).

Currently, more and more properties give their reservationists the freedom to negotiate a room rate with the customer, within reason of course. Hotels would rather sell a room at a rate that is slightly lower than they expected than not sell the room at all. A room night not sold is revenue lost forever.

It is up to the reservation department's staff to make sure that every request from a potential or repeat customer is adequately dealt with and properly documented, that the hotel is occupied to its highest potential, and that overbooking (accepting more reservations than there are rooms available) does not occur. A property's occupancy and revenue are dependent on how well this department operates.

If a property is large enough or busy enough, the reservations department may have its own manager or supervisor. The responsibilities of this position center around staffing and scheduling, report generation, and providing the link between the day-to-day operation of the department and the rooms division manager.

The Front Desk

The front desk handles the critical functions of check-in and check-out. The first impression and the last impression the guest has of a hotel are almost always based on her interactions with the front desk. Centrally located in most hotels, the duties of the front desk include the following:

1. Guest registration (check-in)
2. Room assignment and key dispensing
3. Providing the guest with information
4. Handling guest complaints
5. Updating and checking guest accounts (folios)
6. Collecting and dispersing payments
7. Checking the guest out

A front desk agent is a public relations officer, a cashier, a computer operator, and a security officer all in one.

Besides the duties that most of us are familiar with, another important function carried out at the desk is the night audit. This can be done by the desk agent on duty or by a separate auditor. The person in charge of the audit verifies whether or not guest charges have been posted accurately to the guest's folio. Without a PMS this can be a laborious and monotonous task; if the hotel is computerized, however, the computer system takes care of most of the details much more quickly and accurately. This frees the night auditor for other duties.

Many of the day-to-day operations at the desk are managed and supervised by front desk managers who coordinate activities within the department and work with other departments to make the system as efficient as possible. They determine work schedules for employees and resolve guest problems. They are the eyes and ears of the rooms division manager at the desk.

The Public Branch Exchange (PBX)

Since 1981 the role of the hotel's telephone department has changed dramatically. In that year, the telephone system in the United States was deregulated, which meant that hotel properties could resell telephone services to guests and potentially make a profit. Before that time the PBX primarily had been a switchboard, taking care of incoming and outgoing calls, telephone messages, and wake-up calls. In the 1980s it became a potential revenue center.

Many of today's telephone systems, often referred to as call accounting systems (CAS) are not only connected to, or interfaced with, the hotel's property management system, they are also capable of distributing calls at the lowest cost to the hotel by means of least-cost routing networks. They can price outgoing calls (at a profit to the hotel) and immediately post those calls to the guest account.

This has not only increased the efficiency of the property management system internally, it has also increased the importance of the telephone system to the hotel. At present, more than 2% of total revenue is generated through call accounting systems (Figure 1).

Guest Services

Although every activity in a hotel is related to guest services, there is one department within the rooms division that actually operates under this name.

The guest services department comprises such positions as bell person, concierge, doorman, parking attendant, porter, and elevator operator. Just like the agent at the desk, these employees are in direct contact with the guest, yet they serve in a different capacity.

The person directly in charge of this department is either the bell captain or the concierge, depending on the way the property has structured the department.

Guest services takes care of duties such as handling luggage, operating elevators, escorting guests to their rooms, inspecting guest rooms, parking cars, hailing taxis, and other miscellaneous duties, such as running errands and providing information on local current events.

Since their duties are completely guest related, these employees should be equipped with good interpersonal and guest relation skills and should have good knowledge of the property, its location, and the surrounding area.

If the front office is considered the heart of the hotel, guest service employees are its arms and legs.

Housekeeping

The housekeeping department is involved in maintaining and cleaning guest rooms, public areas, and meeting facilities. Housekeepers often also operate the property's laundry and service its recreational areas (e.g., the weight room, the sauna, and the pool).

The executive housekeeper, in charge of a staff of supervisors and room attendants, has an important position within the hotel operation. Not only does he have the responsibility for linen, laundry, and equipment inventories, he is also in charge of staffing and training. Accurate staffing, planning, and proper training will ensure that rooms are clean on time and ready to be sold again.

In many hotels this department has the largest number of employees. Housekeepers or room attendants clean, on average, about 15 rooms a day, although this number depends on the type of room to be cleaned. This means that properties with more than twenty-five hundred rooms, such as the Excalibur Hotel and Casino in Las Vegas, employ more than 150 room attendants.

Earlier, we talked about the importance of integration and communication. The housekeeping department and the front office update each other almost continuously on the status of guest rooms. It is important for the front office to know the minute a room is clean and ready to be sold again. As stated earlier: a room night not sold is revenue lost forever. The more efficient the housekeeping department, the easier it is for the front desk to assign guests to the rooms of their choice.

Equally, housekeeping needs to know when guests have checked out and how many new guests are expected to check in, so that they can start cleaning rooms as soon as possible.

Cleanliness, promptness, and comfort are essential elements in the guest service experience. It is up to the housekeeping department, together with the front office, to try to avoid one of the most common guest complaints: "My room was not ready."

Maintenance/Engineering

Guests expect their televisions to work, their HVAC (heating, ventilation, and air conditioning) units to function properly, and their showers to have hot and cold running water. If any of these do not function satisfactorily, they will make sure the front office hears about it.

It is a kind of Murphy's Law: if an appliance can break down, it most probably will break down. It is the responsibility of the engineering and maintenance department to prevent and remedy such breakdowns, to make sure that guests have nothing to complain about with regard to the appliances in their rooms, the lighting in the rooms and the public areas, and the locks on their doors.

Engineering and maintenance takes care of a property's physical facilities, not only in the guest rooms but also in public areas, the back of the house, and the exterior of the hotel. They deal with plumbing, electrical systems, and maintenance and repairs inside and outside of the hotel.

The importance of the maintenance and engineering department has increased tremendously in recent years for two reasons:

1. The ever-increasing emphasis on the service aspect means that guest complaints and reports from departments such as housekeeping have to be dealt with promptly. An engineer has to be on duty every hour of the day. HVAC units have a tendency to break down at 3:00 A.M.
2. Utility rates have gone up significantly over the past few decades. Whereas hotels paid as much as 1% of revenue for utilities in the 1960s, they now pay more than 5% of revenue for energy (Figure 1). Control of energy consumption has become of vital importance to the hotel industry. Cost containment through servicing, duty cycling (turning off equipment sequentially for a period of time to reduce energy consumption), and other energy-saving techniques, has been added to the responsibilities of maintenance and engineering.

The engineering department is managed by a chief engineer who is in charge of a staff of maintenance experts. Other departments such as housekeeping, front office, security, and food and beverage provide him with the necessary information so that she can do her job promptly and effectively.

Security

The lodging industry is a hospitality business. Being hospitable not only means catering to the needs and desires of your guests, it also means making sure that they are accommodated safely and that their belongings are secure.

It has become more and more important in this day and age to safeguard the safety and security of guests, the property, and its employees. Thirty years ago security was the responsibility of one person, who was in charge of safety and security and usually other areas as well. Today, hotels have security departments and require all of their employees to complete safety and security courses. Although every employee is responsible for guest safety and security and protection of hotel property, this is only peripheral to his primary job. Security officers now make security and safety a full-time job focus.

Adequate security for a hotel property consists of several elements. These areas include the following:

1. *Security systems:*fences, alarm systems, closed circuit television, and adequate lighting are commonly used
2. *Security procedures:*screening of employees on hiring, training, and orientation with regard to the hotel's security policies, key issuance procedures, what-if scenarios, and contacts with the police department
3. *Security personnel:*can be uniformed guards who deter crime because of their physical presence, or undercover house detectives who monitor not only guest behavior but also the behavior of employees. It is estimated that most thefts in hotels are committed by employees.

In most properties with a separate security department, the person in charge is the chief of security, who usually has a background in law enforcement. Ultimately, security is the responsibility of the hotel's general manager. Ideally though, it should be the responsibility of every employee.

Security has long been the responsibility of the front office, yet more and more of today's hotels have made security an independent department, answering directly to the general manager. This increased emphasis is an unfortunate yet necessary trend.

Conclusion

The effectiveness of the rooms division is the key to the success of a hotel property. Two-thirds of the hotel's operating revenues are generated through the sale of rooms. Most of the property's square footage is devoted to guest rooms and their support services. And rooms generate the largest departmental profit.

This chapter looked at the importance of the rooms division, the interaction of the various departments through integrated property management systems and some of the duties performed by those individual departments.

Reservations, front desk, and PBX are revenue centers within the rooms division. These are the departments that generate revenue by selling rooms and other services.

Housekeeping, engineering/maintenance, guest services, and security are support centers within the rooms division. They are equally important: without support centers, revenue centers cannot exist.

The person in charge of the rooms division is normally called the rooms division manager. This position may also be referred to as resident manager, rooms manager, or executive assistant manager. The title is not very important; the duties of the position are what count.

What then are the duties of the position? We started out by saying that the function of the rooms division is to accommodate guests comfortably, safely, and efficiently. So, rooms division managers are responsible for the selling and maintenance of the rooms, controlling the division's costs, staffing its departments, maintaining security and safety, and facilitating the communication between the individual departments and between the rooms division and the general manager's office.

Many entrants into the lodging industry will find their first positions in the rooms division, and many rooms division managers will eventually enter general management ranks. This is not surprising, because the rooms division truly is the heart of the hotel. Its responsibilities cover all major areas of the operation and provide an excellent introduction to hotel operations. The success of the rooms division is crucial to the property's overall success.

——References———

[1] _1993 HOST Report._ Smith Travel Research.
[2] _1993 HOST Report._ Smith Travel Research.

19

The Role and Functions of Human Resource Management

H. A. Divine
University of Denver

The objective of this paper is to provide an introductory overview of the human resources function in the hospitality industry. Over time, there has been an increasing awareness of the critical significance of this functional area. Once human resource management was seen as a purely mechanical processing function of putting people in jobs, but a new dynamic has emerged. Born of the increased realization that employees and their interaction with guests is the most critical element in guest services, human resources has taken on much greater importance.

Factors cited as being causal to this thinking departed from the conventional wisdom during the 1980s. Before that time, little attention was paid to human resources. There was adequate labor both in terms of quality and quantity. If workers were unhappy, they were easily replaced with others equally qualified. Scant attention was paid to the experience that was provided for guests in terms of interaction with employees. It was an era when quality was measured more in terms of amenities, facilities, and products than in human interactions.

The 1980s were a period when attention was first focused in any concerted way on human resources. Attention was paid to the function because the industry was expanding rapidly, there was a need for additional labor, and the supply of labor from traditional sources was in steep decline. This created a supply and demand imbalance, hence an increase in costs as competition for available labor heightened. In addition to the inevitable increase in labor costs related to an imbalance in supply and demand and the bidding wars that resulted, the federal and state governments increased minimum wage costs during this period. These changes, coupled with the initial thoughts about the effects of labor on perceived quality service, helped focus some executive attention on the human resource area.

These elements plus several others have further heightened the importance of human resources as a functional area in the 1990s. While some personnel pressures on parts of the industry have eased due to recessionary periods, the costs associated with labor have continued to increase and are projected to continue to do so for the foreseeable future. These costs are associated as much with the nature and quality of the labor pool as it is with the numbers. Arguably, the educational system has declined in its effectiveness to the point that possession of a high school diploma may not assure an employer of basic employability of the individual who has one. Additionally, there have been massive changes in the demographics of the labor pool in the United States. The diversity now present in the work force creates new challenges for human resource departments as well as for operating departments. Such factors as literacy and differences in culture and values create new opportunities for managerial creativity at both the operating and staff levels of the organization.

At the same time that the labor supply has proven to provide challenges, two other phenomena have emerged to challenge the hospitality industry.

First, the industry has moved from a developing, growing industry to one that is mature. This means that growth generally comes at a cost to a competitor. In service industries such as hospitality, one of the primary ways in which one competes is to improve the quality of services offered and the perceived value to the customer. Because services depend on the interaction of the front-line employee with the guest or customer, this puts much more pressure on the organization to ensure that employees offering service do so in a quality way. This is, to a degree, further complicated by the fact that guests are becoming increasingly sophisticated and more aware of their purchase options.

Second, there is a trend towards ever-greater government intervention in business in general and the hospitality industry specifically. There are ever-increasing numbers of mandates handed down by government bodies from the federal level to the municipal level, and all in between, which directly affect business and human resources within those businesses. From mandated leaves to health care, to workers' compensation, to increases in the minimum wage at state and federal levels—all affect how an organization does business. They also bring into sharp focus the need to pay closer attention to the human part of the managerial equation.

The role of the human resource department or, in smaller operations, the attention given to human resources by management, is expanding dramatically. The expanded role is driven by increased government intervention at all levels, increased cost of labor, greater diversity in the work force, and greater competitive pressure for quality improvement. Because one of the primary goals of all business is to produce a profit, all of those elements that effect the profitability of an organization must receive attention if there is to be satisfactory return on investment. The environment for business is and will become even more dynamic. In such an environment, human resource considerations will have the same strategic importance in the future as finance, real estate, and accounting have had in the past.

The role or mission of human resource management as a department or function is to contribute to the mission of the organization that it supports. In general, whether the parent entity is a profit or nonprofit organization, the primary objectives are to ensure a highly productive, stable, and motivated work force. The human resources task, then, includes the acquisition (recruitment and selection), preparation (orientation, socialization, training), and maintenance (salary, wages, benefits, evaluation), of a highly effective and efficient work force. While human resources will help in the training and development of management, it is generally beyond the objectives of this department to ensure that the dynamics of the workplace (the interaction between worker and supervisor) are optimal. Rather, as a staff department, it supports line management. Therefore, operating management needs to use the talent of human resource staff just as they rely upon accounting and finance departments.

In addition to the objectives already mentioned, human resources usually is responsible for the organization's compliance with all applicable federal, state, and municipal legislation and regulation of employment. At one time, this was a minor portion of the responsibilities of the human resource departments; however, in recent years it represents a major component that will continue to grow. Not only are there more laws and regulations being passed, but the complexities of their implementation in the hospitality industry and the level of fines for noncompliance make the human resources function increasingly important.

In review, the role or mission of human resources appears simple; however, the methods it uses are very complex.

Functions of Human Resources

Figure 1 shows the major functions of human resources as organized into six major categories.

Planning

Increasingly, executive management of organizations in the hospitality field is including human resource concerns in the corporate strategic planning process. This ensures that human factors within the corporation are given the same priority as finance and other areas. Of all the changes in organizational dynamics over the past 15 years, perhaps the most dramatic has been the recognition of the importance of people to the success of any organization. The recognition that the customer wants quality service, and that this is only achievable through a highly committed, trained, and empowered work force, is a surprisingly recent phenomenon. Human resource considerations have become an absolutely essential portion of the strategic plan.

Other planning tasks that are handled by human resources are long- and short-term personnel needs. These forecasts, coordinated with other major elements in the organization or unit, allow for the timely acquisition and preparation of a work force to serve the needs of the customer. Planning also includes looking at new populations as potential employees for the organization.

Acquisition

This functional area includes those steps that must be taken to attract qualified applications to the organization. A sensitivity to the increasing diversity of the work force in the United States is essential in attracting potentially successful individuals. While the general supply and demand of labor follows general economic conditions in the marketplace, successful organizations do not change their recruitment practices in response to the supply of potential workers. To attract the very best applicants requires as concerted an effort in times

Planning	Strategic Long- and short-term Human Resource plans
Acquisition	Recruitment Screening Selection
Preparation	Orientation Socialization Training
Maintenance	Salary Wages Benefits Evaluation Mediation
Legal and unions	Compliance with federal, state and locality laws and regulations
Separation	Termination for cause (rule or performance) Layoffs/adjustments to work force

Figure 1. The Functions of Human Resource Management

when there are many people looking for work as when there are few. The screening of applicants and final selection are probably two of the most important elements of human resource management. If there is a failure to appreciate the job requirements and the fit between the individual, the job, and the organization, no amount of remedial work later will fix the mismatch. It is at this point that the organization must ensure compliance with all legislation regarding equal employment opportunities.

Preparation

This general function includes all of the activities that prepare the individual to fit into the organization and become a contributing member. As will be seen later in this chapter, the investment made in orientation and socialization are key to reduced employee turnover.

Maintenance

Wage and salary administration and benefits administration are specialized areas, which, when handled well, seem to contribute only slightly but when done poorly or inconsistently lead to disastrous results. Of all the functions, these two and the legal and union areas are the most technical and therefore are generally managed by specialists.

Wage and salary administration is truly a joint effort between the human resource specialist providing workable evaluation systems and tools and line management using these systems and tools to provide periodic and formal performance evaluations to all individuals within the organization.

A role of increasing importance in human resources is that of mediator. In union establishments contractual clauses generally stipulate grievance procedures that eventually involve a disinterested third party for resolution. Progressive firms have established internal systems to provide the employee, or potential employee in certain cases, with a formalized process for resolving difficulties whether in terms of alleged sexual harassment, wrongful discharge, reasonable accommodation, or any other alleged difficulties between employees and their supervisors or other employees. Insofar as there is trust of these individuals by the employees, the system has great promise for resolving employment difficulties.

Legal and Unions

As mentioned previously, these are technical areas that are managed by specialists who ensure that operating management are aware of changes in public policy and regulations which impact them. For example, as more regulations are put into effect regarding teenaged workers it is important that the human resource specialist make line management aware of such changes. Too, it is normal in unionized situations to have specialists who work in the areas of negotiation and overall maintenance of the contract. It is also incumbent on these specialists to keep line management informed of the interpretation of the contract. Likewise, it is important for line management to provide information to these specialists about particularly difficult contract provisions so that they can be negotiated in the future.

Separation

The final major element in human resource management is separation, voluntary or not, of an employee from the organization. Involuntary separation has two major causes. The first is a situation in which shifts occur in business needs and skills needed, causing a mismatch between the skills and abilities of the employee and the needs of the organization. Or, the organization has inadequate business and it must lay off individuals. Generally, every effort is made to find alternative jobs, or retraining is undertaken, but layoffs may occur. In those instances, many firms are providing some form of outplacement service to help employees find other work.

The second involuntary separation is when an employee is terminated for cause. In general, there are two possible elements of cause and they are for violation of rules or for unsatisfactory or inadequate performance on the jobs. The primary function of human resources in these instances is to ensure that individuals are not wrongfully discharged. Were rules and performance standards clearly communicated? Was there a uniformity in the enforcement of rules and standards? Was there documentation of violations or failure to meet standards? In those cases in which immediate termination is not called for, were there warnings? Was there an opportunity for improvement of performance? If all these conditions have been met, individuals can be terminated for cause. While it is the responsibility of the human resources personnel to ensure that all of the requirements are met, line management must actually do the documentation.

This section has provided a brief overview of the various elements that must be dealt with in the management of an organization. In large organizations these functions generally are performed by human resource departments. In small organizations, the functions must still be performed but there may not be a specific department. In these instances someone in the organization must be identified as being responsible for the various elements.

Primary Functions of Human Resource Management

Figure 2 depicts the flow of planning and the execution of the various functions relating to the staffing of any organization. Because this system exists both within the larger corporate system as well as a societal context, many external social, economic, political, and legal forces affect it at all times.

Historically, the hospitality industry has concentrated on the functions shown in the center of the chart: selection processes, orientation, training, evaluation, and the like. However, only recently has the industry become involved in managerial analysis to determine need and overall planning within the personnel function.

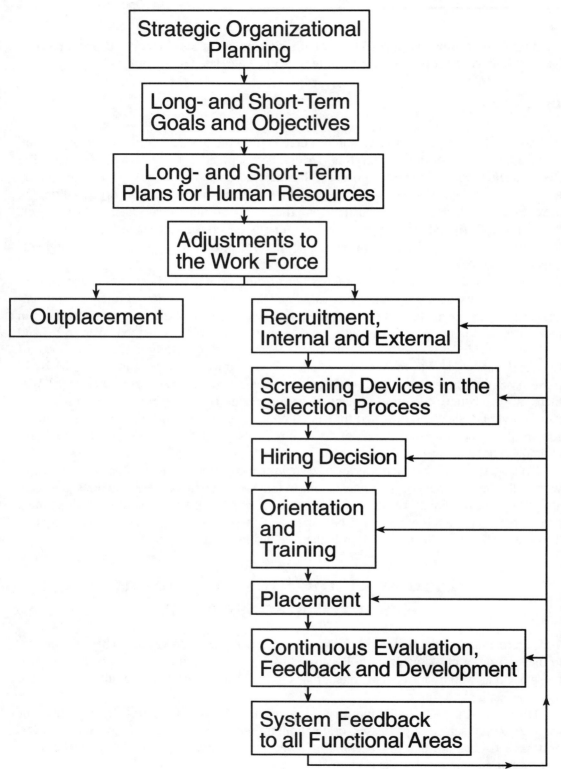

Figure 2. The Flow of Planning and Execution of Functions Relating to Staffing Organizations

Management must engage in long-range human resource planning predicated on both long- and short-term projections of need. The human resources planner must be aware of short-, medium- and long-range corporate planning relative to expansion and other operational changes. It is only possible to project labor requirements if all operational plans are known.

In addition to long-range human resource planning, management must carefully review what is being done in the positions that exist. Studying each job in an organized way is called job analysis. It consists of gathering information relative to the job from an interview with the individual who currently does the job, personally observing of the job being done, and interviewing the supervisor of the individual doing the job. Information thus gathered provides a fair view of the content and context of the job as currently performed. That information then is analyzed to determine whether management agrees with the way the job is performed. The results of the information gathering and analysis form the basis for the job description and the job specification. Simply stated, job descriptions contain information about job duties and responsibilities, relationships between jobs, and general working conditions. The job specification describes necessary qualifications in terms of education, training, skills, experience, and other criteria. The job descriptions communicate the duties to be performed to the person who will do the job. As such, they form the central basis for training and evaluation of workers. The job specification, in outlining the qualifications needed to perform the job, is primarily used in recruitment and selection of individuals for the job. Projections of human resource needs, job analysis and resultant job descriptions, and job specifications are all part of the planning process. If these tasks are not done or not done well, other activities may suffer, as described below.

The next step in the flow of functions is recruitment of individuals to perform the jobs that have been identified. Jobs above the entry level may be filled from two sources. The first is internal, through promotion of individuals currently working in the organization, and the second is from outside the organization. Both sources have advantages. There are morale benefits as well as a knowledge benefit in promotion from within. A lack of promotion from within creates dissatisfaction on the part of individuals within the organization and may cause individuals to leave. A carefully structured promotion or career ladder plan for individuals that indicates a progression of steps from dishwasher to cook has a positive effect upon morale. Another consideration is that individuals from within the organization already know a lot about how it functions, knowledge that a newcomer must take time to learn. This knowledge factor exists on both sides of the employer–employee equation. The employer has knowledge about the individual that is very difficult to find out about outside job applicants—the will to work. The willingness to work, and to work well, is far easier to measure and assess than the motivational aspects of the individual. There are, however, some benefits that may be derived from seeking applicants from outside the firm. The primary benefit is that the firm is opening itself to new ideas at a level in the organization where they may be acted upon. Firms that only bring individuals in at the bottom risk stagnation because all employees with any decision-making power will be imbued with organizational values imposed by superiors. The second factor is that there may not be as qualified an individual with the organization as outside. In this case it would hardly be in the best interest of the organization to proceed blindly with a promotion-from-within policy.

Recruitment from outside takes the form of a carefully planned campaign geared to solicit as many qualified and interested applicants as possible. This means that different sources would be explored for various levels of employees. Entry-level employees are sought through help-wanted ads, public employment agencies, high schools, and colleges as well as senior citizen centers for part-time workers. As one proceeds up the hierarchy of jobs, recruitment campaigns for cooks, bakers, bartenders, and service personnel are directed toward training programs for these jobs in high schools, vocational and technical schools, and community and junior colleges as well as help-wanted ads and union hiring halls. For management positions, college recruitment is done and employing private employment agencies are called on. The campaign should be suited to the level of employee sought. This goes a long way toward reducing the numbers of under- and overqualified individuals applying for the positions available. Another factor is the clear delineation in all advertisements of the qualifications sought.

Attention must be given in the recruitment campaign to organizational objectives relating to affirmative action. It is necessary to expand the sources to include those agencies within the community that act as clearinghouses for minority workers. Affirmative action means that the organization takes positive steps toward creating diversity in the work force through the placement of minorities and women in all levels of the organization. This mandates good training and evaluation processes; however, those programs are useless unless the targeted groups are brought into the organization in the first place.

The hospitality industry has a good record relative to providing opportunities for minorities and women and is actively engaged in expanding upper-level opportunities through training and promotions.

The screening process begins with a pool of potential employees. The first element in screening is gathering data about applicants through an application form, resumes, and biographical sketches. This information, used in conjunction with the job specification, amounts to a preliminary screening. Those who do not possess the requisite skill or experience are eliminated. The process moves through a series of steps including interviews, testing if valid job-related tests are available, and reference checks. In all these steps, a selection-out system operates until the final candidates are chosen. In other words, at the beginning of the process the emphasis is on eliminating those who do not meet various criteria. It is only when the final candidates are selected that the process moves on to finding out which candidate is best. In the hospitality industry much weight is placed on the interview. In fact, more reliance is placed on it than can be supported by existing research. Therefore, interviewers must be carefully trained, and more than one interview and interviewer must be used. A well-thought-out, planned, and organized process is desirable and promises the best long-term results. Unfortunately, in the hospitality industry, sometimes all this planning goes awry and there is an immediate need for someone to fill a particular job. All the planning can do is reduce the incidence of these emergencies, not eliminate them. Therefore, it is an excellent idea for operators to have a back-up labor pool of part-time personnel who can be called in to work on short notice. This allows a temporary respite and an opportunity to start the recruitment and selection process in a logical manner. The alternative reaction to emergencies caused by people not reporting for work or quitting is to hire in haste without attention to proper recruitment or selection methods. The result is "warm-body" hiring, wherein the primary interest is in placing someone on the job immediately. This can have serious repercussions later.

Following the decision to hire, it is necessary to consider orientation and training programs. An orientation program should acquaint the individual with all of the aspects of the job and the company. Due to the high levels of stress present in the interview setting, it should not be assumed that newly hired individuals will remember such things as pay dates, schedules, and the like. Therefore, all of these factors must be reviewed with the new hire. Written material should be available concerning rules and regulations, benefit plans, and other items for which the employee is held accountable. Such written material reinforces the oral communication. Too, use of a checklist in presenting the orientation items assures their coverage in all presentations. Finally, the orientation should include a familiarization with the entire facility and company including an introduction to all coworkers. A large percentage of employee turnover occurs within the first few weeks of employment. This has in large measure been attributed to a failure in orientation or training processes.

Orientation should lead naturally into the next step in the process, which is training. All new employees need some training. If a front desk clerk is hired who has been a front desk clerk in a similar operation previously, the level of technical "how to" training would be minimal. However, it still is necessary to train this individual in the way this operation wants things done. Training programs take many forms including audiovisual programs, various on-the-job training programs, lectures, and simulations. The training methods should fit the training task. Simulations, while valuable for exploring different approaches to customers, are not the preferred method for teaching sanitation codes. Likewise, most audiovisual programs are useful for demonstrating certain techniques only if followed up with actual experience under the tutelage of a trained individual. Training should be based first on what is needed to perform the job and then on advancement possibilities. As such, the training program should be geared to the job description, which spells out the job requirements.

Following the training programs developed to teach both technical and attitudinal components of the job, the individual is placed in the job.

Once the individual is placed on the job as a trained worker, the responsibilities of the human resource department do not cease. All supervisors are responsible for the physical and emotional climate in their work areas. They are responsible for adherence to OSHA safety standards as well as local and state codes. Since at times adherence to the letter of safety standards may cause decreases in productivity, it is necessary to split the responsibility for each. The line supervisor, chef, bartender, or shift manager has the responsibility for productivity, which leads to the profit on which her evaluation is primarily based. It is, therefore, necessary to charge a department with the responsibility to assure safety standards are met. This does not mean that line supervisors need not be trained; rather, they do need to be trained. However, there must be a monitor, just as there must be a monitor for sanitation.

Likewise, the line supervisor is responsible for the emotional environment in the workplace. This includes the leadership style used as well as how disciplinary action is administered. Much has been written about leadership and how leadership style affects the motivation of subordinates and the general organizational climate. This subject is beyond the scope of this chapter, other than to note that the human resource department should monitor the organizational behavioral climate periodically to ensure that it is consistent with the desires of the organization as a whole.

An ongoing function of human resource management is the training of supervisory personnel in evaluation techniques. The function of employee evaluation is extremely important both to the organization and to the individuals involved.

The six primary uses of employee appraisal systems include the following:

1. Periodic appraisal helps create and maintain desired employee performance. Because appraisal will point out deviations from desired standards as well as adherence to such standards, it allows for both correction of deviations and reinforcement of satisfactory work.
2. Appraisals should highlight those areas where there is a need for growth and development. Further training can be given in such areas.
3. The evaluative process itself enhances the supervisor's understanding of the job. It provides the supervisor with a better view of operations.
4. The results of appraisals can be used in planning job changes such as promotions, transfers, and discharges.
5. Appraisal results can indicate needs for compensation adjustments, either increases or decreases.
6. Finally, the results of an appraisal system may be used to validate various other personnel programs, such as selection and training.

There are also five problems or weaknesses for the human resource department to consider in training supervisors to conduct evaluations.

1. The "halo effect" occurs when the evaluator allows one single aspect of job performance to overshadow all other aspects. The halo effect can be either positive or negative.
2. A supervisor can be either too lenient or too strict with the individuals being evaluated. While this may lead to some consistency within the unit, it would lead to distortions, either high or low, if the individuals were compared with others outside the unit.
3. Central tendency occurs when a supervisor rates all individuals within a unit as average.
4. The use the organization is to make of the evaluation data tends to influence the results. If the data is to be used primarily for determining training needs, the evaluations will be somewhat lower than if they are to be used for pay purposes.
5. When individuals evaluate others, they are often influenced either positively or negatively by the individual's most recent behavior.

Human resource departments can sidestep most of these problems through forms that spread the individuals being rated on a continuum through forced distribution. They also can avoid inaccurate evaluations through using them for several purposes and through some type of critical incident process that calls for noting behavior at shorter intervals than the every six months or year for formal evaluations. Another weakness is the most difficult to overcome because its foundation is not job related. It is called interpersonal bias, wherein the evaluation either positive or negative is based upon nonjob factors. Such bias is difficult to guard against and can only be avoided by training supervisors in the fact that interpersonal factors may enter in and they must be discounted. A viable and reliable evaluation program is of utmost importance to any organization. It lets the employee know, in a formal way, how he is progressing.

These functions all relate to the human side of the enterprise: how the organization's needs are determined, through the processes of finding someone to fill the needs, providing them with training, adequate supervision, and evaluation of their progress. Another factor that management must consider in dealing with employees is the subject of unions in the hospitality industry.

Unions and unionization generally are an extremely controversial subject. Operators who do not have unions representing their workers generally vehemently oppose unionization. Likewise, those operators who have recognized and bargain with unions generally would not be disappointed if the unions went away. On the other hand, unions feel that they are doing a great deal of good for the people they represent and cannot generally understand the vehemence of the feelings against them.

Most unions now in existence were formed for the collective economic protection of the membership. Individual employees felt they had little economic power when dealing with management: the union provides a voice that is heard. The single most important aspect in influencing individuals to join unions is a sense of dissatisfaction with the employer rather than some philosophic or social belief. Such dissatisfaction is born of two primary factors. The first is economic, when the employee feels that the reward structure is inadequate. The second is an employee's feeling of powerlessness when dealing with individual supervisors whose actions seem capricious.

The influence of unions on wages and working conditions in the hospitality industry is felt far beyond those facilities that have negotiated agreements. The contract in an area becomes a benchmark against which operators compare their operations and salary and benefit packages. Most of the hospitality industry is nonunion; however, this does not mean that unions do not serve a purpose, nor does it mean that they are unimportant. The presence of a union forces management to be more formal in their dealings with employees in order to satisfy elements of the contractual agreement. As such, it adds rigidity to the employment picture. Some see this as positive and others as negative.

The question of unions in the hospitality industry is a complex one. The role of human resource departments is generally to so structure their programs to eliminate any perceived need on the part of an employee for an intervening third party in the employment situation. Or in the case of unionized companies, to so structure the human resource programs to conform both in spirit and letter to the contractual agreement. One extremely important added feature is the training of supervisors to understand and follow the contract.

As stated, generally unions found a foothold in the hospitality industry due to a perceived failure to provide a positive working environment.

20

Women and Other Minorities in Hospitality Management

Jenene G. Garey, Ph.D
New York University

The advance of women and other minorities in hospitality management over the last 25 years continues to parallel the growth of these groups for all industries—slow and frustrating . . . and getting slower according to many reports. Some experts believed, that by this time, the percentage of women and minorities in management would be increasing more rapidly, but this is not occurring. This chapter provides background details and recommendations for improving the status and pay of women and other minorities. However, we are working with limited information about women in the industry and there is even less about minorities. We do know that the decline of males in the work force and the dramatic increase in the participation of women and other minorities requires corporations and government to consciously examine the issues and take action.

Executives and Managers—Current Status

Restaurants and Institutions (R&I) reports in its 1992 (Dec. 23, 1992) survey that of the 2,039 respondents, men on the average earned $44,600 and women $32,500. In the areas of increases and increase with promotion, men received a higher percentage than did women. The male-to-female ratio on the survey was 65:35. The 1989 R&I JOB$ Survey (August 7) reports that 90% of the female executives are earning less than $40,000 and only 10% earn more than $75,000.

The Bureau of Labor Statistics reports that there are 6.1 million female managers in 1989, up from 3.5 million in 1983. According to the **Economist** (March 28, 1992) quoting the 1989 Census Bureau data, only 18% of American workers earning $50,000 to $75,000 were women and only 12% of those earning over $75,000 were women. A 1987 University of Michigan survey (N = 800) (1, p. 20) of newly promoted executives, for all industries, states that only 3% of the upper level promotions were women, and at the vice-president level the number of women being promoted was decreasing. A 1992 **Fortune** article "When will women get to the top?" (Sept 21, p. 44) reports that in a poll of 201 chief executives of the nations largest companies, only 16% believe that it is "very likely" or "somewhat likely" that they could be succeeded by a female CEO in the next 10 years. "And only 18% think it's `very likely' that even after 20 years a women would be picked. . . ." For the few CEO's in this survey who would admit that the issue is discrimination—they stated, women are working hard and are qualified, but "CEO's, tend to want to pass their job along to someone who's the image and likeness of themselves." On the other hand, 64% said women lacked experience for the CEO position. Senior management positions in these CEO's companies consisted of 4.8% women in 1991, up from 1986 when 2.9% were women.

Business Week (June 8, 1992) in its cover story on corporate women continues to paint a picture of women and corporations only holding the ground that women currently have achieved. In the lower and middle management ranks, the numbers of women are up 15% from 15 years ago. The critical mass is moving upward, with the ranks of chief financial officer and marketing vice presidents being filled by women who graduated from business schools in the past 15 years. BW's survey of 400 women executives in corporations with $100 million or more in annual sales indicates a glass ceiling—56% of women receive a lower salary than men in the same position, and 52% said the rate of progress in hiring and promotion of women has slowed.

Haker states that the percentage growth of women employed as managers and administrators nationwide from 1970 to 1980 rose 91.7%; yet that number represents change of only 3.6% to 6.9% of the work force.[2] However, a 1990 study of 4,000 senior executives reported in *Business Week* (June 8, 1992, p. 78) estimates by the year 2000 women will hold 16% of upper-management positions. *Management Review* (December 1987, p. 44) indicated that one-third of all management positions are held by women, but the senior management in major U.S. corporations is less than 5% female.

The small increase in the number of women executives has not had any effect on the number of women who head a Fortune 500 company. Katharine Graham, chairperson of the *Washington Post,* was the sole woman with that distinction. Marion Sandler of Golden West Financial has joined the ranks, but shares the post with her husband. And like Graham, most other women who head major firms are connected to the company by family ties. Management experts predict the number of women heading Fortune 500 companies will change within the next 20 years as a result of work experience bringing them to the top.

The picture is even bleaker if we identify women who serve on a board of directors. *The New York Times* reported (July 5, 1984) that "Women . . . are Still the Exception." According to a survey completed by Catalyst, a nonprofit research organization that works with corporations to foster women leaders, 46% of the largest American companies still have no women on their boards. Today, women fill only 3% (455 women) of the 14,000 directorships covered by the *Fortune* magazine's 1,000 leading concerns, an increase from 46 women in 1969.

Historically

Over the past 25 years the visibility of women in the work force has been increasing, although slowly. The Commission on the Status of Women established by President John F. Kennedy in 1961, the passage of the 1964 Civil Rights Act, and the subsequent attempt to pass the Equal Rights Amendment have led to changing women's roles in society and progress toward entering traditionally male-dominated occupations.

The book of Genesis and the story of creation of woman from Adam's rib may be a starting point for the differences in the status of men and women. The Bible clarifies the female–male relationship, "For man is not of woman; but woman of man. Neither is man created for woman; but woman for man." (1 Cor. 11). The Koran and Judaism contain similar references to the "place of women in society." As Bem and Bem state in "Training the Woman to Know Her Place,"[3] sexism has become a nonconscious ideology. Parents unconsciously raise a girl child to be sensitive, emotional, and warm, and a boy child to be independent, assertive, and intellectually committed. Consider that we can predict fairly successfully what a girl child will be doing 25 years from today, but not a boy child.

Women are changing, according to a study commissioned by _Cosmopolitan_ magazine and reported in the _New York Times_ (August 18, 1986). Women who reached adulthood in the late 1960s and early 1970s had anticipated marrying and dropping out of the work force as their mothers had done. However, many remained in the work force due to financial need and incentives for career potential. Women now in their twenties, however, have a strong commitment to a career. This younger group has obtained the necessary educational credentials, and they have more control over the timing of their marriage and birth of their children. This later generation has already shown an orientation toward employment plus the family as an institution, which may cause changes in attitudes toward work and how people lead their lives. Moreover, this group has identified what the companies need to do for families, not just for women, when both parents work.

Women's progress toward changing women's roles is a popular topic. Attitudes, the particular view or a framework to caste a belief or opinion, change through influence or persuasion. However, an attitudinal change may not be reflected in a behavioral change. Margaret Mead stated that "to the extent men believe they achieve a sense of their intrinsic masculinity only in those situations in which women know less, earn less, achieve less, and win less recognition than they do, effort to put the recommendations of the Commission (on the Status of Women) into practice will be effectively . . . sabotaged."[4]

Changes in the Work Force, Employment by Women

The outlook for the labor force through 2005 is propelled by an aging of the baby-boom generation, with 2005 having the highest median age labor force ever, 40.6 years. By 2005 69% of the work force is predicted to be 25 to 64 years old, compared to 60.6% in 1975, when 24.1% was under 24. The group under 24 years of age in 2005 will represent 16% of the work force. In 2005 151 million will be working or looking for work, an increase of 26 million or 20% from 1990 (*Monthly Labor Review,* November 1991). Women will increase by 14.8 million to 71.4 million or 26%, a smaller percentage than in 1975–1990 when the growth was 51%. Blacks will increase by 4.2 million to 17.8 million, 32% compared with a 46% increase in 1975–1990; Asians will increase by 4.2 million to 7.2 million, 74% compared to 145% for the previous 15 years; and Hispanics are expected to increase by 7.2 million to 16.8 million, a 75% change. The biggest change is due to changes in the labor force as a result of the 1990 immigration law.

In 1990 57% of all women, more than 57 million in the United States, worked outside the home, a substantial increase from 37.5 million in 1975.[5] Employed women in the civilian work force, age 16 and over, accounted for a change of 50.9% from 1975 to 1990 (*MLR,* November 1991). Some projections for the year 2000 call for the number of employed women to increase to 61%.[5] Black females and males are expected to account for more than 29% of the growth in the work force, and all women will account for 60% of the growth anticipated by 1995.[5,6] By the year 2000 the share of women, blacks, and Hispanics will increase and workers will be older; 50% of the work force will be 35 to 54 years old.[5] However, white women by 2005 are projected to increase "their participation more than any other group" in the labor force (*MLR,* 1991, p. 39).

Census data for all managerial and professional specialties shows that in 1989, the latest year for which census data is available, 45.2% were women, 6.1% of them black and 3.7% Hispanic. *Monthly Labor Review* (November 1990, p. 17) reports that among college-educated employed managers and professionals, black men represent 4.3% of all men and black women represent 8.2% of all women. Overall, college-educated black men earned 72% to 79% of the median earnings of white men. The gap is greater than it was ten years earlier in 1979. For black and white women there were nearly equal median weekly earnings.

The issue of who is going to be available to fill positions in the future is simple— women and other minorities will make up most of the work force. However, companies may not be doing all they can to help. *Fortune* (September 21, 1992, p./ts. 44) says the smartest companies are devoting more time and resources to developing female middle managers and are hiring full-time "diversity managers." Companies also need to give women an equal chance for new assignments. The fact that women work primarily in communications and human resources positions that don't lead upward should not be a barrier. The issue is also one of re-socialization and changing prejudices through workshops that address stereotypical behavior. Another need is for work-family benefit programs. Other factors, discussed elsewhere and in more detail in this chapter, are mentoring and networks.

Since 1950 two-thirds of all women workers have been employed in the service sector. Women traditionally hold clerical and secretarial, teacher, and nurse positions. These are termed the female-dominated positions and explain in part why change has come slowly for women.[5] Restaurant, cafeteria, and bar managers (Bureau of Census, 1982) employed 46% more people in 1981 than 1972; however, the percentage of these positions occupied by females has risen only 24% in the same period.

Pay for women continues at 69% of that for men in the 35–44 year age group, but younger women ages 25 to 34 earn 79.6 cents for every dollar earned by a man. A recent setback that might have narrowed the earning gap has been judicial reluctance to provide equal pay for jobs of comparable value, or "comparable worth," from a 1981 Supreme Court ruling of Title VII of the Civil Rights Act of 1964. Title VII prohibits discrimination on the basis of race, color, sex, national origin, and religion in public and private employment. Lower courts have noted that Title VII's intent is to guarantee equal opportunities in the job market. Some states have been enacting laws to adjust compensation packages. However, the Equal Employment Opportunity Commission (EEOC) in 1985 stated that federal antidiscrimination laws do not require employers to provide equal compensation for jobs of comparable worth. Many experts view the issue as one fruit of the past Republican administrations and look forward to possible changes.

Some positive changes are taking place for women. Since 1960 there has been a radical change to a society in which today almost everyone is paid to work. The Hudson Institute predicted in 1987 that "Over the next 13 years, policies and patterns of child rearing, taxation, pensions, hiring, compensation, and industrial structure will change to conform to the new realities . . ." (p. 87). *Business Week* (June 8, 1992, p. 74) in its cover story reported that in 1981 women represented 1% of the senior executives versus 3% in 1991, and 27% versus 41%, respectively, for managers. Another factor that may cause a faster change is the corporate restructuring (and leveraged buyouts) which has changed male-dominated cultures. Women now are focusing on their careers, although there are still many who don't want to make family sacrifices, and Catalyst president Felice Schwartz thinks women are expressing male qualities such as "goal orientation, competitiveness, the ability to conceptualize, and the aggressive pursuit of responsibility."

Research on Men and Women Corporate Officers

In 1965 the *Harvard Business Review* conducted a survey to determine how women were viewed for "their managerial characteristics and for their suitability for top corporate positions."[6] In 1965, "54% of the men and 50% of the women thought that women rarely expect or desire positions of authority." Twenty years later, this study was repeated, and only 9% of men and 4% of women surveyed think that women don't want top jobs.[7] Some of the other findings include the following:

1. Both men and women respondents expressed a favorable attitude toward women executives (not true 20 years ago).
2. Men are more willing to work for a female boss. However, both men and women believe women are not comfortable working for a female supervisor.
3. Fifty-nine percent of men believe that women need to be exceptional to succeed today (in 1965, 90% felt this way).

Most 1985 respondents did not feel that the passage of the Civil Rights Act, Title VII (previously discussed), changed attitudes; laws can "change behavior and that new behavior often leads to new attitudes." As one female vice president commented, women in management have made tremendous advances over the last ten years, which I believe reflects the excellence and competence of those women who have succeeded. However, sad to say, I do not believe many of those opportunities would have arisen in the first place without equal opportunity legislation and oversight by federal and local governments. This oversight and enforcement, therefore, must continue to exist.

Rosabeth Kanter (Moss) in *Men and Women of the Corporation* studied one corporation's structure and tied her findings to those of other researchers.[8] On the basis of the organizational structure, some of the reasons she gives for why women don't occupy more of the management positions include the following:

- One, managers are concerned about giving up control and attempt to foster homogeneity in the process of maintaining status quo. In selecting new managers they choose people like themselves.
- Two, the opportunity perceived by the person shapes her behavior. If there is a feeling of lack of opportunity, it will limit her aspirations. And people with perceived lower mobility become indifferent to opportunity. When there is a lack of opportunities in the work setting, one seeks satisfying activity outside the work setting. Generally, an employee will develop a self-image that matches the situation, so he rationalizes the setting by assuming he is doing what he should be.
- Three, there are various names given—including mentors, godfathers, rabbis, and sponsors— which Kanter and other authors have indicated are a traditional key to getting ahead for men and are critical to the advancement of women. The mentors serves as a godmother (George Dellea, "On the Ladder to the Top, A Mentor is Key Step," *New York Times* January 26, 1981), who will teach, advise, and support the young protégé. Mentors will fight for the person, help bypass hierarchy or bureaucratic structure, and provide reflected power. All of these are essential for the woman trying to move up. However, research shows that generally leaders promote careers of socially similar subordinates.
- Four, can research demonstrate a case for leadership attitude or style which excludes women? The answer is no; there is a favorable attitude toward women and men who have worked with women. However, there is agreement that a woman has to be exceptional, indeed overqualified as a manager to succeed. Any preference for men is a preference for the power which men

already possess. The woman manager stereotyped as abusing power and bossy, having an authoritarian leadership style, is generally the reaction to any male or female lacking sufficient training or experience, not women managers in general.

A major issue facing women managers today, which Kanter discusses, is tokenism. Women and other minorities when represented in an organization in small numbers become labeled as "tokens." They are highly visible as different, and they begin to be evaluated by those who surround them on the basis of appearance and nonability traits. The woman or black stands out in anything they do or do not do. The token's response to the high visibility is extreme self-consciousness as an outsider. Insiders may try to assert solidarity and exaggerate cultural elements, often using obscene jokes or language, or they may go to the other extreme and quarantine the token because that person is different. The system, not the individual, needs to work to alleviate tokenism. Some suggestions to reduce the incidence of tokenism are batch hiring, role models, women's networks, educating leaders about the problem, and giving full support to the program.

Kanter feels that three central explanatory dimensions affect the system: the structure of opportunity, the structure of power, and the proportional distribution of different kinds of people.[8] The corporate setting as explained by the author provides numerous insights into the movement of women into the traditional male domain. Note, there are no fewer problems for blacks or other minorities who strive for managerial positions. Although few people are willing to admit it, we are all color and gender sensitive. Given this fact, companies need to consciously work to alleviate it.

In other research on men and women, company officers have been shown to have very similar motivators. Women rated challenge most important (for men it was rated second), scope of responsibility second (for men it was most important). Opportunity for upward mobility and compensation were next for women, while men rated compensation, then the level of reporting relationship.[9]

According to work by Roos and Reskin there are "four points at which women face institutionalized barriers to equal participation in the labor force: pre-employment training, job access and assignment, job mobility, and retention."[10] While the first two types of barriers occur in the competitive labor markets, the latter types occur in what is called an "internal labor market." These are positions within a particular firm or workplace. If the positions are in male-dominated occupations, then internal labor markets tend to be hierarchical, with the ladder based on on-the-job training, and custom, as well as skill. Women because of expected childbearing are not hired into entry-level positions on such a ladder; if younger women aren't hired at the bottom level, the process increases the gap between men's and women's earning over the work cycle.

Management Women and the New Facts of Life, a recent *Harvard Business Review* article[11] by Felice N. Schwartz, president and founder of Catalyst, has stirred debates and perhaps some attention from male-dominated corporate offices. Her article, often misrepresented as "the Mommy Track," has helped to bring forward a critical issue for corporate review—women cost more to employ in managerial positions. Schwartz states what is known to be true but often not discussed within the corporation, that "career interruptions, plateauing, and turnover are expensive" and unavoidable because "only women have babies and only men make rules." The main point she makes is that gender differences fall into two categories, maternity leave, which is biological, hence unavoidable, and cultural differences, "traditions and expectations of the sexes" that can be dealt with to reduce their effect on costs. To quote Schwartz (p. 66)—which reiterates points made by Moss earlier

> If we are to overcome the cost differential between male and female employees, we need to address the issues that arise when female socialization meets the male corporate culture and masculine rules of career development—issues of behavior and style, of expectation, of stereotypes and preconceptions, of sexual tension and harassment, of female mentoring, lateral mobility, relocation, compensation, and early identification of top performers.

The author urges companies to examine their experience with women, including "women's negative reactions to negative experience, . . . If women's value . . . is greater than the cost to recruit, train and develop them . . . retain them." Several companies are achieving this goal—Corning Glass, Merck, Navistar—by designing programs and setting quotas to help women managers advance (*Fortune,* September 12, 1988, p. 128; *Business Week,* June 29, 1989, p. 71).

Two recent *Harvard Business Review* articles by Schwartz[12] on women and Dickson [13] on minorities in business discuss how these two groups should use their talents to meet the needs of the capitalist corporations—profit. Both authors propose the means to accomplish the imperative—enhance the bottom line. Dickson relates the how Inroads, Inc., "a national organization for training and development of minority professionals in business and technology" had made a difference for participating companies. Schwartz tells companies there are four actions to take to ensure that women function as effectively as men:

1. "Acknowledge . . . [the] biological fact of maternity"
2. "Provide flexibility for men and women who want it"
3. Give women with leadership traits additional management skills and tools needed for excellent performance
4. Remove barriers in the corporate environment that "exist for women but not for men."

Research on Mentoring

Mentoring is an opportunity by junior-level managers to have access to senior members of the organization. That access may provide entry into social networks and modeling of managerial skills. Women may not have mentors because of lack of access, assumed lack of long-term career commitment by male mentors, and inability by women to recognize the need to form ties with superiors to facilitate advancement. Research by Dreher and Ash on 320 male and female business school graduates showed that respondents with more extensive mentoring relationships experienced more promotions, higher income, and greater satisfaction with benefits. Gender differences were not found.[14]

Work by Ragins and Cotton showed that women perceive more barriers in acquiring a mentor, but were no less successful than men in obtaining one.[15] Protégés with previous mentoring felt they had fewer barriers in obtaining a mentor. In the hospitality field, unpublished research by Bowers and Garey on the relationship of mentors to women managers showed that all those surveyed had a mentor who played a favorable role as a provider of advice and guidance.[16] However, the respondents did not see the mentor acting to cultivate friendships or extend networks as happens in male-to-male mentor relationships.

Hospitality Industry Data

To move from the general to the specific for women and other minorities in the hospitality industry becomes more difficult because of lack of data. The few articles written on women in food and hotel management are frequently anecdotal. The most illustrative data, other than awards that recognize women who have achieved stature, is in the annual JOB$ Survey by _Restaurants and Institutions_ (December 23, 1992). Of all respondents, 52.4% had a college or culinary degree and had worked in the industry for 15.7 years at 3.5 different companies; two-thirds of the respondents were male. Only 51% of the respondents were satisfied with their average raise, 4.8%, compared with their last raise of 5.1% when only 47% were satisfied. Forty-seven percent of the 1992 survey group received a bonus as part of their compensation.

On another important issue from the 1989 _R&I_ survey, job discrimination is still a "major complaint among minorities." Age and sex discrimination increased from 5% to 7%. Discrimination was reported for race, religion, age, and sex. The greatest discrimination was for race, with reports by blacks, 86%; Hispanics, 65%; and Asian Americans, 59%. The next highest percentage of discrimination was reported by whites for age, 59%, and for sex discrimination—51%. _Crain's NY Business_ (September 21, 1992, pp. 1, 37) reports that Wall Street firms are facing more discrimination claims from "Women, minorities and older men, tired of the status quo and ready to confront the system . . .".

In the 1989 _R&I_ survey, job security and clear career paths were motivators. In previous JOB$ surveys, the career worries most often cited by women were low salaries, level of stress, and lack of advancement and recognition. Women in other management careers also articulated these worries. Men answering previous surveys cited job security, number of hours worked, and lack of access to decision makers (power, opportunity) as career worries. A majority of respondents said they found the job challenging; however, almost 50% also rated it frustrating. Salary and bonuses continue to be an issue. Finally, in the 1989 survey _R&I_ agrees that women and minorities are still struggling.

Preliminary findings from two studies conducted using a convenience sample reinforce earlier points made in this chapter. Members of the Women's Foodservice Forum (WFF), participants at the 1993 Forum, and women who are members of the International Food Manufacturers Association (IFMA) completed similar questionnaires on women's perceptions and experiences in the food service industry. The WFF respondents were women who on the average had at least a bachelor's degree and 13 years in the industry. More than half work in quick service and full-service restaurants. More than 60% were in middle management positions, and 69% aspired to be in senior management and 21% a CEO. The group felt that they were paid less than male counterparts. More than 50% felt their career opportunities were the same or better than at other companies, but over 60% felt opportunities within their enterprise were worse for women than for men. Eighty percent believed there was a glass ceiling and the company wasn't doing anything to improve the outlook. Mentoring and equal opportunity were the two most frequently mentioned areas for employers to improve on.

The IFMA group was similar in age, education, and position—middle management. In the company the respondent worked in, 46% replied that there were no women in senior management and 60% occupied middle management positions. Sixty-eight percent replied that there were no women on the board of directors. More than half said there was equal work for equal pay but only 45% felt women advanced at the same rate as men. Only 30% felt they would be promoted to senior management positions. The reasons given were glass ceiling, male-dominated, limited positions, and can't relocate. Despite this drawback, the respondents planned to stay in the industry.

The Women's Foodservice Forum was formed by *Restaurant Business* magazine in 1989 to help answer the problems. Made up of leading women and men in the industry, the mission of the Forum is to be a "national organization that acts as a catalyst to promote the career advancement of women for the benefit of the foodservice industry." The group holds regular national meetings, participates in state and national hospitality association meetings, and has a newsletter. The NRA publication *Restaurants USA* (November 1992, p. 41) lists other networks dedicated to helping women and minorities.

Women as Entrepreneurs

Time (July 4, 1988, p. 54) reports that the number of women becoming entrepreneurs is increasing. The Women's Business Ownership Act of 1988 helped move women into their own businesses by approving many for demonstration projects to provide counseling and training, established a National Women's Business Council, and create incentives to banks to loan money. Many women start their own business because of discrimination that prohibits their advancing beyond the middle management positions in large company. Most entrepreneurs—3.7 million—are women as sole proprietorships (*Time*). The National Foundation of Women Business Owners says by 1990 women owned 5.4 million businesses and employed 11 million people *(Nation's Business,* May 1992, p. 65). Bureau of Labor Statistics data for 1985 shows an average of 128,000 women are self-employed in eating and drinking places and 1983 IRS data lists 56,486 women being sole proprietorships in eating and drinking places. Data on all women's business is very limited. The most reliable comes from the economic census conducted every five years, which undergoes three years of analysis before being reported.

However, on the downside, women only generate one-tenth of all receipts. The most recent U.S. Census Bureau data (1982) stated that about one-half of women who owned companies had gross receipts of less than $5,000, while 0.3% brought in $1 million or more. Women face more problems than men in obtaining financing (most companies are started with less than $5,000), access to government contracts, and the need for "better technical and managerial training to ensure growth of their enterprises."

Sexual Harassment

Sexual harassment is not just a woman's problem—both men and women can be victims. The Equal Employment Opportunity Commission (EEOC) defines sexual harassment as follows: "Unwelcome sexual advances, requests for sexual favors, and other verbal or physical conduct of a sexual nature." In 1972 the EEOC was created to address Title VII of the Civil Rights Act of 1964. Managers must be familiar with this act, as well as with state and municipal regulations. Damages are now being awarded to victims, and federal courts usually find for the victim. EEOC guidelines require that employers provide employees with a work environment free of sexual harassment from supervisors, employees, and customers. There are procedures and time limits that must be followed to file a claim through the EEOC. Bellucci provides a more thorough review of this issue and cases.[17]

A study of sexual harassment for guest-contact employees in New York City hotel properties by Lee and Garey found that women had more such experiences than men and that coworkers were the most frequent source.[18] A comparison of these results to those of Eller completed in 1990 showed higher incidence of harassment in this 1992 study.[19]

Conclusions

Many questions need to be answered and solved before women have an option to become equal to men as managers in the hospitality field or any other field. Some are as basic as what will make women happy, and how to balance a career, marriage, and a family. Today we are seeing a second generation of women who want to succeed. It is not only older women in managerial positions who have experienced women's struggles during the 1960s and 1970s, but a second, younger generation who are better educated and prepared to balance a career and a family—prepared to enter traditionally male occupations and higher-paying jobs. "Most women of all ages are still segregated into female-dominated occupations, where paychecks are consistently lower."[20] A study of the 34 women graduates[21] who represented 5% of the Harvard Business School's 1973 class showed only 26 were working full-time. Of that group, half were married and six others who were working part-time have children. For those with children, women described a delicate juggling act with the finding that their workday was less stretchable and the drain on their energies had resulted in most lowering their career expectations because they weren't able to give the 110% which they felt was needed for their career. For those who were married and pursuing a career toward a top management position, many described their husbands as supportive and stated that meals were frequently eaten out. A Loyola and Northwestern University study entitled All the Right Stuff examined the career progress of one thousand male and female mid-level managers at 20 corporations who were similar. After five years, women's salary raises were 11% behind men's and women had fewer transfers. The authors concluded there was discrimination and gender-related bias.

Finally, the problem is larger than one to be addressed by the individual, husband, or family. It is a national problem of the work force. Equal pay for equal work is important, but solutions also need to examine issues such as child care, flexible work schedules, and care for dependent elderly. Women today and for at least the next 20 years face exciting challenges and alternatives as they decide on a career and roles in life. There are no easy answers, but just as for men, there should be a fair and equal choice.

——References——

1. Hudson Institute.(September, 1988)*Opportunity 2000 Creative Affirmation Action Strategies for a Changing Workforce.* Indiana: Hudson Institute. Prepared for Employment Standards Administration, U.S. Department of Labor.
2. Haker, A. editor.(1983) *US: A Statistical Portrait of the American People.* New York: Viking Press.
3. Bem, S. and D. Bem. (1973) Training the Woman to Know Her Place: The Power of a Non-Conscious Ideology. *Readings in Managerial Psychology. Second edition.* Leavitt, H. J. and Ponoy, L. R. editors. Chicago: The University of Chicago Press.
4. Mead, M. and F. B. Kaplan. (1965) *American Women, the Report on the President's Commission on the Satatus of Women and other Publications of the Commission.* New York: Chas. Scribner's Sons.
5. Hudson Institute. (June 1987) *Workforce 2000: Work and Workers for the Twenty-first Century.* Indiana.
6. Fullerton, H. N. Jr. The 1995 Labor Race: BLS's Latest Projections. *Monthly Labor Review.* U.S. Department of Labor, Bureau of Labor Statistics. November 1985; p. 17.

7. Sutton, C. D. and K. K. Moore. Executive Women—20 Years Later. *Harvard Business Review,* September–October, 1985; p. 42.

8. Kanter, Rosabeth Moss. (1977) *Men and Women of the Corporation.* New York: Basic Books, Inc.

9. Heidrick and Struggles, Inc.(1978) *Profiles of a Woman Officer.*

10. Roos, P. A. and B. F.Reskin. (1984)Institutional Factors Contributing to Sex-Segregation in the Workplace. In *Sex Segregation in the Workplace: Trends, Explanations, Remedies.* Redskin, B. F., editor. Washington, DC: National Academy Press.

11. Schwartz, F. Management Women and the New Facts of Life. *Harvard Business Review.* January–February 1989; p. 65.

12. Schwartz, F. Women as a Business Imperative. *Harvard Business Review.* March–April 1992; p. 105.

13. Dickson, R. D. The Business of Equal Opportunity. *Harvard Business Review.* January–February 1992; p. 46.

14. Dreher, G. G. and R. A. Ash. A Comparative Study of Mentoring among Men and Women in Managerial, Professional, and Technical Positions. *Journal of Applied Psychology.* Volume 75, Number 5: p. 539.

15. Ragins, B. R. and J. L.Cotton. Easier Said than Done: Gender Differences in Perceived Barriers to Gaining a Mentor. *Academy of Management Journal.* Volume 34, Number 4: p. 939.

16. Bowers, P. and J. G. Garey. The Relationship of Mentors and Marital/Family Status to Women Hospitality Managers. Unpublished masters project. 1993.

17. Bellucci, E. Sexual Harassment: A Long Dormant Demon. *FIU Hospitality Review.* 1983 Volume 1, Number 2: p. 66.

18. *Lee, Y. L. and J. G. Garey.* Examining Sexual Harassment in the Guest-Contact Departments of the Hotel Industry. Unpublished masters project. 1993.

19. Eller, M. E. Sexual Harassment in the Hotel Industry: The Need to Focus on Prevention. *Hospitality Research Journal.* Volume 14, Number 2: p. 431.

20. Figart, D. M. (1988) *Economics Status of Women in the Labor market and Prospects for Pay Equity Over the Life Cycle.* Washington, DC: Women's Initiative AARP.

21. Robertson, W. Women M. B. A.'s Harvard '73—How They're Doing. *Fortune.* August 28, 1978; p. 50.

The Foundations of Hospitality Industry Leadership

Ronald F. Cichy
Michigan State University

Introduction

Browse through the business section of any bookstore and you will discover a wealth of books written on leadership in business. These books detail the qualities necessary in business leaders, and they separate leadership traits from general management skills. Only until recently, leadership qualities in the hospitality industry have been undefined.

Beginning in 1989, researchers in the School of Hotel, Restaurant and Institutional Management at Michigan State University have systematically studied leadership qualities of chief executive officers (CEOs) and presidents of hospitality organizations. The study began with a survey of CEOs and presidents of the fifty largest United States lodging organizations. In two additional separate research studies, CEOs and presidents of the U.S.-based noncommercial food service industry and commercial food service industry were surveyed. Two subsequent studies focused on the leadership qualities of Japanese lodging industry and Japanese commercial food service industry CEOs and presidents. Results of these five studies clearly identify common attributes present in effective hospitality leaders, both domestic as well as international. Those qualities most strongly identified were related to vision, communication, trust, and perseverance, and have been identified as the four foundations of leadership in the hospitality industry (Table 1).

Table 1. The Foundations of Leadership in the Hospitality Industry

• Vision
• Communication
• Trust
• Perseverance

Vision

Leaders must have a clear idea of where the organization stands today and where it will be in the short and long term. Vision means direction and articulation in planning. To persuade others to believe in the vision for the organization, leaders must strongly believe in what they want to achieve. A clear set of goals and objectives must be based on vision. Clarity of vision helps leaders describe where the organization is going and helps them persuade others by communicating in a variety of ways.

Once goals are established, time and resources can be directed toward executing the plan. Regular review of the plan also is important in an effort to improve and to achieve an even better outcome next time. Continuous improvement is possible only when results are regularly reviewed and ways are found to improve performance in the future.

Vision is much like making footprints for others to follow. Once a vision is defined, leaders must commit to it and convince others to buy in with all of their energy. This commitment is contagious. Devotion to accomplishment of the stated vision must be done with passion and brute persistence. The vision must be made clear at all levels in the organization.

Vision includes strategic thinking. To become a strategic thinker, learn as much about your industry as possible and gain a better understanding of people. Vision must include watching out and caring for the needs of others to help them succeed. Based on their success, the likelihood of the leader's own success and the achievement of the organization's vision will be enhanced.

Communication

The second foundation of leadership is communication. Leaders listen carefully to others at all levels in the organization. Listening is the most important skill of communication, and listening patiently is critical to a leader's success and the long-term success of the organization.

Leaders listen and act on what they hear from two sources: guests and staff members. Once information is obtained from these two sources, leaders focus all of their organization's efforts on supporting these two groups. The only way to recognize divergence and the modifications needed to rectify it is by listening. Leaders build teams through candor, communication, and commitment.

Successful leaders communicate the big picture or overall desired result to their people. Everyone wants to know where the organization is going—the vision for the organization—and how to get there—the goals and the strategic plan. By listening to suggestions from others in the organization, leaders become sensitive to better ways of doing business.

Trust

Trust is built and reinforced by supporting staff members and encouraging decision making at all levels. Some refer to this level of trust as empowerment. Effective leaders understand their positions and the responsibilities of their staff members by being sincere, open, and truthful.

Trust is not instant; it is built over time and must be nurtured. Trust begins with honesty and reaches fruition through realistic ongoing self-assessment and development of personal conviction. Thus, true leaders understand themselves and their beliefs before attempting to build trust in a personal relationship or an organization.

All strong human relationships are built on trust. Credibility must be earned from others in the organization. Leaders encourage others to perform the responsibilities of their positions and grow in their careers. Leaders share in the fun, the glory, and the defeats.

Perhaps the cornerstone of trust is self-esteem. From self-esteem comes trust, from trust comes commitment, and from commitment comes performance. This formula for building trust and achieving results works well when it has a strong dose of empowerment blended in.

Trust is built on surrounding yourself with great people. Once the people are in place, the leader can help define the tasks, provide the tools and levels of authority and responsibility needed to accomplish the tasks, and then get out of the way. When others are focused and challenged, they will use their own creativity to get the job done.

Trust in business can be categorized in two distinct areas: personal relationships and the community and society as a whole. While personal relationships are obvious, building trust in the community and society as a whole is less clear.

Leaders must give priority to being a good citizen, instead of just being a competitive, uncaring businessperson. Both social morals and business ethics are essential to the success of a business in the long run. Leaders devote themselves to the good of society because their organizations are supported by the communities in which they belong.

Perseverance

A leader is fully committed to the vision and course for achieving the vision, has a plan, communicates it, and sticks with it. Leaders stay with the plan and never give up. The enormous reservoir of energy required for success remains full when leaders are determined to prosper.

Excellence is never an accident. Rather, it is always the result of intelligent action, hard work, and commitment. Leaders dig in, get involved, are competitive, and work to achieve the overall end results. Leaders have a passion for the business sometimes described as a passion for persistence. A combination of clear focus and sustained intensity are the cornerstones for success.

Perseverance requires a leader to believe in convictions and build the emotional and physical stamina to stay the course. While staying focused is sometimes difficult during the best of times, it is even more challenging during crises. One of the hallmarks of leadership is the ability to focus on the overall outcome while under fire. The leader's commitment kindles commitment in others in the organization. As in personal crisis, difficult times in the leader's professional life may draw others closer in a common bond that unifies and strengthens commitment to a vision.

To be successful in the hospitality industry, persistent hard work is required. By working hard and believing in themselves and following their vision, leaders create opportunities and take advantage of situations to achieve goals. Perseverance is simply courage of convictions.

Other Leadership Qualities

A number of other leadership qualities emerged in the studies of various leadership groups. Two qualities—self-awareness and education—were more often identified than others.

Self-awareness is the leadership quality embodied in the statement that leadership is first, foremost, and always an inner quest. Leadership must start from within, with self-awareness and self-understanding. An analysis of self begins the leadership process and helps guide the leader to be more effective in the achievement of goals.

Self-awareness is improved when an individual continuously evaluates inner feelings, motivations, and desired outcomes. Self-improvement is fueled by a knowledge that drives leaders to commit to a vision and live it. Leaders internalize their vision and make desired outcomes tangible by example and by acting as a role model.

The feelings and perceptions of others must be understood and taken into consideration in all relationships. This understanding leads to modifications in the leader's qualities and interactions as relationships develop with others. A variety of inputs coming from staff members, guests, peers, and superiors permits leaders to be effective with different groups being led.

For the leader, self-awareness also extends to awareness of the organization. This includes an analysis of the organization's strengths and weaknesses, its mission, culture, and value system. A leader must be aware of the desired outcomes while considering available resources, as well as the competition. Organizational self-awareness includes a marketing analysis, systems and operational analysis, financial analysis, and most importantly, a human resources analysis.

Education must be continuous if leaders are to stay current and be effective. Continual learning, through education and experience, helps leaders develop a strong platform from which they can move strategically into the future. Leaders are encouraged to continue learning, to be informed, to study world leaders of the past and present, and to never stop wanting to learn.

Complacency will inevitably sink the ship. On the other hand, knowledge will keep the ship afloat and moving toward the desired outcomes. It is critical to learn as much as possible about the business, every day in every way. Education relates to continuous improvement and pays off by helping organizations to stay current, committed, and competitive.

Advice for Future Leaders

In all of the surveys, hospitality industry CEOs and presidents were asked an open-ended question: "If you could give *one* piece of advice to someone who wanted to be a leader like you, what would you say?" They also were asked to provide any additional comments. Although the type of advice varied, several themes emerged. First, the advice could be linked to one of the four foundations for leadership: vision, communication, trust, and perseverance. Second, the message was clear that individuals who aspire to leadership positions can build necessary leadership qualities. For example, if the development of leadership qualities is to begin during the college years, they must be emphasized in the classroom as well as made part of out-of-class work experiences and internships. Additionally, encouragement to participate in extracurricular activities and student organizations that involve some degree of responsibility and teamwork can also assist in the early development of leadership qualities. Further development and refinement of leadership traits take place when mentor—protege relationships are established and nurtured.

Specific comments by hospitality leaders can best be summarized with the following quotes:

> A hospitality professional must remain knowledgeable of industry changes and have an understanding of the business. The leader must also be a `people person' with management skills that will motivate people to want to succeed. The future leader must have a vision, the ability to draw up a plan of action to set the direction, and the ability not only to communicate, but to listen. The leader should be adaptable and willing to compromise and change.

> Food service requires new management to get heavily involved in day-to-day operations. You have to put in the long hours. You have to open and close a lot of restaurants to know the business.

> The traits of effective leaders will be affected by the needs and demands of the eras in which they belong. Therefore, we should be flexible to meet them.

> The important issue as a top executive in the food service industry is to develop effective leadership in our managers. The success of our business depends upon their leadership qualities.

Conclusion

Based on studies of leadership qualities of hospitality industry CEOs and presidents in both the United States and Japan, four foundations of leadership have clearly emerged. These foundations are vision, communication, trust, and perseverance. Future hospitality industry leaders are well advised to begin building these skills early in their careers.

The author wishes to express appreciation to the hundreds of hospitality industry CEOs and presidents, both in the United States and Japan, who responded to the surveys. It is because of their responses that the identification of the foundations of hospitality industry leadership was possible.

The author also wishes to extend his gratitude to the coresearchers who participated in these studies.

——References——

Cichy, Ronald F. Blueprint for Leadership. *Michigan Lodging.* November–December 1988; Volume 13, Number 6: p. 15.

Cichy, Ronald F., Takashige "Teddy" Aoki, Mark E. Patton, and Michael P. Sciarini. Five Foundations of Leadership in Japan's Lodging Industry. *FIU Hospitality Review.* Fall 1992; Volume 10, Number 2: pp. 65–77.

Cichy, Ronald F., Takashige "Teddy" Aoki, Mark E. Patton, and Kerry Y. Hwang. Shidō-sei: Leadership in Japan's Commercial Food-Service Industry. *The Cornell H.R.A. Quarterly.* February 1993; Volume 34, Number 1: pp. 88–95.

Cichy, Ronald F. and Caroline L. Cook. Leadership Qualities: The Non-Commercial Foodservice Industry. *Restaurant Personnel Management.* August 1991; Volume 4, Number 8: pp. 6–7.

Cichy, Ronald F. and Michael P. Sciarini. Do You Fit This Profile of a Hospitality Leader? *Lodging* June 1990; Volume 15, Number 10; pp. 40–42.

Cichy, Ronald F., Michael P. Sciarini, Caroline L. Cook, and Mark Patton. Leadership in the Lodging and Non-Commercial Food Service Industries. *FIU Hospitality Review.* Spring 1991; Volume 9, Number 1: pp. 1–10.

Cichy, Ronald F., Michael P. Sciarini, and Mark E. Patton. Food-Service Leadership: Could Attila Run a Restaurant? *The Cornell H.R.A. Quarterly.* February 1992; Volume 33, Number 1: pp. 47–55.

22

Cultural Diversity in the Hospitality Industry

Frédéric Dimanche
University of New Orleans

Most textbooks present the management of hospitality services as if cultural diversity did not exist. It seems unfortunate that many hospitality graduates will start working in a very complex cultural environment without understanding how this diversity will affect their jobs, their relations with other workers and with guests, and more generally, the quality of the services they will provide. The modern environment is global. In other words, it has become international and multicultural. It is usual for hotels and restaurants to hire a work force and to serve guests who all come from a wide variety of cultural backgrounds. Many readers of this book are likely to represent various cultural backgrounds as more and more international students come to this country to study tourism and hospitality management. As large hotel companies compete in a global marketplace (that is, all over the world), cultural issues and the challenges they present to managers become more crucial.

"Lasting success in working or living with people from another culture ultimately rests on good human relations." This statement made by Stewart and Bennett may sound simplistic, yet nothing can be more true and more overlooked in the hospitality industry.[1] Managers in the United States are learning how to interact and communicate with a greater variety of cultures because the U.S. work force has become more culturally diverse than ever before, and because tourism brings a large number of international travelers. Hospitality students who are about to start their careers can be sure that multicultural issues will become one of the most important and current topics in the industry. Managing in a multicultural environment is difficult, and the future successful manager needs to be aware of the challenges that this task represents.

What Is Cultural Diversity?

A plethora of definitions exists for the word *culture*. Generally, culture can be defined as a specific set of customs, traditions, and values that pertain to a particular people or group. Cultures can be small, and one country can easily encompass several cultures. For example, several cultures are found in the United States: Hispanics, African Americans, Native Americans, and Korean and Chinese Americans represent only a few of them. All have their respective cultural identities, customs, way of life, and languages. Current trends show that the traditional American melting pot seems to have changed: cultural groups don't melt anymore; they all seem now to be claiming the right to retain their uniqueness. For example, the Hispanic population of Florida recently earned the right to use Spanish as an official language in governmental affairs. The Cajuns of Louisiana are reviving their cultural heritage by promoting their food and music, as well as encouraging the teaching of French in schools. Black Americans show their ethnic pride and a new enthusiasm for merchandise reflecting their history and culture. Such examples abound within the United States, and when we go across borders, cultural differences become even more obvious. A traveler to India, the Ivory Coast, or Norway will find himself in very diverse cultural environments, and the behaviors and values of his hosts will reflect this diversity.

Because of all these differences, relationships between individuals belonging to distinct cultural groups may sometimes be difficult. Our own values and perceptions may sometimes preclude our understanding of others' behaviors or attitudes. Many of the misunderstandings between people from different cultures may be due to ethnocentrism. *Ethnocentrism* means assigning validity only to one's own culture. Our way of thinking, our values and perceptions are culture bound, and we look at others through our culturally tinted glasses. Those glasses prevent us from seeing others as they are; we look at them with reference to our culture, and this often leads to cultural misunderstandings and to prejudice. Ethnocentrism coupled with our limited knowledge about others is very likely to prevent us from objectively assessing and understanding cultural differences, which can have serious consequences in a work environment. Shames and Glover talk about cultural tunnel vision in explaining how some managers market services and manage people without considering cultural differences and sensitivities.[2]

For example, a manager has a management style that is very American-specific even though she may be in a diverse cultural environment with Hispanic or Asian employees. The staff might have trouble relating to her management style, and problems may arise because of a lack of communication and understanding of each other's culture. These problems are often referred to as *cultural collision.*

Such shortcomings can also appear between employees and guests. Tourists may be visiting a foreign country and be disappointed with the quality of service provided because of their cultural bias. For example, Americans traveling abroad may complain because waiters do not fill up their glasses with ice cubes when serving water or soda. In fact, this has nothing to do with service quality, but it indicates a cultural difference. The dissatisfaction is therefore due to culture-bound expectations. Inversely, American waiters may have negative attitudes toward French tourists because they often "forget to tip." In France, tipping is not practiced because a 15% gratuity is always included in the check, and French travelers in the United States need to be reminded about tipping.

Hospitality students have certainly already experienced such situations when traveling, working, or meeting international friends on campus. Many of these examples of cultural collision could be easily avoided if both tourists and hospitality professionals were made more aware of their cultural differences.

Cultural diversity is a fact that cannot be ignored by hospitality managers. Being aware of it and learning how to face the problems that may stem from it will certainly be one of the keys to success in the global marketplace.

Why Is Cultural Diversity Important to the Hospitality Industry?

Marketing Services

The past decade has seen hospitality professionals pay increasing attention to the concept of service. They have come to realize that they were not merely providing a manufactured product to their customers, but a bundle of benefits called a service. An extensive research literature has indicated the differences between goods and services. First, services, as opposed to goods, which are tangible are intangible to the customer. A guest can not grasp a service, but only experience it. Although there are some tangible elements in the hospitality product, a night in a hotel or a fine dinner are *experienced* by guests. Secondly, services are perishable; they can not be stocked. Thirdly, they are heterogeneous as opposed to goods, which are homogeneous. There are always some fluctuations in service because of the human component and the interactions between customers and clients. Finally, the service is consumed by the guest at the very same time it is being produced or delivered. This means that the employee is himself part of the hospitality product. These distinctions have some very important implications for the marketing of hospitality services. The most important implication is that *personal relations between service providers and customers become highly significant.* The human relationship between guests and employees is very often what will count most in guests' perception of service quality, and in their ultimate satisfaction. This being understood, it becomes clear why managers now pay more attention to human resource management and to the human element of the hospitality product.

The management of people has now become more important than the management of projects. The difference between success and failure of an organization rests on how well human resources are managed. To succeed, the organization has to adapt to its work force; the quality of guest–employee relationships depends on it. These relationships may be threatened because of cultural problems. Differences in expectations of service quality or lack of effective communication because of language barriers may lead to frustration among personnel and dissatisfaction among guests. Total customer service will require better training of employees, particularly in recognizing and satisfying culturally different customers.

An Increasingly Multicultural Work Force in the United States

Walk through the back of the house of a large American hotel and you are likely to hear people speak English, Chinese, Vietnamese, Indian, or Spanish. If current trends continue, Hispanics will make up about 10% of the total population in 2000, and will become the largest minority group in the USA by 2010. The African American group is expected to increase up to nearly 14% of the population in 2000. These proportions will dramatically increase as we go into the 21st century. Other minority groups such as Asians, Pacific islanders, and native Americans will also grow in the next decades. These population trends recorded by the U.S. Census Bureau indicate that the white non-Hispanic population is not growing as fast as other groups. We are rapidly moving toward a mix of cultural minorities with no majority. This of course is having numerous repercussions in the work place.

An Increasingly Global Industry

The hospitality industry is becoming more international. Companies are going global and develop or convert properties abroad in order to expand their market possibilities. Many of these large hospitality companies from England, France, Japan, or the United States send managers and other executives to work overseas. Some countries do not have the necessary skilled personnel locally, so good opportunities exist for hospitality managers to gain a unique experience abroad. However, these executives will have to be properly trained in order to avoid culture-related problems.

A Growing Number of Foreign Tourists

Working in the hospitality industry also means that managers, supervisors, and other employees will often have to interact with international tourists who have a different cultural background, and who are not always fluent in English. Marketing and providing services to Japanese, German, and American customers each requires a different approach, and marketers as well as managers will need to understand how their clients differ. For example, in 1991, Hilton developed a special marketing package for the Hispanic population of southern Florida. They broadcast commercials on Spanish-language TV channels, and developed a Spanish-speaking 800 reservation service to better attract this market. As hotels and restaurants market themselves in increasing depth, they will have to better understand the specific needs and desires of their foreign and other culturally unique markets.

Trends indicate that international pleasure travel is likely to increase because of relatively cheaper transportation as well as increased vacation time. In addition, the global economy creates more opportunities for business travelers to go overseas. Also, an increasing number of people in countries such as those in Eastern Europe or Asia are becoming potential world travelers because of political changes and economic progress. This represents a culturally diverse pool of potential customers for the hospitality industry.

The Need for Cross-Cultural Training

The expanding cultural diversity of the American population is obvious in the work place. Human resource departments in the hospitality industry are hiring numerous individuals from diverse cultural backgrounds, and this creates the need for managers to be better trained in cultural understanding and cross-cultural communications. This need is even more critical for those who will be starting a career overseas: they will be totally immersed in a different environment with foreign workers, and they will often need the language skills necessary to operate effectively abroad. It is acknowledged in the business literature that the failure rate of American managers on international assignments is quite high. The most common causes for this are a manager's inability to adjust to the new culture and her inability to adapt to the new culture. Improved job training would remedy some of the problems, but most importantly, cultural and language training needs to be provided in a more effective way. Some industry leaders such as Hilton International and Sheraton have understood the urgency of this problem and have already created training programs in order to develop multicultural managers.

What Are the Necessary Intercultural Skills?

A flexible approach to training that stresses social skills needs to be implemented for managers to succeed in a multicultural environment. The goal of this training should be to help them develop skills in order to effectively function within another culture and communicate with culturally different coworkers and customers. According to Lobel, several characteristics for effective global leadership should be emphasized.[3] The most important of all is flexibility. What we believe to be true or right in our culture may not be so in another one. Intercultural interactions may bring misunderstandings and conflicts. The educated manager will know how to be flexible and adapt to such situations. Secondly, it is important for multicultural managers to keep an open mind and to be sensitive and receptive to other cultures. This quality will help avoid the drawbacks of ethnocentrism. Not only should managers be open-minded, but they should also be curious, sincere, and eager to learn from others. Finally, managers should be able to accept cultural differences in a nonjudgmental way. Managers need to learn how to communicate respect for others' values and opinions. Communication and open dialogue are keys to better understanding.

Conclusion

Cultural diversity is a fact that can not be avoided anymore. Each hospitality professional will have to ask and answer this overriding question: "In what ways does multiculturalism influence my work?" At a time when the hospitality industry is becoming more customer and service oriented, managers should take a close look at the importance of understanding cultural diversity. The growing segmentation of markets demands a thorough understanding of consumer cultures and a strong adaptability to change. Managers will have to be trained to develop interpersonal skills, cultural sensitivity, and awareness of cultural differences that affect behavior. Hospitality and tourism students should be encouraged to develop these skills as soon as possible. The best way is of course to learn a foreign language and study abroad. Living in a different country is the best way to prepare oneself for the challenges of working in a culturally diverse environment. Several colleges offer programs in various countries that will provide invaluable experiences to students and prepare them to become successful multicultural managers.

——References——

1. Stewart, E. C., and M. J. Bennett. (1991) _American Cultural Patterns: A Cross-Cultural Perspective._ Yarmouth, Maine: Intercultural Press.
2. Shames, G. W., and W. G. Glover. (1989) _World-Class Service._ Yarmouth, Maine: Intercultural Press.
3. Lobel, S. A. (1990) Global Leadership Competencies: Managing to a Different Drumbeat. _Human Resource Management,_ 29(1), 39–47.

23

Introduction to Hospitality Law

Jane Boyd Ohlin
Florida State University

Introduction

Just as the scope of the hospitality industry encompasses a variety of business interests, the variety of laws that apply to the industry is equally broad. The various legal implications of managing a hospitality operation should be explored in an intensive hospitality law course. This chapter introduces the most pressing legal issues hospitality operators encounter every day and will familiarize the reader with the importance of implementing sound management policies to avoid costly litigation.

Because the hospitality industry is labor intensive, hospitality operators must understand the laws that govern employment. For instance, hospitality operators must abide by civil rights legislation, which forbids discriminatory practices. Specific laws have been enacted that prohibit discriminatory conduct regarding the employment of pregnant women, persons more than 40 years of age, persons infected with HIV, and the disabled, to name a few. Hospitality operators must understand the impact of these laws and learn to comply with the regulations.

Civil Rights Act of 1964—Title VII

Title VII of the Civil Rights Act of 1964 prohibits employment discrimination based on race, color, religion, sex, pregnancy, and national origin. Employers must refrain from basing employment decisions on these factors. In order to defend an allegation of discriminatory hiring practices, an employer must be able to show that the applicant was not hired for reasons other than those prohibited by law. For instance, one would have to show that the person who was hired, was in fact better qualified to do the job or that, at a minimum, the person denied a job was not hired for reasons unrelated to their race, color, religion, sex, pregnancy, or national origin.

The two defenses available to employers are business necessity and bona fide occupational qualification. A discrimination allegation could be defended on the basis of business necessity if safety or profitability requires hiring a specific person. For instance, if an employee was hired specifically to work weekends and then, after the person is hired, the individual could not work those hours for personal reasons, then management may defend on the basis of business necessity. On the other hand, a bona fide occupational qualification (BFOQ) refers to a legitimate or honest job qualification, such as a minimum age requirement necessary for the safe operation of equipment.

Historically, discrimination claims have arisen over hiring practices. Today, however, many employers appreciate the importance of objective hiring practices. Some employers fail, however, to appreciate the importance of applying the laws to *all* aspects of employment. As a result, today, many discrimination claims arise over promotion practices. Managers must remember that the laws apply not only to hiring, but to training, promotion, wages, benefits, and all other aspects of employment. As a result, managers must design their appraisal systems to be objective, consistently applied, and well documented so that in defending a discrimination claim, there is proof that the reason an employee was not promoted, or otherwise rewarded, is unrelated to a discriminatory purpose.

Sexual Harassment

Title VII of the Civil Rights Act of 1964 also addresses sexual harassment in the workplace. Guidelines compiled by the Equal Employment Opportunity Commission (EEOC) include the following statements: Requests for sexual favors and other verbal or physical conduct of a sexual nature constitute sexual harassment when:

1. Submission to such conduct is explicitly or implicitly a term or condition of employment, or
2. Submission to or rejection of such conduct by an individual is used as a basis for employment decisions, or
3. Such conduct has the purpose or effect of unreasonably interfering with an individual's work performance or creating an intimidating or hostile or offensive working environment.

In investigating an allegation of sexual harassment, the EEOC will look at the nature of the complaint and the context in which the conduct took place, in determining whether sexual harassment has occurred. There are two types of sexual harassment of which managers must be aware. Quid pro quo refers to sexual harassment whereby the ability to get a job or to receive a promotion depends on one's willingness to grant sexual favors. A hostile environment in another type of sexual harassment. The conduct does not necessarily result in economic loss, but forces victim to undergo abuse in return for being allowed to work. Pinches, feels, and dirty jokes are all examples of a hostile work environment.

Liability can be established even when there is no economic loss if it can be shown that such sexual harassment adversely affects the psychological aspects of the work environment. Employees who quit under such circumstances may even be eligible for employment benefits if the court determines that "constructive discharge" occurred. Constructive discharge means that the employee worked in such an offensive environment, that she had no choice but to quit under the circumstances.

The employer is responsible for its acts and those of its agents, regardless of whether acts were authorized or even forbidden by the employer and regardless of whether the employer knew or should have known of their occurrence. Regarding conduct between fellow employees, the employer is responsible for sexual harassment in the workplace where the employer or its agents or supervisors knew or should have known about the problem, unless it can be shown that the employer took immediate corrective action.

The employer is responsible for acts of nonemployees, such as purveyors and customers, with respect to sexual harassment of employees in the workplace where the employer, agents, or supervisor knew or should have known and failed to take immediate corrective action. It is important to remember, however, that it is sexual harassment only if the harassing conduct is against the will of the employee.

"Should have known" has been interpreted to mean that if the employer had used proper management techniques, he would have known. Therefore, the EEOC advises employers to affirmatively raise matters by establishing a strong position against sexual harassment, notifying employees of the policy, and implementing procedures for handling any such charges.

Procedures should call for two people to be available to receive a sexual harassment report, this will help ensure that the offender is not the only person the employee can complain to. Employers must inform the employees of their rights and let them know there will be no retribution for defending those rights. Established procedures communicated to all employees, supported by employee training on sexual harassment, may help to mitigate the liability award.

When faced with a sexual harassment complaint, the employer or manager must act immediately to remedy the problems. One instance of harassment usually will not create a hostile environment, if management responds and demonstrates strong disapproval immediately. The disapproval could be firing, transfer, demotion, warning, or probation. Postponing company involvement, however, may prompt the court to rule that the delay amounted to approval of the conduct.

Americans with Disabilities Act

Passage of the Americans with Disabilities Act in 1990 has had considerable impact on the hospitality industry. The law defines *disability* as "a physical or mental impairment that substantially limits one or more of the major life activities." The Act also includes people with a history of physical impairment, such as cerebral palsy and muscular dystrophy, or disease such as mental illness, cancer, epilepsy, or AIDS. It does not include transvestites, homosexuals, or people with emotional or sexual disorders. The ADA is designed to eliminate employment-related discrimination that has historically allowed employers to inquire into the existence of a disability rather than the ability to perform the functions of a job. Today, employers are prohibited from conducting preemployment medical examinations or asking whether the applicant has a disability. The employer must limit preemployment inquiries into the ability of an applicant to perform job-related functions only. The employer may require a medical exam only after an employment offer has been made and then may condition an offer on the results of the exam, but only if all employees are subjected to the same exam requirement.

The law requires employers to provide "reasonable accommodation" to the known physical or mental limitations of an otherwise qualified disabled person who is an applicant or employee, unless the employer can demonstrate that the accommodation would impose an "undue hardship" on the business. _Undue hardship_ is defined as "an action requiring significant difficulty or expense when considered in light of (1) the nature and cost of the accommodation needed; (2) the overall financial resources of the facility, the number of persons employed, and the impact of such accommodation; (3) the overall size of the business; and (4) the type and geographic separateness of the facilities."

To assist operators with understanding what is required under this vague law, guidelines for compliance have been developed by the United States Department of Justice. Even so, operators report confusion over what is required. Many hotels today are challenged by issues such as pool access for the disabled. As litigation ensues, and as judicial precedent is developed, a clearer understanding of the intent of the law should take place.

The Americans with Disabilities Act also prohibits discriminatory employment practices with respect to persons carrying the HIV virus. Because AIDs is not transmittable through food and drink, persons infected with HIV should not be restricted from work unless they have a contagious infection that would serve to prohibit them from working. AIDS testing of employees or of applicants is prohibited, and if an employer learns that an employee or applicant carries the HIV virus, the employer should not divulge this information to anyone else. Employers should treat persons afflicted with AIDS like anyone else, avoid testing for AIDS, and enforce basic health and sanitation procedures for all employees.

Age Discrimination in Employment Act

The Age Discrimination in Employment Act was passed in 1967 and amended in 1978 and 1986. The law prohibits discrimination against employees and applicants older than 40 years. The injured party need only show that age played _some_ part in the discrimination—age does not have to be the sole basis of the discriminatory act. Of course, if an employee is not productive in performing the job, the employer can discipline and terminate the worker. Managers must refrain from asking applicants their age. If there are regulations governing the age an employee must be to serve alcohol or operate machinery, the manager should tell the applicant about the law and the age restriction, then simply ask the applicant if they are old enough to do the work. Managers must be aware of protection available to persons over age 40 with respect to benefit offerings, promotions, and early retirement options. The 1986 amendment prohibits a mandatory retirement age for workers in most occupations and requires employers to continue the same group health insurance for employees over age 70 as that offered to younger employees. Discriminatory practices are actionable in court.

Wage and Hour Law

Because the hospitality industry employs many people and because of the long hours associated with this industry, wage and hour law is of primary interest. Strict labor laws impose minimum age requirements on children in the work force, especially concerning the operation of dangerous equipment in the hospitality industry. Further restrictions apply to hours worked. Operators must thoroughly research this area of the law before hiring young people.

Overtime compensation at the rate of one and one-half times the regular hourly wage for all hours worked in excess of 40 within a 168-hour week is required for most persons in nonsupervisory positions. Employers who attempt to evade overtime regulations by giving employees supervisory titles without true supervisory authority and responsibility will find themselves in legal trouble. Employers must also understand the implications of the Equal Pay Act of 1963, which requires men and women to be paid substantially the same wages for substantially equal work or approximate equal "skill, effort, responsibility and working conditions." Consequently, operators must be aware of the importance of objectively developed job descriptions and wage scales. Legal issues tend to rise over the definition of "equal work."

Negligent Hiring

Employers are increasingly being sued on the grounds of negligent hiring. The elements of a successful negligent hiring suit require that the manager knew or should have known the applicant was unfit and that the unfitness caused the injury or harm. It does not matter whether the employee was acting within the scope of employment at the time of the act. From a management perspective, the best defense is to practice and document sound hiring procedures. For instance, probationary periods will allow the employer to terminate any employee for any nondiscriminatory reason. Also, the employer should check all former employment and personal references of the applicant before extending an offer. The applicant should sign a release allowing the employer to check references. Further, each applicant should sign a statement that false answers on the application are grounds for dismissal.

Likewise, in providing references on former employees, employers must be careful not to defame the character of a former worker. Defamation of character results when a maliciously false statement is communicated to a third person. Prudent managers allow only one person to give out references—as opposed to whoever happens to answer the phone. They also make sure that statements are made in good faith, limited to relevant matter, based on a legitimate business interest, and, most importantly, are true and provable in court.

Negligence

Operators are required to provide safe premises. This requires managers to hire, train, and supervise employees accordingly, while managing the premises in a safe fashion. Employees must be trained to seek out dangerous conditions and inform management. Management can then prioritize risks and respond appropriately. The test in determining whether management acted negligently in failing to protect guests is based on "foreseeable risk." The elements of a negligence action include the following:

1. The operator owed a duty to the plaintiff.
2. The operator acted or failed to act—creating an unreasonable risk of harm.
3. The act or failure to act was the proximate (legal) cause of the injury or harm.
4. Legal damages are ordered to be paid.

The operator occasionally prevails when there was not sufficient time to anticipate the risk and to react. Similarly, operators may not be liable if the plaintiff fails to guard against obvious hazards in plain view.

As business invitees—persons invited onto the premises for the mutual benefit of themselves and the hospitality operator—guests are entitled to be treated with reasonable care. In exercising reasonable care toward a business invitee, the operator is required to affirmatively seek out dangerous conditions, even if they are concealed, and to remove the danger. Making the guest aware of the danger serves only to minimize liability. The responsibility applies to dangerous conditions that are known or that reasonably ought to have been known. Operators are also required to provide furniture and appliances which may be used in the ordinary and reasonable way without danger.

Licensees are persons who enter the property with permission, but for their own purposes, such as a pizza delivery person or the guest of a registered guest in a hotel. The duty of the operator in this case is to warn of concealed dangers that the operator knows of. The operator must also refrain from unreasonably dangerous conduct. Toward trespassers, persons who enter without permission, no duty is owed, but the operator cannot intentionally harm or set a trap for the trespasser. Be aware, however, that known trespassers can become licensees if allowed to continue trespassing on the property.

In light of escalating crime rates, hospitality operators must adjust the concept of "foreseeable risk" to reflect known criminal activity in their area. For instance, if purse snatching has been known to occur in the parking area of the business, then the operator should take reasonable steps to protect the guest from purse snatching. The operator should install sufficient lighting in the parking areas, install fencing when appropriate, and employ security staff as needed. Courts will evaluate the precautions taken by the hospitality operator in light of the foreseeable risks involved.

Accurate key control in hotel operations is essential in combating criminal activity. Hotel operators must install solid locks on doors, and implement an efficient method of coding keys and changing locks on doors when keys are not returned. More than 80% of all theft involving guest rooms has been attributed directly to hotel employees with access to rooms or hotel employees working in collusion with third persons. For this reason, it is apparent that a well-managed key system which holds employees accountable is essential to guest security.

Contract Law

Contract law is also of great concern to hospitality operators because many hotels and restaurants enter into contracts with large groups for business. Disputes arise over cancellation policies, refund policies, and services contracted for. For instance, the marketing department may promise banquet seating for a party of 500. This poses problems for the food service staff when the banquet hall only seats 475 persons. Communication between departments is essential for operators seeking to limit the risk of litigation over contract disputes.

Because contracts in the hospitality industry are often created many months or even years before the event is scheduled to take place, and because turnover in the industry is so high, it is imperative that contracts be in writing. Every detail should be spelled out and written in plain language. All words that are necessary to communicate a full understanding of the rights and obligations of all parties must be stated. Of course, all modifications to the contract should be in writing and signed as well. Operators get into trouble when they accept changes to the contract over the phone, then neglect to include them in the contract.

The contract should provide for a deposit. A cancellation clause should be included that allows either party the right to cancel within a specified time with written notice. Such a clause can be arranged with a graduated increase in forfeit of deposit money. A liquidated damages clause, which is an advance agreement between the parties as to the damages the hospitality operator will be entitled to if the contracting party cancels, is also recommended. The clause should require the canceling party to pay all reasonable attorney fees and the costs of litigation. To protect customers from unscrupulous overbooking practices, some states require that if a hotel accepts a room deposit, it must hold the room. If no room is held, the hotel must refund the deposit and make every effort to find other accommodations. The hotel could be heavily fined for each guest denied.

Conclusion

This chapter should serve as a brief introduction to some of the laws hospitality operators must familiarize themselves with in order to avoid costly litigation. The reader should pursue the study of hospitality law thoroughly in a course designed for this purpose. In addition to further development of the laws discussed in this chapter, other areas of law the operator should be familiar with include dram shop (alcohol) liability, liability for guests' property, eviction of guests, Uniform Commercial Code regulations, truth-in-menu, tip credit reporting, immigration regulations, occupational safety issues, and a myriad of other areas. Most importantly, operators should seek the advice of legal practitioners in their own state because many aspects of hospitality law are governed by state statutes.

24

Ethics in Hospitality Management

William E. Miller
Northern Arizona University

"Everyone does whatever he want to—whatever seems right in his own eyes."

Judges 17:6 (LB)

When people are affected, when interests collide and choices must be made between values, ethical considerations are at stake. That means nearly all the time for people in business.

Report of the Business Roundtable
February 1988

Individuals are responsible for their own integrity. They will be influenced by many people and events but, in the end, their integrity quotient is of their own making.

Admiral Arleigh A. Burke
U.S. Navy (Retired)

Introduction

Ethics is the hottest term in business discourse today. In Latin it means "the study of ideal conduct." Business ethics has also become one of the hottest topics in business and hospitality schools.

During the 1980s, scores of books and hundreds of articles from the professional journals and industry magazines were written on the topic of business ethics—or more often the lack of ethics (the doing of wrong as opposed to right). In addition, a dozen or more applied ethics centers were created at universities throughout the country to study and teach about business ethics. In 1988, The Marion W. Isbell Endowment for Hospitality Ethics—the first of its kind in the nation to focus on ethical issues in the hospitality industry—was established at Northern Arizona University to assist hospitality management students in understanding and practicing the moral reasoning skills necessary to be successful and effective in the hospitality industry. While this new concern for ethics seemed to be everywhere in the 1980s, Andrew M. Sikula predicts that "the 1990s will be an era in which management ethics will be the focus of administrative activities."[1] Rushmore M. Kidder, founder of the Institute for Global Ethics, predicts that the 1990s will become an Age of Ethics and that individuals void of ethical constraints will be able to wreak unprecedented damage on our society.[2]

The ethical reputation of the hospitality industry is determined by the individual actions of the owners, managers, and employees of the lodging and food service business and the owners, managers, and employees of travel and tourism businesses. The actions of each are important because those actions combine to establish and define the ethical reputation of the hospitality industry as a whole.

The Language of Ethics

A person may understand very well what ethics means, yet not be able to define it. Conversely, a person may be able to define ethics, yet not know what it means.

In order, then, to avoid the semantic confusion that often inundates discussions about ethics, it is necessary to define the essential terms involved.

Ethics	Ethics is the name we give to our concern for good behavior. We feel an obligation to consider not only our own personal well-being, but also that of others and of human society as a whole. *Dr. Albert Schweitzer*
	Ethics concerns standards of behavior consonant with values which we hold to be important. *Kirk Hanson,* Director, The Business Enterprise Trust
Hospitality Ethics	Hospitality Ethics is the study of ethics as it applies to that segment of business referred to as the hospitality industry. It aims at developing reasonable ethical standards for the hospitality industry. *W. E. Miller,* Director Isbell Ethics Center
Code of Ethics	A written standard of conduct consisting of those rules or principles (values) by which men and women live and work in mutual confidence. *W. E. Miller,* Director Isbell Ethics Center

Values

Values represent learned attitudes or beliefs which individuals consider to be important. The values that we hold are inward motivations that drive our outward actions. Those values which relate to beliefs concerning what is right or wrong (e.g., honesty, integrity, fairness) are "ethical" values. Values which are ethically neutral (e.g., ambition, happiness, pleasure) are "nonethical" values.

W. E. Miller, Director
Isbell Ethics Center

Character

Character has three interrelated parts: moral knowing, moral feeling, and moral behavior. Good character consists of knowing the good, desiring the good, and doing the good—habits of the mind, habits of the heart, and habits of actions.

Thomas Lickona, State University
of New York, Cortland

Why Should the Hospitality Industry Be Concerned with Ethics?

With increasing frequency we are being bombarded by headlines targeting questionable and sometimes criminal behavior in the hospitality industry:

48 Biltmore Hotel Investors Sue Accountants for $15 Million

Hooters Restaurant Chain Is Sued: Ex-waitresses Say They Were Harassed

Holiday Inns Danced the Tax-Avoidance Two-Step

Bob Evans Farms Family Restaurant Executive Quits After Pot Raid

During the 1980s and early 1990s, ethical vacuums were at the core of many business calamities ranging from companies such as Dow Corning, Phar-mor, Drexel, And Beechnut to executives such as Boesky, Milken, Helmsley, and Keating. The hospitality industry was not immune during this period as chronicled by the headlines cited, nor were the major accounting firms—Arthur Andersen, Ernst and Young, or Price Waterhouse—all of whom are active in the hospitality industry.

There are three primary reasons why the hospitality industry and its future managers should be concerned with ethics:

1. Bottom-line self-interest—our industry and our managers need to avoid scandals such as those of the savings and loan industry with the resultant fines, penalties, and possible jail terms.
2. An inclination on the part of most people to act ethically—our self-esteem and self-respect depend to a great extent on the private assessment of our own ethical behavior. Most people will alter their conduct if they discover it is inconsistent with the company culture.
3. The total quality management (TQM), employee involvement, and empowerment movements currently being implemented throughout the hospitality industry demand an unprecedented degree of integrity and honesty within a company—a process that often exposes internal ethical shortcomings.

If those who manage in our industry convey the idea that adherence to a high standard of personal and professional ethics is not an option in our industry, a clear message will be delivered to managers and employees of what is really important.

I'm Just a College Student—Why Talk to Me About Hospitality Ethics?

Recent studies conclude that the ethical quality of society has worsened in the past few decades. In fact, evidence suggests there is a continuing downward spiral with regard to the ethical and moral behavior of the college-age generation.

A comprehensive report by Josephson Institute of Ethics titled, *The Ethics of American Youth: A Warning and a Call to Action,* concluded that an unprecedented proportion of today's youth has severed itself from the traditional moral anchors of American society—honesty, respect for others, personal responsibility, and civic duty are all found lacking. For evidence of this erosion in ethical values, consider some of the highlights of the report:

1. **Dishonesty.** Cheating in college is rampant (about 50% at most colleges). Anywhere from 12% to 24% of resumés contain materially false information and there is an increasing willingness to lie on financial aid forms and in other contexts where lying benefits the applicant. Because teachers and employers have their own agendas, liars and cheaters are rarely caught and are seldom punished.
2. **Civic Duty.** Young people are detached from traditional notions of civic duty. They are less involved, less informed, and less likely to vote than any generation previously measured.
3. **Ethical Values.** A significant proportion of the present 18- to 30-year-old generation has adopted attitudes and ethical behavior patterns that subordinate the traditional moral principles of honesty, respect for others, and personal responsibility. Today's youth exhibit self-centered values stressing personal gratification, materialism, and winning at any cost.[3]

Further evidence of ethical and character erosion in America is found in the book, _The Day America Told the Truth—What People Really Believe About Everything That Really Matters._ This treatise, based on a national survey, takes a statistical look into the heart and soul of America's populace. The authors' findings produce a disturbing portrait of a nation devoid of common morality. Among the "revelations" reported in this study are the following:

1. Lying has become an integral part of the American culture. We lie without even thinking about it.
2. The number one cause of business decline in America is unethical behavior by executives.
3. There is an epidemic problem with "moral ambivalence." Most Americans see the great moral issues of our time in shades of gray rather than as clear-cut moral choices.
4. The majority of Americans are malingerers, procrastinators, or substance abusers in the workplace.
5. Americans have little respect for the property of others. They have a penchant for taking anything that isn't nailed down—from work, at stores, and on the road.
6. Religious people are much more moral than nonreligious people.
7. Women workers are more ethical. They are less likely to steal, to malinger, to lie to their bosses, or to leave work early. Women can be trusted more. It is imperative that women be looked to for leadership in American business right now.[4]

Will Students Carry Over Ethical Skills to the Workplace?

Most students enter their first jobs with a value system in place and a fairly well-developed character. They want to be ethical; they want to be proud of themselves and what they do for a living. Self-esteem and self-respect depend on the private assessment of one's own character. Very few people are willing to accept the fact that they are not ethical.

In a recent survey of psychological research, James R. Rest concluded that moral development continues throughout formal higher education and that a commitment to ethical behavior can be enhanced by well-developed educational interventions.[5]

Consequently, many students will alter their conduct if they discover it is inconsistent with their espoused values. Acting ethically requires certain intellectual skills that develop both with maturity and formal education. Thus, the most critical period in the formation of operational or applied ethics occurs as students are about to leave college and begin their careers. If ethical principles have been internalized, they will be readily carried over into the workplace.

The Core "Consensus" Ethical Principles

Managers and supervisors in the hospitality industry routinely face decisions with ethical implications. How they handle those decisions can have a significant impact on the profits, productivity, and long-term success of an organization.

One of the tasks ahead for hospitality school educators is an approach to ethics and ethical decision making in the workplace that builds upon the moral capacities of the students preparing for management careers.

The Josephson Institute of Ethics advocates ten major ethical principles or values that form the basis for ethical decisions and establish the standards or rules describing the kinds of behavior an ethical person should and should not engage in. These values are honesty, integrity, trustworthiness, loyalty, fairness, concern and respect for others, commitment to excellence, accountability, leadership, and reputation and morale.[6] The job of the hospitality school instructor, or for that matter, the industry executive, is to encourage the kinds of behavior an ethical person should emulate and discourage those that they should not.

The Notion of Stakeholder Analysis and Principled Reasoning

Stakeholder analysis in business decisions can help us understand how insensitivity to the multiple claims on corporate actions can lead to unintended consequences and unnecessary harm to those within the company as well as those on the outside with an interest or "stake" in the business. Typically, in the hospitality industry the impact of decisions would affect the following stakeholders: guests, employees, owners and managers, lenders, vendors/suppliers, stockholders, and decision makers.

The use of principled reasoning (choosing) in the decision-making process can focus the decision maker's attention on the rights and interests of the stakeholders and consequently better inform the individual decision maker. However, good analysis does not guarantee good decisions. Sometimes decision makers willfully do what is wrong. Michael Josephson suggests that there are three major reasons that fundamentally decent people fail to conform to their own moral principles: unawareness and insensitivity; selfishness consisting of self-indulgence, self-protection, and self-righteousness; and defective reasoning.[6]

Principled reasoning and stakeholder analysis does not always lead to principled or moral decisions or for that matter, ideal conduct. It is, however, a powerful analytical tool to help the decision maker see all the ethical implications of the decision.

How Does One Decide What's Ethical?

Here are some of the decision models for resolving ethical issues that we have identified. They provide a practical guide to determining and doing the right thing:

1. The Golden Rule: The most basic and perhaps the most practical of all ethical theories. It is as valid in business decisions as in personal ones. The Golden Rule or Rule of Reciprocity simply stated is: "In everything, do to others what you would have them do to you." (Matthew 7:12) Variations of The Golden Rule are also found in the writings of Confucius and Aristotle.

2. The "Ethics Check" questions[7]:
   - Is it legal? Will I be violating either civil law or company policy?
   - Is it balanced? Is it fair to all concerned in the short term as well as the long term? Does it promote win–win relationships?
   - _How will it make me feel about myself?_ Will it make me proud? Would I feel good if my decision were published in the newspaper? Would I feel good if my family knew about it?

3. The Josephson Institute Ethical Decision-making Model[8]:
   - All decisions must take into account and reflect a concern for the interests and well-being of all stakeholders. (This is simply an application of the Golden Rule.)
   - Core ethical values and principles always take precedence over nonethical ones.
   - Is It is ethically proper to violate an ethical principle only when it is clearly necessary to advance another true ethical principle which, according to the decision maker's conscience, will produce the greatest balance of good in the long run.

Conclusion: A Need for Positive Ethics

The reason we have seen so much emphasis on ethics in the hospitality industry recently is not that hospitality managers and employees are less ethical than managers and employees in other industries, but rather that the hospitality industry has given so little thought to developing a corporate culture that rewards "positive" ethical behavior. "Positive" ethics means concentrating on doing what you should do simply because it is the right thing to do. It's knowing the difference between what's right and what's expedient.

A conversation took place recently between two hotel and restaurant management (HRM) majors in a senior seminar on ethics in the hospitality industry. One asked the other if she would steal $1,000,000 if no one else in the world would ever find out. It's a good question, for it strikes at the heart of all ethics. She gave the right answer when she said: "Ethics are not determined by who knows. Ethics are absolute even if no one else would ever find out."

The future of the hospitality industry depends on men and women who are not passive but active, who are prepared to make choices and take responsibility for those choices. That requires individuals who have a value system and the courage of their convictions to do what is right even when there is great pressure to do otherwise.

——References——

1. Sikula, Andrew M. A New Environmental Ethical Era. *Proceedings. Long Beach, Calif: Fourth Annual National Conference on Ethics in America. 1993; p. 92.*
2. Kidder, Rushmore M. A Look Back, a Look Forward, and a Bow. *The Christian Science Monitor.* June 11, 1993; p. 13.
3. Josephson Institute of Ethics. The Ethics of American Youth: A Warning and a Call to Action. California, October 1990.
4. Patterson, J. and P. Kim. (1991) *The Day America Told the Truth.* New York: Prentice-Hall.
5. Rest, James R. Can Ethics Be Taught in the Professional Schools? *The Psychological Research Journal.* 1988; p. 42.
6. Josephson, Michael. Teaching Ethical Decision Making and Principled Reasoning. Ethics: *Easier Said Than Done.* Winter 1988, p. 29–30.
7. Blanchard, K. and N. V. Peale. (1988) *The Power of Ethical Management.* New York: William Morrow and Company. p. 27.
8. Josephson, Michael. (1991) Making Ethical Decisions. Pamphlet. California: Josephson Institute of Ethics. p. 20.

The Ten Core Values for Hospitality Managers

There is a strong consensus in Western society concerning moral values and principles, which historically has provided a practical guide to determining and doing what is right.

The following list of moral values or ethical principles has been translated into operational language by the Josephson Ethics Institute. They incorporate the characteristics and standards that most people associate with ethical behavior. They have been somewhat adapted so as to more closely relate to the ethical decision maker in the hospitality industry.

Honesty	Hospitality managers are honest and truthful. They do not mislead or deceive others by misrepresentations.
Integrity	Hospitality managers demonstrate the courage of their convictions by doing what they know is right even when there is pressure to do otherwise.
Trustworthiness	Hospitality managers are trustworthy and candid in supplying information and in correcting misapprehensions of fact. They do not create justifications for escaping their promises and commitments.
Loyalty	Hospitality managers demonstrate loyalty to their companies in devotion to duty and loyalty to colleagues by friendship in adversity. They avoid conflicts of interest; do not use or disclose confidential information; and, should they accept other employment, they respect the proprietary information of their former employer.
Fairness	Hospitality managers are fair and equitable in all dealings; they do not abuse power arbitrarily nor take undue advantage of another's mistakes or difficulties. They treat all individuals with equality, with tolerance for and acceptance of diversity, and with an open mind.

Concern and respect for others	Hospitality managers are concerned, respectful compassionate, and kind. They are sensitive to the personal concerns of their colleagues and live the Golden Rule. They respect the rights and interests of all those who have a stake in their decisions.
Commitment to excellence	Hospitality managers pursue excellence in performing their duties and are willing to put more into their job than they can get out of it.
Leadership	Hospitality managers are conscious of the responsibility and opportunities of their position of leadership. They realize that the best way to instill ethical principles and ethical awareness in their organizations is by example. They walk their talk!
Reputation and morale	Hospitality managers seek to protect and build the company's reputation and the morale of its employees by engaging in conduct that builds respect and by taking whatever actions are necessary to correct or prevent inappropriate conduct of others.
Accountability	Hospitality managers are personally accountable for the ethical quality of their decisions as well as those of their subordinates.

The ten ethical principles listed were adapted from a publication of the Josephson Institute of Ethics, 310 Washington Blvd., Suite 104, Marina del Rey, California 90292, (213) 306–1868.

—Appendix B———

Ethical Dilemmas in the Hospitality Industry

Here are some prime examples of dilemmas replete with ethical overtones, which often confront hospitality industry employees. If you or one of your employees were faced with these, would you do the right thing? How would you encourage positive ethical behavior as it relates to these situations?

1. Would you call in sick just because you have unused sick leave?
2. The general manager is collecting money for (United Way, Boy Scouts, Rescue Mission, a political party). Is this ethical?
3. Other managers take home bathroom amenities for their personal use. Would you?
4. The night auditor just explained that when a guest overpays a bill the money is dropped into a special account used for an employee "flower fund." Is this right?
5. A purveyor delivers one "free" case of wine to your residence *after* you placed an order for 50 cases. Do you keep the case?
6. Your chef suggests using leftover turkey as a substitute in the chicken salad. Would you approve?
7. Your manager tells you nothing is unethical or wrong in the restaurant business if you can get away with it and make a bigger profit for your restaurant. Do you agree, disagree, or agree with reservations?
8. When news of a sexual harassment complaint reached your hotel manager, he dismissed it with a crack about "these wacko feminists." As a new food and beverage manager, would you say anything?
9. You have always disliked Maria and were relieved to see her laid off. Now, without warning, you are asked to give a reference for Maria over the phone. What would you do?
10. Through a computer error your hotel has overcharged a regular corporate customer. You tell the front desk manager and she tells you to mind your own business. Should you?

25

Hospitality Marketing Management

Robert D. Reid
James Madison University

Introduction

Two independent restaurateurs were discussing business trends when one said, "Business sure has been slow since that new chain restaurant opened across the street two months age. We used to serve 350 to 400 people on the weekend nights, but now we're only averaging about 250. What do you think I should do to build sales?" Hospitality managers ask similar questions every day, as they attempt to operate successful restaurants and hotels.

When managers ask questions such as the one above, they often hope for a simple and easily implemented solution. Unfortunately, this is usually not so. There could be literally hundreds of potential reasons. Marketing, like the other management functional areas, is complex. It encompasses a variety of tasks and responsibilities. Within this chapter, we shall briefly explore several concepts and issues related to marketing management within the hospitality industry.

The first section examines the broad spectrum of marketing: what marketing is, the marketing concept, and the marketing cycle. The second section provides an introduction to services marketing. Specific differences between how products and services are marketed will be discussed. The third section examines the marketing management cycle. It also provides a brief overview of the elements of the marketing manager's position. The fourth section examines issues that are having an impact on marketing activities within the industry.

The Broad Spectrum of Marketing

What Is Marketing?

Marketing is defined in several ways. The American Marketing Association defines it as the performance of business activities that direct the flow of goods and services from producer to consumer. Marketing has also been defined as the merging, integrating, and controlled supervision of all efforts by the company that relate to sales.

Marketing involves a complex set of activities. To define adequately marketing, one must examine the activities that are encompassed by it. These activities include the following:

1. Discovering the wants and needs of the customer
2. Creating products and services (product–service mix) that satisfy these wants and needs
3. Promoting and selling the products and services to generate a level of income satisfactory to the management and stockholders of the organization [1]

The first and foremost activity of marketing is to understand the customer. The customer's wants and needs must be thoroughly understood. Many marketing and management authors have noted that truly excellent companies thoroughly understand their customers. This is often referred to as being "close the customer." Excellent companies learn from those they serve. They listen to learn and improve the way they serve the customer. When given the opportunity, guests of hotels and restaurants will tell the management what features are appreciated and what aspects of the operation could be improved. It is important for marketing-oriented managers to learn to listen to guests and then act on their suggestions. Many new ideas for services and amenities come from guest suggestions.

The second activity of marketing is the development of the products and services (product–service mix) which will be offered to the guest. Each year new product–service mixes are developed and then enter the competitive marketplace. In the past decade, the development and expansion of various types of lodging options, such as all-suite hotels, and budget brands, such as Hampton Inns, Comfort Inn, and Sleep Inns, have added diversity to the array of product–service mixes available within the lodging sector. Most of the major hotel chains have expanded their product offerings by segmenting the market and offering specific brands to meet the needs of targeted potential guests. Within the food service sector of the hospitality industry, similar developments have occurred.

The third activity of marketing involves the promotion, advertising, and selling of the product–service mix that has been developed. A tremendous amount of creativity and innovation is called for to be successful. The advertising media are filled with all types of advertisements, so the key to success is reaching the potential customer with your message and promoting action. The desired action is the purchase of the firm's product–service mix. Promotional activities can take many forms, both internal and external to the business. Restaurant chains within the fast food sector often run coupon promotions featuring discounts with the goal of increasing sales within the chain's units, often at the expense of the competition.

Another aspect of this marketing activity is personal selling. The hospitality industry is a people-contact business. The purchase of hotel rooms and meals involves face-to-face contact between the guest and the hospitality employee. Each of these contacts offers the opportunity for personal selling.

The final part of the definition of marketing implies that an acceptable level of income must be produced. This is central to the reason for being in business. All businesses, including nonprofit ones, have goals for sales and profits. These are targets that the businesses need to reach to be successful. If management is successful in achieving the first three elements of the definition, then it has a much higher probability of reaching an acceptable level of income.

Marketing is a complex function of management. Marketing, along with operations, accounting and finance, human resource management, administration, and research and development comprise the six key result areas for which managers are held responsible.

The Marketing Cycle

To fully understand marketing, it is necessary to move beyond a simple definition and see how specific parts are put into action. As discussed above, marketing involves the performance of several activities. These are shown in Figure 1.

Managing the Marketing Mix

Management of the firm's marketing activities can be described as mixing the elements for which the marketing manager is responsible. Traditionally, the marketing mix consisted of four elements:

1. *Product.* The unique combination of products and services
2. *Place.* The manner in which the products and services are sold, including channels of distribution
3. *Promotion.* The methods used to communicate with the tangible markets
4. *Price.* A pricing policy that encourages consumers to purchase the product and results in profitability for the firm [2]

This marketing mix was widely applied for many years. A more contemporary view holds that the marketing of services, such as hotels and restaurants, differs from products and therefore calls for a modified marketing mix. Lewis proposed a hospitality marketing mix that consists of four components [3]:

1. *Product–Service mix.* This is the combination of all products and services offered by the hospitality operation. This includes both the tangible and intangible elements.
2. *Presentation mix.* This includes those elements that the marketing manager uses to increase the tangibility of the product–service mix as perceived by the consumer. This submix includes elements such as location, atmosphere and decor, price, and personnel.
3. *Communications mix.* This submix involves all communication that takes place between the hospitality firm and the potential consumer. It also includes the elements of advertising and market research. It is important to understand that this submix is an established two-way communications link with potential consumers.
4. *Distribution mix.* This submix element involves the manner in which the product–service mix is distributed. This is called the "channels of distribution." For example, often hotel rooms are not sold by the hotel company directly to the end consumer, but through a travel agent who actually places the reservation. [3]

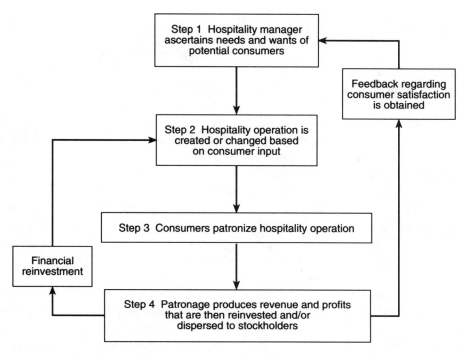

Figure 1. The Marketing Cycle

(Adapted from Reid, Robert D. (1989) *Hospitality Marketing Management.* Second edition. New York: Van Nostrand Reinhold, Inc. p. 9.

The Marketing Concept

The term *marketing concept* has been used for many years. It is a very simple concept: the number one priority of business should be to satisfy the customer. Often, companies lose sight of this important goal, focusing instead on other aspects of marketing such as monitoring the activities of the competition. While it is critical to monitor what the competition is doing, those activities should not become the primary focus of the business.

Peter Drucker proposed that the purpose of business be to create customers. This puts the marketing concept into perspective, for if there are no customers, there will be no sales. If there are no sales there will be no profits.[4] Although managers often speak of profits as the primary goal of the business, this really should not be the case. The primary purpose for being in business should be to create customers and keep them satisfied.

If a business, such as a hotel, can create and satisfy customers it is more likely to have a level of sales that allows it to be successful. Placing the primary emphasis on satisfying the customer is more likely to result in profitability than placing the emphasis on profitability and hoping that you can satisfy the guest in the process.

Marketing's New Priority

Until quite recently, marketing took a back seat to other management functions. Company presidents and officers often came into their positions from accounting or operational backgrounds. Those with a marketing background were often not considered for top positions in companies. This has changed. Today, we find that company presidents often come from the marketing management ranks. The most noteworthy example is John Skully, president of Apple Computer. In the future, presidents of companies must have a strong marketing background.

There are several important reasons behind this shift. First, the consumer market today is very fragmented. The so-called mass market does not really exist. Instead, the market is made up of a vast array of small homogeneous market segments. Second, the intensity of competition is much higher today than it was a few short years ago. In recent years, there has been a substantial increase in the number of available hotel rooms in the United States. This growth in the supply of available hotel rooms has exceeded the growth in demand, resulting in declining occupancy rates and a crunch on corporate profits. This intense competitive situation calls for some marketing savvy. The situation in the food service segment is equally competitive. As one chief executive officer of a fast food company noted, the main thrust today is taking business away from the competition, and that fact, more than any other, is modifying the business. Each firm has to out-execute the competition, and that is why marketing is more important than ever before.[5] Many food service companies have increased their advertising and promotional budgets in recent years. Besides the increase in advertising budgets, a larger percentage of the budget is being allocated to support promotional efforts.

Within this new marketing emphasis, companies believe their greatest opportunity for success lies in developing specific and innovative product–service mixes for well-defined market niches. This can be seen in the market segmentation strategies being used by hotel companies.

Unique Aspects of Service Marketing

Hospitality Services Marketing

The large size, sustained growth, and economic impact of the hospitality and tourism industry have been well documented. As a part of the service sector, the hospitality industry has been part of the fastest growing sector of the economy.

Growth in the service sector has been the result of several factors. Perhaps the factor having the greatest impact on the hospitality industry is franchising. The proportion of franchised operations has continued to grow at the expense of independent operations. The widespread proliferation of franchises has resulted in the increased use of mass media to establish brand identity and loyalty. As an example, Choice Hotels, Inc. has grown very dramatically in recent years using franchising as the means of growth.[6]

Marketing of hospitality services, such as hotel rooms or restaurant meals, differs dramatically from marketing products such as automobiles or washing machines. There are several reasons for this difference.

Nature of the Product

The nature of services differs from products. When consumers purchase a new car or washing machine, they buy an object, a device, or other tangible thing. It can be touched, viewed, and examined in great detail. When the same consumer purchases a service such as hotel accommodations, the nature of the service is quite intangible. When the guest checks out of the hotel, he has purchased a service in the form of hotel accommodations. He has purchased the service provided by the hotel staff in the form of check-in, check-out, food and beverage service, swimming pool, and other amenities. Once the guest leaves the hotel, there is nothing tangible that he can show to others, or to himself, to remind him of the experience at the hotel.

Consumer Involvement

Services also differ from products because of the manner in which consumers become involved in the purchase and delivery of the service. Unlike settings where consumers merely purchase a product off the shelf and take it home, in the hospitality industry, the consumer is part of the delivery system. This often takes the form of self-service in restaurants or hotels. Similarly, when guests order a meal in the dining room, they interact with the server in selecting the menu items, how they will be prepared, and so forth.

Quality Control Problems

Unlike products that are manufactured on an assembly line, services are produced and consumed at the point of sale. In the factory, if a product is defective, it can be removed from the assembly line and set aside to be repaired or scraped. This is not true with services. If a server in a restaurant is having a bad day and treats the guests poorly, negative feelings toward the restaurant will result. If the door attendant of a hotel is away from his position, for whatever reason, and is unable to help the guest unload his luggage from the car, the guest may have a very negative initial impression of the hotel's service level.

To maintain consistency of service, most companies have developed extensive standard operating procedures (SOP's), which provide specific detail about how the products and services are to be delivered to the consumer. These standards are established in order to maintain consistency with the various units operated by the companies. Other companies have followed the lead of the Japanese by implementing a total quality management (TQM) program that focuses all of the attention of the company's employees or associates on satisfying the needs of the guests. Ritz Carlton was recognized in 1993 as a recipient of the prestigious Malcolm Baldridge Award, as documentation of their commitment to improving and enhancing guest service. Marriott has also implemented a total quality management program in all of their full-service hotels and resorts, with very successful results. Associates are given the authority to take whatever steps, within broad parameters, they deem necessary to satisfy the guests.

Inability to Develop Inventories

Unlike product industries where inventory can be stockpiled in anticipation of high demand periods, the hospitality industry vs services cannot be stockpiled. If a hotel has 300 guest rooms, it really does not matter if 400 potential guests want to make reservations for tonight. The hotel has a finite capacity of 300 rooms. If the hotel sold 225 of the rooms last night, the potential revenue from the 75 rooms that were not sold is lost forever. The rooms cannot be reclaimed and held in inventory for the future.

Different Distribution Channels

Product companies manufacture, distribute, sell, and service in different facilities. These facilities are often spread over a broad geographic area. Service organizations, such as hotels and restaurants, conduct the same functions within one facility. Hospitality service organizations must manage the interaction between server and guest so that the guest receives the type of service that she has come to expect. In addition, management may also be called on to control the behavior of guests if that behavior begins to negatively affect the use of the service facility by other guests. For example, if a guest in a hotel decides to have a party in his room and the room is next door to someone who wants a quiet and peaceful night, a problem could easily result.

Responsibilities of the Marketing Manager

The management of the marketing function is in many respects similar to other areas of management responsibility. The key to being successful is to view the marketing management process in three steps. The steps are planning, execution, and evaluation. These are illustrated in Figure 2.

Planning

Very few individuals or businesses are successful through luck alone. Success is usually the result of a carefully thought-out plan. The planning process begins with a clear idea of what is to be accomplished. It begins with broadly defined goals that provide guidelines about the direction in which the organization would like to move. These goals are long term in scope. The goals then are refined into more specific short-term objectives. The objectives usually state in clear and measurable terms what is to be accomplished, who will be responsible

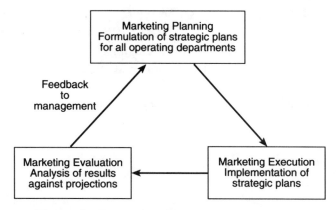

Figure 2. The Marketing Management Cycle

(Adapted from Reid, Robert D. (1989) *Hospitality Marketing Magagement.* Second edition. New York: Van Nostrand Reinhold, Inc. p. 19.

for seeing that the tasks are completed, and by what specific date the objectives will be reached. Once the objectives have been agreed on, action plans are developed. Action plans provide specific detail concerning how the objectives will be achieved. Details are discussed, which, when put into action, have a high probability of achieving the desired results.

Execution

Once the details of planning are completed, the next task is to put the plans into action and get the job done. This is normally the most enjoyable part of the challenge of marketing management. The depth and breadth of tasks associated with executing a marketing plan are tremendous. Aspects include hiring and training marketing and sales staff members, refining and implementing promotional plans, placing advertising in selected media, engaging in personal selling, and managing all of the aspects of the marketing mix.

Evaluation

Once the marketing plan has been put into action, the evaluation phase begins. To what extent did the action plans achieve the desired results? Why did certain elements work well, while others did not? These are examples of the types of questions that need to be answered during the evaluation phase. The evaluation phase involves market research focused on analyzing the variance between budgeted and actual performance, evaluation of the effectiveness of advertising, and promotional and personal selling activities. Another key element of the evaluation phase is an assessment of the environment in which the business operates. This includes an assessment of the impact that competition has had on the business as well as the impact which broader issues such as the economy have had.

Trends in Hospitality Marketing Management

To develop a thorough understanding of marketing, further study is required. Included in this study will be the specific marketing courses required within a hospitality management academic program. Beyond understanding broad concepts, one must also become a student of marketing trends that affect the industry. The following section will briefly examine three trends that are currently having an impact on the hospitality industry.

Market Segmentation

In the past, hotel accommodations were aimed at the broad market. With few exceptions, there was little attempt to fine tune the product–service mix to meet the needs of a particular type of traveler. In the past ten years all of this has changed. Market segmentation involves the division of the total potential market into smaller, more homogeneous segments called target markets.

Segmentation has traditionally been based on the following variables:

- *Geographic variables,* such as city or town of origin
- *Demographic variables,* such as age, sex, income, and education level
- *Behavioral variables,* such as frequent, moderate, or infrequent travelers
- *Price variables,* such as high, medium, or low price of the product–service mix
- *Benefit segmentation variables,* such as the consumer's perceived need for certain hotel amenities
- *Psychographic variables,* such as those variables based on lifestyle, attitudes, or personality

During the 1980s and early 1990s, most major hotel companies began to deviate from the strategy of having only one brand or type of lodging product–service mix. Instead, they developed specific brands to meet the needs of specific market segments. This trend toward niche brands is likely to continue.

Marketing the Complete Amenities Package

No longer are hotels built only as lodging facilities. They are built instead as total product–service mix packages offering a wide array of amenities that consumers have come to expect. Amenities typically included are a choice of several food and beverage outlets, fitness and exercise centers, retail shopping outlets, as well as a wide array of other services. Each additional service or amenity must be evaluated in terms of its contribution to the total cost to the operation and its perceived value to the prospective guest.

Increasing Emphasis on Promotions

In both the food service and lodging segments of the hospitality industry the use of promotions is increasing. Within the fast food segment, a wide array of promotions and packaged specials are used to build store traffic. This increase in traffic often comes at the expense of the competition. The name of the game is building market share, that is, the percentage of the total potential market that patronizes an establishment.

The lodging segment has also seen the benefit of promotional efforts. Nearly all of the larger chains have developed frequent guest programs in which guests are awarded points based on the number of nights they stay in chain properties. These points can then be accumulated and used toward gifts, complimentary lodging, and travel. As an added bonus, many frequent guest programs are linked with frequent flyer programs offered by the major airlines. In this way, a traveler can earn points toward complimentary lodging and air travel by using specific hotels or airlines.

Other trends continue to influence the industry as well. Those discussed comprise only a small sample. As a student entering the dynamic hospitality industry, it is important that you begin to look for trends. The skill of being able to sense what is happening and what is likely to happen in the competitive environment is an acquired skill, one that will allow you to gain a competitive advantage.

Conclusion

This chapter has provided a brief introduction to the broad field of hospitality marketing. The marketing of services, such as hotels and restaurants, differs greatly from traditional product-oriented marketing. As a student entering the hospitality field, it is important to develop a solid foundation in basic marketing concepts.

Using this as a base, later coursework in marketing will allow you to further develop your marketing skills and prepare you for a successful career in the hospitality industry.

References

1. Reid, Robert D. (1989) *Hospitality Marketing Management*. New York: Van Nostrand Reinhold, Inc.
2. Assael, Henry. (1993) *Marketing: Principles and Strategy*. Second edition. Orlando, Fla.: Dryden Press.
3. Lewis, Robert C. and Richard E. Chambers. (1989) *Marketing Leadership in Hospitality*. New York: Van Nostrand Reinhold, Inc.
4. Drucker, Peter. (1974) *Management: Tasks, Responsibilities, and Practices*. New York: Harper and Row.
5. Annon. Marketing: The New Priority. *Business Week*. November 21, 1983.
6. Rothwell, Tony. Presentation. Silver Spring, Md. February 13, 1990.

26

Merchandising: Influencing the Consumer Purchase Decision Inside the Restaurant

Donald I. Smith
Washington State University

*Research indicates that between 25% and 50% of guest
expenditures are made during the purchase decision.*

Webster defines *merchandising* as "Sales promotion, a comprehensive function including market research, development of new products, coordination of manufacture and marketing and effective advertising and selling."

Influencing Consumers

For the purposes of this chapter, the definition will be narrowed to the function of influencing the consumer's purchase and repurchase behavior after the selection decision has been made. Thus, merchandising includes all sales and promotional activities that influence a guest on-premises.

Let me explain what merchandising is not. It is not advertising, price promotion, or any others means of influencing consumers through product perceptions, trial, or retrial. It is not another form of media event, because these activities all occur off-premises.

It is possible to influence the consumer purchase decision by manipulation. A seller can have a selfish motive and in the short-term cause the guest to purchase something or spend more than they intended. This activity, in the long run, will almost always cause postpurchase dissatisfaction or dissonance.

Postpurchase Dissatisfaction

Research suggests that consumers go through several buying stages:

1. Awareness of a need
2. Product options

3. Screening of costs and benefits
4. Decision and expectations
5. Purchase
6. Postpurchase evaluation

Because most of the time (not always) the degree of out-of-pocket risk is relatively low in food and service purchases, the purchase intent generally is uncomplicated and is quickly made. However, a family of five going through a drive-thru for a snack or a meal can be relatively expensive today. Merchandisers who effectively push the buyer to spend more than she intends will often experience a long decline in guest count.

Two considerations in a merchandising program or system are the following:

1. Does the additional purchase contribute to the guest's total restaurant experience? The critical success variable to merchandising is understanding your target guests' needs and wants, and not just your own desire to increase the average check. In other words, merchandising should be of mutual benefit to both buyer and seller. For example in fast service and convenience restaurants much attention and training is placed upon suggestive selling. Counter people are taught to influence the purchase of side items (cheese, fries, or guacamole), sell desserts, and up-size the drinks. A guest who expected to spend $3.50 ends up spending $5.50 and later says, "It's really expensive eating at that restaurant. I can't afford to go back." This is postpurchase dissonance.
2. Is the merchandising program manageable for the crew? One of the quickest ways to kill a suggestive selling program is to associate more pain than reward for the employees who are to execute it. If more pain than reward is associated with the sale of a product, don't expect your people to promote it. For example, if you promote a Mexican pizza which generates a high gross profit, but its production time delays the table turnover, thus cutting into the service person's overall tips, the suggestive selling program of that product will not be successful. The items to be merchandised should be readily available.

Selection

In terms of the buyer behavior model, the merchandiser designs the restaurant experience to optimize the enjoyment of the guest as well as increase the average guest check.

Research indicates that up to 73% of frequent buyers make their entire purchase decision after the restaurant has been selected. However, we can take a lesson from the supermarkets who obtain approximately 50% of their income through impulse purchases. These add-on sales do not just happen by accident. They are planned into the grocery shopper's experience through price promotions, signs, sampling, and location. The same influencing opportunities exist in the hospitality business. Added cocktails, wine, appetizers, desserts, take-home items, and repeat business can be made to happen through merchandising.

A definition that catches the philosophy of merchandising is, "merchandising provides the consumer the opportunity to increase their satisfaction of the product experience through additional purchases without creating post-purchase dissonance."

Planning Objectives of Operational Marketing

Planning and establishing clear and measurable objectives are essential to an effective program. Before a merchandising program is implemented, the overriding imperative is that the seller understand the guests' needs, wants, and expectations. Each employee's goal should be to exceed those expectations. The primary objective is to increase the consumers' frequency of visits.

With this imperative in mind, let's examine five merchandising objectives:

1. To enhance the guests' experience and perception of value
2. To increase average total gross profit per guest
3. To create trial and repeat purchase of a new product
4. To increase the party size
5. To create word-of-mouth advertising

In trying to fulfill our objectives, we should ask the following questions:

- What are we trying to accomplish?
- Is it consistent with our enterprise's mission and strategy (reason for being) and way to achieve it?
- Does the program meet our guests' needs?
- How will we know whether we have accomplished merchandising objectives?

Six merchandising tools are described herein that are interwoven into the guest's service experience. Used properly, they will lead to increased guest satisfaction and higher profits. They are

- Suggestive selling . . . A friendly suggestion
- Product packaging . . . What the eyes sees, the eye buys
- Sampling . . . An unexpected gift of hospitality
- Point of purchase material
- Menu
- Price
- Social evidence

Suggestive Selling

Hotels and restaurants have a distinct merchandising opportunity because all guests come into contact with a sales host, whether this is an order-taker in fast food, a front desk clerk at a hotel, or a service person at a sit-down restaurant. These are the enterprise's most effective influencers. They can, through suggestive selling, influence the purchase decision. (I prefer the term "sales and service host" to waitress or waiter because it is more descriptive, and it defines the true responsibility.) Suggestive selling definitely can influence the guest's purchases. One experiment indicated that the average guest check increased by 50% when a service person simply suggested products to the guest. The critical elements of any suggestive selling program are "the three E's":

- *Engineering* the program. This assures that what you want to promote can be delivered easily. When service people are asked to promote items that delay service and are time-consuming in production, they tend to resist suggesting them.
- *Education and training* in the art of suggestive selling. A five-step guide to training should be employed:
    1. *Orientation.* Provide the salesperson with the *why,* i.e., why we are embarking on the program.
    2. *The tell.* Provide product knowledge, and explain in detail the suggestive selling behaviors you wish them to learn.
    3. *The show.* Demonstrate those suggestive selling behaviors in the most accurate way.
    4. *The try.* Allow the learner to try.
    5. *The reenforcement or redirection.* Provide feedback on their performance.
- *Enforcement/reenforcement.* Whenever an employee is asked to learn some new task, there are two questions that they have to address:
    1. Can I do it?
    2. If I do it . . . what's in it for me?
- In addressing this second issue there are two ideas I would like to put forth. First, merchandising programs should include performance incentive contests, rapid performance feedback. In addition, the supervisor's encouragement and "mystery shoppers"* are useful reenforcement tools.

Second, selecting the right people for sales host positions is the basis for a successful merchandising program. While it is not the purpose of this chapter to discuss the selection process, one cannot escape the subject when discussing effective selling. The sales host must have intelligence, enthusiasm, persuasive communication skills (verbal and nonverbal), a desire to influence others, and most of all, empathy. What's more, they must contribute to a climate of entertainment, which can affect the guest's desire to prolong the dining experience and purchase additional products.

The ABC's of Suggestive Selling

Create a Climate of Enthusiasm

The single most important factor in maximizing the guest's expenditure is establishing a climate of enthusiasm—a climate of hospitality and goodwill that is created by friendly managers and service people whom the guest perceives as wanting to contribute to their enjoyment. If the guest thinks she will have an enhanced experience through a product benefit, she will thus be more satisfied with the product than without it.

---

* Mystery shoppers are individuals not familiar to the restaurant or hotel employees or management who are hired to be a guest and evaluate and report on the performance of a crew based upon prearranged standards. Their reports are used to reward, reenforce and correct behaviors, i.e., the counterperson is to suggest a beverage when the guest does not order one.

Respond to Needs

The guest's needs and wants are varied. People purchase hospitality services for a variety of motives; they are hungry, in a hurry, conducting business, entertaining, providing social paybacks, relaxing, escaping, changing pace, or celebrating. Professional sales hosts know that the more they understand guest motives and personalize the experience, the better the climate for merchandising.

Remember Abraham Maslow's theory of a hierarchy of needs. We must take care of the guest's *primary* needs first. For example, if a guest needs to get back to work in a hurry, don't influence her to purchase a product that takes time in preparation, no matter how good it is. Or another example, a businessperson taking a client out to lunch may prefer to have a leisurely dining experience with two cocktails before the meal. Restaurant prestige, exclusivity, ambience, and personal service are his needs. On the other hand, a secretary on a 45-minute lunch break probably is driven by convenience, time, and price/value. In any case, assume people enter a restaurant hungry. It is important to neutralize this hunger need. For example, to merchandise alcoholic beverages, astute merchandisers provide some light food ("drink stimulator") to curb the appetite while guests have a cocktail or two.

Feed ego as well as appetite. Another critical guest need is being made to feel important. The great Win Schuler was a master of recognition. He stressed remembering guests' names and faces, going out of one's way with little personal things, like having a special salad prepared "just for you," that would make the guest feel important.

Develop credibility and trust/know the product line. To efficiently persuade guests to purchase products, the sales host must establish credibility with the guest. The host must be believable.

Credibility and respect are developed through product knowledge. Training should stress product benefits as well as ingredients, method of preparation, and time. It should also cover pronunciation, provide first-hand taste experience, guest benefits, preparation time, and diet considerations.

Sales hosts must memorize the menu items and their benefits. One progressive chain (TGI Friday) tests all applicants prior to hiring on their knowledge of items, key differentiating ingredients, preparation methods, and price. They require the prospective sales host to pass the menu knowledge with a score of at least 90%.

The Friendly suggestion. Sales hosts can influence guest purchases by suggesting their favorite item, sharing inside information, and stressing certain products over others that the sales host feels are more beneficial to the guest's needs.

Scarcity or not on the menu. Another effective method of developing credibility is to offer the guest an item that is limited in quantity or not on the menu. This is a planned merchandising effort. One highly successful restaurateur used to have a different salad prepared in the kitchen ready to go. He or his sales hosts could suggest that the guest not order a salad but to let them prepare a special one for the party. It was relatively easy to deliver the treat to the table without any delay in production.

Influencing with the AIDA System

A simple four-letter acronym represents a system for merchandising.

A is for Attention. The promoter or promotion must get the buyer's attention. This can be accomplished in a variety of ways. In advertising, often some provocative photograph or color layout grabs the attention of the reader. Fast food "street merchandising" calls attention to the restaurant through eye-catching signs or building streamers. In personal sales, it is often the salesperson simply asking for attention ("a moment of your time") or the non-verbal ability to capture the attention of the buyer.

- *Enthusiastic voice*—excitement is transferred through intonation to get the buyer's attention.
- *Innovative packaging*—attention can be drawn with an unusual menu.
- Universal restaurants bring a tray of delicious desserts to the table rather than the less effective dessert menu. They have accomplished a 24% dessert sales increase during a recent test run.
- McGuffy's Restaurants use a menu they call the "McGuffy Reader," which looks like the first grade primer of the same name, as a means of gaining attention. The drink menu is called "The Dirty Little Book" and is filled with handwritten graffiti of guests. The book certainly calls attention to the beverage menu.
- The former Shamrock Hilton of Houston, Texas, placed their swimming pool menu on t-shirts worn by attractive pool attendants.
- Sales hosts at the Fun Magic Time Machine in San Antonio, Texas approach the table and blow up a balloon, on which is the wine list. If the guests choose not to have wine, the balloon is released with its characteristic noise and shouts of "cheapskate."
- An effective menu we used at Chateau Louise in Chicago, Illinois, as an attention getter was the beautiful "Picture Frame Wine Menu." The sales hosts approach the table with an eye-catching frame, which listed wines and drew attention to the wine list.
- *The flame.* Flambé of food is always an attention getter in a restaurant and also an excellent way to stimulate desire to experience special entree or dessert selections.
- *Sound of the sizzle.* The original sizzling steak planner is a traditional means of making heads turn.
- *Size* can be used as an attention getter both exceptionally large or small. One of the most creative I've seen was a small (1/pr//pr/ X 2/pr//pr/) wine menu that listed only three wines: (1) red, (2) white, and (3) pink. Below the simple list were the words, "Please order by number so as not to confuse our wait staff."
- *Smell.* The sweet smell of freshly baked bread or pastry is a way of getting attention. For example, the pungent smell of curry or bouillabaisse can elicit a response.

I Is for Interest. The next step in the process is to pique the customer's curiosity, thus holding his attention and causing him to wonder. For example, asking the guest a provocative question that suggests a new, exciting experience or taste treat is an effective means of creating interest. Such questions include the following: "How many times have you. . .?" "Would someone be adventurous and try our. . .? "Have you ever tasted. . .?"

Interest also can be created by packaging of products in unusual and unfamiliar ways. Cause the guests to wonder, what's that? G. D. Graffiti's, a gangster concept restaurant, has its sales hosts bring a violin case to the table followed by the statement: "I'm going to make you an offer you can't refuse!" This action causes the guest to wonder what's inside the case.

D Is for Desire. Robert Cialdrini in his provocative text on influencing entitled *Influence Science and Practice,* researched why requests presented in one way influenced compliance and those presented another way did not. He has metamorphosed these compliance techniques into weapons of influence. I heartily recommend this text to anyone who wants to be a professional in sales. His principles of influencing include the following:

- *Reciprocation.* This principle states that most people try to repay a kindness offered by another. The sales host who does an unexpected favor for the guest ("the uninvited gift") creates a debt that most people are driven to repay. For example, a former student who worked his way through college as a waiter would occasionally purchase dessert for a special party of guests; the treat was "on him." Needless to say, he came home with exceptional tips.
- *Social proof.* The principal of social proof states that people frequently decide on appropriate behavior by observing what others are doing. If, for example, they see wine being served at many tables, they will frequently get on the bandwagon and purchase wine themselves.
- *Liking.* People tend to say yes to individuals whom they like and feel as if they know. Physical attractiveness, the belief we are alike, and repeated friendly contact are all effective influencers.
- *Scarcity.* People assign more value to opportunities that are less available. If we have just four bottles of the 1983 Margaux left in the bin, it can seem to be of more value to the wine drinker than an older, more familiar product.

Building a desire can come from associating a guest benefit with the product. Without an associated benefit, the buyer may have had her interest piqued but see no reason to purchase.

- The *visual appeal* of appetizing food is an effective and wordless way of building desire. For example, dessert merchandisers know that the best way to sell dessert is to practically place desserts under the guest's nose. The usual dessert menu cannot compete with the dessert bar or a mouth-watering tray, which offers immediate access to a small pleasure.
- The *speed appeal.* Make the item easy and fast for the guest to get. In the case of add-on sales like desserts, wine, coffees, and after-dinner drinks, you must assure guests that the item is easy and quick to obtain. A well-known Chicago restaurant chain used to have their sales hosts come to the table with an Irish coffee cart with all the "fixin's" right in front of the guest. With the suggestion of "Can we make your coffee Irish?" Irish coffee sales soared. The visible wine cellar and cheese or dessert bar are good examples of making the item easy to get.
- *The descriptive benefit.* Well-trained sales hosts are skilled in describing a taste experience. Words like *fresh, cool, crisp, crunchy, piping hot,* and *just made* are all action-oriented words that can build a guest's desire.

A Is for Action. Nothing happens until the sale is made. Therefore, the most critical element of merchandising requires that the sales host call for action to buy.

- The *positive assumption* concept requires that sales hosts, when asking for the order, make the assumption that the guest is going to buy. For example, when suggesting a cocktail, the sales host will ask, "Are you ready to order your cocktail?" or "May I take your cocktail order now?" Do not assume an either/or alternative. For example, "Are you going to have a cocktail now?" is wrong.
- *Ask the "which" question.* The sales host should ask, "Which one of you is going to be the first to try our delicious apple cream cobbler?"
- Avoid asking questions that can be answered yes or no.

Listening to the guest's real response. A guest can make any of four types of responses to a suggested purchase:

- *A positive no.* This is a clear and decisive refusal, in which the guest leaves no possible question of choice. We instruct our sales hosts to cease any further effort to encourage a purchase. We never want to make the guest feel uncomfortable, intimidated, or that they have to defend their decision.
- *A qualified no.* This is a hesitant answer that implies some interest and, therefore, an opportunity to make an additional sale. One recommended response to this is to offer an alternative. For example, "Are you ready to try our freshly made strawberry shortcake?" The answer: a hesitant "no—I don't think so." Quick alternative: "I'll bet you would like some fresh strawberries in champagne" or "A coconut Amaretto coffee?"
- *The positive yes.* This response clearly indicates that the guest knows exactly what he wants. Once again, no effort should be made to suggest a shift in decision. The positive yes should be met with a reinforcement of the choice. For example, the guest says, "I'll have a 1967 Pinot Chardonnay." The sales host's response is to reinforce the selection, perhaps saying, "That is an excellent choice, you will enjoy that wine." If the guest leaves an alternative to the suggestion such as pie, we may suggest an ice cream or a whipped cream topping, but it would be limited to enhancing the guest's choice.
- *The qualified yes.* Offers the sales host the greatest opportunity to exercise suggestive selling. It is under these conditions that the effectiveness of sales training appears. The well-trained sales host is ready to offer suggestions from a list of alternatives best suited to fit the diner's occasion.

Product Packaging

"What the eye sees, the eye buys." This old merchant's rule of thumb is not an exaggeration. We do know that a guest can be influenced to purchase an item if it is packaged in an exciting way, one that exceeds the guest's expectation. It has been said that people eat with their eyes. This figure of speech could be restated because people can be influenced to purchase with their eyes, noses, ears, and tongues (through sampling). Many items can be merchandised through eye appeal such as size, color, texture, flambé, or unique service ware. Merchandisers can also appeal to sound by presenting sizzling platters. The appetizing odor of products, such as fresh breads and steaming spice blends stimulate purchases. Providing guests with a sample taste is often used as a sales promotion technique. Food does not have to be exotic; as a matter of fact, it is often more marketable when it is familiar (i.e., steak, hamburger, chicken, seafood, prime rib). Packaging can consist of creating something new with familiar food, perhaps by using unusual ingredients (chicken, à la whiskey),packaging, or flambé. The following are certain principles that food marketers should heed in their desire to create a perceived difference through product packaging.

All menu items should pass the D&B test. When planning a menu each item should be *different and better* than that served by the competition. For example offer a menu of delicious ethnic appetizers, each accompanied by a half ounce of the country's most popular drink, i.e., sake or tequila.

Do not merchandise everything. While I suggest all menu items be special in some way, merchandise items that are highly popular and profitable. An important exercise in menu analysis is ranking all menu items by their contribution margin (gross margin) and featuring those items with the highest contribution margin.

Exceed the guest's expectations. This requires competitive shopping. Attract the eye by the height of the center of the plate, for example, a thick steak or a mile high pie.

Provide glamorous garnishes for attention and interest. Capture the eye through garnishes. Follow the philosophy of the famed restaurateur Mike Hurst, "thou shalt not use parsley," and use fresh fruit and vegetables to create exciting sensory appeal and enhance the taste experience. Think fresh—pineapple, melons, grapes, broccoli, or cauliflower.

When product differentiation is difficult to achieve through the menu item or the garnish, look to unique service and glassware. The Bella Grande Glass and five or six grapes inside can make something special of a jug wine. Eggs and omelets served in skillets or bread on a plank are examples of this approach.

Perhaps there is no better way to influence a guest's purchase in an entertainment-oriented restaurant than to flambé and prepare items at the tableside. I have often heard restaurateurs say that this service style requires experienced and formally trained service personnel. This is not necessarily so.

Make the product a part of the ambience. Call the guest's attention to products by designing them into the decoration. One packaging concept recently developed for a pizza chain featured a 16-foot salad bar. It was packaged with a great awning reminiscent of an old-fashioned grocery store, with crates of fresh produce lined up behind a melange of ingredients. The salad bar promised a unique gustatory experience and was the featured decor item in the dining room. Guest salad frequency increased from one of ten purchases to one in three. Restaurants can be designed so as to visually stimulate the guest purchase by using product packaging as decor.

Sampling or Pump Priming

The concept of pump priming illustrates the old adage, "you put a little water in the well pump to get a lot of water out." One of a packager's best means of stimulating the sales of products is by giving away a drink, special salad, or appetizer early in the meal period. For example, send a complimentary flaming dessert to a guest's table early in the evening and observe the increased number of flaming desserts you will sell the rest of the dinner period. When this becomes an act of hospitality, it can result in reciprocity compliance.

Another means of sampling is the taste. Sonny Look of Look's Sirloin House would begin every guest visit with a small sample of some excellent wine, "compliments of Mr. Look." This practice sold bins of wine.

Pump priming includes providing gifts on slow evenings. On slower evenings at the Chateau Louise, I would have several dozen escargot made up and pass them out in the dining room. That not only introduced people to order escargot; it created much favorable word of mouth.

Point of Purchase

Another tool of merchandising is to call attention to a desirable product through table tents, posters, and other suggestive items. Almost everyone is familiar with the fast food companies' posters of food at the entry and the Translites at the menu board. There are also more subtle ways to suggest an item at the point of purchase. For example, at Chateau Louise, we substituted the wine glass for the water glass. We enhanced the purchase suggestion by placing the guest's napkin in the glass, which created an attractive table top. This simple effort caused a 10% increase in wine sales.

Use a rifle shot, not a shotgun approach, to point of purchase merchandising (P.O.P.). It is better to reinforce the same offer through P.O.P. several times, perhaps in four different ways, than to promote many different products. The New York Sheraton's restaurant named "Sally's" sets a good example. A life-sized dyecut of an attractive woman advertising Sally's restaurant is at the entrance. Translite posters of Sally's products appears at the elevators, with mouth-watering four-color pictures of menu items. Table tents feature Sally's in the hotel rooms, and additional graphic reinforcement is located at the entrance of the room. When the purchase decision is being made, you can be certain that the benefits of Sally's will readily come to mind.

Merchandising Suggestions

Attention-getting Tools

- Such tools include blackboards and promotions (i.e., wine of the month), posters (pictures of popular foods), life-size dyecuts, and wine barrels filled with the wine of the week.

Table-top Merchandising

- Such merchandising can take the form of the wine bottle, the wine glass (emphasized with napkins), and table tents.

Some Points for P.O.P.

- Merchandise fewer items more frequently.
- Avoid clutter of P.O.P. materials (the discount-house look).
- Use the KISS concept in graphics, because simplicity is the essence of good design. Maximize the use of open space—it makes your message easy to read.
- The headline is critical, because four of five readers of advertising don't get past the headlines.
- Use a consistent format to make it easy for your reader to get the message.
- Get attention in the headline and supportive graphics.
- Put the elements of promise in the headlines. Use words such as _free, new, $$ off,_ or _treat._
- Comply with trademark requirements.

- Support the objective with graphics, letting the graphics tell the story if possible. An attractive product presentation is one of the best ways to influence the guest's purchase. Four-color photography is most effective, and most expensive.
- Good graphic ideas can be found in magazine ads, clip art, and the yellow pages.
- The paper grade and print implies the quality of the offer.
- Use contrast devices to get attention. These devices include black backgrounds, reversals, and color.
- Use logos to simplify communication where possible.
- Avoid quickly penciled, handmade posters; it is a statement about your food and service.

The Menu

A menu should be designed to capture the reader's interests and influence the purchase decision. Direct the guest's eye to buy the most profitable and popular items. This can be accomplished through layout and design.

- Emphasize the products you want to sell through placing them near the optical center of the page.
- Designate the proportion of space to merchandise desirability.
- White space is an attention getter.
- Contrast calls attention.
- Graphics are valuable influences.
- Use color deliberately. For example, red is an exciting, attention-getting color.
- Copy should be simple, descriptive, yet interesting.
- Type must be legible. The smallest type should be 12-point.
- Clip-ons can be an effective menu merchandiser, but care should be used to avoid clutter.

Menus are limited marketing tools, but they have the following drawbacks:

- Limited to one-way communication
- Static eye-appeal
- Can't answer all the questions
- Often difficult to read (confusing or too artistic, etc.)
- Limits the guest's opportunity to spend more

New menus should result in increased guest counts and higher average checks. There are four reasons to add items to a menu:

- Influence greater demand
- Increase the contribution margin
- Neutralize the competitor
- Create excitement

Price

Added-Value Alternatives

Provide guests the opportunity to purchase the greater value. Merchandisers know that by offering the guest a second-greater value alternative of a product, they can influence some guests to purchase the better value. This is effective with highly popular entrees and side items such as appetizers and drinks. For example, if a cafeteria offers a 6-ounce cup of coffee for $0.50 and a 12-ounce cup is merchandized at $0.80, the guest receives the greater value and the restaurant receives a higher contribution margin (CM) per guest. An estimated 40% of guests in the cafeteria line will agree to purchase the larger size. It follows that a cafeteria serving coffee to 1,000 guests per day can influence an estimated 400 to purchase the 12-ounce cup for $0.80. Six hundred guests will continue to purchase the 6-ounce coffee at $0.50 for a total of $300.00. Total daily coffee sales can be increased to $620.00 instead of the $500.00 earned when only one size was offered. For every 1,000 guests, the better-value alternative has the potential to increase sales by $120.00 per day, or $43,800 per year.

The concept of the *better-value alternative* is being effectively used by quick service restaurants to merchandise soft drinks by adding a second or even a third soft drink size, for example, regular, large, and giant.

Table service restaurants have effectively merchandised the added-value alternative in many ways. For example, Chateau Louise effectively merchandised three sizes of the prime rib: the Henry VI cut (8 oz.), the Henry VII (14 oz.), and the 22 oz. cut with seconds, the Henry VIII cut. One of the keys to the effectiveness of this merchandising was increasing the value for each larger cut. It must be noted that as we move the customer to a larger purchase, the cost of goods percentage will rise, but, more importantly, the contribution margin for each guest rises. Remember, that we bank dollars, not percentages.

The Table d'Hote Value

Offer the guest the greater value by pricing a package of menu items for a lower price than the items purchased separately. Package alternatives can include wine with dinner, a special cocktail at lunch or brunch, or steak sold by the ounce or by the meat grade (prime or choice). Additional package alternatives are pie with or without ice cream, take-out foods (take a pizza home for the freezer at a reduced price when one is purchased in the restaurant), french fries (size), salad sizes, a two-tiered salad bar—an à la carte price and a lower price when purchased with an entree, ice cream with fresh fruit or a liqueur topping, and a half sandwich and soup or salad etc.

27

Introduction to Hospitality Financial Systems

Raymond S. Schmidgall
Michigan State University

Introduction

Every business consists of operations including sales and expenses, and each uses resources in its activities. For individual hospitality businesses, the accounting, including the reporting of these activities, is accomplished through the hospitality financial system.

This financial system consists of records and forms, computers including software programs, and especially people working to record, summarize, and communicate financial information to both internal and external users.

The internal users are decision makers usually referred to as managers, who need financial information to make decisions affecting the future. For example, what was the average daily rate (ADR) and how did it compare to the budget? If the ADR differed significantly, these managers must determine why and take action. The hospitality financial system should provide both the ADR and the budget numbers. The manager then determines the causes of the difference and takes action.

External users, including both investors and creditors, need financial information. Investors need to know the future prospects of the business so they can optimize their investments, while creditors, such as suppliers, must know the ability of the business to pay its bills so they can determine the amount of credit to extend. Even the government needs information to determine that the proper amount of taxes has been paid.

This chapter covers the basics of a hospitality financial system, including classifications of activities and major financial statements. Brief examples are provided of the three major financial statements.

Basics of the System

Accounting may be defined as the process of identifying, recording, classifying, summarizing, and communicating financial information about an economic entity to decision makers interested in making informed judgements and decisions.

First, events of a financial nature that must be recorded are identified. The sale of food to a hotel guest and the payment to a supplier for beverages received are two examples of events that will be recorded in the financial records. Often hundreds of similar events in a business day of even a small business are recorded.

Next, the process of recording entails entering the information into the financial records. Most businesses today use computers for recording this information, but in the past large manuals called journals were used for hand-written journal entries.

During the recording process, the activity recorded is classified. The major classifications and a brief description and examples of each are as follows:

Revenues	Inflow of cash or promises to pay in exchange for goods or services rendered. Revenues are often referred to as sales, e.g., room sales and food sales. Revenues also include interest income.
Expenses	Outflow of cash or promises to pay in exchange for goods or services received. Expenses include wages expense, utilities expense, and telephone expense.
Assets	Resources owned by the economic entity. Assets include cash, accounts receivable, and equipment.
Liabilities	Obligations owed by the economic entity to creditors. Liabilities include wages payable, taxes payable, and mortgage payable.
Owner's equity	The residual value of the assets over liabilities that have been paid that belong to the owners.

Several business activities that must be recorded and classified include the following:

Activity	**Major Classifications Affected**
1. _Sales_—A hotel guest buys lunch on account.	_Assets_—a promise (from guest) to pay (the hotel) is received _Revenues_—future inflow of cash
2. _Purchases_—The hotel purchase food on account.	_Assets_—food is obtained _Liabilities_—an obligation pay in the future

3. *Cash disbursements*—The hotel pays its telephone bill.

Expenses—an outflow of cash
Assets—resources are reduced

4. *Cash receipts*—A hotel guest checks out and pays her bill.

Assets—cash is received
Assets—a promise to pay by the guest is satisfied

5. *Payroll*—Employees are paid wages for the week.

Expenses—cash is paid
Assets—resources are reduced

During a business day in most hospitality businesses, hundreds and even thousands of economic events are identified and recorded in the entity's books. All these activities are classified within the five major categories discussed above. Periodically, the results of these activities are summarized in financial statements for communication to decision makers within the economic entity and to external parties.

Financial Statements

The financial statements are the scoreboards of the economic entity. They reflect the results of activities in three basic ways as follows:

- Income statements—reports revenues and expenses
- Statement of cash flows—reports both cash received and disbursed
- Balance sheets—reports assets, liabilities, and owners' equity

The income statement reports the operating results of the business for a period of time. Expenses, such as salaries, utilities, and taxes, are subtracted from revenues, such as room revenues and food sales, to equal net income. Internal decision makers (such as department heads and the general manager) are interested in operating results as this reflects their performance in managing the business. The operating results will be compared to the budgeted figures and to last year's operating results to determine just how well the business has performed. External parties, including investors (owners) and creditors, are also interested in results reported on the income statement. For investors, and even potential investors, the results reflect net income, which accrues to owners. Generally, profitable businesses are able to pay their obligations as they become due so creditors find the income statement results to be useful.

The statement of cash flows reports the receipt and disbursement of cash from the three major activities of operations, investing, and financing for a period of time. The net result shown on this statement is the increase or decrease in cash. Users of financial statements want to know not only the change in cash but how the three major activities cause the cash to change. Generally, users prefer to see cash increases in a business come from operations rather than simply from more financing, because cash from operations has been earned while cash from financing must be repaid in the future.

Obligations owed to creditors are paid with cash while disbursements of profits to investors, called dividends, are cash payments. Thus, positive cash flows in the current period suggest future payments can be made. Managers of the business are also interested in this statement because it reflects the cash flows for activities for which they are responsible.

The third major financial statement is the balance sheet. The balance sheet reports the assets, liabilities, and owners' equity of the business at a particular date. The assets are the resources of the economic entity and include cash, accounts receivable (hotel guest promises to pay), and property and equipment. Liabilities are the obligations of the business to pay creditors while owners' equity is the residual value of assets in excess of liabilities.

Creditors find this statement useful as it reflects their claim to assets (liabilities) as well as showing the amount of assets. The greater the excess of assets over liabilities, the greater the comfort to creditors in realizing they will be paid on a timely basis.

Investors in the business are interested in the balance sheet because it shows their claims to assets: assets less liabilities equals owners' equity. Managers of the economic entity need to know how assets compare with the claims to the assets (both liabilities and owners' equity). They want a balance sheet that shows the business has significant resources compared to its obligations, thus suggesting the creditors will be paid and owners will receive periodic dividends. The better the business is operated, then, the higher the profits and the more cash is available to pay obligations and dividends. In addition, the better the business is operated, the higher the compensation of the managers.

Financial Statements Illustrated

An introduction to financial management should include examples of these three statements. Figure 1 is the condensed income statement for the Example Motel. Revenues total $510,000 while expenses equal $435,500 resulting in net income (also called profit) of $74,500. This statement is highly condensed to keep it simple. Income statements prepared for external parties are often highly condensed in order to retain the confidentiality of operating details. Income statements prepared for decision makers within the economic entity are often quite detailed, and will include a detailed schedule for each operating department such as the rooms and food departments of a lodging business.

Figure 2 is the balance sheet of the Example Motel. As with all balance sheets, it shows assets, liabilities, and owners' equity. The assets (resource of the motel) equal $265,000 while total liabilities equal $152,000. The difference between assets and liabilities equals owners' equity of $113,000. The net income of $74,500 earned during 19X1 is shown in this section of the balance sheet. The assets are subdivided between current and property and equipment. Liabilities are divided between current and long-term, and the owner's equity section of the balance sheet reflects the owners' claims to assets. Jim Smith is the sole owner of the Example Motel.

Example Motel
Condensed Income Statement
for the Year of 19X1

Revenues:	
Sales	$500,000
Interest income	10,000
Total revenues	510,000
Expenses:	
Salaries and wages	150,000
Depreciation	30,000
Interest expense	30,000
Other expenses	200,000
Income before income taxes	100,000
Income taxes	25,500
Net income	$ 74,500

Note: Expenses total $435,500 including income taxes.

Figure 1. Income Statement

Figure 3 is the Statement of Cash Flows. The bottom line of this statement reveals an increase in cash of $4,500 for the year. If balance sheets had been shown for two consecutive periods, which is the general practice in business, the difference in the cash amount of the balance sheet would be $4,500. To keep this statement fairly simple, a few lines of activity are shown for the three major categories of operations, investing, and financing. This statement shows cash inflow from operating activities of $104,500 starting with net income (from the Income Statement) of $74,500. Cash flows invested in equipment and building totaled $110,000 for 19X1, while financing activity includes the reduction of long-term debt of $10,000 and an inflow of cash from debt financing of $20,000.

Example Motel
Balance Sheet
December 31, 19X1

Assets

Current assets:

Cash		$ 5,000
Accounts receivable		10,000
Inventory		5,000
Total current assets		20,000

Property and equipment:

Land	$ 20,000	
Building	300,000	
Furnishings and equipment	50,000	
Less accumulated depreciation	125,000	
Net property equipment		245,000
Total assets		$265,000

Liabilities and Owners' Equity

Current liabilities:

Notes payable	$ 24,000	
Accounts payable	8,000	
		$ 32,000

Long-term liabilities:

Mortgage payable		120,000
		152,000

Owner's equity:

Jim Smith, capital at January 1, 19X1	38,500	
Net income for 19X1	74,500	
Jim Smith, capital at December 31, 19X1		113,000
Total liabilities and owner's equity		$265,000

Figure 2. Balance Sheet

Example Motel
Statement of Cash Flows
for the Year of 19X1

Cash flow from operating activities:

Net income		$ 74,500
Adjustments to reconcile net income		
to net cash flow from operations:		
Depreciation	$ 30,000	
Increase in current assets.	5,000	
Increase in current liabilities	5,000	
Net cash flow from operating activities		$104,500
Cash flow from investing activities:		
Purchase of equipment	10,000	
Purchase of building	100,000	
Cash flow from investing activities		<110,000>
Cash flow from financing activities:		
Payment of long-term debt	10,000	
Proceeds from debt financing	20,000	
Net cash flow from financing activities		10,000
Increase in cash		$ 4,500

Figure 3. Statement of Cash Flows

Summary

Hospitality financial systems provide financial information to decision makers both within and external to the hospitality business through three major financial statements. The income statement reflects operations of the business. The balance sheets shows the resources and claims to the resources of the business, while the statement of cash flows reflects the sources and uses of cash from three major activities—operations, investing, and financing.

The key to a successful hospitality financial system is the communicating of relevant economic information to decision makers. Though it involves forms, reports, computers, software, and more, the prime ingredient is people. The bookkeepers, accountants, and other financial experts make the hospitality financial system successful.

——References——

Schmidgall, Raymond, and James Damitio. _Hospitality Industry Financial Accounting._ East Lansing, Mich.: The Educational Institute of the American Hotel and Motel Association.

Schmidgall, Raymond. _Hospitality Industry Managerial Accounting._ East Lansing, Mich.: The Educational Institute of the American Hotel and Motel Association.

Uniform System of Accounts and Expense Dictionary for Small Hotels, Motels, and Motor Hotels, Fourth edition. Educational Institute of the American Hotel and Motel Association, 1407 S. Harrison Rd., East Lansing, MI 48823

Uniform System of Accounts for Clubs. Club Managers Association of America, 7615 Winterberry Pl., Bethesda, MD 20817

Uniform System of Accounts for Hotels, Eighth edition. Hotel Association of New York City, Inc., 40 W. 38th St., New York, NY 10018

Uniform System of Accounts for Restaurants. National Restaurant Association, 311 First St., N.W., Washington, DC 20001.

—Appendix A—

The Uniform Systems of Accounts

Internal users of financial statements need considerably more detailed financial information to make operating decisions than do external users. More detailed financial statements, especially income statements, are provided by the uniform systems of accounts (USA). The USA are standardized financial systems prepared for various segments of the hospitality industry, including hotels, motels, restaurants, and clubs.

The major benefit of this system is the standardized format of the income statement and accompanying department schedules. A department schedule reflecting the details of revenues and expenses is provided for each profit center in the hotel, that is, each part of the hotel that generates revenues and incurs expenses. Examples include the rooms department, food and beverage department, and telephone department. Department schedules are also provided for service centers, that is, departments that provide service and incur costs but do not generate revenues. Examples in a lodging operation include marketing, administration, and maintenance. Financial information from the department schedules figures are summarized on the income statement of the business.

Figure 4 illustrates the income statement for lodging operation, while Figure 5 is an income statement based on the uniform system of accounts for restaurants.

There is considerably more detail in these income statements than you find in the income statement shown in Figure 1. The underlying reason for more detail is management's needs. A responsive hospitality financial system will produce information to meet the user's needs.

Vacation Inn
Income Statement
for the year ended December 31, 19X1

	Schedules	Net Revenues	Cost of Sales	Payroll and Related Expenses	Other Expense	Income (Loss)
Operated departments						
Rooms	1	$1,041,200	$ 0	$ 185,334	$ 79,080	$ 776,786
Food and beverage	2	626,165	208,448	218,532	66,513	132,672
Telephone	3	52,028	46,505	14,317	6,816	(15,610)
Total operated departments		1,719,393	254,953	418,183	152,409	893,848
Undistributed operating expenses						
Administrative and general	7			47,787	24,934	72,721
Data processing	8			20,421	11,622	32,043
Human resources	9			22,625	4,193	26,818
Transportation	10			13,411	7,460	20,871
Marketing	11			33,231	33,585	66,816
Property operation and maintenance	12			31,652	49,312	80,964
Energy costs	13			0	88,752	88,752
Total undistributed operating expenses				169,127	219,858	388,985
Income before fixed charges		$1,719,393	$ 254,953	$ 587,310	$ 372,267	504,863
Rent, property taxes, and insurance	14					200,861
Interest	14					52,148
Depreciation and amortization	14					115,860
Income before income taxes						135,994
Income tax	15					48,707
Net income						$ 87,287

Figure 4. Uniform System of Accounts for Hotels

Summary Statement of Income
Steak-Plus Restaurant
for the year ended December 31, 19X1

	Schedule Numbers	Amounts	Percentages
Revenue			
Food	D-1	$1,045,800	75.8%
Beverage	D-2	333,000	24.2
Total revenue		1,378,800	100.0
Cost of sales			
Food		448,000	42.8
Beverage		85,200	25.6
Total cost of sales		533,200	38.7
Gross profit	D-3	845,600	61.3
Other income		5,400	.4
Total income		851,000	61.7
Controllable expenses			
Salaries and wages	D-4	332,200	24.1
Employee benefits	D-5	57,440	4.2
Direct operating expenses	D-6	88,400	6.4
Music and entertainment	D-7	14,200	1.0
Marketing	D-8	30,000	2.2
Energy and utility services	D-9	37,560	2.7
Administrative and general expenses	D-10	56,400	4.1
Repairs and maintenance	D-811	28,600	2.1
Total controllable expenses		644,800	46.7
Income before rent and other occupation Costs, interest, and depreciation		206,200	15.0
Rent and other occupation costs	D-12	82,200	6.0
Income before interest, depreciation, and income taxes		124,000	9.0
Interest		21,600	1.5
Depreciation		31,200	2.3
Total		52,800	3.8
Net income before income taxes		71,200	5.2
Income taxes		14,240	1.0
Net income		$ 56,960	4.2%

Figure 5. Uniform System of Accounts for Restaurants

28

Overview of Cost Control Procedures

David V. Pavesic
Georgia State University

Why Study Cost Control?

All hospitality operations need to have a cost control program. Control is a process or function that is used to regulate, verify, or check that which is accomplished through some method, device, or system. The first step in correcting any problem is to realize that you in fact have one. One often assumes that there is no problem until something is discovered to be missing, and then the damage has already been done. Without controls in place to detect variances and shortages, owners and managers remain open to losses. When a loss is discovered, one must take appropriate action to limit adverse effects on the financial well-being of the operation. Operational success does not happen by chance; it happens as the result of some very careful planning.

Cost control is not a one-time response that is to be employed when a business begins to experience declining sales and shrinking profits. Cost control is an ongoing *process* that must become so ingrained in the minds of all employees that it becomes institutionalized as a permanent part of the culture and philosophy of a company. The control philosophy becomes institutionalized when all employees innately place a premium on getting the greatest value for the least cost in every aspect of the company's operations without sacrificing quality or customer service.

A large part of remaining in business today is the ability to keep waste to a minimum and to use resources as efficiently as possible. Keeping costs under control allows products and services to be sold at a lower price. When you offer recognizable value to your customers, revenues will grow from repeat business.

It does not matter how intelligent you are or how many hours you put in each week physically on location at the place of business. Physical presence alone is insufficient for adequate control. No one can possibly see everything that can cause costs to be out of line. Even if it were possible to observe all business activities and transactions, you still could not ascertain on the spot the effect on financial results. One must have written cost reports and records to detect what the eye cannot always see. The difference between success and failure in most hospitality enterprises can be as little as 3% of sales. That small percentage can be the difference between being solvent and going out of business.

The further removed an owner or manager is from the actual operation of a unit or department, the greater the need for proper cost control records. Cost control records become a substitute for the eyes of the absent owner or manager. If this were not the case, thousands of franchisees would operate unchecked by their franchisers. In corporate chain operations, management is generally further removed from the front lines where the work is actually being performed. In such cases where absentee ownership is common, cost control records are used by absentee owners to assess the effectiveness and efficiency of the unit's management.

Management's Role

Effective cost control systems must start at the top of the organization. No control program can function well unless management supports and enforces the standards and procedures. Employees are quick to notice when standards are not followed and when management fails to act to bring variances from standards into line. Employees will deviate from set standards only as much as management allows.

Regardless of the type of hospitality enterprise, cost controls will be a major part of management's total responsibilities. Cost controls encompass all areas from the back door to the front, from purchasing to checking deliveries, making the bank deposits, paying the bills, and all the activities in between.

Control is a basic management function that is accompanied by the functions of planning, organizing, directing, and coordinating. These are interactive management functions. In order to have proper control, it is necessary to plan short-term and long-term goals, to organize resources to achieve them, and to direct and coordinate individuals and departments in the pursuit of those goals and objectives.

In addition to the functions of planning and directing, policies, procedures, rules, and regulations are also control tools. Such tools allow management to appraise performance of individuals and departments relative to achievement of goals and objectives. Ongoing appraisal is an important part of the control process. A hospitality enterprise must establish goals and must develop a program to achieve those goals within the time frame and the budget in which it has to work while still maintaining the qualitative standards of performance. Thus, proper control implies the exchange of information for planning, implementation, and appraisal of goals and objectives.

Purposes of Cost Control

Cost control is not the computing of percentages and ratios. It involves making decisions after the percentages and ratios have been compiled and interpreted. Cost accounting and bookkeeping are not cost control in themselves, but the means of gathering the information needed for control to take place. Therefore, a more complete definition of cost control can be delineated by citing its purposes:

1. To provide management with the information it needs to make day-to-day operational decisions
2. To monitor the efficiency of individuals and departments
3. To inform management of what expenses are being incurred, what incomes are being received, and whether they are within standards or budgets
4. To prevent fraud and theft by employees, guests, and purveyors
5. To be the basis for knowing where the business is going, not for discovering where it has been
6. To emphasize *prevention,* not correction
7. To *maximize profits,* not minimize losses

A key aspect of a cost control program is *prevention* and not correction. Prevention is brought about through advanced planning. Correction is after-the-fact activity, *after* the damage has already been done.

Control in hospitality enterprises is placed over all items of income and expense. The major areas are food, beverage, and labor. Consider that the cost of a 1,000-room convention hotel is around $164 million; over the life of the hotel, however, more money will be spent on food, beverage, and labor than on land, construction, and furnishings.

Cost Analysis

Many operators become converts to cost control only when it is too late. When losses are excessive, the business is like a terminally ill patient. All cost controls can do at that point is keep the business going a little longer, but eventually the inevitable occurs: bankruptcy.

There is a difference between cost *control* and cost *reduction.* Cost control is more the accumulation and interpretation of information, filling out department reports, taking inventories, costing out recipes, and the like. Cost reduction is the action taken to bring costs within acceptable standards.

A story about Christopher Columbus serves to illustrate the preventive aspect of cost control. When Columbus set out for the New World, he had no idea how to get there, how long it would take, or what to expect along the way. He had to battle rough seas and risk running aground on sandbars and coral reefs. When he finally got to where he was going, he didn't know where he was. The one thing that many entrepreneurs attempting to open their own businesses have in common with Columbus is their courage to take the risk for something they believe in very strongly. Today, one cannot expect to succeed in business without an operational plan any more than one could sail around the world the first time without the aid of maps and charts. The competition is too great, and one will likely run into financial difficulty within a few months. By being prepared and having a plan, not only will a business be able to avoid making fatal mistakes but it will be prepared for the problems along the way.

Many times just limiting the amount of damage will allow one to remain in business when other, less prepared operators fail. When the economic conditions that foster business activity are poor, few businesses completely avoid the adverse effects. However, forewarned is forearmed. We batten down the hatches to minimize loss or dock at a friendly port until the danger passes. Such are the economic recessions, inflation, unemployment, interest rates, and tax laws that hospitality enterprises must endure. Only the well-prepared will survive in rough economic times. Cost controls are an important component of the survival kit. Today, if Christopher Columbus were a restaurateur, he would find himself competing against entrepreneurs who have current charts and the latest equipment and expertise to help their businesses succeed the first time. Richard Melman, president of Lettuce Entertain You Enterprises and a very successful and innovative restaurateur, told an auditorium full of restaurant people at a recent National Restaurant Association convention that 80% of the success of any restaurant concept is determined before it opens its doors to the public.

Cost control is not a one-shot application but an ongoing program that requires five elements for success:

1. Advance planning
2. Devices or procedures to aid in control
3. Implementation
4. Employee compliance
5. Management enforcement

A cost control program cannot be sustained unless you have the complete cooperation of management and employees.

Although cost control is critically important to the profitable operation of any business, it alone will not ensure profitability. Cost control and quality control are not mutually exclusive, and they often complement one another. In fact, cost controls have been found to fall in line in operations that have a commitment to quality. Cost control is only part of the total operational strategy of a successful business. You can have adequate cost controls and still go out of business due to the lack of another, equally important component that is the primary reason corporate and independent operations fail: *inadequate sales revenue to retire debt and return a minimum profit.*

A business must have adequate sales revenue, which implicitly requires a marketing strategy to accompany a cost control program. Cost and efficiency follow when there is an emphasis on quality, customer service, innovativeness, participation, and a customer-focused management philosophy.

Low costs will not make much of a difference without adequate sales volume and customer counts. Costs cannot go below a point where a business sacrifices the quality of its goods and services to achieve cost goals and objectives. In the long run, customers will start going to competitors as they find poor value for their money, poor quality products, and poor service.

In order to be effective, a cost control program must possess the following five characteristics:

1. Relevant information is provided to management.
2. Information is reported in a timely manner.
3. Information is easily assembled and organized.
4. Information is easily interpreted.
5. The benefit of the information is greater than the cost of the control.

Some operators become too bottom-line oriented and forget about the qualitative aspects of the business. Don't be penny wise and dollar foolish when it comes to controlling cost. The marketing perspective keeps you in touch with the competitive world and acts as a reminder that we cannot forget the importance of quality in the products we sell and the service we provide to the customer.

The Importance of Standards

Setting standards is an integral part of any cost control program. The dictionary definition says that a standard is simply *a measure that establishes a value.* Standards establish a minimum acceptable level of performance or results. Standards become the yardsticks that management uses to measure the qualitative and quantitative levels of performance for departments and individuals. Wherever there is an expense there needs to be a standard that will serve as a benchmark for comparison with the actual results achieved. Employees need to be aware of the standards and to be held accountable for them.

In establishing standards, one defines a predetermined point of comparison that will be measured against the actual results achieved and resources consumed in the process. The difference between resources planned and actual amounts used or the variance between some qualitative measure and the level of quality achieved will be appraised relative to the standard established.

Management must reduce or eliminate the negative discrepancies between the predetermined standards and the actual results. A positive variance occurs when performance exceeds the standard. Management will praise or reward those who are responsible for a positive variance. Although standards can show where individuals or departments have not met expectations and corrective action must be taken, standards are more important as a preventive measure that reduces or eliminates the number of times corrective action must be taken. Do not leave it up to employees to develop their own qualitative and quantitative standards. Employees can offer new ideas and information that will benefit the operation, but management remains the final authority on standards.

It is not likely that management trainees will be allowed to establish standards, especially in a national corporate chain operation. Management's main responsibility will be to see to it that employees adhere to existing standards. We use terms like *tight ship* and *by the book* to indicate that things must be done a certain way. Management must set the example for the employees to follow.

Every operation must establish its own standards relative to its own financial and operational idiosyncrasies and its position in the marketplace. This is necessary because all of the variables that will influence cost standards differ from hotel to hotel and even within a chain of restaurants. Rent, taxes, interest rates, depreciation schedules, and the like all uniquely affect the bottom-line profitability of an operation.

The importance of standards as an integral component of any cost control program is illustrated by the following five steps:

1. Establish standards of performance and results for all individuals and departments.
2. Charge all individuals to follow established standards to prevent waste and inefficiency.
3. Monitor adherence to standards as a preventive control measure.
4. Compare actual performance against established standards.
5. Take timely and appropriate action when deviations from standards are detected.

Cost control is not very complicated, as it is all basic management functions. You have to be able to identify your costs and be able to detect where costs are out of line. Do not lose track of the qualitative and revenue-enhancing perspective when implementing a cost control program. Cost controls are not an end in themselves. Once costs have been contained, the only way to increase the bottom line is to increase sales revenue.

──References──

Dittmer, P. G., and G. G. Griffin. (1989) *Principles of Food, Beverage, and Labor Cost Controls for Hotels and Restaurants.* Fourth edition. New York: Van Nostrand Reinhold Publishers.

Hendricks, K. *Waste not, want not. Inc.* (March 1991); pp. 33–42.

Keiser, J. (1989) *Controlling and Analyzing Cost in Foodservice Operations.* Second edition. New York: Macmillan.

Keister, D. C. (1990) *Food and Beverage Control.* Second edition. Englewood Cliffs, N.J.: Prentice-Hall.

Levinson, C. (1989) *Food and Beverage Operation: Cost Control and Systems Management.* Second edition. Englewood Cliffs, N.J.: Prentice-Hall.

29

Introduction to Hospitality Property Management

Melissa Dallas Bandy
Bowling Green State University

Introduction

Property management in the hospitality industry, analogous to facilities management or plant engineering in other industries, addresses effective management of buildings, equipment, and land. The term properly implies asset management, because the property is the primary physical asset contributing to the realization of profit.

The purpose of property management is to maximize guest satisfaction and employee productivity through a carefully controlled physical environment while practicing environmental responsibility. The physical environment of most hotels, restaurants, and clubs, however, is quite complex and requires a wealth of systems and engineering knowledge.

Accordingly, the components of a successful property management system are driven by the desired outputs of guest satisfaction, increased employee productivity, and environmental responsibility, rather than by prescribed inputs such as systems design. After all, guest satisfaction and employee productivity can combine to increase revenues and decrease costs, ultimately leading to a faster recouping of investment and a larger contribution toward a fair profit. Environmental responsibility can also have a direct effect on revenue. More importantly, however, environmental concern is now legally and ethically paramount for most major firms and, therefore, cannot be ignored.

Guest Satisfaction

Guest satisfaction can be realized in many ways through effective property management techniques. Guest safety, convenience, and comfort are all components leading to satisfaction and, ultimately, to increased revenue through higher guest folios or checks and increased patronage.

Guest Safety

Guest safety is an issue of increasing importance in this decade. Hotel and restaurant operators and owners are predicted to assume even more responsibility for guest safety in the next century as the scope of innkeeper's liability grows and demographics change. Specifically, more women are pursuing careers requiring extensive travel, and the average age of Americans will continue to increase as the youngest baby boomers pass age 50 around 2010. A common concern of both of these groups is safety.

Technological advances have made certain safety features, such as keyless locking systems, possible. Traditional keys, which can be easily copied, transferred, or "lost" for future use, are being replaced with key cards, allowing random anonymous coding for each check-in. Additionally, some properties are adopting systems enabling guest room access using a credit card as a key.

Television surveillance cameras are also increasingly important to ensure guest safety. Even though the presence of such cameras can deter some crime, physical monitoring of the screens is still necessary.

Electronically controlled sensing devices are commonplace now and are continually being upgraded to include fire, tornado, hurricane, and earthquake warning devices. The ultimate sensing device is networked into the property's management system (PMS) to allow immediate identification of physical problem areas in the hotel or restaurant. The exact location of the problem often implies the type of emergency measure to be enacted. For example, a fire in a hotel room will require different emergency measures than a fire in a vast public space or in an elevator shaft.

Guest Convenience

The most profound technological advances addressing guest convenience are the property management system for hotels and point-of-sale system (POS) for restaurants.

Property Management Systems

Most PMSs in hotels begin with computerized front office systems, often interfacing with a central reservation system (CRS). The CRS captures complete guest data before the guest arrives at the hotel, speeding the check-in process.

Additionally, many hotels have incorporated computerized guest services through the guest room television. For example, guests can order room service to be delivered within a specified time, can review their folios, and can check out of the hotel by merely pressing a few buttons on the remote control. Most PMSs also offer the guest telephone services such as voice mail.

Point-of-Sale Systems

Point-of-sale systems (POSs) have brought advanced technology to the food service industry, adding to customer convenience. Many food establishments now boast POSs, allowing the customer to place an order at a computer terminal and determine the method of payment. For credit card payments, POSs are often networked to afford quick verification, saving the customer time and minimizing frustration. The customer's order is then transmitted to the kitchen, prepared and delivered to the customer much faster than by the use of traditional ordering methods. Although some consumers complain of the impersonality of such systems, most, especially during lunch, will forgo traditional service contact for expediency.

Guest Comfort

Guest comfort, another goal of effective property management systems, is achieved in a variety of ways. Since the 1970s, when many buildings were sealed to conserve energy, air circulation has become an increasingly important issue. Uncomfortable levels of humidity or temperature can quickly frustrate guests, resulting in guest discomfort or, ultimately, in lost business. A less tangible result of an uncomfortable environment involves psychodynamics, the subconscious mental or emotional processes underlying human behavior as a response to environmental influences. Specifically, guests may choose not to return to a hotel or restaurant, unable to cite specific reasons for their dissatisfaction. Such behavior can be partially attributed, through psychodynamics, to uncomfortable environmental influences, making such a response difficult to address.

To combat such undesired results, many properties are installing energy management systems (EMSs) to control the heating, ventilation, and air conditioning (HVAC), electricity, lighting, water supply, and refrigeration. In some hotels, the EMS controls the heat and lighting in guest rooms, greeting the guest when the guest enters the room and conserving energy by turning the system off when the guest leaves the room. These functions serve a dual purpose; to contribute to guest comfort and to decrease energy costs for the property.

Water supply is also regulated by EMSs, heating water during peak periods at a different rate than during slow usage periods. Most EMSs boast a tracking device that can monitor usage rates by time periods to maximize their effectiveness for management.

Employee Productivity

Employee productivity can be enhanced through effective property management techniques, resulting in decreased labor costs and, most often, in increased job satisfaction. In effect, property management should be used to most effectively facilitate the interaction between the guest and the employee and between the work environment and the employee.

Guest–Employee Interaction

Guest–employee interaction is a constant in the hospitality industry; its importance cannot be stressed enough. Virtually all positions in a hotel or restaurant ultimately affect the guest, although the employees often lose sight of this. For example, although a housekeeper does not encounter guests as often as a restaurant server, a housekeeper's effectiveness directly contributes to guest satisfaction. The importance of many of the behind-the-scenes job is being recognized by the industry.

Certain aspects of property management can directly enhance the productivity of all employees. For example, many PMSs link room status from the front desk to the housekeeping department, enabling quicker room turnover. Room status should also be linked to the maintenance or engineering department, immediately generating work orders to be completed. Such networking allows maximization of revenue because prioritization can be implemented into the system, perhaps listing the rooms with the highest rack rate to be cleaned or repaired first.

The implications of a PMS for the front office staff are obvious. Many larger hotels, for example, have opened their front desk, enabling their staff to more personally serve the guest. In effect, the marble barrier, the front desk, is discarded in lieu of computerized check-in and increased guest interaction. Additionally, folios are much easier to run with a PMS and are more accurate, because most accounts are automatically posted at the time of guest usage.

The PMS allows more thorough reporting functions for all areas of the hotel, including the sales and marketing department and food and beverage areas. For example, full guest information can be used by the sales and marketing department for many purposes, including directing future promotions and generating guest profile reports. Sales and catering departments are becoming increasingly integrated into PMSs, since virtually all aspects of sales and catering affect other hotel divisions. In the past, poor communication between the sales and catering office and other departments led to frustrated employees and angry potential clients. With the introduction of PMSs into sales and catering, however, events can be booked more smoothly and more completely, resulting in greater assurance of guest satisfaction and a marked decrease in employee frustration.

In the food and beverage area, POSs can be used to calculate and valuate inventory, suggest order quantities based on a par stock (the minimum amount of an item required for operation), develop and cost recipes and menus, and for other forms of budgeting and forecasting.

Work Environment/Employee Interaction

Interaction between the work environment and the employee is crucial, affecting productivity and job satisfaction. After all, an employee cannot perform well if the lighting is inadequate or if the equipment is in need of repair.

Property management can be used to monitor lighting levels throughout all work areas. For example, the candlepower used in the kitchen prep area can be programmed to vary during certain periods of the work day, increasing the intensity during day shifts and decreasing intensity during nights when the prep area is out of use.

Preventive maintenance programs should be part of all property management systems, generating extensive preventive maintenance schedules for all equipment within the property. The maintenance or engineering department is responsible for these programs, following a rigid schedule of equipment lubrication, system safety checks, and pool maintenance, for example. Property management systems can also be of use in laundry facilities, prioritizing wash loads and inventorying supplies.

In short, the interaction between the work environment and the employee should be barrier free and should facilitate productivity and job satisfaction. The use of information from the science of ergonomics will enhance this interaction because ergonomics focuses on designing the work environment to fit the worker. As more attention is given to ergonomics, property management systems will contribute to the ideal fit between the work environment and the employee.

Environmental Responsibility

The last goal of effective property management is environmental responsibility. Increased governmental regulations, effective lobbying efforts, and general concern about limited resources have combined to force environmental awareness and responsibility on businesses. While some conservation methods can be almost cost prohibitive, many can result in actual cost savings.

Property management systems can be interfaced to manage waste water treatment. For example, guest room water waste can be retreated and recycled for use by the groundskeeping staff. While such recycling is environmentally sound, it also results in lower water bills for the property.

Environmentally responsible strategies include an array of programs from basic recycling plans to the use of solar energy. Thermodynamics, the conversion of heat into other forms of energy, will also be a viable strategy for hotels and restaurants in the future, conserving energy and lowering overhead costs.

Importance of Property Management

Property management directly affects the bottom line of the profit and loss statement. For example, renovation is almost always more expensive than preventive maintenance programs. Guest service technology can increase guest satisfaction while decreasing labor costs. An entire hotel or restaurant fire is vastly more expensive than installation of an automatic sprinkler system activated by a sensor and networked to proper authorities. Maintaining equipment results in a safer work environment, leading to decreased workers' compensation costs, increased employee productivity, and decreased absenteeism.

A hotel or a restaurant is an investment and must be treated as such. The 1993 average construction cost per room in a hotel was $100,000; $10,000 per seat in a restaurant. The immensity of the investment combined with an increased risk of failure in the hospitality industry due to overbuilding have forced many hotels and restaurants to adopt formal property management systems.

Property Characteristics Determine the System Components

The extensiveness of a property management system is based on features of the property itself. The age of the building, its geographic location, and its size contribute to the complexity of the system. Additionally, the level of service the property offers, its customer mix and expectations, the corporate culture, and occupancy rates further define the extensiveness of property management used. Quite obviously, a more extensive system should be used for an older, larger building in a volatile climate with a high level of service and relatively high occupancy rates.

This observation is confirmed by the fact that more than 97% of full-service resorts are computerized as compared to 88% of all lodging facilities. Recent literature suggests that strong growth is expected in guest-related technologies including "smart" rooms, which feature labor-saving and energy-saving devices in addition to improved guest service.

Career Opportunities

Career opportunities in property management are primarily found in larger properties, more than 300 rooms, or in large restaurant chains. The title of the positions or departments can include either engineering or maintenance, but since "maintenance" connotes technical, not managerial, expertise, "engineering" is preferred. In small hotels, less than 150 rooms, the chief engineer reports directly to the general manager. The chief engineer must be more technically qualified at a smaller property because the engineering and maintenance staff is always small, consisting of hourly labor working as groundskeepers or general laborers. Most major functions are contracted to a firm specializing, for example, in building renovations or HVAC.

In a small restaurant, most engineering and maintenance functions are assumed by line employees, who conduct programs such as periodic preventive maintenance at a store level. Similar to small hotels, most other engineering or maintenance functions are contracted from the outside.

In larger hotels, however, engineering staffs can be quite large. In fact, three to four engineering staff are needed per 100 guest rooms. The chief engineer heads the engineering department, reporting directly to the resident manager or to the general manager. The chief engineer's duties are mainly managerial in nature, and include budgeting, forecasting, and strategic planning. The assistant director of engineering reports directly to the chief engineer, assuming managerial responsibilities including scheduling, project leadership, and direct supervision of the supervisory staff. Each engineering supervisor is directly in charge of a functional area such as carpentry, audiovisual, grounds, or systems, which includes both electrical and computerized systems. These positions demand technical expertise in each functional area, because less is contracted out in larger hotels.

Most large restaurant chains also include an engineering department in their corporate structure. Geographic logistics create difficulties in managing such departments, however, and many act as a contracting referral service for individual stores. However, when a major renovation or systems change is scheduled, the engineering department will often manage the entire project.

Security personnel can be included in the engineering department or, in large hotels, may be a separate department. In the latter case, the director of security assumes the managerial functions and reports directly to the resident manager or to the general manager. Again, in smaller hotels and most restaurants, basic security is assumed by all line employees and, if more personnel are needed, the function is contracted out.

Conclusion

The current competitive environment in the hospitality industry is expected to continue. As investors demand a greater return on their investment and as consumers demand higher service levels, the importance of property management will continue to grow. A successful hospitality manager must realize that effective property management systems can maximize guest satisfaction and increase employee productivity while addressing environmental concerns. Effective property management demands proactive approach if the manager is to maintain a comfortable and safe environment for both guests and employees, simultaneously allowing recovery of investment and a fair profit to the property's investors.

30

Computers in the Hospitality Industry

Michael L. Kasavana
Michigan State University

During the past decade nothing has enhanced the professionalism nor increased the productivity of the hospitality industry more than the computer. Computers have changed the way hotels and restaurants plan, coordinate, evaluate, and control their business.

Hospitality computer systems are composed of software (programs) and hardware (equipment). Software basically refers to the instructions within a computer system that tell the hardware devices what to do, how to do it, and when to do it. Computer hardware is visible, moveable, and easier to distinguish than computer software.

The lodging industry is served by property management systems (PMS) technology, while food service depends on restaurant management system (RMS) design for its automation application. Each of these systems is discussed below.

Property Management Systems

No longer must a hotelier depend on a myriad of metal racks, an assortment of mechanical machinery, or a set of monotonous clerical procedures for folio management. From the moment a guest first contacts a property through to account settlement, a computer system is capable of monitoring, charting, and recording all guest–hotel transactions. The traditional guest cycle (arrival, occupancy, departure) has evolved into an expansive sequence of presale, point-of-sale, and post sale phases.

Guest Cycle

The guest cycle encompasses that period from the moment a potential guest first contacts a hotel until final reconciliation of account. From a practical point of view, the guest cycle serves to clarify the intricate series of communications within the hotel network. The cycle originates with presale events (reservations, prepayments, or account creation),

Presale	Point-of-Sale	Postsale
Reservations	Room assignment	Account settlement
Prepayment	Occupancy	Account reconciliation
Account creation	Charge purchases	Zero account balances
Arrival	Charge postings	Check-out

Figure 1. Overview of Hotel Guest Cycle

evolves into point-of-sale activities (room, food, beverage, and other revenue centers), and concludes with postsale transactions (check-out, account reconciliation, and guest history). Figure 1 contains an overview of the guest cycle by phase.

Property management systems are typically segmented into front office, back office, and interface application areas.

Front Office Applications

While not all PMS configurations operate identically, there appear to be four common software modules: reservations, rooms management, guest accounting, and general management.

Reservation modules are constructed according to a hotel's reservation (time) horizon and enable a rapid processing methodology for confirming or denying room requests. Reservation capabilities can be acquired through telecommunications interface to a central reservation network or through direct in-house operation. Regardless of the data's origin, the PMS electronically manages reservations data and is capable of producing a myriad of timely and accurate room, revenue, and forecasting reports.

Rooms management modules have room status as their primary focal point, so attention to housekeeping and occupancy activities is a critical variable. In addition, room rack and information rack equivalents are part of a complete rooms management package. Since the rooms module replaces most traditional front office equipment, it often becomes a major determinant in the selection of one PMS over another.

The guest accounting module provides the hotel with increased control over its guests' accounts and significantly modifies the night audit routine. Guest accounts are maintained electronically, thereby eliminating the need for folio cards, trays, or posting machinery. Guest accounting modules are capable of automatically monitoring predetermined folio credit limits and allow for multiple folio formats. Connecting revenue centers to the basic PMS scheme will provide remote data entry, which would be otherwise unavailable.

General management modules cannot operate independent of other front office modules. Since general management applications tend to be report-generating packages, their functionality is affected by the resident data collected through the reservation, rooms management, and guest accounting modules. The general management module is also capable of interconnecting the front and back office portions of a PMS configuration.

Back Office Applications

Like automated front office approaches, back office applications vary significantly. Typical back office modules are general ledger accounting, payroll, inventory control, and financial reporting.

General ledger accounting involves the specification of a chart of accounts and a systematic approach to transaction recording. The Uniform System of Accounts for Hotels (AH & MA) provides a logical approach to PMS back office design. A transactional accounting scheme must track accounts receivable, accounts payable, and cash and adjust entries. Some general ledger packages also offer a means for budget creation and comparative analyses. The general ledger module is a critical variable in the identification of an effective back office system.

Payroll accounting is a major concern in a back office application. The fact that hotel employees qualify for unique benefits, rates, withholdings, deductions, and report requirements renders this a complex system function. Time and attendance records are needed for the computation of gross pay. Pay rates, job codes, employee meals, uniform credits, tips, taxes, and the like are applied in the derivation of net pay. The maintenance of an accurate payroll register and the production of payroll checks are proprietary and confidential within the data processing area.

Inventory control is essential to efficient hotel operations. Back office applications treat inventory in several ways. Some key items by price, others by units, and some allow the user to select their preferred basis. The three most common inventory operations are inventory status, inventory valuation, and inventory variance. Inventory status involves an accounting of how much of each item is in storage. Oftentimes this information is combined with par stock or minimax levels as an aid in replenishment/purchase ordering. Inventory valuation deals with the extension of price against stock on hand. The critical factor here is knowing which price is used. Back office systems tend to employ either an inventory item's actual purchase price, a system computed average price, or a market replacement value for each item. The aggregation of price times stock yields an inventory valuation. The difference between a perpetual inventory tracking and a physical inventory is termed inventory variance. In other words, a beginning inventory level minus stock attributed to sales plus additional purchases will produce an estimate of stock available. A storeroom check (physical inventory) may not equate with the system's projected (perpetual inventory) inventory level. Variances should be investigated because they indicate a lack of inventory control.

The determination of bottom-line profitability and fiscal well-being of the business is found in the financial reporting module of a back office application. Most systems are capable of producing flash reports as well as predetermined interval reports. There can be differences, however, in report formats, user programmability, and compliance with industry standards. Balance sheet and income statement formulation are common to all financial packages. Additional formats can include cash flow analyses, fixed asset analyses, spreadsheet analyses, disbursement analyses, and the like. Users are often more interested in being able to alter financial report presentations than almost any other PMS application. The degrees of freedom accorded the user varies from none to full system flexibility. The proper level of hotel input is a function of need and user competency.

Interface Applications

Although the number of interfaces to PMS schemes is continuously expanding, the most popular applications are point-of-sale, energy management, call accounting, electronic locking systems, personal computer software, and in-room bars and movies.

Data captured at point-of-sale (POS) locations becomes critical to the maintenance of accurate and timely computer-based guest accounting and financial tracking modules. The ability to communicate this data to both front and back office components can result in numerous benefits from comprehensive reporting.

Significant results have been derived from energy control technology interfacing. The interconnection of guest room controls through the rooms management module in the front office has led to a reduction in energy consumption and hence has produced cost savings. Energy management systems (EMS) operate so effectively that maintenance and engineering personnel are able to direct their attention elsewhere.

There is no other PMS interface that has received more attention than telephone call accounting. Call accounting systems (CAS) enable the hotel to take control over local and long distance services and to apply a contribution margin to switchboard operations. CAS are responsible for the placement and rating of outgoing dialing, and interfacing to a PMS guest accounting module assures online posting to the proper folio. The telephone area of a hotel, traditionally a loss leader, has become a potential profit center.

Electronic locking systems (ELS) are changing the way hotels maintain control over guest room access. At check-in, guest room door locks are changed and new keys produced via a computer located in the front office. This technique ensures enhanced guest safety and strengthens the hotel's ability to monitor room usage. It is anticipated that the interfacing of ELS technology to PMS designs will lead to more efficient self-check in systems.

For hoteliers, the personal computer (PC) has become a popular means to expand data processing capabilities. The ability to transfer data from the PMS to the PC (downloading) for special application outside the PMS enables a unique level of sophistication. Similarly, the movement of data from the PC to the PMS (uploading) also presents unique advantages. Generic PC software includes spreadsheet analysis, word processing, database management, and communications programs. Many of the features of these packages are not available in hotel property management systems.

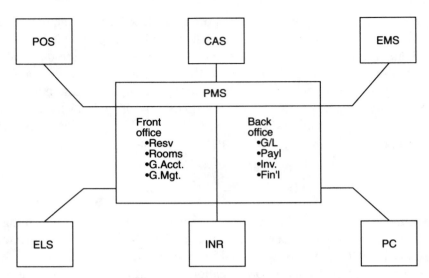

Figure 2. Anatomy of a Property Management System

Computer vendors have been paying increasing attention to interfacing in-room (INR) beverage and in-room movie systems to PMS schemes. Much of the interest has been prompted by the outright demand for in-room amenities and the growth of cable networks and satellite earth stations. The interfacing of in-room bars and movies to the PMS guest accounting module has evolved into a reliable billing mechanism for specialized revenue centers.

Figure 2 provides a summary of a property management system with related interface applications.

Restaurant Management Systems

Computers in Food Service

It's been said that the three most important success factors in the food service business are control, control, and control—over such things as operations, marketing, menu, finance, accounting, labor, production, service, settlement, pricing, and inventory. Restaurateurs are discovering that the best means to gain these controls is through computerization. Computers store large amounts of data and can provide accurate information in a timely fashion, as needed.

Just as the sophistication of restaurateurs has shifted from a fixation on menu and meal planning toward bottom-line profitability, so too have computer applications. No longer must an operator rely on haphazard forecasting, intuitive marketing research, seat of the pants decision making, or indiscriminate data for strategic planning. Automated food service information systems are rapidly becoming part of the industry landscape.

Single-Unit RMS Applications

Traditionally, a food service operation has been segmented into serveice (front of the house) and management-(back of the house) oriented functions. When faced with the decision of which area to automate first, practitioners have been inconsistent in approach. Some operators claim that unless they computerize their service functions first, they will not be able to properly account for sales, cash, or menu-item popularity or provide an acceptable level of service. Others take a different stance and point to the back office area as the best candidate for automation. Their reasoning is that unless there are sufficient supplies of inventories, fixed assets, labor, and profitability there won't be a restaurant in the future. Consideration of the merits involved in both arguments has led to the development of integrated restaurant management systems (RMS) designed to minimize data rehandling and the elapsed time from data input to informational output.

Service Applications

Electronic cash registers (ECR) and point-of-sale (POS) systems are used to monitor the order entry to production to service to settlement linkage in a restaurant. Although there are technological differences in basic ECR and POS designs, there are also many commonalities. ECR/POS system hardware typically includes order entry devices, central processing unit(s), memory unit(s), and local and remote printers. Order entry devices can be configured as cashier terminals (unit with cash drawer), precheck terminals (without cash drawer), or hand-held terminals (FM transmission). Standard processing options available are stand-alone, master–slave, and processor-based configurations. While each configuration is specific in information and control flows, each also has its relative strengths and weaknesses. Although not always perceived as crucial in the selection process, the size, location, and nature of memory units can significantly affect system capability. Memory unit alternatives include sequential access media (magnetic tape), random access media (magnetic disk), and rapid access media (bubble memory). With respect to output there are four types of ECR/POS printers: slip, receipt, workstation, and journal printers. The most-used type is the slip or guest check printer. This printer is often equipped with automatic slip feed (ASF) and/or automatic form number reader (AFNR) components. Receipt printers produce a flimsy, narrow register paper copy and are either part of or located close to the register they serve. Undoubtedly the most revolutionary printer to affect cash register technology is the remote workstation printer. Remote printers can be soft copy (video display) or hard copy (printed page) in their functionality. In either case they are designed to communicate production requests to workstations within kitchen, bar, or other areas. The fourth type of printer is the journal printer. This printer is responsible for generating a continuous audit trail of all transactions entered into the system. The journal printer also takes responsibility for printing system directed reports.

ECR/POS software options include server/cashier/outlet accountability, revenue analysis, sales reporting, prechecking, check tracking, menu mix analysis, recipe explosion, inventory control, and time/attendance recording.

Management Applications

Management, or back office, applications are directed at nonservice food service uses, including general ledger accounting (payables and receivables), cash management, sales and revenue analyses, fixed asset accounting, inventory control, menu planning, payroll, budgeting, and financial reporting. A number of food service operators interested in back office applications initially become involved with generic software. Similar to hotelier PC applications above, restaurateurs are becoming increasingly involved in expanded data processing activities. The most popular generic software offerings for restaurants are electronic spreadsheets, database management, and word processing. Spreadsheets provide a framework for analyzing budgeting, financial, and related matters. They enable a user with little or no previous computer background to construct powerful electronic ledgers. Database programs are especially useful for handling long lists of items that may be applied or referenced in a number of ways. A list of food ingredients, menu item recipes, market research studies, meal plan schedules, and the like are candidates for database programming. Word processing software enables an operator to perform text creation, editing, and printing with relative simplicity. Word processing modules have been especially instrumental in menu printing, direct mail campaigns, and other promotional projects. Although there is no definitive study concerning the implementation of customized food service systems versus generic software, it appears that most operators depend on specially designed RMS packages for support. Figures 3 and 4 provide quick guide summaries of food service hardware and software concepts discussed above.

Integration is the Key

Given the kind of data captured in the service area and the specific needs of managerial applications, there is potential for overlap or duplication of effort. Recent technological advances have led to the development of fully integrated food service systems: systems that interconnect service (ECR/POS) networks with management- (back office) based micro-, mini-, or mainframe computers. This bridge enables the sharing of guest transaction data with operational and financial information. The outcome of this union tends to exceed the expectations of even the most optimistic management.

Service	Management
Order entry devices	**Data entry devices**
• Cashier terminal	• Cathode ray tube
• Precheck terminal	• ECR/POS interface
• Hand-held terminal	• Telecommunications
Processing options	**Processing options**
• Stand-alone network	• Microcomputer (PC)
• Master–slave network	• Minicomputer
• Processor-based network	• Mainframe computer
• PC pos network	**Output options**
Output options	• Video display
• Operator display	• Line print terminal
• Slip printer	• Graphics printer
• Receipt printer	• Communications file
• Remote printer/display unit	• Magnetic media
• Journal printer	

Figure 3. Quick Guide to Food Service Hardware Systems

Service	Management
Prechecking	**General ledger accounting**
• Order entry	• Chart of accounts
• Production link	• Accounts receivable
• Service settlement	• Accounts payable
Check tracking	**Inventory control**
• Open checking	• Beginning inventory
• Closed checking	• Purchases/transfers
• Missing check report	• End inventory
Menu analysis	**Payroll**
• Menu score mix	• Time/attendance
• Recipe explosion	• Withholdings/tips
• Menu engineering	• Payroll register
Revenue analysis	**Financial reporting**
• Server productivity	• Flash reports
• Day part reporting	• Income statement
• Settlement reconciliation	• Balance sheet

Figure 4. Quick Guide to Food Service Software Systems

Multiunit RMS Applications

While what is applicable for the single-unit RMS operation might also apply to the unit within a group, there usually is not as great a need for as much number crunching. Programs that are critical to a single-unit manager may lose impact at a district, regional, or national office. Delineating which functions are appropriate at any given level appears to be unique to each food service company. While central offices tend to capture strategic data (payroll, revenue, product cost, and statistical information) typically there is a decentralization of operational data maintained at the unit level. Communication to home office is becoming an essential component in multiunit RMS automation networks. Typically, data is consolidated at the unit level and prepared for transmission to headquarters. While some chains continue to require stores to mail in their reports, many are beginning to adopt online data transmission. Telecommunications, involving telephones and modems, is quickly becoming the desired vehicle for moving data from one location to another.

Cash register consolidation can take place at a host register, in a register consolidator, within an electronic store-and-forward (ESF) device, or at a peripheral computer. Data transmission from unit to headquarters can be via common carrier telephone line (point to point) or involve electronic mail (point to mailbox) techniques. Once received at the central office, data is typically placed into a micro-, mini-, or macrocomputer for further processing and/or storage. Such important applications as labor tracking and scheduling, sales by day part, comparative outlet statistics, and cash reconciliation are performed.

Advances in PMS and RMS Technology

Self check-in and check-out terminals, enhanced guest room amenities, sophisticated life safety systems, and extended energy management applications highlight anticipated developments in hotel PMS technology. Off-premises dining, quality of food, and shrinking contribution margins are perceived as critical RMS concentration areas.

Recent developments in automation that may bear on hotel and restaurant operations can similarly be delineated. There appear to be at least five broad advancement areas: integrated software, local area networks, user interfaces, advanced networking technologies, and expert systems.

The concept of integrated software is important because it deals with the capability of analyzing data in a variety of formats. With integrated software, the user is capable of performing several data processing functions on the same data with minimal data handling. Local area networking involves the interconnectedness of dissimilar hardware, software, and operating systems to achieve synergistic throughput. LANs have been proven to increase productivity, increase utility, enhance shared resources, and enable interactive communications. As hotels and restaurants continue to tie together different systems and locations, the importance of networking becomes paramount. The ability to incorporate already purchased hardware and software into a more powerful system will lead to cost savings and extend the life of the computer components.

User interfaces, as the name implies, describes those products designed to provide the user with simple, reliable interaction with system operations. Examples of newer products under this heading are self-check terminals, hand-held order entry terminals, optical character recognition (OCR), touchscreen CRT units, magnetic strip readers, and verbal recognition (VR) devices.

Although still in its infancy, advanced network technologies probably will affect on all future system developments. These new technologies include current and near-future processing options including the following:

1. Data processing—information primarily in numbers
2. Word processing—information primarily in text
3. Image processing—information primarily in pictures
4. Audio processing—information primarily in sound

It is anticipated that all four of these capabilities will be available in most network designs.

One of the most recent advances in computer systems is termed expert systems. An expert system is one in which the computer is applied to tasks normally requiring human intelligence. A possible outcome of such systems is better decisions in far less time. The objective of this approach is human engineering. Human engineering means that because an expert system could operate in place of a person, people would be free to devote their time to more productive work. How will expert systems affect the hospitality industry? So far there has been little research done to suggest its impact. It may be quite some time before this technology controls a unit or a multiunit conglomerate, but scientists warn that it's coming.

Summary

Eventually all segments of the hospitality guest cycle will have some degree of automation. New hotel and restaurant developments may range from purchase order to purveyor telecommunications, to electronic funds transfer (EFT) settlement techniques, to online personnel management functions. Regardless of techniques adopted, management is reminded of the three computer *nevers:* never be the first user of any system; never be the largest user of any system; and, more importantly, never be the last user of any system!

31

Why Is Service Important to the Hospitality Industry?

Taylor Ellis
University of Central Florida

Have you ever telephoned a restaurant and had the phone ring ten times before anyone answered it? Then, you were put on hold before you could even reply? Have you ever called an airline to request the most cost effective method of flying to another city, only to be asked what day and time you wanted to fly—the phone operator offering no solution to your problem? When you have called someone for information, and that person is not available, has he or she failed to return your call? These are all examples of poor service.

Importance of Service

Now, what is good service? The answer to this question is not an easy one. Most people only notice service when they don't receive it. Service in today's business situations is expected. This is especially true in the hospitality industry. Cambridge Reports, of Cambridge, Massachusetts, asked fifteen hundred people, "How well do service companies meet your needs and concerns as a consumer?" Only 8% rated their service companies as excellent. Fifty percent reported good, but 42% said fair or poor. More than one in three people agreed with the statement that "service industries care less than they did a few years ago about meeting my needs." A 1987 Gallup Poll asked 1,045 people what makes them decide not to return to a given restaurant. The results were similar in the hospitality industry. The number one reason, identified by 83% of respondents, was poor service: not food quality, not ambience, not price.[1]

What is poor service? Cambridge Reports asked people what they think of when they hear the word *service*. The most frequent response was some variation of the following: personal attention, responsiveness, or politeness of employees. These terms would appear to describe the hospitality industry.

What is the impact of poor service on business? The initial impact of poor service, that the customer does not return, is only the tip of the iceberg. Additional research indicates that 96% of dissatisfied customers never complain. Of those individuals who stop doing business with a hospitality business, 68% do so because of poor service. In fact, customers are five times more likely to stop doing business with a hospitality company due to poor service than poor product quality or high cost. These research findings indicate that poor service drives customers away without giving the business operators an opportunity to salvage the situation because customers don't complain. The hospitality professional may not have the opportunity to make the situation right. She may not even know what went wrong!

This inability to correct poor service will in turn drive away more customers. This situation is bad enough, but unfortunately the story doesn't end here. The average unhappy customer tells nine people about the experience, and a full 13% tell 20 or more people. Compare this to research that shows that the average happy customer only tells five other people about their positive experience and you can see the problem.[2]

What is the cost of the lost guest? Various studies have placed the cost of obtaining a new customer at five to six times the cost of keeping an existing one. Organizations that have developed and implemented effective customer service programs have seen profits jump 25% to 100%. Even unhappy guests can be maintained as customers if you are able to resolve their problem. Research has shown that between 50% and 70% of all customers who complain, and have their issues resolved, will remain customers. It is little wonder that some individuals in the hospitality industry have stated that a guest who complains is the best thing that can happen to their business? Not only are they able to retain that guest as a customer, they are able to eliminate up to 20 negative images about their business, reduce costs of maintaining customers, increase profits, and solve the problem so that it doesn't happen to anyone else. For these reasons, it is imperative that hospitality industry managers understand and implement service quality standards and programs in their businesses. Remember, customer service in the hospitality industry is a must. Good service is a requirement of getting and keeping business; in fact, it is the product itself.

Why Is Service So Hard to Maintain?

Quality products are easy to identify. They are usually the same each time you purchase them. They are manufactured under conditions of strict quality control, and once made, they can be stored. These are just some of the differences that exist between products and services. For our purposes it is enough to know that products and services differ substantially. In this section we will concentrate on the functions that create problems for service providers.

First, you must remember that in any organization, customers take two forms, internal and external. The internal customers are just as important as the external customers. Internal customers can be defined as those individuals who work for your company and with whom you interact on a daily basis. It is important that other employees are treated as well as external customers. Guests are able to observe the interaction between employees and will often attribute behaviors to that interaction that may not be true. This can lead to misunderstandings and a perception of poor service by the guest. Another critical factor concerns the fact that all employees are involved in the provision of services for guests. Because of this, if employees do not treat each other with respect they cannot treat the guest with respect. Animosity between employees can cause guest service problems.

Since a service doesn't exist until it is called for by the guest, it needs no shelf space, has no shelf life, and most certainly, is not an asset that can be inventoried. Because the sale, production, and consumption of services take place simultaneously, with the purchaser playing a role in the production of the service itself, there is considerable room for something to go wrong. Some of the more common problems include misunderstandings, differing cultural backgrounds, and perceived slights. Because of the involvement of the guest in the process, the hospitality employee must constantly evaluate the impact of what is taking place on the guest and change his or her approach accordingly. If an employee is not capable of performing this function for some reason, it is likely that the guest will have a less than satisfactory experience. Quality control in the hospitality industry entails watching the service process unfold and evaluating it against the customer's level of satisfaction.

This establishes another important aspect of service: the customer's expectations. It is important to recognize that the receiver's expectations, and perceptions, of service are integral to his or her satisfaction. To create a distinctive level of customer service, management must understand, and even on occasion shape, the customer's prepurchase expectations, influence the customer's evaluation of postpurchase quality, and ensure that the process of being served is not only easy and painless but, when possible, enjoyable.

The methods used by management to ensure quality service are numerous, so only a few will be discussed here. One of the commonly overlooked aspects of service is the marketing or advertising campaign of the hospitality enterprise. Market segmentation analysis indicates that one enterprise cannot be all things to everyone. Consequently, it is important to select one market segment and cater to it. The image that a property, restaurant or hotel, portrays is shaped by the marketing and advertising approach. Don't promise too much. If a guest's expectations are met then she will be satisfied. If the property does not meet her expectations, she will be lost as a customer.

How are a guest's expectations established? The answer is, in one of two ways depending on what prompted the guest's arrival in the first place. If the guest is on a repeat visit, his expectations were established on the first visit. This can present problems for management. Since service is produced and consumed at the same time, whatever happened during the guest's first visit to create a satisfied guest may not be repeatable. For example, the interaction between the guest and the waitress who served him during his first visit is not possible because the waitress is not currently working. A complicating factor is that the longer people stay away from a specific destination, the less they remember about negative experiences. We all have a tendency to glamorize past experiences. This creates an image that is harder to achieve the second time around.

The second way a guest's expectations are created is through management decisions. These most often take the form of facility design and promotion. We have all been conditioned by the lavish physical appearance of a facility to expect great things, only to be disappointed. Likewise, advertising can create expectations that cannot be met by the property. For example, an authentic French restaurant would not serve Southern fried chicken and other similar dishes. In this instance, management may have established expectations that cannot be met, ensuring a dissatisfied customer. It is critical that management take pains to ensure that the guest's experience over time remains the same and is within the projected image. If you can't deliver quality, don't promote quality either in advertising or appearance.

Service satisfaction is the result of a dynamic, not static, encounter. The consumer evaluates both the process and outcome, and values both. Guests take whatever data is available to them, judge it by their own personal standards and expectations, and decide whether or not they are satisfied. For example, a coffee-stained menu may not be considered inappropriate in a truck stop or diner, yet is inappropriate at a fine restaurant.

Services are usually provided for one individual at a time, so being able to respond to that unique situation is essential. The main variability in performing service functions is related to both customers' and providers' attitudes. Attitudes are very difficult to interpret and control. Customers or employees seldom know what the other's attitude is toward them. However, that doesn't stop them from making a judgment based on what they think it is. The process of providing service covers a lot of territory. It may even carry over to the perceived nervousness of the employe. For example, think about how a new employee would feel when asked to serve the company president on her first day on the job. How would the company president perceive the employee's apparent nervousness?

Table 1 provides the basic characteristics of services as identified by Murdick et al.[3] It is important to note the number of areas where something can go wrong. Because of these potential trouble spots, service management must take a total organizational approach that makes quality of service, as perceived by the guest, the number one driving force for the operation of the hospitality business.

Management's Responsibility in Providing Service

Good service is not an accident, it doesn't just happen. To be effective, service must be planned and managed. Factors contributing to good service include everything from the design to the delivery of the service; from maintaining efficient operations to ensuring that the quality of the service is both high and consistent. Every hospitality company must have a strategy for providing service that matches the desire of the target market with the strengths of the company.

The strategy for delivering service to the guest is more than just a mechanism for dealing with customers; it is the competitive advantage of the business. This approach to hospitality management, marketing, control, and direction of service as a full, profitable business must be fully understood by hospitality managers. If used properly, the company's approaches to service can become the major differentiation for new and existing hospitality businesses. This process of separating and focusing on service to the customer as a line of business makes it possible to optimize customer satisfaction and profitability.

Table 1. Characteristics of a Service

Services are intangible output.

Services produce variable, nonstandard output.

A service is perishable. It cannot be carried in inventory, but is consumed when produced.

There is considerable customer contact throughout the service process.

The customer participates in the provision of service.

Skills are sold directly to the customer.

Services cannot be mass produced.

Acute personal judgment is employed by individuals performing the service.

Service firms are labor intensive.

Decentralization facilities are located near the customers.

Measures of effectiveness are subjective.

Quality control is limited primarily to process control.

Pricing options are elaborate.

Source: Murdick, V. (1990) *Service Operations Management.*

Zemke and Schaaf have identified five key steps to obtain optimum customer-service interaction.[1] First and most important, listen to guests. Take every opportunity to understand and respond to guest needs and expectations. Keep in mind that guest wants are constantly changing, and may require creative solutions.

Second, management must establish service standards or procedures, behavior, and appearance. Once established, all employees must be regularly measured against the standards. To be effective, these standards cannot be created in a vacuum. It is the employees who must implement the standards, and they are the ones closest to the guest. If management does not attempt to obtain employee input when creating the standards, they are doomed to failure. On the other hand, if employees are vested in the standards through their creation, success can be assured. No one wants their ideas or standards to fail. The standards should also apply to management. To be effective, front-line employees must see and believe that management is a part of the process and has standards that they also must meet.

Third, all standards must be measurable, for example: define how long customers should wait or service should take. This step creates a yardstick that shows how well the company or the individual employee is doing. When establishing the measurement portion of the standards, make sure the goals are realistic. It does no one any good to set standards so high that everyone fails. Remember that quality service is an ongoing process, so you are always striving for improvement. The concept of acceptable error cannot apply; the goal must be 100% performance. Because of this, measurement aspects of the standards can always be raised.

Fourth, management must provide clear-cut incentives and performance review standards. The standards must be fair to all employees and applied evenly. If any employee perceives that the incentives or performance review standards are not being fairly applied, the entire system will fail. In addition, the incentives must be sufficient to entice employees to achieve them. Remember, at the most basic level we are all motivated to act in a particular way because our action will either result in a gain (reward) or avoid a loss (punishment). When dealing with service employees, it is much better to use positive reinforcement (reward).

Fifth, follow-up must be done to provide visible performance incentives for the best service performance. All employees desire recognition. Remember that awards can be given either individually or to a group. Recognize and encourage group excellence. Present the recognition in some type of award ceremony. This serves to indicate to other employees that the plan is real and that they can also achieve similar results. Remember the incentive must be substantial enough to create interest among all employees.

Keep in mind throughout this process that the problem is matching management and employee perceptions with consumer perceptions of what the service concept and service level are and should be within your property. If all three groups are in agreement, you will succeed in maintaining your customers and reducing the number of dissatisfied guests.

Simply stated, one of the best reasons to give good service is that it makes you feel better. Becoming somewhat obsessed with providing superior service is a lot more satisfying than operating a hospitality business on the assumption that guests are creeps and are out to get you.

Service Components

Most effective service organizations base their operation on four key points. First, make time to listen to, understand, and respond in a timely manner to changing customer wants, needs, and expectations. Second, hospitality businesses must create and communicate to the guest a well-defined, customer-inspired service strategy. This is usually accomplished through advertising and the physical appearance of the facility. Third, every attempt must be made to develop and maintain guest-friendly service delivery systems. This means developing procedures to make the guest more comfortable not the staff. Last, it is very important to hire, train, inspire, and develop guest-oriented front-line people.

Following these guidelines ensures that the guest can enhance her stay by having positive experiences. From the initial to the final contact with the staff, guests should feel that the property has done the following:

1. Shown sensitivity to and awareness of the customer
2. Understand service provisions for the customer
3. Interacted with the customer on a friendly, service-oriented basis
4. Made the staff aware of the need for continuing feedback on service performance
5. Provided the guest with a method for reporting problems, complaints, or service needs and requirements.[4]

Summary

Let's answer the question posed at the beginning of this chapter: What's an adequate service level? It is the level of service that will satisfy customer's needs or expectations. A hospitality manager must know what satisfaction really means to his customers. Once the true meaning is understood, it can be translated into performance and specific service levels.

Keep in mind that how service personnel appear and what they say or do at the point of contact with the guest creates the image of the property for the guest. Once established, a continuing relationship depends on maintaining the guest service level throughout all guest–employee interactions. In this way, both the actual and perceived service performance will be the same. As a result, you will have satisfied, repeat guests. That is the objective of the hospitality industry.

——References——

1. Zemke, R., and D. Schaaf. (1989) *The Service Edge.* NAL Books: New York.
2. Timm, P. (1992) *50 Simple Things You Can Do to Save Your Customers.* Hawthorne, N. J.: Career Press.
3. Murdick, R., B. Render, and R. Russell. (1990) *Service Operation Management.* Allyn and Bacon: Boston.
4. Blumberg, D. (1991) *Managing Service as a Strategic Profit Center.* McGraw-Hill: New York.

32

Quality Service Management in Hospitality Operations

Ray D. Langbehn, *Metropolitan State College of Denver*
Yvonne L. Spaulding, *Metropolitan State College of Denver*

Introduction

Customer Service for many years has consisted of an obscure sign above a counter in the back of an establishment, staffed by an often harried employee who did nothing all day but field complaints from irate customers. Usually the customer was made to feel responsible for whatever actions took place, and as a result, chose not to patronize that particular business in the future.

Has This Ever Happened to You?

Two friends, Kate and P.J., decided to go to dinner at the Good Food restaurant for a light snack. It was 9:30 P.M. on a Monday evening, and the restaurant was not particularly crowded. Kate ordered a hamburger, well done, which had hash brown potatoes on the side. P.J. ordered a combination appetizer plate with fried zucchini strips, mushrooms, and garlic toast. Kate had mentioned to the wait staff that she was allergic to onions (anticipating that onions may be served with her burger) and to please not put any onions on her plate. They each ordered a glass of wine while waiting for their entrees.

When the wait staff brought the combination plate, it did not have any fried zucchini strips on it. Instead, it had asparagus strips. P.J. inquired as to why they eliminated the fried zucchini. The wait staff left the table to check on it, returned, and replied that they were out of zucchini. He made no offer to replace the asparagus with something else, or do anything else. P.J. was not fond of asparagus, so he ate everything but the asparagus.

When the wait staff came to remove P.J.'s plate from the table, P.J. suggested to him that, in the future, if the restaurant was out of a certain item, they might tell the customer before serving it. The wait staff replied that no one told him that they were out of zucchini—they simply plated it and he brought it out. While this was happening, another wait staff brought out Kate's burger. It was rare. She asked that it be sent back and cooked more. A while later the burger was delivered. By this time, both P.J. and Kate had finished their wine and desired another glass to finish with their food. Their wait staff could not be located. Once the recooked burger was delivered to Kate, the wait staff disappeared. She never returned to the table to check on the doneness of the burger. Kate, at this point, also noticed that there were several slices of onion on her plate. This was the last straw.

P.J. and Kate decided that they wanted to express their concerns to the management. Because they could not locate their wait staff, P.J. approached the hostess stand and asked for the manager to stop by their table. No one came for several minutes. Eventually Rachael, the manager, appeared at the table with an order of fried zucchini. This was the item that the wait staff said was no longer available.

Kate and P.J. politely explained to the manager that they were finished with their meal, thanked her for the zucchini, and expressed their concerns for such a disappointing experience at her restaurant. Manager Rachael apologized and inquired as to what they wanted her to do. P.J. asked that his appetizer plate be removed from the bill. Manager Rachael agreed.

The wait staff returned later with the bill. Stamped on the bill in two different places in large, bright red letters were the words, "PROMO."[1]

What Happened in This Situation?

What happened was that the customers were not served as they expected to be served—and these customers probably will not return to the restaurant. In addition, as shown by the wait staff and manager Rachael's responses to the customers, this employee behavior will continue in the future, and more and more customers will be disappointed in the service and not come back.

Why Did It Happen?

First, and most importantly, the wait staff was obviously not trained properly, and particularly not in the area of having basic knowledge of daily menu items: what is still available and what is not. Secondly, there does not seem to be much communication between line workers and wait staff regarding what was requested on the ticket and what actually was plated for the customer.

In addition, as exemplified by the wait staff's response to the customer regarding the unavailability of an item, the wait staff chose not to take responsibility for what happened by saying, "no one told him that they were out of zucchini—they simply plated it and he brought it out."

What Can Be Done About It?

Management needs to begin a comprehensive and intensive customer-driven quality service program that encourages every person within the organization to think like the customer and to practice the concepts and theories that follow.

What Is Customer Service and Why Is It So Hard to Deliver?

Service is now a major buzzword for nearly all businesses and organizations. The hospitality industry is a major player in the part of the economy called the service sector. The service sector now makes up the greater part of the economy and creates most new jobs. And yet, poor or mediocre service is fairly common, whether at a convenience store, a government office like the department of motor vehicles, or a fast food drive-up window. Good customer service is a notoriously difficult thing to deliver consistently at all times. Why? Let's start with a definition.

Quality customer service is an action or set of actions taken by one person for the benefit of another person that meets a need, solves a problem, or produces a positive experience. Karl Albrecht defines total quality service as "a state of affairs in which an organization delivers superior value to its stakeholders: its customers, its owners, and its employees."[2] Several important ideas are encompassed in Albrecht's definition. One is the concept of value. When customers' expectations are fully met or exceeded, they perceive value in the service received. No matter what we _think or believe_ about the quality of the service we are providing, the customer's perception of the service experience is what matters as they form an impression about our organization. Another concept in Albrecht's definition is that everyone in the organization benefits from quality service, not just the customers. There are both external service to customers, and internal service from one employee or department to another, that produce an atmosphere or environment of total quality service throughout the organization.

For the hospitality industry we can think about a server in a restaurant, a desk clerk in a hotel, or a travel agent making your travel arrangements. While for each customer certain elements of service may be more or less important, we can generally agree that certain factors are commonly expected, and necessary to a quality service experience. Quality service is positive, polite, friendly, timely (quick for some, well paced or unhurried for others), helpful, solution oriented when problems occur, nonjudgmental, accepting, knowledgeable, gracious, welcoming, anticipatory of customers' needs, and provides good follow-through. A quality customer service employee needs to possess all these skills and the ability to judge which elements are most important for each customer. We begin to see why quality service is easier said than done.

The very nature of service is that it is an experience and not a thing. It is intangible. It is perishable and can't be inventoried; that is, it can only be produced when the customer needs it. In economic terms, production and consumption are simultaneous. The customer becomes a part of the organization as the service is being produced, even though she does not appear on the organization chart or have a job description. The demand for service is cyclical; busy and slow periods of business are dictated by the customer's needs and not the organization's needs. Because each customer has somewhat different expectations, it is difficult to standardize service without depersonalizing it, and it becomes difficult to measure quality when different customers require different types of service. And then there are the difficult and demanding customers who are determined to have a bad experience or intimidate their server. Food servers in restaurants regularly rank as having the fifth or sixth most stressful occupation in the United States.

Compare this situation to that of a toy factory, for example. The manufacturing organization is already preparing for the next holiday season before the current one is over; current best-sellers indicate models that it would be profitable to manufacture next; large inventories are stockpiled months ahead of time; the customer never enters the factory; and defects in a toy from last season can be permanently corrected. The process of production in the factory is completely separated from—and is usually an entirely different organization from—the toy store that sells the toy to the customer. In addition, a grumpy factory worker does not in any way affect the final service to the customer in the toy store. But, in the store, or in our hotels and restaurants, rude, apathetic, cold, or condescending servers do affect entirely the service experience of our customers. When a server acts like a machine, parroting stock phrases, or is unable or unwilling to solve problems when they occur, hides behind company policy, or dismisses our concerns, our service experience is a bad one.

Teaching Old Dogs New Tricks

It is possible to consistently deliver high quality customer service, despite the type of problems we have discussed. For an existing organization that needs to improve its service, this may require a fundamental change, or paradigm shifts, in the way all members of the organization think and do business. A paradigm is a set of beliefs and values about how and why things happen the way they do; it helps determine how we act and behave. For example, if we believe that most customers are demanding and unreasonable, we tend to be defensive and rigid in our service in order to keep those customers in line.

Today's customers are far more sophisticated than in the past. They have traveled more and have had a wider variety of service experiences. In order to remain competitive, and have our customers perceive greater value in the services we provide, many management experts advocate the need for a paradigm shift in our organizations. If we see that the way to profit is not to sell more rooms or meals (the old paradigm), but to deliver superior value to our customers (the new paradigm), *long-term* profit is better assured because of satisfied customers who will return and refer others to us. Truly, without customers we cannot stay in business, and without satisfied customers we cannot remain profitable.

The new paradigm to support quality service works at making sure that all parts of the organization include the customer and service in their planning and execution, whether we are discussing rules, systems, pricing, the menu, the billing system, employee training, or lighting, signs, entrances, and parking lots.

In planning this paradigm shift there are a number of places to start. For an existing organization, we can start by identifying what is happening now by determining the cycle of service and "moments of truth" of our customers. The cycle of service is the entire service experience, from the customer's first contact with the organization, through each point at which the customer receives a service and can form an impression of our organization (the moments of truth), until his last contact with us. Do we do a superior job at each of these steps, or are certain points of service less than good? Is there a regular breakdown at certain points? When something goes wrong or a problem occurs, it becomes a "critical moment of truth." How we solve the problem or fix the situation will be critical to the impression the customer has of our organization and its service.

Mission Statements and Service Strategies

An effective mission statement is a statement of the beliefs, values, and practices of an organization. It says what the organization exists and stands for, who it serves, and how it will go about accomplishing these tasks in a way that creates value for its customers, and allows them to perceive differences and relative superiority between one organization and another. All members of the organization, from top management down through all employees, should know, understand, and believe in the mission statement. It must be practical and achievable to be workable, and should establish realistic and attainable goals. An effective mission statement is fundamental to a successful paradigm shift.

Hospitality organizations recognize that they cannot be all things to all people. One type of organization concentrates on speed of service; another concentrates on elegant and gracious service. Good mission statements help define the market segments the organization wishes to concentrate on serving. New organizations often start with a mission statement as the first step in planning. Existing organizations find that new or revised mission statements help to refocus employees on what is and should be most important.

While the mission statement is a broad and relatively short statement, service strategies define the goals in further detail and include action plans, or strategies for how to achieve the goals. Service strategies also allow the organization to establish standards of performance for employees to help assure that the strategies and goals of the organization are consistently achieved. The standards of performance in turn assist in the development of job descriptions that do more than just outline the mechanics of what is to be done. Such job descriptions include how, and to what standards, tasks are to be performed, so that the mission statement is supported at all times by what the organization actually does.

Who Will Deliver Good Service and How Will We Do It?

Human relations skills are essential when considering the aspects of quality service management in hospitality operations. More specifically, possessing the knowledge and having the ability to exhibit effective nonverbal communication techniques when dealing with customers is vitally important when implementing a quality service management strategy in hospitality operations. Finally, addressing business etiquette and protocol situations provides an effective capstone to the rudiments of interpersonal communication concepts. It is becoming increasingly important to consider the inclusion of interpersonal communication and human relations concepts in hospitality education curricula, as well as in employee training in the hospitality industry.

When looking at aspects of communication, several components can be investigated. These include verbal components, or use of voice; kinesics, or bodily activity; proxemics, or use of space; physical appearance; and chronemics, or the use of time.[3]

When looking at effects of verbal (or voice) communication, a customer may be turned off merely by the sound of an employee's voice—perhaps a sarcastic, sing-song, or whiny intonation. Kinesics, or bodily activity, also plays an important role in the way in which a person communicates nonverbally.

The type of facial expression displayed by the employee to the customer, her use of the hands while communicating, body position, eye behavior, and stance can send several different messages, particularly when communicating interculturally.

Proxemics, or the ways in which we use space, can also provide valuable information about the type of communication that is occurring. For some cultures, standing close together is not only acceptable and expected, but to move away abruptly, or distance yourself from that particular customer, may be interpreted as an insult—that the person has done something to displease you. Standing too close to the customer can also be perceived as a threatening behavior. In addition, these situations can be even more complex when considering gender differences, and relating those differences to diverse cultures.

Being aware of what is acceptable in a business setting, and what is appropriate business protocol, can also make the difference between creating a customer-friendly environment or causing an international incident. For instance, in Central and South America, it is perfectly acceptable for someone to be 30 minutes late for an appointment. Also, it is typical practice for business to be discussed in a social setting, particularly dinner, and this business meal can last several hours.

In the United States, it is usually in poor taste to be even 15 minutes late. In Israel, for another example, discussing business over a meal is perfectly acceptable. In Italy, it is important to consider in which part of the country you are doing business. Business entertaining is done in restaurants, not in private homes. Also, if you were dealing with a customer in Rome, the business day there ends around 7 P.M., while in Milan, business hours are more comparable to those in the United States. In order for us to exhibit effective business protocol, we must be aware of the intercultural differences.[4]

There are several components that can lead to an increase in the level of awareness of employees when dealing with customers, to ensure more effective, quality service. These components include the ability to recognize direct and indirect communication styles; sensitivity to nonverbal cues; awareness of cultural and linguistic differences; interest in the culture of others; sensitivity to the myths and stereotypes of the culture; ability to articulate the elements of his own culture; awareness of the relationships among cultural groups; and accurate criteria for objectively understanding what is considered to be "good" or "bad" in another culture.

Knowing effective communication techniques and the will to use them also improves the ways in which we deal with any conflict situations that arise.

When dealing with a dissatisfied customer in particular, it is much easier to achieve a workable solution when you are able to listen effectively to her, establish what the problem is, and what she really wants to have done about the situation. Once that has been established and understood, then the conflict can be effectively resolved through mutual need satisfaction.

This method ultimately achieves several benefits: increased commitment to carry out the decision; higher quality decisions; warmer relationships; quicker decisions; and the elimination of the need to "sell" the decision that was made, because each person had the opportunity to take part in the final decision.[5]

Effective listening is another component of communication that is absolutely vital in achieving quality service management in hospitality operations. We must learn to listen with an open mind, without prejudice, judgment, or bias. We must learn to question, paraphrase, and ask for clarification, in order to avoid misunderstandings and misinterpretations of messages.

How Can We Keep the Spirit of Service Alive and Well?

There must be a regular system for refocusing on service. This can be accomplished by demonstrations in role-play exercises during orientation periods, and during ongoing training and development seminars. Overall, employees must be taught to think like customers. Numerous concepts of team building can implement this focus on service and quality service management in hospitality operations. Team building can be accomplished in the following ways:

1. Assign each team a significant piece of the work while arranging the work environment to foster lots of interaction among team members.
2. Try to ensure that each team member is able to perform each of the jobs performed by the team.
3. Allow team members to evaluate each other as part of their evaluation.
4. Create a common goal. Encourage cooperation by establishing rewards that can be won by doing the job together.
5. Remove any rewards that would encourage people to work against each other.
6. Discourage anything that is counterproductive.
7. Discourage withdrawal by or isolation of group members.
8. Rotate members among groups.
9. Discourage any win–lose competitions between individuals.
10. Encourage allocentric communication, focusing on _them,_ rather than yourself (assuming that you are the leader or manager).[6]

By concentrating on these suggestions and possibly implementing them into your daily training regime at your particular property or business organization, quality service management can be achieved and maintained, and the eventual outcome will be a customer-driven organization.

How Are We Doing and Are We Making Progress?

In order to assure that our goals are being met, that our training methods are effective, and that we are consistently maintaining and improving the quality of our customer service, we must have a regular system of assessment and measurement in place. Focus groups of regular customers are interviewed in depth and encouraged to be candid and honest about the organization. Personal and telephone interviews can indicate satisfaction and areas for improvement. Surveys or questionnaires can be regularly solicited from customers on specific issues or areas of concern.

All three methods, as well as comment cards, are most useful when there are incentives for the customer to participate and return the comments or ratings. A variety of objective and subjective methods, including management regularly talking with guests, will provide the feedback necessary to assure quality customer service.

——References——

1. Disend, Jeffrey. (1991) *How to Provide Excellent Service in Any Organization.* Radnor, Pa.: Chilton Book Co. pp. 254–255.
2. Albrecht, Karl. (1992) *The Only Thing That Matters.* New York: Harper Business.
3. Littlejohn, Stephen W. (1992) *Theories of Human Communication.* Belmont, Calif.: Wadsworth Publishing Co.
4. Yager, Jan. (1991) *Business Protocol, How to Survive and Succeed in Business.* New York: John Wiley and Sons.
5. Gordon, Thomas. (1979) *Leader Effectiveness Training.* New York: Wyden Books.
6. LeBoeuf, Michael. (1985) *The Greatest Management Principle in the World.* New York: Berkeley Books.

Travel and Tourism Management

Part V

33

Introduction Travel and Tourism Management

Leland L. Nicholls
University of Wisconsin-Stout

Travel and tourism are interwoven. Travel is a common theme in all definitions of tourism. The variables of time, distance, residence, purpose, and length of stay are also other considerations of travel and tourism. In general, travel is a multidimensional phenomenon that simultaneously evokes images of adventure, romance, mystery, and exotic places as well as the mundane realities of business, health, personal safety, and security. Tourism has been commonly used to describe the field of travel. (Gee, 1984) Tourism is an industry that occurs at destination areas—areas with different natural and cultural features, which attract nonlocal visitors (tourists) for a variety of activities. (Murphy, 1985) Recreational time is often categorized as very short (up to one hour), short (a few hours), a full day, several days (usually a weekend), and a week or more (usually an annual vacation). Full-fledged tourists are usually those who are away from home beyond the period of a full day and have traveled a distance of five or more miles for the purpose of personal enjoyment.

Jafari, a scholar on tourism theory, noted that travel and tourism is still in the process of being marked and remarked. And we find ourselves disagreeing with each other on many points as to its nature and scope. (Jafari, 1977 and 1938). Mieczkowski further noted:

> The term *travel* encompasses *tourism* from one point of view and is only part of it from another. Travel is a very wide notion connected with displacement of peoples, much beyond the scope of tourism; it may be undertaken for reasons of war (movement of armies), exploration (Columbus was not a tourist), migration, commuting, etc. Refugees, migrants, vagabonds, explorers, nomads, and soldiers have been travellers, but not tourists.

> Travel has been with us since prehistoric times, whereas tourism is a socio-economic phenomenon largely associated with the modern industrial age and differs from travel quantitatively and qualitatively. At the same time, however, travel constitutes only an element of tourism and frequently not even the most important one, especially with respect to single destination tourism where a relatively long stay in the vacation area (the static aspect of tourism) extends between relatively short and unimportant "nuisance" travel by jet (the dynamic aspect of tourism). In the majority of cases, travel constitutes only the means to an end: the sojourn.

Thus, it seems we have a good case for eliminating the term *travel* and substituting the term *tourism* in conformity with the usage in other languages. There is one obstacle, however, to overcome. According to international definition, visitors can be divided into two categories: (1) excursionists (day tripper, same-day travellers) and (2) tourists (travellers who stay overnight or more than 24 hours). The statisticians compute tourist revenues and expenditures as tourists. This is a problem which causes researchers to use the awkward combination *travel–tourism* to designate the whole field. The wide acceptance of the term *tourism* in most non-English languages indicates that this obstacle has been ignored for practical reasons. (Mieczkowski, 1981)

It is further noted (Edgell, 1993) that tourism has been included as part of the service sector and is included in the U.S. trade account as "business services." Yet, in terms of the balance of trade account, a more specific definition would be "travel and transportation." In official U.S. trade statistics, under "Types of Business Services in International Trade," there is a separate category referred to as "travel and transportation" with the following definitions:

Travel

Services provided to U.S. citizens traveling abroad (U.S. imports) and international visitors to the United States (U.S. exports).

Passenger transportation

Transportation provided by foreign carriers to U.S. residents for transportation abroad (U.S. imports) and by U.S. carriers to foreign residents (U.S. exports).

While these definitions serve to describe tourism data as a part of trade statistics in the United States, they generally represent the definitional approaches taken by many countries in the world.*

Travel and tourism is closely related not only to economic development, but also to cultural pursuits, international policy initiatives, worldwide understanding, goodwill, and peace. It includes the buying, selling, and management of services and products (to tourists), which might range from managing a resort, restaurant, hotel, or airline to renting cars to operating a convention center, cruise ship, or theme park. The industry demands exceptionally skilled, creative, innovative, and flexible managers because of perishable products, such as airline seats, restaurant tables, and lodging rooms. Besides its product perishability, the industry demands a wide range of products from other sectors of the economy. Food, water, airplanes, ships, buses, computer reservation systems, construction, medical supplies, and scenic vistas are only a few of the many natural and man-made products and services interconnecting the diverse and dynamic industry.

---

*For a more complete discussion of definitions see Leiper, Neil, Defining Tourism and Market Related Concepts: Tourism Market, Industry, and Tourism System in *VNR's Encyclopedia of Hospitality and Tourism*, Khan, Olson, and Var, eds., 1992.

In summary, precise definitions of travel and tourism are virtually impossible because of disagreement among societies and academic circles throughout the world. Travel has evolved from a long-established tradition of curious movement by the wealthy and privileged from place to place for business and pleasure to a postindustrial practice of mass tourism.†

Scope and Nature of Travel and Tourism Management

Tourism combines demand (the prospective tourist's desire to travel), supply (services provided by the tourist industry), and end product (an enjoyable travel experience). The industry's structure is divided into supply and demand, with four basic travel motivators (figure 1).

In the past 50 years the U.S. economy has shifted from a manufacturing basis to a service-based economy. Today, services account for approximately 70% of the U.S. gross national product and 76% of employment. In the next decade nine of every ten jobs created will be in the service sector of the economy.

Tourism ranks as the first, second, or third largest industry in 47 states in the United States. Tourism employs more than 4.7 million Americans directly and 2.2 million indirectly. It is the second largest private employer in the nation and generates more than $50 billion a year in wages and salaries. (Edgell, 1985 and 1993) In 1992, 476 million travelers generated $279 billion or 7% of world trade and 100 million jobs.

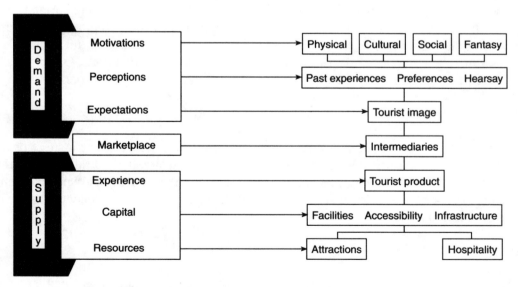

Figure 1. Scope and Nature of Travel and Tourism Market
Source: Murphy, 1985

---

†See Metelka (1990) for a comprehensive reference on travel and tourism terminology and definition.

Travel and tourism is a complex and multidimensional phenomenon. Tourism, however, actually comprises only one segment of the travel market. In spite of impressive economic statistics, travel and tourism have received little attention from many policy-making organizations.

This chapter introduces the reader to the general characteristics and complexities of travel and tourism. The author also aims to provide insights into some of the trends in the travel and tourism industry. Travel and tourism will be first analyzed in a spatial context, with examples of community, regional, national, and international scale. Management issues, challenges, and trends will be discussed at the end of the chapter.

Economic Development

Local Travel Tourism Development

Virtually every city, town, and village in the world has some resource, activity, attraction, event, celebration, or unique feature capable of motivating the traveler or tourist. When properly planned and managed, local benefits from tourism usually include employment, income, diversification of economic base, tax revenues, visibility, and culture. There are nearly 1.5 million travel-related business firms in the United States. (Edgell, 1993) The cases described here represent recent planning, management, and promotion of tourism at different stages of development, scope, and geographical scale to produce tourism revenue.

The communities discussed have recognized the value of increased tourism and have built the travel industry into their economic development plans. Community travel and tourism development often focus on the creation of destination points that function as anchor sites in neighborhoods or districts to attract visitor and convention trade. Other ways to develop tourism include using special events and local culture as image creators.

Neighborhoods

At the micro-scale, communities and cities often develop tourism along a street or avenue. Usually less than a mile long and less than ten blocks square, these destinations attract trendy restaurants, bookstores, specialty shops, theaters, art galleries, and special events (i.e., ethnic block parties). Grand Avenue in St. Paul, Minnesota, is an excellent example of tourism at a micro-scale.

Historic Districts

Rugy, Tennessee, has a population of 60 people. The community was founded as an English colony in 1880 by social reformer Thomas Hughes (author of *Tom Brown's School Days*). The citizens have recently undertaken a massive effort to protect and promote its greatest asset—its rural, historic identity. The local preservation organization, Historic

Rugby, has been working since 1966 to restore the colony. Seventeen of the town's original buildings have been restored, including eight structures from the 1880s and a Victorian-era library with 7,000 period volumes.

Recently, Historic Rugby, through the nearby city of Allardt, received a $456,768 community development block grant from the state of Tennessee for major restoration in the city's National Register Historic District. This public–private development project consists of the renovation of a historic restaurant, Harrow Road Cafe; acquisition and restoration of the Newbury House for visitor lodging and an English tea room; reconstruction of the original Rugby Commissary as a retail outlet for handmade traditional crafts and other locally produced products; and connecting boardwalks, walkways, and off-street parking. The 1907 schoolhouse is being transformed into a visitors' interpretive center.

Rugby is attracting visitors to the town who are in the area to visit Big South Fork National Park. All of these developments are expected to increase tourism in Rugby, which in 1983 attracted approximately 15,000 travelers. (Partners for Livable Places, 1985)

Developing Tourism Anchors

In Memphis, Tennessee, a forgotten and unused stretch of land has been transformed into Mud Island Theme Park—a site that attracted more than one million visitors during its first year of operation. The $63 million project was built by the city with the approval of taxpayers and was planned as a major tourist attraction, a component of downtown traffic control, and a clean-up of derelict conditions.

To get to Mud Island, visitors either ride a monorail or paddlewheel riverboat, or walk along a one-third-mile-long covered passageway connecting the site to downtown Memphis. Mud Island celebrates the mighty Mississippi River through cultural activities, restaurants, and shops. Tying all of the components together is River Walk, an exciting five-block-long scale model of the river that reflects every topographic detail of the fabled "Mother of Water." The attraction also offers visitors the Mississippi River Museum, native southern cuisine, play and picnic areas, and a 4,300-seat amphitheater. The Mud Island development serves the dual purpose of attracting tourists by highlighting the river and the people along its banks, and of revitalizing a formerly squalid area. (Partners in Livable Places, 1985) Charlotte, North Carolina; Birmingham, Alabama; and Bloomington, Minnesota, represent other examples of recent anchor development.

Reinforcing Local and Cultural Tradition Through Special Events

Salley, South Carolina, (population 500), has two sources of revenue—The Salley Manufacturing Corporation, a maker of women's clothing, and the annual "Chitlin Strut." Initiated 20 years ago by local government officials, the one-afternoon country music festival originally received little support from the community's citizens. The celebration has grown considerably and now is an all-day affair with a parade, beauty contest, dance contests, and souvenir sales in addition to continuous music and chitterlings. Local residents now support the event whole-heartedly. Community teams are assigned weeks in advance, which promotes keen but friendly competition among various units to see who can sell the most. Today festival-goers number approximately 40,000 and consume more than 4.5 tons of "chitlins," in addition to 150 barbecued pigs and 1,500 chickens.

Since the celebration's beginning, Salley has not had a tax-rate increase, and the festival proceeds have paid for new fire and garbage trucks, a new city hall and firehouse, street signs, Christmas decorations, and trash containers. The festival's success has helped Salley obtain some of the best highway signage of any locality of its size in the region. Money is not the only benefit generated by the "Chitlin Strut"—community pride and a sense of purpose have been enhanced, and many of the town's social and cultural barriers have been dissolved. (Partners in Livable Places, 1985)

These examples represent community-scale tourism development seeking to properly create more employment, a larger tax base, additional support facilities, urban revitalization, and community spirit. Though increasing tourism in a community can have pitfalls, through proper planning and management tourism can also become a community asset—economically, socially, and culturally.

Assessing and Protecting Tourism Assets

The Spoleto Festival in Charleston, South Carolina, is patterned after an Italian festival. The popular event represents an excellent example of local intercultural interpretation and cooperation to promote the arts.

Financing Promotional and Marketing Efforts

Since the savings and loan scandals of the 1980s, finding investment capital for tourism projects has been difficult. More accurate feasibility studies are needed for all scales of tourism projects. Some cities, however, have been more successful than others in formulating sound financial plans for tourism projects. Bloomington, Minnesota, for example, was recently successful in developing a financial plan and economic incentives to attract and construct the Mall of America, a multimillion dollar urban entertainment center. The 78-acre center has approximately four million square feet of retail shops, amusement park, and entertainment facilities. Additional lodging, sports, and convention facilities are being planned for the future near the Minneapolis–St. Paul International Airport. Other examples of creative financing include Baltimore, Maryland (baseball stadium); Monterey, California (aquarium); San Jose, California (entertainment center); and Anaheim, California (theme park).

County Travel and Tourism Development

Located along the 45th parallel of north latitude is Door County, Wisconsin. The county is known for its natural similarity to Cape Cod in Massachusetts. The combination of natural and man-made tourist attractions has attracted millions of visitors to the county.

Door County, population 25,739, has the highest per-capita land value in Wisconsin. It has 25 inland lakes, 32 streams, and 20,000 acres of water in bays and harbors of the peninsula. Forests occupy one-third of the 447 square miles. The county has approximately 20,000 motor vehicles that travel on 1,257 miles of roads and cross 14 bridges. About 350 resorts, motels, lodges, and campgrounds in the county provide 6,000 rooms. Three thousand campsites are available in 13 privately owned campgrounds and four state parks. More than 250,000 campers visit the county annually. It is not unusual for the county to host 60,000 visitors on a busy summer weekend. The Chamber of Commerce spends nearly $155,000 to annually promote tourism. Three thousand jobs and 1,000 businesses are directly related to tourism. The 1.6 million visitors generate an estimated $170 million in direct tourism revenue. (Hastings, 1993)

The county is more than famous for its cherry and apple orchards, 4,000 acres of sunflowers, 200 charted shipwrecks, and fish boils. Tourists and property owners come together in restaurants, parks, beaches, cultural and craft activities, spectator events, and recreational facilities. Although the county may have been settled as early as 7,000 B.C. by Plano Indians, it has been a major tourist destination since the 1969 article in *National Geographic Magazine* entitled "A Kingdom So Delicious." (Lotz, 1981)

The popular tourist destination, not unlike others, is so attractive that tourists return to visit and live. One of the dilemmas facing the tourism industry is where to develop real estate. The advantages and disadvantages of sites in the county have been identified (Table 1).

Management of such sites often is the basis of travel and tourism development in many popular destination areas. Sixty percent or more than 15,000 nonresident owners of property now temporarily inhabit this county along with natives, transplants, and retirees. In summary, few counties are as closely tied to travel and tourism management as Door County, Wisconsin.

State Travel and Tourism Development

The early 1990s has been a period of economic recession for much of the United States. Some of the travel and tourism characteristics likely to propel the industry into the year 2000 are as follows (Waters, 1992):

- More weekend trips
- Short trip duration
- Declining distance (average pleasure round trip, 80 miles in 1991)
- Decline in air travel

Table 1. Door County Recreation—Real Estate Sites

Where to Locate	Advantages	Disadvantages
1. Shoreline	Sound of waves Dock Swimming, water sports View of water	Costly High taxes Erosion Dampness
2. Bluff	View of lights, islands, water, sunset, sails Westside peninsula	High-priced, taxes Wind Glare, wells
3. Wooded	Sound of rain on leaves, wind Beauty of nature—woodlot Birds Wildflower Animals	Dampness Limited view
4. Meadow	View Reasonable prices, taxes Native plants and animals	Not exciting
5. Farmland	Joy of ownership, expansion of land Orchards, trees Vegetables Lower prices and taxes Privacy View	Upkeep
6. Inland lakes	Water sports No erosion Little dock upkeep	Little available Lots small Earthen dams
7. Island	Seclusion Privacy Prices Taxes	Inaccessible Weather Logistics of Supplies, equip- ment, services Expensive Time consuming Mail delivery Radio and TV reception Lack of protection
8. Subdivisions	Close neighbors Citylike Prices and taxes vary Small lot sizes	Crowded Small lots Less privacy
9. Village	People in tourist season Services Newspapers, etc. TV Mail Protection (police and fire) Schools Roads, streets, highways Library Fuel Sewage Recreation, parks Auto repair	Crowded Small lots Less privacy

- Decline in business trip distance (average 862 miles)
- Decline in the time available for a vacation

Positive indicators for U.S. travel and tourism include the following:

- Increases in foreign spending to nearly $70 billion
- Employment in the industry has held steady
- Increases in rural travel
- Improved census data
- Improved ski resort business
- Record use of national parks and forests
- World leadership in conventions (New York, Dallas, Chicago)
- More than 20 million people will retire by 2002
- Increases in casino and riverboat gambling visits
- Increases to visits to factory outlet malls (Pigeon Forge, Tennessee)

To better appreciate the role states have in tourism, tourism activity in the three leading revenue-generating states will be discussed here. California, Florida, and New York lead the nation in tourism revenue generation (Table 2). It should be noted, however, that tourism revenue generation is not necessarily directly correlated with state expenditures for tourism (Table 3). These three states rank thirty-second, fifth, and eighteenth respectively for state travel office budgets.

Although California earns more from tourism than any other state ($77 billion in 1989), it has suffered economic setbacks, a weak real estate market, high unemployment, and military base closings. Overcrowded highways, air pollution, water shortages, high cost of living, urban riots, a huge state deficit, and business migration have dimmed the prospects for tourism in the near future. Positive influences, however, include climate, growth in foreign trade, location relative to the Pacific Rim and Mexico, and political clout. Famous art galleries, museums, theaters, movie and television studios, theme parks, desert resorts, hotels, restaurants, convention centers, vineyards, national parks, and sports and recreation facilities will continue to renew the tarnished image of California for future economic leadership.

Tourism is Florida's largest industry, with more than 40 million visitors in 1991. The state's climate, rapid increase in population, no income tax, the super-destination of the Orlando area, car racing, the space center, and professional and amateur sports facilities all add to the nearly $50 billion annual revenue of Florida tourism.

New York ranks eighteenth in state tourism budget but is third in revenue. Canadian shoppers, overseas visitors, cultural attractions, boating opportunities, historical attractions, convention facilities, and scenic attractions all contribute to annual tourism revenues of nearly $40 billion.

Illinois, Texas, Nevada, New Jersey, Pennsylvania, Virginia, and Ohio have significant travel and tourism revenues and management opportunities. Regionally, the South Atlantic states attract the largest percentage of travelers (21%).

Table 2. Domestic Tourism Spending in United States for Trips More Than 25 Miles from Home, 1989

State	Tourism Spending in State ($ billions)	Rank	State	Tourism Spending in State ($ billions)	Rank
Alabama	$6.57	27	Montana	2.19	42
Alaska	2.19	45	Nebraska	3.29	39
Arizona	8.76	20	Nevada	19.73	6
Arkansas	4.38	36	New Hampshire	2.19	44
California	77.27	1	New Jersey	18.08	7
Colorado	9.86	18	New Mexico	4.01	37
Connecticut	6.03	29	New York	36.71	3
Delaware	1.64	48	North Carolina	12.60	13
Florida	49.32	2	North Dakota	1.64	49
Georgia	14.25	11	Ohio	14.79	10
Hawaii	10.96	16	Oklahoma	4.93	32
Idaho	2.19	41	Oregon	6.57	28
Illinois	21.92	5	Pennsylvania	17.54	8
Indiana	7.12	26	Rhode Island	1.09	51
Iowa	4.93	33	South Carolina	7.67	23
Kansas	4.38	34	South Dakota	1.09	50
Kentucky	6.03	30	Tennessee	10.96	15
Louisiana	8.22	22	Texas	31.23	4
Maine	2.74	40	Utah	4.38	35
Maryland	8.77	21	Vermont	1.64	47
Massachusetts	12.60	14	Virginia	15.89	9
Michigan	13.15	12	Washington D.C.*	5.48	31
Minnesota	7.12	25	Washington	8.76	19
Mississippi	3.84	38	West Virginia	2.19	43
Missouri	10.96	17	Wisconsin	7.12	24
			Wyoming	2.19	46
Total				$548.00	

Note: Foreign visitors spent $35 billion in the United States in 1989, bringing total tourism spending in the United States to $583 billion.

*Metropolitan area

Source: Travel Industry World Yearbook—The Big Picture

Table 3. Projected State Travel Office Budgets by Rank

Rank	State	1991–1992	% Change from Previous Fiscal Year	Rank	State	1991–1992	% Change from Previous Fiscal Year
1	Texas	$26,754,334	31%	26	Arizona	5,727,300	9
2	Illinois	25,000,000	3	27	New Mexico	5,722,300	43
3	Hawaii	23,031,938	-18	28	Alabama	5,689,324	5
4	Louisiana	13,478,067	44	29	Maryland	5,114,156	-19
5	Florida	12,794,732	20	30	Ohio	5,050,000	-6
6	Pennsylvania	12,400,000	-11	31	West Virginia	4,161,129	24
7	Alaska	10,460,959	-16	32	California	4,100,000	-45
8	South Carolina	10,348,944	14	33	Utah	3,999,737	-10
9	Virginia	9,908,973	28	34	South Dakota	3,550,000	1
10	Colorado	9,679,000	12	35	Iowa	3,482,404	-17
11	Wisconsin	9,404,583	10	36	Indiana	3,250,000	-7
12	Massachusetts	9,025,000	69	37	Wyoming	3,131,886	-24
13	Minnesota	8,874,435	6	38	Idaho	2,984,113	7
14	Arkansas	7,977,315	3	39	Rhode Island	2,857,000	9
15	Tennessee	7,661,000	-29	40	Vermont	2,490,600	1
16	Georgia	7,321,240	-8	41	New Hampshire	2,441,215	-14
17	Kentucky	7,224,300	9	42	Oregon	2,432,500	0
18	New York	7,005,520	-47	43	Kansas	2,385,834	12
19	North Carolina	6,751,000	1	44	Washington	2,243,386	-22
20	Missouri	6,455,600	-1	45	North Dakota	2,050,000	37
21	Michigan	6,333,600	-28	46	Maine	2,012,491	25
22	Oklahoma	6,287,098	12	47	Connecticut	1,813,356	-1
23	New Jersey	6,212,000	-11	48	Mississippi	1,731,905	-25
24	Montana	5,752,912	12	49	Nebraska	1,591,177	5
25	Nevada	5,730,907	13	50	Delaware	808,000	-14
	Grand Total					$342,693,270	0.0%
	Average					$6,853,865	—

Source: U.S. Travel Data Center

National Travel and Tourism Development

Tourism on a national scale is aptly represented by the world's leading destination, France (Table 4), which jumped from fourth to second in tourism revenue between 1986 and 1991. During this period, France had an annual average growth rate of nearly 17%, exceeded only by Singapore, Thailand, and Australia (Table 5). The French world market share of tourism receipts now totals nearly 9%, or half the U.S. share. (Waters, 1992)

Table 4. World's Top Tourism Destinations, 1991
International Tourism Arrivals (Excluding Excursionists)

1991 Rank	Country	Thousands of Arrivals		1986 Rank	Average Annual Growth Rate % 1986/91	Share of World Total (%)	
		1991	1986			1991	1986
1	France	55,731	36,080	1	9.09%	12.42%	10.58%
2	United States	42,114	26,158	3	9.99	9.39	7.67
3	Spain	35,347	29,910	2	3.40	7.88	8.77
4	Italy	26,840	24,672	4	1.70	5.98	7.24
5	Hungary	21,860	10,613	11	15.55	4.87	3.11
6	Austria	19,092	15,092	5	4.81	4.26	4.43
7	United Kingdom	16,805	13,897	7	3.87	3.75	4.08
8	Mexico	15,962	12,659	9	4.75	3.56	3.71
9	Germany	15,635	13,458	8	3.04	3.49	3.95
10	Canada	14,989	15,621	6	-0.82	3.34	4.58
11	Switzerland	12,600	11,400	10	2.02	2.81	3.34
12	China	12,464	9,000	12	6.73	2.78	2.64
13	Portugal	8,814	5,409	14	10.26	1.97	1.59
14	Czechoslov.	8,200	5,330	15	9.00	1.83	1.56
15	Greece	8,036	7,025	13	2.73	1.79	2.06
World Total		$448,545	$340,891		5.64%	100.00%	100.00%

Source: World Tourism Organization

Tourism improvements in France are being driven by higher average incomes, deregulation, international economic cooperation, removal of travel barriers, improved rail and air infrastructure, central location, the 1992 Winter Olympics, and the opening of Euro Disney. The opening of the Channel Tunnel also will be a strong influence on travel from the United Kingdom.

Summary

This chapter has examined travel and tourism management through analysis of small scale (community) development to the large scale (national). Forecasts for the future of world tourism appear to reflect slow but steady economic gains. Travel volume is projected to reach 752 million arrivals and $720 billion in receipts by the year 2000. Europe will lead us into the next century as a destination and in travel receipts (Table 6). (Edgell, 1993)

Table 5. World's Top Tourism Earners, 1991
International Tourism Receipts (Excluding International Transport)

1991 Rank	County	Millions of Current U.S. Dollars		1986 Rank	Average Annual Growth Rate % 1986/91	Share of World Total (%)	
		1991	1986			1991	1986
1	United States	$45,551	$20,454	1	17.37%	17.47%	14.61%
2	France	21,300	9,724	4	16.98	8.17	6.94
3	Italy	19,668	9,855	3	14.82	7.54	7.04
4	Spain	19,004	12,058	2	9.53	7.29	8.61
5	Austria	13,956	6,954	6	14.95	5.35	4.97
6	United Kingdom	12,588	8,163	5	9.05	4.83	5.83
7	Germany	10,947	6,294	7	11.71	4.20	4.49
8	Switzerland	7,030	4,227	8	10.71	2.70	3.02
9	Mexico	5,934	2,984	10	14.74	2.28	2.13
10	Canada	5,537	3,860	9	7.48	2.12	2.76
11	Hong Kong	5,078	2,287	11	17.30	1.95	1.63
12	Singapore	4,386	1,767	13	19.94	1.68	1.26
13	Netherlands	4,300	2,219	12	14.15	1.65	1.58
14	Thailand	4,295	1,421	14	24.76	1.65	1.01
15	Australia	4,164	1,300	15	26.22	1.60	0.93
	World Total	$260,763	$140,023		13.24%	100.00%	100.00%

Source: World Tourism Organization

Table 6. World and U.S. International Visitor Arrivals and Receipts
1960–2000

Year	World Arrivals (Millions)	U.S. Arrivals (Millions)	U.S. Share (%)	World Receipts ($ Billions)	U.S. Receipts ($ Billions)	U.S. Share (%)
1960	69.3	5.6	8.1	6.9	1.0	14.8
1965	112.9	7.8	6.9	11.6	1.5	13.3
1970	165.8	12.4	7.5	17.9	2.3	13.0
1975	222.3	15.7	7.1	40.7	4.7	11.5
1980	287.8	22.3	7.7	102.4	10.6	10.3
1985	329.6	25.4	7.7	115.4	17.9	15.5
1986	340.8	26.0	7.6	139.8	20.5	14.7
1987	366.8	29.4	8.0	171.6	23.7	13.8
1988	393.9	34.1	8.7	197.7	29.7	15.0
1989	427.9	36.6	8.5	210.8	36.6	17.3
1990	455.6	39.5	8.7	255.1	43.4	17.0
1991	455.1	42.9	9.4	261.1	48.8	18.7
1992(P)	475.6	45.4	9.5	278.7	55.2	19.8
1993(P)	503.6	47.9	9.5	334.0	60.1	18.0
1994(P)	533.4	50.9	9.5	389.0	67.3	17.3
1995(P)	564.8	54.2	9.6	445.0	75.3	16.9
2000(P)	752.0	77.4	10.3	720.0	132.1	18.3

P = Projected (Receipts are in 1992 USA dollars).
Source: Complied by Ron Erdmann, market research analyst, U.S. Travel and Tourism Administration from World Tourism Organization and U.S. Travel and Tourism Administration data on world and U.S. international tourism arrivals and receipts, March 1993.

Some recent influences on travel and tourism will shape future management opportunities and concepts. Consider the following examples, cases, and issues:

- Free flow of travelers between nations (Western Europe)
- Trade pacts (United States, Mexico, Canada)
- Growth in democracy (India)
- New travel frontiers (Russia)
- Natural disasters (U.S. midwest floods and Hurricane Andrew)
- Large world events (World Cup Championship in United States)
- Ecotourism (Costa Rica)
- Civil war (Yugoslavia)
- Overbuilding tourism goods and services (hotel rooms in Detroit, Michigan)
- Growing influence of travel agents and tour operators (United States)
- Growth in U.S. food service companies in foreign markets (Taco Bell to Mexico)
- Labor turnover in food service

- Growth in U.S. lodging companies in foreign markets (Radisson in Moscow)
- Decline in hotel occupancy levels
- Growth in limited service lodging chains
- Forecasting
- Law
- Decline in world airline traffic
- Growth in passenger car registrations and miles traveled
- Growth of rental car use
- Growth of motorcoach tours
- Increased demand for rail service
- Increases in cruise ship boardings
- Tourism as a force for peace
- Sustainable rural tourism development
- Community values (no-growth vs. growth)
- Authenticity of tourism experience and products
- Individual sense of place
- Information systems
- Gaming and tourism
- Quality service
- National investment policies
- Promotion
- Service tourism vs. real estate—recreation tourism
- Heritage tourism
- Agritourism
- Sustainable tourism
- Big events
- Terrorism
- Health safety and security
- Tourism education
- Religious tourism
- Service management models
- Festivals and special events
- Tourism policy, planning, and promotion
- Telecommunications
- Seasonality

Some of the most recent management subjects addressed by current travel and tourism leaders, educators, and researchers include information technology, computerized reservation systems, terrorism, frequent flyer programs, incentive travel, telemarketing, airline deregulation, image development and maintenance, contract compliance, meeting management, ticket distribution deficiencies, and direct discounting. Other issues and subjects include sociology, history, geography, anthropology, political science, and economic perspectives of tourism; tourist guides; consumer research; interrelationships of leisure, recreation, and tourism; semiotics of tourism; domestic tourism; socio-cultural-environmental impacts of travel and tourism; and tourism in centrally planned economies.

The travel and tourism industry remains extremely complex and will require a constant regeneration of management leaders. Approximately 700 colleges and universities in the world are now offering studies leading to a better understanding of travel and tourism.*

——References——

Council on Hotel, Restaurant and Institutional Education. (1991) *A Guide to College Programs in Hospitality and Tourism 1991–1992,* New York: John Wiley & Sons. 1991.

Edgell, David L., Sr. (1985) *International Trade in Tourism: A Manual for Managers and Executives.* Washington, DC: U.S. Department of Commerce, U.S. Travel and Tourism Administration.

____.*World Tourism at the Millennium: An Agenda for Industry, Government and Education.* Washington DC: U.S. Department of Commerce, U.S. Travel and Tourism Administration, 1993.

Gee, Chuck Y., Choy, Dexter J. L., Makens, James C. (1984) *The Travel Industry.* Westport, Conn.: AVI Publishers, Inc., 1984.

Hastings, Robert, Executive Director, Door County Chamber of Commerce. Telephone interview, July 17, 1993.

Jafari, Jafar. Anatomy of the Travel Industry. *Cornell H.R.A. Quarterly, XXXIV(1),* 1983:73.

____. Paratourism and Its Contributions to the Hospitality Industry. In *The Practice of Hospitality Management,* Pizam, et al. eds., p. 427, Westport, Conn.: AVI Publishing Inc. 1982.

Kahn, Mahmood, Olsen, Michael, and Var, Turgut. (1992) *VNR's Encyclopedia of Hospitality and Tourism.* New York: Van Nostrand Reinhold.

Lotz, M. Marvin. (1981) *Your Piece of the Peninsula: A Door County Reference Book for Property Owners and Buyers,* Fish Creek, Wis.: Holly House Press.

Metelka, Charles J. (1990) *The Dictionary of Tourism,* 3rd edition. Wheaton, Ill.: Merton House Travel and Tourism Press.

Mieczkowski, Zbigniew Ted. Some Notes on the Geography of Tourism: A Comment. *Canadian Geographer, XXV(2)* (1981):189–190.

Murphy, Peter. (1985) *Tourism: A Community Approach,* New York: Methuen & Co.

Partners for Livable Places. Destination: Where? Putting Cities Without Surf, Slopes and Slot Machines on the Map. Washington DC: 1–28.

Pizam, Abraham. The Management of Tourism. Special Issue, *Annals of Tourism Research,* VII, No. 3, 1980, 377–500.

Travel and Leisure. (1985) *World Tourism Overview 1985.* New York: American Express Publishing Corporation.

University of Minnesota Tourism Center, Rural Tourism Development. (1991) *Training Guide.* St. Paul, Minn.: Minnesota Extension Service.

Waters, Somerset R. (1992) *Travel Industry World Yearbook.* New York: Child and Waters, Inc.

---

*See A guide to Programs in Hospitality and Tourism, CHRIE, 1991.

34

Meeting and Event Planners

Lalia C. Rach
University of New Haven

Introduction

In the past 15 years organizations have come to recognize the need to employ qualified professionals who can design and implement meetings and special events. The primary reason for employing a professional meeting or event planner is to ensure that the function runs smoothly and efficiently. A poorly planned meeting or event reflects badly on the organization and can result in diminished resources for associations and decreased status for a corporation. The success of a meeting and event planner depends on his ability to organize and produce an endless series of activities while attending to thousands of minute details. Individuals in either occupation must be creative and flexible, able to manage time and conflict, have a superb eye for detail, and thrive on change and risk. Both types of planners must understand the focus, purpose, and participants of the organization sponsoring the meeting or event in order to plan a successful gathering.

Members of either profession will most likely join one or more of the following associations: International Festival Association (IFA), International Special Events Society (ISES), Professional Conference Management Association (PCMA), and Meeting Planners International (MPI). Numerous publications have been developed specifically for the profession including *Corporate Meetings and Incentives, Meeting Manager, Meeting News, Meetings & Conventions, Special Events, Successful Meetings,* and *Tradeshow Newsweekly.*

Meetings

A meeting is defined as a planned function of two or more people designed to further communication. A meeting whose participants are from two or more countries is categorized as an international meeting.[1] Although modern technology enables individuals to communicate instantly, the need for face-to-face, personal interchange has not diminished. Meetings remain the most common means of communication between two or more people. In fact, more and more meetings are held every year due to the increased need for people to interact with others, to learn about advances within their professions, to personally communicate with different constituents, and to transmit new ideas, skills, and methods. The sponsoring organization and the purpose for which the meeting is held determine the number of participants, the type and length of the meeting, the site of the meeting, and the type of facility. Associations and corporations are the two primary organizations that sponsor meetings.

Meetings are held to solve problems; resolve conflicts; and to train, inform, promote, change, and motivate employees, members, and customers. It is vitally important for the meeting planner to understand the purpose of the meeting as well as the expected outcomes because this information is the basis for every decision made during the planning of the meeting. The meeting site, the meeting room design, food and beverage selections, and the quality of accommodations should be selected based on the meetings' purpose.

Events

A special event is any unique activity created for a specific or general audience which occurs on an annual, periodic, or one-time basis. A community may develop a festival to attract tourists and to provide cultural activities for locals. A company or an association may decide to include a special event during the course of their annual meeting. The destination of the meeting may well determine the nature of the special event. A convention in Washington, D.C., might feature an evening spectacular at Mount Vernon, the home of the first U.S. President George Washington. Participants cruise down the Potomac River enjoy cocktails and hors d'oeuvres, dock at Mount Vernon for dinner, dance on the lawn overlooking the river, and close with a midnight cruise back to Washington, D.C. A corporation might want to introduce a new product by staging a gala for buyers or sales personnel. Many corporations sponsor annual incentive trips for top personnel. The entire trip is a continuous special event, with each day's activities designed to outdo the previous one's.

Events are developed to celebrate history, honor achievements, create memories, encourage visitation, and promote growth. An event planner must have a clear understanding of the significance of the event, as this will determine the degree of extravagance. The choice of venue and the quality of decor and entertainment will depend on the intent of the sponsoring organization. Events include social occasions where birthdays, anniversaries, and personal achievements are celebrated; retail productions such as holiday extravaganzas and store openings; corporate affairs to introduce new products, honor personal achievements of employees, and provide incentives; sporting events; government anniversaries; charitable organizations' fund-raising events; and events such as festivals and parades.

Although all events are to some degree special, certain events are of such proportions they are designated as mega-events. A mega-event is distinguished by the large numbers of participants and spectators, and the demands the sheer numbers place upon the destination's accommodations, transportation system, retail shops, and restaurants. A mega-event may be a once-in-a-lifetime spectacular hosted by a specific city or region. The Olympics, the Super Bowl, or the World Cup are classified as mega–sporting events that are held on an established timetable, at different locations. There are mega-events that occur at the same place on a recurrent schedule such as the presidential inaugural, which occurs in Washington, D.C., every four years; the Mardi Gras in New Orleans, an annual explosion of fun before the 40-day period of Lent; and the yearly Macy's Thanksgiving Day Parade in New York City.

Types of Meetings and Events

As the meeting and event professions have grown in complexity and become more specialized, each has developed a distinct set of terms. The term *meeting* has many variations including convention, congress, conference, lecture, workshop and trade show. All are meetings but that's where the similarity ends. A convention is a business or professional meeting generally held for a three- to five-day period on an annual or biannual basis with a large number of attendees. Conventions feature a general session and breakouts (smaller groups focusing on one problem or issue) or workshops. A convention may or may not be accompanied by exhibits or a trade show. A conference is similar to a convention but may or may not feature breakout sessions. It is convened to address one issue or problem and attendees are expected to participate and discuss.

A congress is the same as a convention but used to specify an international convention outside the United States. A talk by one or two people followed by question-and-answer session is a seminar. A lecture is a structured, formal presentation by experts. The question-and-answer session is optional. Workshops feature small groups that exchange information and receive training. Case studies, role playing, and other group exercises are used to increase knowledge or skills in specific area. A trade show can either accompany a convention or stand alone. It is used by suppliers to exhibit products.

The term *event* has various interpretations including ceremony, celebration, gala, and festival. Each is an event of a slightly different structure. A ceremony generally occurs at the beginning or ending of a convention, corporate meeting, or a mega-event and features an elaborate activity that either sets the tone or cements an image. Celebrations focus on the social occurrences of life, such as anniversaries, birthdays, graduations, and reunions. Generally, attendance is by invitation only. A gala is an event on a grand scale involving multiple sites and large numbers of people. The U.S. presidential inaugural is perhaps the best publicized gala. Festivals honor individuals, incidents, and milestones. They occur on an annual basis for periods of one day to a week, are open to the public, and usually revolve around a central theme.

Meeting and Event Planners

The Professional Convention Managers Association (PCMA) estimates there are 225,000 full- and part-time meeting planners in the United States.[2] Most are employed by associations and corporations; however, a significant number are self-employed or work for universities and government agencies.

The primary duties of a meeting planner include marketing; program development; selection of the meeting location; arranging housing and transportation; choosing food and beverage for receptions, breaks, and meals; contracting with destination services; and determining meeting room layouts.

Marketing begins months before the convention is held in order to attract participants and exhibitors. Site selection will be influenced by the destination's organized approach to attracting and servicing meetings. The meeting planner will look for cities and facilities that provide products and services necessary to the success of the meeting. The most frequently used destination services are hotels, destination management companies, decorating firms, local ground operators, audiovisual companies, entertainers, and security firms.

Food and beverage selections greatly influence the overall success of the meeting. The food must be selected with the participants in mind. Items that are too exotic or too ordinary for the group will cause dissatisfaction.

The style or manner in which a meeting room is set up should be determined by the purpose of the meeting. For example, a meeting that is designed for training would most likely require the room to be set in a classroom or schoolroom configuration. This means the room is set with rectangular tables 6 to 8 feet long and 18 to 36 inches wide. This set-up is best for training sessions and lectures at which attendees are expected to take detailed notes.

Characteristics of a successful event planner mirror those of a successful meeting planner. Most event planners are self-employed. Although a meeting planner may at times be an event planner, generally the reverse is not true. Event planners are involved in creating special or unusual happenings that may or may not occur during a meeting. The primary duties of a special event planner include determining the proper site; facilities rental; identifying appropriate transportation; creating a concept that features lights, sound, decorations, special effects; and subcontracting for services such as catering, music, entertainment, and video recording.

Statistics

More than one million meetings were held in 1991, with almost 81 million attendees. Spending by sponsoring organizations and attendees in the United States alone exceeded $38 billion. The average delegate spent an estimated $1,133 over the course of a convention. According to a 1992 survey by *Meetings & Conventions* magazine, more than 800,000 off-premises corporate meetings, 225,000 association meetings, and 11,000 conventions were planned and held. Forty-nine percent of the corporate meetings were training seminair and management meetings, while 61% of association meetings were educational seminars and professional or technical meetings. A breakdown of the number of meetings, expenditures, and attendance by type of meeting is presented in Table 1.[3]

The growth in meetings has been accompanied by an increase in the number of meetings held abroad. The number of meetings held outside the United States has nearly doubled since 1987. Corporate meetings outside the continental United States increased from 33,500

Table 1. Overview of the U.S. Meeting Market for 1991

	Associations	Conventions	Corporations
Number of meetings (thousands)	806.2	10.2	215
Spending in U.S. dollars (billions)	15.3	11.0	8.7
Number of attendees (millions)	22.6	8.6	49.6

Source: The Meetings Market '92

Table 2. 1991 Association Delegate Spending

	Dollars	Percentages
Hotel room and incidentals	317.78	51
Hotel restaurants	68.31	11
Other restaurants	70.96	11
Hospitality suites	32.26	5
Entertainment	31.17	5
Retail stores	50.98	8
Local transport	26.89	4
Other	24.62	4
TOTAL	$622.97	100

in 1987 to an estimated 68,500 in 1991. During the same time frame, association meetings held abroad more than doubled, from 1,500 to 3,860. In 1991 more than 6,000 international associations held meetings in various destinations around the world.

Meetings and conventions are big business. A recent study estimated the economic impact of association-sponsored conventions on a destination to be $622.97 per delegate.[4] Table 2 provides a breakdown of the spending by a delegate in 1991.

The statistical information available for special events is quite limited. The International Special Events Society (ISES) has 1,200 members, of whom 40% identified themselves as planners and 60% as suppliers.

Market Segments

The major meeting and event market segments are association conventions and meetings and corporate meetings and shows.

Associations

Associations are not-for-profit organizations designed to promote professionalism, education, and networking for individuals in specific careers and specific jobs. There are nearly 23,000 national associations worldwide, and approximately 100,000 at the regional, state, and local levels.[5] The American Society of Association Executives (ASAE) divides associations into two categories: trade associations and professional societies. Trade associations represent a grouping of business firms. The main function of the trade association is to establish industry standards and ethics codes, host conventions, and perform research. The Travel Industry of America (TIA), the American Hotel and Motel Association (AHMA), and the National Restaurant Association (NRA) are hospitality and tourism industry–related trade associations.

Professional societies are formed by individuals with common interests or careers. Groups that make up professional societies include trade, professional, educational, scientific, and military associations. Professional societies provide networking opportunities and continuing education programs. The Council of Hotel, Restaurant and Institutional Educators (CHRIE) and the Society of Travel and Tourism Educators (STTE) are examples of educational associations of interest to hospitality and tourism teachers.

Associations host two main types of meetings: major conventions with or without trade shows and other off-premises meetings. Conventions and exhibits are an association's main source of revenue and are held to disseminate knowledge and information among members. Other types of meetings are board and committee meetings, professional meetings, and educational seminars. Reasons for association meetings include providing information to members, gaining recognition for the association, and earning revenue. Association meetings generally are planned years in advance, and on a regular cycle, to attract participants to the event. Attendance is voluntary, with attendees either paying their own way or supported to some degree by their employer. The destination and accommodations must be reflective of the members' status, affluence, and sophistication.

Corporations

Corporate meetings vary considerably in size depending on their purpose. The most common types of corporate meetings are professional and technical, sales, product presentation, and board meetings as well as training seminars. Corporate meetings account for the great majority of all meetings held in the United States and the world. They differ significantly from association meetings in size, planning time, location, and participation. Generally, corporate meetings are small, involving fewer than 60 participants. Most importantly, they are scheduled as needed or on demand with a relatively short lead time. Attendance is quite predictable because employees must participate and their expenses are paid by the company.

Conclusion

Although meetings and events are not new concepts, it was not until recently that an individual could choose a program of study in these fields at the post-secondary level. At certain universities (e.g., Georgia State, University of New Haven, Central Florida), a student may now select a major or minor in meeting and event planning that will allow her to develop a career as a meeting and event planner.

——References——

1. Catherine H. Price. *The AMA Guide for Meeting and Event Planners.* AMACOM. p. 435.
2. Penny C. Dotson. *Introduction to Meeting Management.* PCMA. p. 4.
3. The Meetings Market '92. *Meetings and Conventions.*

35

Travel Agency Management

Andrew N. Vladimir
Florida International University

Introduction

It once was easy to define a travel agency. You could say that any establishment that was accredited by the Airline Reporting Corporation (an organization or conference set up by airlines to collect money on their behalf for tickets issued) was a travel agency. By that measure, 1991 was a good year. According to *Travel Weekly,* there were 32,066 agency locations booking $85.9 billion of travel compared to 6,700 agencies booking $5 billion in 1970. Since the airline industry was deregulated in 1978, the number of travel agencies has more than doubled from 14,804 to 32,066. But by other measures there may be more than 35,000 agencies if you add in those who are cruise-only travel agencies. Some of these agencies do not issue any airline tickets and thus do not require recognition by the Airline Reporting Corp. They sell only cruises; the airline tickets to the ports of departure are issued by the cruise lines in conjunction with the sailing documents. However, for the purposes of this chapter, we will define agencies by the traditional method. Thus our discussion of what they do and how they do it will refer to the most common garden variety of agency, which sells a broad range of travel products and services including airline tickets, hotel rooms, cruises, tours, train and bus tickets, as well as ancillary products and services such as travel insurance, foreign currencies, and passport photos.

According to the 1991 U.S. travel agency survey conducted for *Travel Weekly* by Louis Harris and Associates, the average revenue per agency was $2,680,000. However, most travel agencies are small businesses, with 64% of all locations reporting revenues of less than $2 million and only 11% reporting more than $5 million.

What then is a travel agent? What exactly do they do and how do they do it?

In the very simplest terms, an *agent* according to most dictionary definitions is "one that acts for or as the representative of another."[1] Travel agents therefore *represent* airlines, cruise lines, hotels, car rental companies, tour operators, and others who offer travel and tourism services. As representatives their job is first and foremost to dispense information about these various services to the public at large. In this sense they are *information brokers*. However, because they represent and are agents for other companies, they are also *distributors* and *salespersons* and as such they receive their compensation from the organizations whose products they distribute and sell.

History

It can be shown very easily that the travel agent really revolutionized the selling of travel, and more than any other single factor is responsible for the shape of modern travel as we know it today.

The first travel agent is universally recognized as being Thomas Cook. Cook was an English Baptist preacher who in 1841 organized a rail tour from Leicester to Loughborough of 570 people to attend a temperance meeting. Cook recognized that with the emergence of railroads and steamships there was a need for someone who was willing to make arrangements for people who wished to explore England and the Continent and were somewhat nervous about traveling on their own to foreign places. Soon Cook had established himself as sales agent for these new and convenient forms of transportation, and in 1856 he offered the first grand tour of Europe. About the same time (1850) the American Express Company was formed in the United States. Originally started with the purpose of shipping merchandise and money across the continent and then to Europe, the company soon grew to the point where it also offered travelers checks and dispensed information on foreign destinations. Not until 1915, however, did the company decide to go into the business of handling tourist travel and offering tours.

Originally travel agencies were closely regulated businesses because they collected money for carriers and also handled the disbursement of funds in the form of travelers checks. But over the years most regulation has disappeared and with it the protection offered agencies of exclusive sales territories. Today, almost anyone with approximately $40,000 or the ability to borrow it can start a travel agency. In fact one recent trend in the travel agency business has been the emergence of franchising. New owners with no background at all can buy a franchise, get professional training and support, and then open their doors within a few months.

Types of Travel Agencies

There are various types of travel agencies in business now, and new variations seem to spring up all the time with technological advances and the ease of entry into the business. Here are some of the most common:

Full-Service Agencies

Although these agencies handle all types of travel, in most cases a little more than half of their business comes from vacation and personal travelers booking airline tickets and hotel rooms. Before airline deregulation in 1978, fares were more or less standard on the same routes and thus business travelers were often accustomed to calling airlines directly to make their travel arrangements. Agencies were used more for convenience than any other reason. However, with today's complicated and competitive fare structures it is a formidable task for anyone to figure out by themselves which airline offers the best fares and the most convenient schedules without the aid of a computer. The complexity of ticket purchase has led many more travelers to buy their tickets through travel agencies. Today, American Express and Thomas Cook are two of the largest full-service agencies in the world, with branch offices in all major countries.

Commercial Agencies

These agencies specialize in commercial business and frequently have little or no walk-in clientele at all. Agents deal with corporate customers on the telephone and book primarily airline tickets, hotel rooms, and car rentals. Very often they also handle meeting arrangements for their clients. Rosenbluth Travel in Philadelphia is an example of a highly sophisticated commercial agency with a separate meeting planning facility.

In-plant Agencies

In-plant agencies are located in the offices of large corporate clients so that ticketing and other arrangements can be booked instantly and in person. They are branch offices of regularly established commercial agencies. In some cases agencies do not need to open an in-plant office staffed by an agent, but instead install satellite ticket printers (STP's) in clients offices. Under this arrangement the client calls the agency to arrange travel but instead of the agency printing the ticket in its office and then delivering it or mailing it to the client, the ticket is instantly printed on a satellite ticket printer in the client's office. In 1989 satellite locations accounted for 11% of total travel agencies.

Group and Incentive Agencies

These travel agencies specialize in creating customized travel programs for both groups and corporations. For example, many companies reward their top salespersons with trips to exotic places. Others hold annual conventions in Hawaii and the Caribbean for all managers and their spouses. Then there are church groups that wish to visit religious sites such as the Vatican and veterans groups who wish to return to the beaches of Normandy. Group and incentive agencies specialize in this kind of business. Two of the largest are Maritz and E. F. McDonald Company.

In addition to these kind of agencies, which are the best known, there are several other types of travel agencies that need to be mentioned here:

Direct-Response Agencies

These are agencies that do not have any walk-in offices but market their products directly through the mail, often to senior citizens. Many of them offer extended-stay options for their clients, who may wish to spend a month in Spain in their own apartment. One of the largest programs of this kind is offered by the American Association of Retired Persons (AARP). In addition, there are direct-response agencies that operate with toll-free 800 telephone numbers and offer little or no advice or service but instead rebate up to half of their regular 8% to 12% commissions to customers who are willing to do their own homework. Travel Avenue in Chicago, Pennsylvania Travel in Paoli, Pennsylvania, and The Smart Travel in Coconut Grove, Florida, are examples of agencies that operate in this manner.

Tour Operators

Although travel agencies represent many tour operators, in many cases the operators sell directly to the public, thereby acting as their own travel agents. These tours are frequently sold by mail as well (often through university alumni associations) and are often advertised in magazines such as *Condé Nast Traveler* and *Smithsonian*. Much adventure travel such as African safaris, treks to Nepal, and trips to the Galapagos Islands are marketed in this fashion. Companies like Society Expeditions and Tauk Tours are good examples of these kind of operations.

Cruise-Only Agencies

Because there are now more than 100 cruise ships operating out of U.S. ports alone, many agencies have been formed in recent years that handle only cruise business. Since an essential part of selling cruises is knowing the layout of every ship so that the most favorable cabins can be selected (the ones with the least noise and motion) and also understanding which ports of call offer the most interesting attractions, very knowledgeable agents are needed to service prospective passengers. Almost all cruise tickets are sold through travel agents because of these complications, and most travel agents simply do not have enough experience nor have they inspected enough ships to be able to give authoritative advice on this subject. For this reason many agencies have sprung up in recent years that handle only cruises and go to extra lengths to train their agents to become familiar with ships, their menus, on-board services, and ports of call. Since only 5% of Americans have taken a cruise and the business is growing rapidly, these agencies tend to do very well in markets where cruises are popular.

Consolidators

Although most consolidators do not deal directly with the public but rather with other travel agencies, some do and advertise regularly in Sunday travel sections of major metropolitan newspapers. These consolidators have negotiated special arrangements with certain airlines that allow them larger commissions on certain routes and flights or simply have been able to obtain more favorable fares or larger commissions based on unsold seats, volume, and other considerations. In London they are known as "bucket shops." While most of these operations are legitimate, there have been some instances of consumer fraud in this area. Moreover, many established agencies refuse to deal with consolidators, despite the fact that they can obtain cheaper fares through them, on the grounds that they are technically illegal or may not offer an adequate level of protection for their clients. In addition, unlike space booked through traditional sources, sometimes flights may not be confirmed until a few days or even a few hours before departure.

Travel Clubs

These clubs charge an annual fee (usually $35 to $50) and in return offer their members packaged vacations at special prices. The vacations are usually developed on short notice by the clubs working with tour operators who have unsold airline seats and hotel rooms and are willing to sell them to clubs, often at substantial discounts. Discount Travel International (DTI), R & R Travel, and Stand-Buys are three well-known agencies in this category.

What Travel Agencies Do

We have already mentioned the principal products and services sold by agencies in the descriptions above. These need some elaboration and clarification, however. As mentioned earlier, airline tickets make up more than two-thirds of sales for most travel agencies. In order to be able to sell tickets for all major airlines throughout the world, agencies need to be accredited by the Airlines Reporting Corporation (ARC) and the International Airlines Travel Agent Network (INTAN). Monies collected from passengers are forwarded weekly to these organizations through area settlement banks which distribute them to the airlines which they belong to.

Ninety-six percent of all travel agencies subscribe to one or more the of the five computer reservation systems (CRS), which for the most part are owned or controlled by the major airlines. The most widely used systems are Sabre (35% of all sites) and Apollo (23%). The other three systems and their market shares are System One (19%), PARS (17%), and DATAS II (9.2%). In addition there are two major multinational European systems, AMADEUS and GALILEO, owned by a group of European carriers, and a Far Eastern system called Abacus, owned by Singapore Airlines. All of these airline systems are linked together. Thus it is possible for an agent to compare schedules and fares from different airlines along with seat availabilities make an instant reservation, issue a ticket, and in some cases a boarding pass as well. Computer systems are a major expense to agencies, however—a typical agency with $2 million sales has five computer reservation terminals (CRTs) per location and spends more than 6% on computer leasing and necessary forms and supplies. However, the rental fees charged by airlines to travel agents are negotiable depending on the volume of business or the market share that agency is able to generate for the airline supplying the system. Many agencies also use air fare auditing programs purchased from independent suppliers that recheck the information provided by their primary airline system for lower air fares and more convenient flight times.

However, these are only the major chains. On the whole, the lodging industry has not kept up with either the airlines or travel agents in computer technology. Many hotels still do not have computerized property management systems (PMS's), and even those that do in most cases do not have hardware and software which is compatible with the airline reservation systems. Industry analysts expect this to change in the future—as travel agencies become more involved in making hotel reservations for their clients, the lodging industry is expected to accelerate programs to interface with their CRS systems. Meanwhile, just about every travel agency subscribes to the _Official Hotel & Resort Guide, Hotel & Travel Index,_ or a similar publication from which they draw information about rates. Rooms and cars are then booked by telephone, or in the case of foreign countries by mail, telex, or facsimile. Some hotels are represented by hotel representatives, who are able to confirm reservations on behalf of their clients instantly.

Travel agents also deal in cruises. These are tremendously popular for agents for several reasons:

1. Because a cruise is an all-inclusive vacation, the agent makes commission on the entire amount the client spends on the vacation—not simply on the transportation and lodging portions.
2. Cruises are high-ticket items. An airplane ticket may cost several hundred dollars but a seven-day Caribbean cruise costs more than $1,000 in most cases.
3. Commissions are higher on cruises. Whereas the standard commission agents earn on domestic airline tickets, car rentals, and hotel reservations is 10%, overcapacity in the cruise business and fierce competition have forced most lines to offer greater commissions and other incentives to agents who are able to sell cruises. This same discounting have made cruises an exceptional vacation value.
4. Cruises tend to provide a high level of satisfaction. That means customers are more likely to be pleased with the arrangements the agent has made and use that agency again for future travel.

Tours are another popular product with travel agents. Like cruises, tours often are all-inclusive. Basically tours fall into three classifications: independent, escorted, and package. Escorted tours appeal to people who are inexperienced travelers or who do not enjoy traveling with groups of strangers. However, there is a third group of experienced travelers who recognize that tour operators are able through volume discounts to secure airline seats and hotel rooms at a far lower cost than individuals travelers and thus join these tours simply to take advantage of the low prices that are available. Some escorted tours are very expensive, however. Lorraine Travel in Miami has put together around-the-world escorted tours on a Concorde jet that cost $40,000 per person and up. Independent tours, known in the trade as FIT's (foreign independent tours), are usually tailored exactly to the needs of the client and require a good deal of detail work by agents. Daily itineraries have to be worked out, hotel reservations, cars, and sometimes sight-seeing excursions or theater tickets need to be arranged along with air, train, or steamship transportation. Many agencies charge a special fee for this kind of careful planning in addition to the regular commissions they may earn. Package tours are very similar to independent tours in that visitors do not travel with a large group or a guide but by themselves. The difference is that the elements of the tour (air, hotels, and often a car) have been assembled by a packager or tour operator. Certified Tours in Ft. Lauderdale, Florida is such a packager. They assemble their own tours as well as those Dream Vacations for Delta Airlines. When an agent or a customer calls the Delta Dream Vacation desk they actually get a Certified Tour sales agent who books them an airline ticket and a hotel for a package price that is considerably lower than if the same things were purchased separately by calling the airline and the hotel directly.

In addition to all of the major services mentioned above, travel agents also book train tickets for both Amtrak and European railroads. They are the main source of distribution in the United States for Eurail and BritRail passes. European ferries such as the cross-channel steamers are also booked by agents, and many will even arrange to charter private boats for sailing in the Greek Islands or Caribbean. Most agents arrange visas that their clients need to visit certain countries as well as give advice on inoculations that may be required. The sale of travelers checks and foreign currency is still handled by many agencies, along with trip cancellation insurance, and in some cases guide books and other travel items.

How Travel Agents Are Trained

Many travel agents start their careers by attending one of the many vocational training schools that teach the basic skills required. While these schools, which offer courses lasting anywhere from a few weeks to several months, will not guarantee placement, many agencies do recruit beginning agents from their graduates. Community colleges also offer travel agent training programs. Courses in these schools generally focus on the technical skills needed to make airline reservations and issue tickets as well as basic geography because many prospective agents have not had the opportunity to travel. Travel suppliers have learned that the best way to train agents is to give them an opportunity to see the places they are asked to sell. The two trade associations of travel agencies, The American Society of Travel Agents (ASTA), and the Association of Retail Travel Agents (ARTA) both sponsor numerous meetings and events where agents learn to improve their skills. So does the Cruise Line Industry Association (CLIA) which runs "schools at sea" where agents learn to sell cruises while taking one. Airlines offer agents a 75% discount on fares and hotels. Cruise lines have special rates so agents can become familiar with their products. Many times destinations and tour operators or airlines will get together to offer, for a small price, familiarization trips, known as FAM trips, to agents where a group is taken to a particular place and given a chance to inspect all of the hotels and other sights. These are working trips—it is not unusual for agents to visit more than a dozen hotels plus a couple of restaurants and a sight-seeing attraction in a single day. Most agents who go on such trips take careful notes and are often expected to write reports for other agents in the office when they return. In addition to all of these methods, there are numerous trade shows in the industry. At the Henry Davis Shows, many suppliers get together, erect small booths, and pass out literature about their hotels and destinations. Also airlines, tour operators, and destinations frequently hold in-depth training seminars for agents.

There is a formal certification program for travel agents as well, run by the Institute of Certified Travel Agents. Agents who complete this five-year study program earn the designation of CTC (Certified Travel Counselor), which is considered the most prestigious in the industry.

How Travel Agents Get Paid

Many travel agents advertise that "our services are free." This is not exactly correct. While services are generally free to consumers, agents are paid a commission as noted earlier from all major vendors. Consumerists have noted that this may cause a conflict of interest in that the amount of commission may influence the agent's advice, which is supposed to be impartial. In recent years many agencies have banded together into consortiums, which are groups of agencies that use their combined strength to negotiate lower rates for their clients and higher commissions for their agencies. Two such associations are Travel Trust International and Hickory. The result of this sometimes is that agents may be tempted to suggest airlines and cruise lines where they have negotiated special deals for themselves which may or may not be in the interest of their clients. Good agents adamantly refute any charge that they might be tempted to do this. They say their first interest must be their client or else they will not get any repeat business. Nevertheless, many consortiums have preferred suppliers and instruct their agents to offer the products of these suppliers before any other simply because they are more profitable to sell.

The truth is that travel agencies earn very little profit on what appears on the surface to be substantial sales. Thus unless agencies are carefully managed and preferred supplier arrangements are negotiated, the amount of money an owner takes home can be disappointingly small. Let us take an average agency with $2 million in sales. Such an agency might collect as much as $215,000 in commissions and overrides. Management consultant Armin D. Lehmann writing in *Travel Agent* magazine[2] suggests that it is possible for this size enterprise to make as much as $45,000 if they operate on the following budget:

Compensation, including employee benefits 48.5% = $82,450
Location 10.25% = $17,425
Promotion and advertising 7.56% = $12,750
Phone 6.25% = $10,625
Computer 6.1% = $10,370
Accounting and legal fees 5% = $8,500
Education and training 2.5% = $4,250
Entertainment/gifts to clients 2.25% = $3,825
Office supplies 2% = $3,400
Dues/subscriptions/reference materials 1.8% = $3,060
Insurance and bonding 1.6% = $2,720
Delivery charges 1.5% = $2,550
Miscellaneous donations, etc. 1.4% = $2,380
Postage/express services/freight 1.25% = $2,125
Bank charges and contingencies 1.1% = $1,870
Equipment repair and maintenance 1% = $1,700
Total expense $170,000
Gross profit $45,000

While this is an ideal budget, the fact is that few agencies of this size achieve these figures in reality. The reasons are many. First of all, note that the compensation figure suggested is $82,450. This not only includes actual payroll but contributions to social security and workman's compensation, employment agency fees, commissions paid to outside sales persons, and health plans and other insurance paid for by the employer. In addition, this includes the salary of the owner/manager. An average agent produces $350,000 to $400,000 in sales annually. An agency this size therefore would require five agents. Even if the owner is one of them, the average salary including benefits which should amount to at least 20% is $16,490. This figure correlates closely with the 1992 *Travel Weekly* Louis Harris survey, which reported that straight salary for full-time agents ranges from $12,428 for agents who have been with an agency for less than one year to $25,007 for agents who have been with an agency ten years or more. Managers receive a median straight salary of $20,573.[3] In addition to this, many owners travel extensively themselves (this is one of the main incentives for going into the business) and offer to pay the cost of some FAM trips for their agents, who would hardly work for such low salaries otherwise. These expenses are charged to the agency but since there is no allowance for them in this budget those costs all come out of profit. So that while this budget is achievable if an owner runs a very tight ship with highly productive agents, realistically, most owners are fortunate if they are able to take home $25,000 from their $2 million agency. Indeed *ASTA Agency Management,* which profiled typical agencies in the $1- to $2-million dollar range, reported that the average remuneration to owners was $24,606.[4] Agencies this size comprise almost one-third of all one- and two-outlet stores. The average agency in this group reported being in business 11½ years and achieving a retail booking revenue of $1,260,000. The bottom line according to the magazine was that "More than a few of these agency owners subscribe to the sentiment that typically they have all of the headaches and not much of the fun. . . .the remuneration to principals is not something to boast about."[5]

The Future of the Travel Agency Business

To a large extent the future of the travel agency business is tied to global economic and political events. If people continue to travel more in years to come, then the agency community as a whole is bound to benefit. But if major political disruptions or recessions slow down travel, then the agency community will suffer as well. In bad times travel expenses are one of the first things cut by businesses, and vacation travel is put on hold as well by consumers.

Barring these kinds of events, however, many of the trends that are prevalent throughout the travel and tourism industry will affect travel agencies as well. For example, there is a major trend toward consolidations and mergers in the airline business and in the hotel business. The same can be expected among travel agencies. In 1991, for example, 29% of U.S. travel agencies reported that they had acquired another agency that year. In that same year the industry witnessed the largest agency acquisition in its history—the purchase by American Express of Houston-based Lifeco, a firm with annual air sales of more than $1 billion.[3] These large agencies can be expected to come up with new, innovate packages and fares that will be available only through their offices, making it even more difficult for smaller independent agencies to stay competitive.

Globalization is another trend in the travel business. For the first time in 1989 more visitors from abroad came to the United States than the number of Americans traveled abroad. To take advantage of this new shift in travel patterns, agencies will have to form alliances with tour operators and travel agencies abroad and learn how to deal with "inbound tourism" where besides making arrangements for their local clients to travel overseas, they will have to be able to arrange sightseeing tours within their own regions for foreign visitors.

Another trend is that more and more businesses are turning their travel and meeting arrangements over to agencies, which in turn will book more hotel rooms than in the past. Since the hotel industry itself is rapidly changing to introduce products that will respond to shifting demographics and lifestyles, agents will need to be better informed about the products they sell. This means training costs will increase considerably for the industry as a whole.

There is no doubt that tomorrow's traveler—even today's—is much more sophisticated than ever before. With the advent of the home computer and other technology such as the Travel Network on cable television, people know more about what they want and how to get it. Travel agents will no longer be able to succeed by simply taking orders. They will have to become experts on matters that informed consumers cannot easily find out for themselves. This is a serious challenge, but one that can be met. Although the larger agencies will definitely enjoy some advantages in buying power, smaller independents that recognize they are in the business of providing service and information should be able to enjoy a prosperous future as well. But there will be fewer of them. The future is bright, but the playing field will be smaller and there will be no room on it for amateurs.

——References——

1. *American Heritage Dictionary,* (1976) Second college edition. Boston: Houghton Mifflin Company.
2. Armin D. Lehmann. Your Travel Agency Budget: A Blueprint for 1990. *Travel Agent.* October 30, 1989; pp 29–30.
3. *Travel Weekly.* August 13, 1992; pp. 116, 118.
4. Mort Weiser. It's a Living. *Travel Weekly's Louis Harris Survey.* June 29, 1988: p. 137.
5. Daniel Fitzgibbon. How $1- to $2-Million Agencies Are Performing. *ASTA Agency Management.* March 1989; p 36.

Hospitality Industry
Career Menu

Part VI

36

Club Management: A Unique Career Choice

Larry Joe Perdue, *George State University*
William E. Kent, *Auburn University*

The more than twelve thousand private clubs in the United States exist primarily to meet the social and recreational needs of their memberships. Protected by the First Amendment to the Constitution of the United States (the right of free association), private clubs usually have two criteria for membership. These criteria include a common bond among members and a selection process. The common bond may be the desire to play golf or tennis or the enjoyment of food and beverage services in a relaxing, uncrowded, comfortable atmosphere. The selection process is determined by the membership and administered through a board of directors.

Individuals and families join clubs in order to enjoy the company of friends in comfortable surroundings. It is often said that a private club serves as an extension of the members' home where they may entertain guests, relax, and feel special. They do not want to wait in the lines that are often found in commercial restaurants. They want to be able to play golf when they choose without difficulty in acquiring tee times, as is often the case with public golf courses. Club members like special attention. They enjoy being recognized by name by the staff and having their special drink or table waiting for them when they arrive. Club members expect and pay for special and unique service.

Various membership categories exist within private clubs. The most common include the following:

Full or resident member	These members have full use of club facilities, have voting privileges, and usually pay the highest dues.
House or social members	Found in some clubs, this category of membership usually provides for the use of club house facilities, including food and beverage service, but usually does not allow for golf privileges.

Nonresident member	They usually live a specified distance from the club, thereby utilizing facilities to a lesser extent than that of other membership categories and generally pay lower dues.

Additional categories of membership might include the following:

Senior members	Individuals who have been members for a specified number of years and have reached a certain age. They might pay lower dues and usually lose any right to vote in club elections.
Junior members	Those individuals, usually sons and daughters of full members, who have not yet attained the age of regular membership.

A unique aspect of private clubs is the dedication to excellence both in quality of product offered and services provided. Although sound fiscal management is essential in private club management, the emphasis for management is often to provide uncompromising service on a break-even basis rather than a profit-centered orientation.

The Nature of Clubs

Private clubs may be classified in several ways. Clubs may be thought of as social or recreational, yet many fall into both categories. Clubs are also frequently divided into town or country clubs. While this division is helpful, it refers primarily to location and only hints at the nature of the club. Also, many clubs do not fall in either the country or city category.

A classification of clubs would include two major characteristics, purpose and ownership. The following is a brief description of clubs classified by purpose:

Country clubs This is the most commonly found club in the United States. There are more than 6,000 private country clubs.[1] Their activities center around golf, but country clubs also typically offer members tennis counts, a swimming pool, and fitness centers. Some may have racquetball courts, jogging trails, and other special-interest sports facilities. It is common for country clubs to offer both formal and informal dining as well as a variety of beverage facilities. Golf and tennis pro shops traditionally offer not only golf equipment, but club logo merchandise.

City clubs There are some 2,000 city clubs in the United States,[1] the purpose of which is to serve the business and social entertainment needs of members in an urban setting. While food and beverage facilities are center stage, city clubs frequently offer reading rooms and some may offer athletic facilities and overnight accommodations.

Yacht clubs Located on substantial bodies of water, yacht clubs are organized around the members' ownership of and interest in boats. While "yacht" club evokes images of sleek craft 100 feet in length, there are clubs located on lakes where the average boat may be 25 feet in length. A yacht club typically has slips for member's boats, refueling facilities, dining rooms and lounges, and may offer dry dock and repair services as well.

Military clubs These clubs are owned by the U.S. government and were built to enhance the morale of persons serving in the armed forces. They may be divided into enlisted personnel clubs, noncommissioned officer clubs, and commissioned officer clubs. Military clubs typically feature food and beverage facilities but may also offer golf, tennis, and swimming to members and may even have a package liquor store.

Others There are tennis clubs, hunt clubs, beach clubs, faculty clubs, and a host of other special interest clubs. The facilities are devoted to accommodating the special interests that founded the club.

Most of the clubs described above fall into either of the two categories of ownership described below.

Member-owned clubs Most clubs today, especially the older ones, are owned by their members and are governed by a board of directors elected by the members. In a manner similar to corporations, members are considered to be shareholders, with each member having a vote as regards to the election of board members and major items of club business. There are, however, certain membership categories, described earlier, that do not include voting rights.

Corporate or developer clubs Corporate or developer clubs are owned by one or several individuals or a corporation. A developer often builds a club to market it to potential home buyers as an amenity. A home buyer may automatically become a member or may have to pay a modest initiation fee or dues. The member, however, will not have an equity position in the club and will usually have little if any influence on how the club is run.

There are, however, corporate or developer clubs in which the facilities are leased to the membership, which in turn controls the club's affairs.

Club Organization

While a particular club may introduce variations on a theme, most operate under a similar organizational structure. If a simplified organizational chart were to be drawn, it would look something like the chart on the next page.

This hourglass configuration is unique to private clubs and portrays the somewhat complex line of authority that originates with the most important stakeholders in the club—the members.

Members reign supreme in a member-owned club. The club was founded by and for the members and the power to continue, enlarge, change, or disband the club resides with them.

The board of directors and club president are members elected by their peers to see that the mission of the club is carried out. The board and president are interested in club policies, strategic issues, and the direction the club is taking. Through the club committee structure, the various activities and interests found in a club can find expression via the board. It is the board's responsibility to monitor the activities of the various committees, and the board may

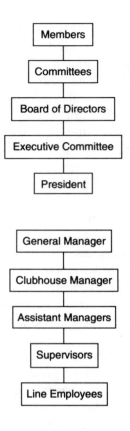

act as a watchdog when and if a committee has its own budget. Typical club committees include golf, tennis, clubhouse, social, finance, long-range planning, and any number of other special interest areas.

The general manager is the chief operating officer of the club and reports to the club president. In many ways, the general manager also reports to the board of directors, particularly in matters regarding budget and policy issues. The relationship between the club general manager and the board of directors is a crucial one, and it can have more influence on the success, growth, and tone of the club than almost any other factor.[2] The general manager's job is to carry out the policies established by the board to manage the day-to-day activities of the club, and to supervise the employees of the club as they serve the needs of the members.

The clubhouse manager, found in medium-sized and large clubs, reports to the general manager. This person typically is responsible for the food and beverage, housekeeping, and engineering departments in a club.[2] Although the clubhouse manager may delegate responsibility and authority to assistants and department heads, this person is still ultimately responsible for all operations within the clubhouse.

One or more assistant managers may be found in larger clubs and are assigned specific duties, frequently in the food and beverage outlets in a club. This position is commonly considered an entry-level job for a college graduate.

Managing a Club as a Business

Most private clubs do not consider making a profit a priority objective. In fact, *Clubs in Town and Country 1992,* indicates that on average, the food and beverage departments in country clubs report a 0.2% loss. It is only by factoring in membership dues that most clubs can report an annual profit.

The reasons for this are simple. The purpose of clubs is not to earn a profit but to provide facilities, activities, food, and beverages to members at a level of quality that would not otherwise be available to them. By paying dues (and usually a substantial initiation fee), members literally subsidize amenities that are among the finest found anywhere.

There are, however, clubs operated by professional management firms that do have a profit objective. There are also corporate or developer clubs, described earlier, wherein the owner seeks a true profit.

Regardless of the presence or absence of profit motive, all club managers have a fiduciary responsibility. *Fiduciary* refers to or involves a confidence or trust. In other words, no matter how large a budget the manager has to work with, no matter how opulent the club furnishings, the club manager is professionally honor-bound to manage the club's assets in a prudent, businesslike manner. He is the guardian of the club's assets and must act professionally in every respect.

One of the tools created to help managers in this regard is the Uniform System of Accounts for Clubs. Published by CMAA, the purpose of the uniform system is to provide a consistent guide for the logical and accurate reporting of club income and expenses. Two important objectives are achieved through use of the uniform system: income and expenses are allocated and reported in ways that come as close as possible to reflecting what actually occurs in the club, and by using a uniform system, board members, managers, controllers, and outside auditors can speak a common language when discussing the club's finances. There is one additional benefit for the manager who takes a position at another club—he can quickly adapt to the new club's financial structure if that club also uses the uniform system of accounts.

Club Management as a Career

Are private club managers different from managers of hotels and restaurants? There is evidence that the values and characteristics of club managers do indeed set them apart from their colleagues in the hotel and restaurant fields. A study by Raymond Schmidgall[3] points out vividly how the professional priorities among hotel, restaurant, and club managers differ on one common management point. Schmidgall asked managers from all three industry segments if they would feel compelled to take action to correct a 2% or less variation in projected food costs in their operation. A full 74% of the restaurant managers and a substantial 46% of the hotel managers responded they would be compelled to take action. Yet only 15% of club managers would feel so compelled. Does this mean that club managers do not care about food costs? No, the truth is that the club manager must first and foremost achieve a level of quality that will please her members. Because members are willing to pay for a premium dining experience, that expectation must be fulfilled. With little or no profit motive, the club targets quality, even if food costs rise as a result. Naturally, no club manager will tolerate any costs that are out of control.

Other characteristics are shared by many club managers. They tend to be knowledgeable in the finer aspects of food and beverages, including familiarity with haute cuisine and fine wines. They tend to have considerable skills in diplomacy, as they manage a facility in which each customer considers himself to be an owner. The club manager who cannot cope with a new club president annually, who will not attempt to please a variety of special interests, and who cannot be successful in learning and using members' names will not be a club manager for long. The club is a second home to its members, and the club manager must be devoted to creating the friendly yet dignified environment that members are seeking. One last important point regarding member relations; unlike hotel and restaurant managers whose actual contact with guests may be limited, club managers interact personally with members on a continual basis.

The pace of the club manager differs significantly from that of the hotel or restaurant manager. In hotels and restaurants, large crowds and hectic days translate into success and profits. In clubs, orderliness, quality, and a sense of dignity translate into success (member satisfaction). Therefore, the daily pace for the club manager is slower, but one should not envision a life of leisure in the club business. The club is established for the members, not the management, although the management has the pleasure and privilege of working in a most pleasant environment. It is not unusual for a club manager and her family to have access to the club and its facilities, though the wise manager does not overstep this privilege. Many clubs are closed on Mondays and all managers may take a full day off. There are times, however, when part of even that day must be spent at the club—hosting a special golf outing, for example.

Career Ladders

A career in private club management is both rewarding and demanding. The entry route into the profession usually involves one of three paths. Promotion from a nonmanagement position in the club, although once the most common entry route, is now less frequent. Transfer from another segment of the hospitality industry is common and can provide excellent management experience. However, private club management is a unique part of the hospitality industry. Clearly, the most advantageous entry route into the private club management profession is the successful completion of a four-year degree in hospitality management coupled with private club work experience. Summer employment in the pool snack bar or part-time food and beverage wait staff experience provide excellent credentials for entry-level management positions. From the entry-level assistant manager or manager trainee position, individuals will usually progress to the clubhouse manager position and then to the general manager position. In some clubs, the entry-level positions may include those of supervisor, assistant department head, or department head.

Salaries, Benefits, Rewards, and Drawbacks

Salaries and benefits for private club management positions are comparable to or slightly above those found in other segments of the hospitality industry. An excellent source of information on salaries and benefits for private club management positions is the Compensation and Benefits Survey published regularly by CMAA.

Private club management is both a financially and personally rewarding career. Private club managers are given the opportunity to serve as head of a hospitality organization that provides services at a level often unequaled in other segments of the industry. They are able to work in some of the most aesthetically pleasing environments found within the hospitality industry. They work with and serve leaders from all segments.

Club Managers Association of America

The Club Managers Association of American (CMAA) is the only professional association representing private club managers in the United States. Its mission is to advance the profession of club management by fulfilled educational and related needs of its members.[1] Through a national staff located in Alexandria, Va. a national board of directors and committee structure, and local chapters located throughout the United States, CMAA provides educational programming, career assistance, a certification program, an annual conference and exposition, a governmental affairs department, a research and publications department, an insurance program, and a student chapter program.

The Club Management Institute (CMI), the educational arm of CMAA, is dedicated to a life-long learning program for its membership. The Business Management Institute (BMI) is a competency-based, five-stage program offered on university campuses by CMAA that provides up-to-date club management education at every level of a club manager's career. The five levels include BMI I (The Basic Club Management School), BMI II (The Leadership Edge), BMI III (The Chief Operating Officer Concept), BMI IV (Managerial Excellence: Tactics for Today), and BMI V (Strategies for Tomorrow, Realities of Today). Faculty for the BMI program includes university faculty, industry consultants, and senior club managers.

The certification program administered by CMAA leads to the designation of Certified Club Manager (CCM). Club managers who have attained the CCM status are recognized throughout the private club profession as leaders having distinguished themselves through experience, education, association activity, and successful completion of a comprehensive examination. Qualification to take the certification examination is determined through a requirement formula. Education credits are granted for a college degree (a degree from a four-year hospitality program earns the most credits), successful completion of the BMI requirements, CMI-specified and endorsed workshops, and attendance at national conference education sessions. Association activity credits are awarded for CMAA membership, participation in chapter meetings and national conference sessions, and leadership roles in the association. When the required credits have been earned, a rigorous examination covering seven subject areas is administered. Those areas are private club management, food and beverage operations, accounting and financial management, human resource management, management and marketing, external and government influences, and facilities management. The CCM designation is permanent and carried throughout the club manager's lifetime. CMAA's certification program recognizes continued educational achievement through Recertification, and Honor Society, and the Master Club Manager (MCM) distinction.

How to Get Started

A degree in hospitality administration is quickly becoming a prerequisite for entry into the private club management profession. Elective courses in business and recreation management should supplement the traditional hospitality management curriculum. Many hospitality programs now offer specific elective courses in private club management. Many of the nation's leading hospitality programs have CMAA student chapters on campus. These chapters offer education programs specific to private club management. They provide field trips to local clubs and presentations by club managers. They provide opportunities to attend the national CMAA conference and to compete for scholarships. Credits that may later be applied toward certification requirements are granted by CMAA for student chapter educational meetings. As previously indicated, work experience in private clubs while in school is a critical area of preparation for the private club management profession. Opportunities abound within the private club industry for individuals who are willing to prepare themselves academically and experientially and dedicate themselves to excellence in service to the membership of private clubs.

——References——

1. Club Managers Association of America, Alexandria, Va.
2. Club Managers Association of America. (1989). *Club Management Operations.* Fourth edition. Dubuque, Ia.: Kendall/Hunt. pp. 17, 26.
3. Schmidgall, Ray. Control, Control, Control. *The Bottom Line.* August 1987; p. 7.

37

Theme Park Management Overview

Duncan R. Dickson
Walt Disney World Company

"While there is very little grown-up in a child, there is a lot of child in every grown-up"* This is the premise of the theme park. The modern theme park industry opened to the public on July 17, 1955 when, in a then-rural area of Orange County, California, Disneyland opened amid the many cries that it was a folly and would never amount to a thing.

The modern theme park may only be 25 years old, but it owes its being to a much older tradition. The theme park is an outgrowth of the ancient carnivals, tournaments, and circuses of Europe and Asia. These were all primarily entertainment events—gatherings of individuals to share news, trade items they had made and grown, and to join together for simple enjoyment.

As the United States progressed into the twentieth century, the run-of-the mill amusement park and carnival started to become seedier and less a place for families than a place for children and juveniles, resplendent with hucksters, cheap games, cheaper food, and rides built for thrill. Literally, a place for amusement, not entertainment.

From the same imagination that brought us Mickey Mouse, Snow White, and real-life nature adventures came the genius of the theme park. Folklore has it that the theme park was created as Walt whiled away his time as his daughters rode the merry-go-rounds and he sat on the park benches. Walt thought that there must be a better solution than the adults paying the tab and sharing boredom while the children romp and joyously have a good time. Walt wanted a place where grown-ups could be children and not be thought of as such. He wanted a place where children of all ages could enjoy themselves.

So what is the theme park of today? Is it simply an outgrowth of the carnival, a revamping of the old amusement park? Some of the current genre that are considered theme parks are upgrades of the old but the overwhelming majority of the parks built since 1955 are truly new and different. They offer their guests real family entertainment—a place where children of all ages can go to enjoy themselves, relax, escape from the burdens of the world, and even be educated. The successful theme park of today does all of these things.

---

*Eric Sevareid on the *CBS Evening News* announcing the death of Walt Disney.

351

As the population of the United States grows older, all theme parks will have to make transitions to offer more diverse types of entertainment and become more sensitive to the older audience. To many this means that the parks will become more and more educational, as well as becoming more diverse in their individual offerings. The acquisition of all the Sea Worlds by the Busch Gardens/ Anheuser Busch group expands the number of Busch theme parks beyond The Old Country, which has the influence of Western Europe, and The Dark Continent, which is an African-theme park and zoo, to educationally oriented marine theme parks in Orlando, San Diego, Ohio, and San Antonio. Opryland has expanded out of its base in Nashville, with a live action theme park in San Antonio called Fiesta Texas.

Probably the most important entrant into this theme park for the older American is the culmination of Walt Disney's Florida dream, Epcot Center. Opening in 1982 Epcot Center has proved to be a catalyst at encouraging the older American to enjoy the theme park and expand their horizons that theme parks are not just for kids anymore. This pioneering experiment continues to set the pace for the theme parks of tomorrow and highlights the efforts that can be made in theme parks. Even the expansion of the American theme park to Japan and Europe is incorporating things that have been learned at Epcot Center.

The expansion of the movie-related theme parks shows an overwhelming curiosity by the public to be involved in the movies and how movies are made. The Disney-MGM Studios Theme Park has been overcrowded since opening. Universal Studios in Orlando has pushed MGM Studio Theme Park to upgrade their offering in Orlando and to consider upgrading their California park. Expansion of this concept is already slated for EuroDisneyland, and the Busch Gardens people are looking to expansion in Spain for their concept of theme park.

The experiments by Disney in both Anaheim and Orlando have proven that theme parks can be and are a springboard to more than simply the growth of a theme park. In both areas growth of hotels and convention centers and other tourism infrastructure has led to incredible growth of the area. Today the Orlando area, a city of roughly 1.2 million people, leads the United States in total concentration of hotel rooms with more than 70,000 hotel rooms in the area. The Anaheim area of southern California is not far behind and ranks in the top five, depending on which study you read. Both of these areas are stimulated by the placement of a theme park, and the areas have simply grown and grown.

The theme park business depends on how well the guests enjoy themselves. All parts require repeat attendance to stay open. Even The Walt Disney World Resort, the most popular destination resort in the world, must have repeat visitors. Thus the key to successful operation of a theme park is to have your guest's leave wanting more; in other words, you must continue to attract the same visitors.

Most parks have a basic theme around which they organize their attractions. For our purposes, an attraction is anything that makes an individual return to a theme park. These attractions blend and become unified to create a total atmosphere—whether it be total immersion into fantasy, a rejoicing of the American spirit, or a dedication to the sea. Through this central theme will weave the rides, restaurants, shops, and live shows that entice the visitor to return. To ensure the return of the guest year after year, the theme park must continually update its attractions. Because food and merchandise are not the primary drawing cards for theme parks, this means rides and live entertainment must serve this purpose and be either redone or changed.

Because many parks depend on a short operating schedule—140 days between May and September is not uncommon—the great cost of adding new rides becomes financially risky. Those that do operate year round attempt to add major rides every three to four years. The others create this newness by modifying and bringing in new live shows. By keeping the park fresh and in the mind of the visitor, "new," the operators will ensure a stream of people attending the park.

Aside from this requirement to keep adding and changing, the theme park must provide the guest other essentials as well. The most important of these is perceived value. Unless the visitors believe they have gotten an entertainment bargain, they will not return. The value is generally a great deal of entertainment for a single price with no add-ons. The price must be sufficiently low to allow an entire family to attend without bankrupting them. Of course, the price is going to be higher for the more attractions provided. Value is also perceived when unadvertised extras occur, such as parades and entertainment groups. It makes no difference whether an individual spends two dollars or twenty dollars, they must leave saying, "I really had a good time and it was worth every penny."

The value must extend from the price of admission through the price and quality of food and merchandise. It is all too easy to think that just because there is a captive audience, you can serve them anything and charge what you want—regardless of quality. This "what the traffic will bear" attitude, while initially profitable, will not create return guests. The comparisons to Burger King and Sears come all too easily not to give the visitor the best quality at the best possible price.

The American public loves a value. It is the easiest thing to sell. Every member of the family needs to be able to find value in some aspect of the theme park. A four-year-old finds value in the character he sees. A twelve-year-old thinks a thrill ride is the high point of the park visit. To a teenager, it is the live show. The couple in their twenties think it is the escape from reality. The parents of the teenager like the intricacies of how the whole appears to be larger than the sum of its parts; while the grandparents are enraptured by the patriotic displays. Value is the reason for the all-important return visit.

Theme Park Careers

Career groups in the theme park industry fall into three primary areas: attractions, food service, and merchandise. Of course, these are not the only career opportunities, but they are the distinctive, highly visible areas of operational management. Other career fields include, but are not limited to, accounting, engineering, maintenance, marketing, horticulture, personnel, computer science, and many others.

Custodial Management

Most people would tend to overlook this extremely important area of theme park operations, as they may overlook a housekeeping department in a hotel as being necessary but not truly a management task. But in the theme park business custodial is perhaps one of the most important departments we have. You will find, if you question Disney executives, that the guest letters indicate the most important things that the Disney guests comment on are the cleanliness of the parks and the friendliness of the cast. Custodial is a well-managed process that ensures that the park is as clean as it possibly can be at all times. By maintaining the cleanliness, the guests will help keep it clean as well. The sweepers are out in force immediately after a major event, such as a parade. The entire park is steam cleaned after hours during the third shift. You will find that in well-run theme parks, custodial is a three-shift operation, with individuals ensuring that all is taken care of, all is clean, and that the park is as clean and sparkling every morning as it possibly can be.

Training for the custodial crew is as important and time consuming as it is for any other area of a theme park. Not only does a custodial crew member need to know and understand the variety of equipment that they use (and this can be quite sophisticated from automatic sweepers to vacuum-operated disposal systems to the variety of chemicals used), but also custodial hosts are the ambassadors of goodwill. Per individual, they probably get more questions about what time things happen and where things are than any other employee within the park. So it becomes important that all of the custodial staff be aware of what is happening, special events, and opening and closing hours so that they can fully address the questions that the guests will have. Custodial crew members are the unsung hero of the theme park industry.

Entertainment—Live Show Management

Integral to any theme park is the entertainment or live show component. Opryland theme parks are a leader in this element of entertainment, but the Disney theme parks are also on the cutting edge of this attraction. At the new Disney-MGM Studio Tour, the use of live entertainment to create a feeling that one is in mid-1930s Hollywood goes a long way to creating the atmosphere, as the guest wanders down Hollywood Boulevard. The live entertainment can be as subtle and simple as a mime performing or as sophisticated as a full on-stage choreographed show. The entertainers enhance the guest experience and allow the guest an alternative to roller coasters and other types of attractions. Of course the entertainers include actors and actresses, singers and dancers, individuals who wear the very bulky and very hot costumes of the various characters as well as lighting and sound technicians, choreographers, directors, producers, and stage managers, all of whom are necessary to get the show up and going.

The live show area of a theme park quite often brings life and personality to the park, thus ensuring that each and every guest has an exciting and fulfilling experience.

Attractions Management

Encompassing everything from parking lots to roller coasters, the individuals in attractions management must be constantly aware of the efficiency of their operation. If the theme park is entertainment, then the attraction managers are the keepers of the show. They are responsible for maintaining the entertainment aspect of the theme park.

Systematizing the operation is the most important function of the attractions managers. They must ensure that the system creates the greatest amount of efficiency without interfering with show, safety, and courtesy.

Theme parks work on a volume-per-capita basis. They must attract the maximum number of attendees and have them flow through the park with the greatest of possible ease. To do this, each attraction manager must know the ride capacity for their attractions and be able to make best use of the capacity. They need to know how to have people wait in queues without thinking of how much time is being spent. Once each area—parking, transportation, tickets, and each individual attraction—maximizes its capacity, the attendance and efficiency of the entire park is enhanced.

Because the theme park business is such a labor-intensive business, the attraction managers spend most of their time dealing with the human relations aspects of business—training and scheduling. Training is a constant function, ensuring that all employees contribute to the safety of the operation, that they are courteous to all guests, and that the attraction is properly maintained at all times. Scheduling is a considerable problem because of the large fluctuations of attendance. Although many theme parks still operate for a limited number of days per year, more and more are year-round parks. Scheduling plays an important role in a year-round park, because the permanent work force must be maintained. The employees must work changing shifts to accommodate varying opening hours and attendance patterns.

Creativity and human relations must be the hallmark of attractions managers. They must be able to anticipate and react to constantly changing situations. Although they have fairly accurate projections, weather and the whims of the economy can wreak havoc on the best of plans. Good ability to train, schedule, and communicate meshes with the ability to react and anticipate—essential for attractions managers.

Food Management

Food managers in the theme park industry do not differ significantly from their counterparts in other aspects of the hospitality industry. The notable difference is the volume that is served. Almost everyone who visits a major theme park eats there. Consequently, a theme park's food operations must be prepared to handle as many as 93,000 guests in one day.

Beside the volume, a theme park must offer a full range of restaurants. Fast food restaurants, of course, are preeminent because the typical guest is interested in only a fueling station. There must be an availability of service restaurants as well, though, to serve the guest who wants a break from the attractions.

Because of the guests' necessity to eat while they are in the theme park, the value of the food to the guest is as important as anything.

Systematizing the operation to meet the demands of peak periods is also important for the food manager. Scheduling employees to meet the needs of the guests is extremely difficult. The theme park guest wants the food served as fast as possible so she can get back to the entertainment. New computerized cooking equipment and cash-handling systems must be scrutinized to improve existing operations. Only by improving efficiency will food managers be able to improve their contribution margins.

Merchandise Management

Many people think of merchandise as a necessary evil, but done correctly it can be as big a revenue producer as food.

In a properly laid-out theme park, merchandise shops become a profitable plus-sale diversion from the roller coaster: a place to get out of the heat and the lines, a place to browse and rest.

Sweatshirts, balloons, and other trinkets can provide a bountiful resource for the theme park. Once again, quality and value are keys to the success of the merchandise operation. The guest must feel that he is receiving a bargain at the theme park merchandise shops.

As with the food locations in the theme park, the merchandise shop must have a motif that is in harmony with the attractions near it. All three—merchandise, foods, and attractions—must blend and complement each other so that the guest is encouraged to flow from one area to the other. The merchandise in the shops must also change from one area to the other.

Solid management in attractions, foods, and merchandise helps to create an integrated team that produces a successful theme park operation. The synergy created by the three is the single item that attracts guests and maintains the flow of return guests as well as new ones.

Summary

The theme park has come a long way from the Gardens of Tivoli in Copenhagen and the prater in Vienna. It has become a place where the family can gather and enjoy themselves and each other. We have recognized that family entertainment is now an important aspect of American life.

The success of the theme park depends on the quality, value, and efficiency of each park. Perhaps the best summation of this chapter comes from Walt Disney—"Well, I think by this time my staff, my young group of executives, and everyone else, are convinced that Walt is right. That quality will win out. And so I think they're going to stay with that policy. Give the people everything you can give them. Keep the place as clean as you can keep it. Keep it friendly. Make it a real fun place to be."

38

Resort Management

Chuck Y. Gee
University of Hawaii

The Distinguishing Characteristics of Resorts

Resorts trace their history from Roman spas in the second century A.D. Originally created as havens for rest and relaxation for the citizens and legionnaires of Rome, the purpose for and attraction of resorts have not changed much over the centuries. Today, we distinguish resorts from other lodging forms by the pleasure markets they serve. Indeed, the resort has often been described as the only human institution that is created solely for the pleasure of its users. Because patrons of resorts generally come there to enjoy leisure pursuits, the location of the resort relies less on convenience than on climatic and recreational attributes. For many years, resorts remained strictly the domain of the wealthy; it was not until the mid-twentieth century that they were frequented by the middle class, primarily owing to a rise in disposable income and establishment of the paid vacation.

Operators agree on three factors common to successful resorts: reputation of the resort, attractions of the locale, and recreational facilities offered by the resort. These factors influence the marketing and management of resorts as well as buildings and facilities design, space allocation for guest rooms, storage, recreation, sports amenities, entertainment, public attractions, shopping, health care, and other special services that add to guest satisfaction and help build repeat business. Although repeat business is important to all types of hotels, it is essential to the survival of a resort. In a resort, repeat business helps perpetuate resort traditions. Management must therefore direct considerable effort toward the development of strong guest and employee relationships, as well as providing services, facilities, and amenities that will keep guests happy during their stay. Moreover, the resort manager today must be keenly aware of special marketing techniques and modes of advertising as she competes for customers who have many vacation options.

The resort manager has all the problems of the typical urban hotel operator, but these problems are compounded by a seasonal labor force, weather cycles that can affect recreational activities and thus the length of the operating season, ongoing developmental concerns, and often delicate community relations. In the decade of the 1990s, environmental concerns will take precedence over many other issues as resorts located in fragile areas are affected by major problems such as pollution, oil spills, congestion, and so forth.

In the following sections, we will cover some of the distinguishing characteristics of resorts, including markets, location, recreation, food service, service, seasonability, maintenance, and organization. Then we will discuss the various impacts—economic, social, cultural, and environmental—that resorts on their host communities,and the resort developer/owner's investment concerns.

Markets

The resort concept as applied to the operation of hotel connotes the provision of facilities, services, and amenities that serve individuals, families, and groups who are on holiday and vacation. Today, many resorts look to the convention and group travel business as an important secondary market to fill the troughs in their business cycle. Urban resort areas, on the other hand, are increasingly focusing on the convention and group meetings market as the primary market. There are two basic advantages that resorts have to offer to convention and meeting buyers. Firstly, because resorts are self-contained they already have all the necessities for successful functions. Most can provide sophisticated conference facilities, top-notch service, a glamorous location, and first-rate meetings professionals. Even more important is the fact that resorts offer an environment and amenities that permit business to be combined with pleasure. It is not unusual for a group meeting at a resort to program its business agenda around recreational and leisure activities. The mountain ski resorts catering to convention groups, for instance, find that business meetings can be scheduled early in the morning so that guests can take to the ski slopes by mid-morning if they wish.

This attention to the business market has apparently paid off, with resorts now receiving a substantial portion of the meeting and convention business. A 1987 survey of resorts reports that the business and conference segment now accounts for more than 30% of guests.[1] Another segment increasingly sought by the resort operator is the incentive travel market, which can account for as much as 25% of an individual resort's revenue. The full-service resort is especially suitable for this market because everything is under one roof. Incentive travel is a motivational device generally used by companies to reward employees, dealers, distributors, and customers who exceed specified performance objectives. As in the case of conventions and meetings, the incentive travel market has its own professional planners offering consultant services to coordinate between the company sponsoring the incentive and various resorts. These planners are extremely influential in determining the destination and specific property selected for a company incentive program.

It has been found that the increase in business-related travel to resorts enhances the resort's leisure travel traffic in two ways—increased length of stay and return visits for vacation purposes.

Resort operators should be aware that travel agents greatly influence the resort choice of their clients. Therefore, keeping travel agents informed may be essential to a resort's economic well-being. A resort can boost awareness of it among agents by providing up-to-date brochures, scheduling familiarization tours, and making service representatives available. It can further encourage travel agents to recommend the property with prompt payment of travel agent commissions.

Location

In the years following the fuel crisis of 1973 in combination with stagflation and recessionary cycles, vacations like other commodities began to be looked upon as an investment in terms of time, money, and value received. Many Americans sought comparable vacation destinations closer to home that would require less money and less effort to reach, and which offered value for price. In recent years, other factors have influenced the tendency to travel closer to home. A study by the Marriott Corporation in 1987 reported that Americans were taking more frequent pleasure trips, but the trips tended to be of much shorter duration. The preference for shorter trips results from the significant increase in the number of dual-income households, making it difficult to coordinate long vacations, as well as increasing time and work pressures.[2]

This trend toward shorter and closer vacations has resulted in the emergence of a new breed of "urban resorts," which have adopted numerous resort concepts. Cognizant of the fact that *resort* means recreational facilities, city hotels are creating rooftop fitness centers with jogging tracks, exercise equipment, and whirlpool baths, while others are arranging for special membership privileges with nearby tennis and swim clubs in order to attract more of the leisure market. Urban resorts may include such diverse types of properties as airportels, motels on the outskirts of cities, and condominiums. These urban properties either provide their own recreational facilities, or access to such nearby community facilities as indoor and outdoor pools, tennis courts, bowling lanes, golf courses, swimming pools, whirlpool and sauna, and jogging or exercise trails. These resorts are designed to attract both transient travelers and budget-conscious vacationers seeking an alternative to remote resorts.

Although the urban hotels have increasingly adopted resort concepts, the traditional resort settings of mountains, desert, countryside, and seashore still appeal to most pleasure travelers. Such locations frequently are distant from major sources of supplies of food and other goods. In such instances, they must essentially be self-contained and provide for their own basic support service such as police and fire protection, health care, utilities, transportation, and warehousing.

Finding employees for a remote resort may be a particularly difficult problem if there are no nearby residential communities. Housing, transportation, and other services must then be provided to workers on resort land.

Despite such problems, there are numerous reasons why resorts developed in remote locations. These include cheap land, government incentives, special climatic conditions, topographic advantages for specific sports or recreation, natural scenic attractions, and feasible linkage by road or air. Remoteness in itself has an appeal to the vacation traveler who seeks an environment different from the urban or suburban environment of his job and residence, which is often noisy, polluted, and congested.

Recreation Provisions

Although urban resorts with limited recreational facilities continue to spring up, few transient hotels are able to provide and maintain the diversity of amenities and facilities which have come to be expected by resort vacationers. Some of these recreational facilities are for internationally popular sports activities such as golf, tennis, squash, skiing, sailing, and fishing. The costs of developing and maintaining an 18-hole golf course, outdoor and indoor tennis courts, squash courts, ski lifts, marinas, or breeding ponds for trout fishing were never nominal, and over the years these facilities have become increasingly expensive to install, maintain, and operate for profit. Major resorts are not only expected to provide one or more primary recreational facilities on which their reputations are often built, but also to offer auxiliary or secondary recreational facilities for swimming, table tennis, shuffleboard, horseback riding, archery, skeet shooting, crafts, and other varied activities.

In addition to these traditional recreational offerings, resorts are always looking for innovative services and amenities to include as part of their resort experience. Club Mediterranean—the ultimate international vacation for many—has taken advantage of the growing interest in computers and offers computer workshops at several of its villages around the world. Along with computer lessons, other educational activities are offered by Club Med, including foreign languages and self-improvement training.

Many resorts catering to families offer special recreational programs for children, thus allowing their parents to enjoy recreational pursuits on their own. Club Med has many of its properties designated as family-oriented resorts, some of which offer a "miniclub" where "minimembers" have their own special area of the "village" with a clubhouse, private pool, and beach.

While most resorts charge guests by the individual activity, some resorts have followed the Club Med example of packaging recreation into their accommodations rate. The total package quotation does hold particular appeal for families and planned-budget vacationers.

Indoor and outdoor physical fitness and health amenities are a growing trend in resorts. Interest in physical fitness continues to grow and shows no sign of slowing down. Resort operators responding to these interests are providing everything from jogging tracks to fully outfitted gymnasiums with professional staff. For many resorts these fitness centers are a profitable addition to the property, generating direct departmental profits and serving also as a valuable marketing tool.

Resorts around the world also provide various recreational activities for the more venturesome. These activities range from white-water rafting to other innovative water sports such as parasailing, windsurfing, and exploring underwater scuba trails.

At certain resort destinations, casino gaming is almost essential in developing a well-rounded tourist plant. Nevada and New Jersey are currently the only states permitting casino gaming in the United States. Florida, Louisiana, and West Virginia are among the states that recently considered legalization of casinos, but these casino proposals failed to win resident support. The move towards legalization of gambling is receiving strong support from the resort industry, as operators see increased tourism competition from the Caribbean and other destinations with casino attractions. Casino gaming, as it is argued, will bring in additional jobs and revenue for the area and will also help make the destination less seasonal.

Food Service

Because of the longer average length of stay at resorts, guests tend to reject the standard menus offered by transient hotel food service operations. The resort manager is required to pay special attention to creating longer menu cycles and a greater number of food specialties. To relieve dining monotony, special events, theme dining, and cook-outs are an important aspect of resort food service. While cook-outs and special dining events can be carefully planned in every detail, the weather or other factors may force alternative courses of action to be adopted.

The most important trend affecting the food and beverage department in today's resorts is also an outgrowth of the nation's health and fitness consciousness. As many resort guests demand lighter, more nutritious and yet diversified menus, resort chefs are making significant modifications to their menus and providing quality meals that are low in calories, cholesterol, saturated fats, and salt. Many, in fact, have altered their philosophy regarding food preparation and presentation to include smaller portions and new ways of merchandising meals.

The methods of charging for meals or allocating revenues for food operations generally are different for resorts than for transient hotels. Most transient hotels follow a European plan whereby the room rate includes no meals, and the use of restaurants by guests is entirely voluntary. Resorts, especially those with remote locations, may adopt an American plan or modified American plan, which includes all or some of the meals in the accommodation rate. There is also the Bermuda plan or continental plan, which offers accommodations with a full American-style breakfast included in the price of the room.

Service Orientation

A business traveler staying in a city hotel will require convenience, efficiency, and prompt service at critical times. The resort guest, on the other hand, wants attention, service, and care throughout the day. Attitude is as important as proficiency. Hospitality is everything in a quality resort. But hospitality is also costly in terms of labor expenses. Payroll costs for resorts, which are escalating annually, currently run from 30% to 40% of total revenues, depending on the rate structure of the resort.

The staff of a resort property usually includes a social director or recreation director specifically to handle the entertainment and recreation needs of guests. Besides general activities, many resorts also offer customized services such as an individualized fitness regimen and beauty treatment or such amenities as flying in daily copies of the guest's home-town newspaper. Well-managed resorts provide "at-home" hospitality where guests become a part of the extended family of the resort. Returning guests often look on members of the staff as long-time friends. Every employee in a resort operation, therefore, must be motivated to the philosophy of total hospitality, supportive human relationships, and unstinting service to guests around the clock. Personalized service—the remembrance of and catering to the likes and dislikes or idiosyncracies of each guest as an individual and not as a statistic—is the key to success in the human equation of resort operations.

Seasonality of Operation

Transient hotels operate all year round. Many resorts are seasonal by definition, i.e., winter and summer resorts. The length of the operating season may fluctuate between 90 and 180 days, often depending upon climatic conditions or other factors. Sometimes the season is too short to earn sufficient revenue to cover investment costs, operating costs, and return a profit on capital. Most resorts are now attempting to move into a four-season mode by developing new markets during the off-season periods. Some winter resorts, for instance, have developed summer attractions, including recreational amenities, festivals, and seminar and learning centers in their attempt to become year-round resorts.

The problems of managing a seasonal enterprise are numerous. There is the special problem of hiring and retaining a reliable labor force, season after season. Each season a new group of full-time or part-time employees must be hired and trained. Motivation of employees is made more difficult as the seasonal nature of resort employment curtails promotional and advancement incentives.

Winding down the inventory of food and supplies toward the end of the season is a management headache. Security of property and caretaker maintenance while the facilities are shut down present other major problems.

Maintenance of Facilities

Regardless of the length of a resort's season, an ongoing renovation program is essential for the maintenance of a quality product and to justify a resort's rate structure. Such a program can range from routine maintenance involving staff painters to renovations directed by professional interior designers. Thus, in order to keep their facilities fresh and attractive so that guests will continue to patronize their resorts, owners must invest large sums for annual renovations, additions, or refurbishment.

Organizational Framework

Resort organizations may be divided or grouped according to front of the house (i.e., rooms division, guest services) and back or heart of the house (i.e., food and beverage, physical plant maintenance) areas. Additionally, a third division—which may be termed outdoor facilities and recreation—is required to cover the recreational functions and facilities that do not fall under either designation.

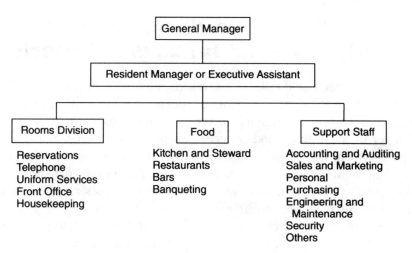

Figure 1. Transient Hotel

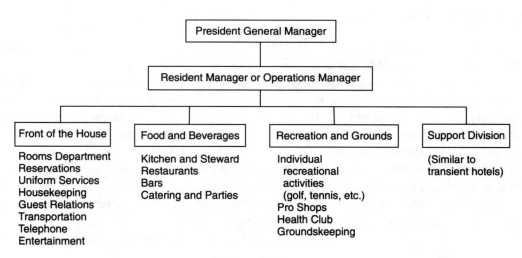

Figure 2. Resort

The operation and maintenance of recreational facilities are labor intensive, and many also require professional management. Figures 1 and 2 illustrate how a resort differs from a conventional hotel in its basic structure. The location of specific units within the basic structures and layers of management will, of course, vary widely according to size and type of facilities and amenities offered.

Economic, Social, and Environmental Impacts of Resorts

Aside from their operational differences, resorts are further distinguished from transient hotels in terms of their substantial economic, social, and environmental impacts on surrounding areas and the host community. In some communities, a resort is the primary employer and buyer of local goods and services. As such, the resort's management policies concerning employment and procurement will have direct consequences for the community's economic health. Moreover, social changes are induced in the host community through resort development, employment, residents' interaction with guests, and economic growth. These social changes may be both positive and negative, but they are always difficult to pinpoint, and to measure, as they pertain to such subtle elements as lifestyle, attitudes, values, culture, and quality of life. Unlike social impacts, on the other hand, environmental impacts are readily recognized. The development of resorts generally requires large tracts of land for hotel facilities, sport facilities, recreational use, and in some instances, vacation homes. Infrastructural development for resort destinations may also introduce urbanization with its associated problems of population growth, which will in turn affect the environment.

Economic Impact

The long-range economic success of a resort depends to a great extent on its acceptance by the local community. While it is true that the resort provides employment and brings in needed revenue to support local business in the area, it is equally true that the community provides a source of labor for the resort, local customers for the resort's restaurants, and community services that might not be otherwise available. The development and maintenance of good relations between the resort and its host community are important functions of the resort's management and ownership.

In planning and developing a resort, the costs and benefits of the proposed development should be identified and weighed by the resort developers, owners, and managers and by the local community in which the site is located. If the costs outweigh the benefits, alternative projects or alternative sites should be considered. If benefits outweigh the costs, then the analysis process will contribute to the successful planning, development, and strategic operation of the resort.

The modern approach to minimize the negative aspects of resort development has been to involve the community in the general planning and decision-making process. Residents must be made to feel that they have a stake in the success of the resort. Grassroots leaders and other vocal community members, who are likely to have fears about the impact of the development on their community or existing power structure, should be identified and contacted first. So important are these points that today social scientists are often retained as consultants to resort developers to assure the successful integration of community goals with those of the project.

Revenue generated by the resort and its subsequent recirculation within the community will have economic and qualitative impacts on the life of the community. The dollars that the guests spend are new dollars to the area's economy. From one-half to two-thirds of these dollars may be respent in the local community by the resort in the form of payroll, purchases, and consumption of local services and goods. Management should be cognizant of the prosperity that a resort development can bring to a community, but it should also be careful not to overestimate or inflate the economic benefits. In many resorts a fair amount of food, supplies, equipment, and sometimes labor must be imported from other areas. This represents an "export leakage" and a loss to the local economy. Resort operators should therefore make every effort to purchase locally when possible.

Social Impacts

The social impact of resort development is at best difficult to measure. Many factors need to be taken into consideration: the remoteness of the resort's location, the size and level of economic development in the nearby community, the availability of labor, other existing industries, trades and services, and traditional social patterns within the community. For example, the first-time employment of large numbers of women in a rural community where men have traditionally been the sole family breadwinners may significantly change the roles of family members. Other impacts can be an increased divorce rate, crime, and juvenile delinquency. Although a resort will also bring positive effects, the culture shock for the community often outweighs these benefits. Progressive resort developers today recognize the importance of adding a social scientist to the planning team for new developments.

Culturally, the impact of resort development is even more difficult to assess. Resort development creates an economic demand for the trappings of local culture. This can paradoxically enhance and degrade local art forms and customs at the same time. Ersatz culture and art may be created for economic gain, but on the other hand, local artists, musicians, and craftsmen have an outlet for their services and products. This core of employed artists can spark a general renewal of interest by residents in their own cultural heritage.

Resort development may spark a two-way migration of residents that profoundly alters the character of the community. Two categories of new residents are drawn to the resort area. Buyers of second homes for vacation or retirement are generally affluent and culturally more similar to tourists than to established residents. The second group is made up of newcomers drawn to jobs in the community. Both of these groups will gradually take an active part in community life—something transient visitors do not normally get a chance to do. Further social and political changes may occur as the wealthier of these new residents become the new social and political elite of the area, displacing the older establishment.

As new residents arrive, some established residents may decide to leave. An initial emigration may occur as resorts increase the value of all nearby property, making the sale of land an attractive proposition. Young people with fewer ties to family and traditional employment may go to work in the resort or may move out of the community altogether to a more urban setting.

Environmental Impact

Resorts invariably create heavy demand for water and energy resources, and for transportation and communication services. To meet these demands, resorts require sophisticated infrastructure systems which are not only costly capital investments, but will affect the environment in terms of land and other natural resource use and open space. In all but the most developed urban settings, existing roads, airports, depots, electricity, gas, water, sewage disposal, and telephone lines will probably not be adequate to support new resort development. Developers typically provide these within the resort site, while local government has generally been willing to provide (or at least subsidize) offsite construction of expensive supporting infrastructure as an incentive to attract outside investments.

Unfortunately, for many resorts the development that ensues is not always expected or ultimately beneficial to the resort or the community. The growth of Disney World as a theme park and resort, for example, has created raging controversy with regard to its environmental as well as economic and political impacts on central Florida. Investment in resort-oriented infrastructure requires government to make trade-offs whose benefits do not always outweigh costs. In opting to spend public capital for resort-supporting infrastructure, governments are sometimes forced to divert funds away from other projects of potentially greater direct benefit to the local population such as farm irrigation systems, schools, or community centers.

Beyond the public cost-benefit question, the environmental impact of resort development remains a basic issue, regardless of the resort's location. In a less developed area, resort development can be an answer to some of the life-threatening environmental problems, including poor water supplies, inadequate sanitation and sewerage facilities, bad housing conditions, and vulnerability to natural disasters. In a developed area, on the other hand, these fundamental environmental problems have for the most part already been solved. An assessment of the environmental impact of a resort in a developed area should consider secondary environmental problems that are side effects of growth—congestion and pollution.

Every resort manager should realize that the success of resort operations will ultimately depend on maintaining both a pleasant social and physical environment. The best resorts always appear to have a healthy respect for the natural attributes of the land and its ecological balance. Natural environment, which is an important aspect of the resort attraction, is fragile and too easily destroyed if responsible planning is neglected. It behooves the resort developer to conform to tight environmental standards, both for the long-term viability of the resort and to maintain good community relations.

Investment Concerns

Resort developments are typically characterized by tremendous capital investments with heavy costs in fixed assets for land, building, and guest amenities. Returns on investments are usually low in early years. At the same time, the payback period is usually much longer, with low cash flows during the early years in comparison to transient hotel developments.

Resort hotels are generally considered to be riskier investments than other types of large-scale construction. They require tremendous investment in non-revenue producing space with continuous capital outflows needed for renovations to keep them attractive over the years. Not only is hotel occupancy more sensitive to fluctuations in the economy than office buildings and apartments, but competition is intense in the industry and aggressive new resort properties often having a marketing edge over older resorts that have not seen reinvestment from their owners.

One of the most pressing development problems facing resort management in the early 1980s was the difficulty in obtaining financing because of high interest rates and a tight money supply. The scale of resort development had grown over the years beyond the capacity of hotel chains to provide capital for expansion. As a result, many big chains opted to expand by franchising the hotel name or operating resorts under management contracts, with little or no equity position. Others adopted mixed-use policies to include the sales of fractional ownership, time-sharing, or apartments.

The characteristics of resort investments, however, with low cash flows in early years and heavy investment in fixed assets (particularly land) had made them most attractive to certain investors. These were investors with large sums of investment capital seeking real estate tax advantages, long-range economic gains in terms of potential equity buildup, or an investment that could act as a hedge against inflation, since resorts can react quickly to marketplace changes with price increases. With federal tax reform passed by Congress in 1986, however, many of these attractive investment features have been lost. Resorts are currently being financed by more traditional sources, and overall, investor emphasis has returned to the actual cash flow performance of the operation. Creative financing deals are on the decline, and foreign investment is increasing. While conflicting viewpoints exist regarding the future of resort financing, the one thing which seems certain is that financing will fluctuate with changing tax laws and economic conditions.

An alternative form of financing for resorts today is through the development of condominiums, which are sold as apartment units to individual buyers and placed into a rental pool managed and marketed by the resort. Management and individual investors share in the risks and the profits. The obvious advantages for management are the reduction of capital costs and the risk-sharing by the individual investor of an unoccupied room with ongoing fixed costs.

Time-sharing is another means of developing new resort projects. Individuals purchase guaranteed accommodations at a resort of their choice for the time period of their choice for a specified number of years. This purchase can take one of two forms: an ownership interest in the resort property, or a prepaid license to use a resort unit. Many time-share purchasers participate in international vacation exchange services, which gives them the opportunity to exchange weeks with time-sharers in other locations. It has been estimated that there are 2,100 resorts worldwide providing time-sharing vacation intervals to 1,350,000 purchasers.[3] Bad publicity regarding time-sharing frauds and bankruptcies has had a negative impact on time-share sales. As a response, many states now regulate time-share sales.

Another tool for lowering capital requirements and increasing overall return on investment for the developer is the sale of vacation homesites. Golf courses, tennis courts, and boat marinas are often required resort amenities, but may not be profitable operations in themselves. Resorts may use them as loss-leaders to attract guests. Similarly, the hotels themselves may not be great profit centers, but will greatly enhance land values in the resort, which the developer may exploit by selling resort vacation homes.

Resorts of the Future

Many of today's leading architects and designers talk about the resort of the future in terms of the creation of a total environment, not simply a hotel property. To create such an environment, mere knowledge about the mechanics of design will not be enough. The planner or developer must also appreciate the underlying leisure philosophy and vacationer behavior which shape the resort concept. Successful resorts in the future will be those that sell a total experience composed of a bundle of tangibles and intangibles to provide guests with a holiday period of creative escape from their everyday lives. Hawaii's mega-resorts, for example, represent such a response to the vacation marketplace. Mega-resorts attempt to offer a fantasy experience by featuring such manmade attractions as water wonderlands patterned after the hanging gardens of Babylon; seven-acre swimming lagoons stocked with porpoises, sea turtles, and brilliant reef fish; Clydesdale-drawn custom-built open air carriages; and theme villages. Imagination is combined with innovation in most mega-resorts.

While some resort developers and operators will be leaning toward the creation of mega-resorts, other resort concepts that are likely to flourish as the industry becomes more segmented include health resorts and executive retreats. Health resorts will continue to grow in various directions. Spas and health centers will more commonly cater to the average resort guest whose interest is in maintaining health and fitness, but service will also be expanded to provide for the unwell guest, the elderly, and the young. Some health experts see an eventual partial merging of the resort and health care markets.

In contrast to the mega-resort trend, smaller and highly personalized resorts catering to the executive retreat market, which seeks a pleasant environment but minimal distractions and no crowds, may become an important growth segment. The idea here is to provide a space for private meditation and the realignment of physical and spiritual balance.

Summary

The successful development and management of a resort requires a keen understanding of the distinctions between resorts and other lodging forms. Location, seasonal patterns, and changing vacation travel patterns significantly affect management, marketing, and operational policies. The needs of resort guests are more complex than those of business travelers. The average stay is longer and so more varied activities, food service, and recreational amenities are required. Resort guests also expect more personalized attention from the staff around the clock.

It is essential that management concern itself with the impacts of the resort on the host community, and do everything possible to make these impacts positive, whether they be economic, social, or environmental in nature. The host community will also be affected by the increased level of employment, traffic, public services, and infrastructural particularities of the resort. If the resort management and the host community jointly decide and cooperate on key issues relating to growth, expansion, or encroachment on public rights, both parties may coexist with mutual benefits.

——Additional Reading——

Gee, Chuck Y. _Resort Development and Management_. Second edition. The Educational Institute of American Hotel and Motel Association. 1988.

——References——

1. Laventhol and Horwath. (1987) _The U.S. Resort Lodging Industry._
2. Marriott Corporation. (1987) _The Marriott Report on Leisure Travel: The Demise of the Traditional American Vacation._
3. Ron Haylock. Developments in Worldwide Timeshare. _Travel and Tourism Analyst._ 1988; Number 2.

39

Casino Hotel Operations and Management

Sheryl Fried
Widener University

What segment of the hospitality industry includes two unique cities, riverboats, and Indian reservations? The answer is casino gaming, and it is the fastest-growing segment of the hospitality industry. The most famous gaming cities are Las Vegas, Nevada, and Atlantic City, New Jersey. The former houses most of the largest hotels in the world, and the latter is the busiest destination resort in the United States. One city is surrounded by desert and mountains in the west, and the other is located on the east coast alongside the Atlantic Ocean. These cities are part of the expanding, exciting, and challenging casino gaming industry.

History

Gambling as a form of entertainment, sport, and fund raising can be traced through the development of Western civilization as far back as ancient Egypt. Many of today's casino games have their roots in Europe. In the fourteenth century, the Italians and the French are credited with originating playing cards. In the 1600s the English played a popular game called hazzard. This game is the forerunner of the casino game of craps.[1]

Native Americans had many games of chance within their cultures. Also the Spanish, French, and English explorers brought with them their own form of gambling games. As the country grew, gambling became a small and quiet part of U.S. history. Many forms of gambling could be found in the back rooms of the first New England taverns, on the paddleboats and steamships in the heyday of the Mississippi riverboat era, and in boomtown saloons of the Wild West. Quite often these gaming establishments were operated illegally in private rooms.

Places Where Gaming Is Legalized

Casino gaming has been limited by government legislation. Unlike the hotel industry, casino hotel gaming is limited to several key areas. Nevada and Atlantic City are two major on-land geographic locations for casino gaming in this country.

Nevada

In Nevada, gambling has been both legal and illegal. In 1869 gambling was legalized and then outlawed again in 1910. The status and form of legal and illegal gambling changed several times until 1931 when it was finally legalized and remains legal today.[2] Nevada has several major gaming cities, each with its own personality. To better understand this industry it is important to know a little bit about some major gaming resorts.

Today, the major gambling resorts in Nevada include Lake Tahoe and Reno in the north and Las Vegas and Laughlin in the south. The city of Lake Tahoe is situated on the shore of a large mountain-rimmed lake at the border of Nevada and California. This city has less than a dozen hotels and casinos. In addition to gambling, Lake Tahoe also offers fine downhill ski slopes in the winter and water sports in the summer. Not far from Lake Tahoe is Reno, Nevada. This town, known as the "biggest little city in the world," has most of its casino hotels located in the downtown area.

In the southern portion of the state, Las Vegas, the entertainment capital of the world, is an internationally known gambling and entertainment mecca. There are more than 50 major casino hotels, and most of the large properties are located on the strip or in the downtown area. Las Vegas will have eight of the ten largest hotels in the world by the year 2000.[3] The largest hotel in the world is the Excalibur, with more than 4,000 rooms. In 1994 the MGM Grand Hotel Casino will open with 5,000 rooms.

Las Vegas is a convention destination city. It is one of the big three convention cities in the United States. By the end of decade when several construction projects are completed, it is predicted that Las Vegas will be the number one convention destination in the United States.

Las Vegas is also a showcase for top name entertainment from Jay Leno and Diana Ross to Broadway musicals and revue shows. This city also houses professional sporting events such as heavyweight boxing, golf, and tennis tournaments.

Recently the city has been marketed as a family resort. Many of the casino hotel properties offer entertainment for all ages including circus acts, water parks, theme parks, and shopping malls. These attractions blend nicely with the sunny desert and casino gaming environment.

The other major and rapidly growing gaming community in southern Nevada is Laughlin, located on the Colorado River across from Arizona. This little desert town has ten major casino hotels and is the third-largest gaming revenue producer in Nevada.

Gaming is legal in the entire state of Nevada and many other communities have casinos and hotel casinos. However, the size and scale of the casino hotels are small in comparison to the cities mentioned above.

Atlantic City

Atlantic City, New Jersey, "The world's playground," saw its first casino hotel open in 1978. Currently there are ten casino hotels that line the boardwalk, and two are located along the bay. One of these properties, Trump Taj Mahal, contains the largest single casino space in the world.

Atlantic City is located in one of the most densely populated areas of this country, with 25% of the population within a day's driving distance. It is therefore no surprise that since 1989 more visitors traveled to Atlantic City than any other city. In numbers this translates to approximately 35 million visits per year.[4]

Atlantic City is also an entertainment and sports center. Throughout the year top name singers, comedians, and entertainers as well as boxing champions are billed at these find resort hotels. In the summer this resort is filled to capacity, with the white sandy beaches and boardwalk providing the major nongaming attractions.

Other U.S. Gaming Locations

Most people know that casino gaming is legal in Atlantic City and Nevada, but it is also legal in many other on- and off-land locations in the United States and its territories. They include Puerto Rico; Deadwood, South Dakota, three mountain communities in Colorado; riverboats; and Indian reservations.

Although Puerto Rico is the only area that has traditional casino hotel resorts like Las Vegas and Atlantic City, the other gaming towns are still developing into gaming and tourism destinations.

Deadwood, South Dakota, has limited gaming and only a handful of small hotel properties. Local and state governments use the taxes from gaming money raised for historic preservation of the community's wild west heritage.[5]

Three historic mining towns in Colorado—Cripple Creek, Black Hawk, and Central City—legalized gambling in 1991. There are fewer than 20 casinos operating in these three mountain communities.

Riverboat Gaming

The state of Iowa was the first to offer riverboat gambling, in 1991 at Fort Madison. Legislation in that state restricts each patron to a $200 limit on gambling losses and a $5 maximum bet on a floating riverboat. Other states were soon to follow in legalizing riverboat gaming on a county-by-county basis, and they include the states of Illinois, Missouri, Mississippi, and Louisiana. As of early 1993, 15 riverboats were afloat on the Mississippi River and off the Gulf Coast. It is predicted that many more states will follow in this wake of gaming fever along the river. As more communities host these floating casinos and competition for gamblers' money increases, gaming restrictions and limits on gamblers will loosen.[6]

Indian Reservations

There are close to 150 casinos run by native Americans nationwide. The proliferation of Indian gaming was made possible by the 1988 passage of the Indian Gaming Regulatory Act. Native American reservations that offer casino, pari-mutuel, or other public gambling can be found in the following states: Arizona, California, Colorado, Connecticut, Idaho, Iowa, Louisiana, Minnesota, Mississippi, Montana, Nebraska, North Dakota, Oklahoma, Oregon, South Dakota, Washington, and Wisconsin. These casinos range from offering video lottery and keno to providing a full range of casino games, hotel accommodations, and food and beverage and entertainment outlets.[7]

One of the largest and more famous casinos owned by Native Americans is located in Ledyard, Connecticut. The Foxwoods Casino is a large tourist complex on the Mashantucket Pequot reservation. The casino has just under 200 gaming tables and more than 3,000 slot machines that operate 24 hours per day. In the summer of 1993 the reservation will offer gamblers other nongaming amenities including swimming pools, theater, show rooms, theme park rides, and a re-created Ice-Age Pequot village.

Native American gaming is the fastest-growing segment of the gaming industry. This is because Native Americans may operate the same form of gaming and casinos in any state that legally allows that form of gaming. For example, if a state allows churches to operate bingo or a fire hall to hold a "Las Vegas-style" gambling fund-raising night, then an Indian reservation in that state may operate the same games for profit. Therefore since all states except Hawaii and Utah allow some form of legalized gambling either for charity or for private business, it is potentially possible for Native Americans to operate casinos in almost all of the 50 states. Provided that Congress or the Supreme Court do not significantly change the 1988 act, reservation gaming will be a prominent gaming market force within the United States.

Cruise Ships

Gaming is also a major part of the cruise ship industry. Luxury casino cruise liners set sail from the east and west coasts of the United States. It is also possible to sail off the coast of Mississippi and Texas and gamble on a floating casino cruise to nowhere and back. Many other places like Japan, Hong Kong, Australia, Europe, and the Caribbean are popular ports of call for casino cruise ships.

Around the World

Casino gaming and casino hotels can be found around the world. They are as close as the Caribbean and Canada and as far away as England, France, Monte Carlo, Africa, Malaysia, and Australia. The casino gaming industry is limited by the laws of many countries, but gaming can be found in many places across the United States and around the globe.

Casino Gaming Ownership

Many of the companies involved in the ownership and operation of casino hotels are traditional hotel companies. In the past they have included Holiday Inn and Ramada. Today, hotel giants such as Hilton, Promus, and Hyatt own and operate some of the finest casinos in the world.

The casino gaming industry is also known for attracting some flamboyant, famous, and interesting owners. Some of the more famous casino hotel ownership has included gangsters such as "Bugsy" Segal, who opened the Flamingo Hotel in Las Vegas and was later gunned down mob-style in 1947. Famous entrepreneurs have had major ownership of and influence on the development of the casino hotel industry. One notable man was the eccentric recluse Howard Hughes, who in the course of his lifetime owned airlines, a movie studio, four casino hotels, and much of the land in Las Vegas in the 1960s and early 1970s.[8]

Even today billionaire Donald Trump and entertainer Merv Griffin are among the colorful and unique owners and operators of casino hotel properties. Due to the legalization and regulation of the industry today, many casino hotel properties are also owned by publicly traded multi-million dollar corporations such as Caesars World, Showboat, Promus, and Aztar.

Casino Hotel Properties

The uniqueness of the gaming industry is illustrated by the interesting locales and individuals who operate the properties. However, the size of the physical plant and customer market segment also make the casino hotel business a peerless segment of the hospitality industry.

The trend today in the casino hotel industry is, the bigger the better. It is common for casino hotel properties to have 500 or more rooms. Las Vegas has several hotels with more than 3,000 rooms. These guest rooms range from the standard motel-type rooms to the most luxurious theme suites of the grandest scale. Room amenities in the luxury suites typically include whirlpool baths, mini spas, several big-screen TV entertainment centers, two or more bathrooms, several living rooms and bedrooms, dining room, wet bars, and the best view in town. They may be decorated with original antiques or modern one-of-a-kind designer furnishings. These suites are usually located in a separate part of the hotel and may include butler service, private registration, lobby, and bar area.

Hotel Area

The operation of a casino hotel is very different from a noncasino hotel. At a standard hotel, the major goals of the front desk, room reservations, and sales departments are to give quality service and sell all available rooms. In a casino hotel, quality service is important but 100% occupancy is not. Rather, the goal is to hold rooms and ensure that they are available for the casino hotel patron. In a casino hotel all guests are not considered equal. Satisfying the wants and needs of the valued casino patron is one of the most important tasks of the front desk. Many times this means not selling clean available rooms to the general public. For example, many of the super theme suites are never sold and are left vacant many a night even though they may sell for $1,000 to $25,000 per night. The reason for this is that a casino customer may gamble up to ten times as much as the revenue from one room night. A customer worth that much should never be denied a room. These suites are held just in case a casino customer may want a room and does not have a reservation or decides to stay at the last minute. On an average weekend in Atlantic City about 80% of a casino hotel's rooms are reserved by the casino for valued casino customers. These rooms are either given away free or rented at a discounted rate to high rollers and other casino patrons.

Food and Beverage

Casino hotels often include casinos with more than 50,000 square feet of gaming space. Many of the large properties have convention and meeting facilities and extensive food and beverage outlets.

A 500-room property typically has four to seven food service outlets. They may offer volume restaurants such as a 24-hour coffee shop, Jewish-style deli, and extensive buffet in addition to several smaller gourmet restaurants. Many casino hotels have a variety of international haute cuisine restaurants to cater to the wealthy casino patrons. Some of the more popular gourmet rooms include authentic classic French, Italian, and Chinese cuisine. Because many casinos are open 24 hours, hotel casinos offer several restaurants that never close.

A typical casino coffee shop could serve more than 2,000 meals each day. Many of the average to larger casino hotels gross between $30 and $40 million in food and beverage sales a year and room service sales of up to $10 million. These outlets require trained and qualified chefs and managers to handle the large volume of food sales. Quite often, casino hotels have large purchasing and food and beverage control staffs to assist the food and beverage department in supplying food products and controlling costs.

Beverage outlets in a typical casino include casino bars, lounges, and showrooms. Usually entertainment, bands, singers, and comedians are booked for these rooms. Some of the showrooms hold 2,000 customers each. Usually these rooms have a two-drink minimum and cover charge. On a sold-out performance night, this requires the cocktail servers to serve 4,000 drinks per show, in dim lighting, while the entertainers perform. This is no easy task to manage six days a week, two performances per night.

Another unique aspect of casino properties is that some of the food and beverage products are given away for free. For example, many casinos offer free alcoholic beverage service to their patrons while gambling. Also, many of the gourmet rooms have an average check price of more than $100 per guest and never charge their customers for the food served. This is because good casino customers are given complimentary meals when they gamble large sums of money at the casino.

Convention Space

Convention and banquet facilities in the larger properties tend to augment the casino customer base and serve as a major draw for guests. This is particularly true for Las Vegas, which has a large convention center. Many of the large properties, like the Hilton International, Mirage, Bally's Grand, The Sahara, Tropicana, and Caesars Palace, have thousands of square feet of convention and meeting space. These properties participate in citywide conventions like the Consumer Electronics Show, which draws as many as 100,000 people in one week's time. These hotels also are large enough to handle their own smaller conventions. Las Vegas, Reno, and Atlantic City all expect to expand their citywide and hotel convention capacity in the 1990s.

Large hotel and casino properties typically offer health spas, tennis, golfing, and swimming amenities for their customers. The larger properties even have teen and day care centers for the family. Many of these properties are theme resorts. For example, the Excalibur has a medieval theme, Trump Taj Mahal is decorated in an exotic Indian style, and Circus Circus is designed around a circus tent. The Mirage Hotel includes such attractions as a tropical rain forest, a volcano, and live white tigers.

Other Features

A typical 500-room property has four or five retail shops. In some larger hotels the properties may include mini shopping malls inside the facility. Some of the more common types of retail stores may be a gift shop, men's store, ladies' fashion shop, jewelry store, and hair salon.

Due to the sheer volume of business and the nature of the casino customers it is not uncommon for these properties to own and operate fleets of limousines, 1,000-car parking garages, and gas stations. From this description, one may conclude that casino hotels are far from the typical airport, or downtown, convention hotel with the same number of rooms. This is because casino hotels cater to a special guest market.

Special Guest Market

The casino hotel customer market includes the vacationer, business and convention traveler, and casino customer. Most of the casino hotel properties are located in resort areas and therefore the customers who frequent them expect the same amenities and facilities that a typical resort hotel would provide. However, because a casino hotel has gaming it attracts a very unique type of customer, the gambler. These customers keep the casino hotels full and hotel occupancies are on average 80% to 90% a year. This is significantly higher than the national occupancy average.

Casino gamblers range from the bus customer who rides public transportation to play the slot machines to the wealthiest international business traveler who is flown in one a chartered jet, wined, dined, and pampered while wagering at the tables in the casino.

The High Roller

The latter of the two gaming customers is often referred to as a high roller. This is a casino customer who may wager $50,000 to $100,000 or more in a casino per visit and may visit five or ten times a year. Needless to say, this is a very valuable customer to a casino hotel property. Because one individual high roller may generate $100,000 to millions of dollars in revenue, the casino often "comps" room, food, and beverage expenditures. The term _comp_ is short for _complimentary_. Although the high roller may spend all of his money in the casino, he does not have to pay for anything else in the hotel facility. Some high rollers who gamble large sums of money also receive gifts such as Rolls Royces and trips to Europe in addition to complimentary goods and services while staying at the hotel. Other gamblers who wager several thousand dollars may only receive complimentary lunch or dinner or a discounted room rate.

Sometimes groups of high rollers and potential high rollers from one geographic area are offered several day packages for free. These trips are called junkets, and they include transportation, room, food, and beverage. The casino arranges these trips in the hopes that the high rollers will gamble more than the cost of the junket. Most of these customers are flown in by plane. In Atlantic City some junkets arrive by bus.

Organizational Structure

Given the size and scope of these casino hotel properties and the unique customer market, it is no surprise that the organizational structure of a hotel casino is much larger and slightly different from a standard hotel of the same room size. The managers and employees often handle many more customers and provide a wider range of customer service than any of the other hotel market segments.

In addition to the customer differences, casino hotels have many restrictive government regulations that dictate their structure and even specific job positions and organizational design. The typical organizational chart of a large Nevada casino hotel is shown in Figure 1.[9] Note that the director of loss and prevention has authority equal to the directors of finance, sales and marketing, casino operations, and hotel operations. The loss and prevention department is responsible for surveillance of the casino gaming areas. This area is also known as the "eye in the sky" because the employees monitor using cameras and catwalks above the casino floor.

New Jersey gaming regulations are different from Nevada's and in many ways more restrictive. Figure 2[9] shows the typical upper-level organizational chart for an Atlantic City casino hotel.

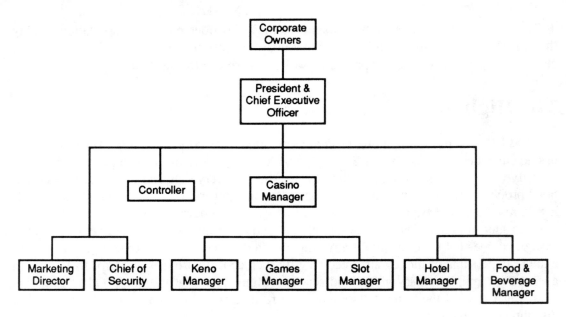

Figure 1. Typical Organizational Chart for Nevada Casino Hotel

Atlantic City (figure 2) also has checks and balances built into the organizational chart to ensure that the casino is audited properly and run honestly. Note that the director of internal audit and the director of surveillance report directly to the board of directors and are above the president of the company. The reason for this is that the audit department audits the casino and the surveillance department monitors the casino activities in the form of security and protection in the same manner as the loss and prevention department of the Nevada casino hotels. These departments would not be able to function fully if they had to report to the managers they monitor. Therefore, they report to the board of directors, who do not operate the daily casino hotel activities.

Also notice that in Atlantic City there are other unique department head titles in addition to the expected vice president of casino operations. Two positions that may seem unusual are the general counsel and vice president of government regulations. Because Atlantic City is regulated by the Casino Control Commission and monitored by the Division of Gaming Enforcement, it is necessary for the casinos to have legal advice on property. Both those departments ensure that the casino hotel abides by the many government rules and regulations. The cost to a casino if found guilty of breaking the rules can range from a $1,000 fine to loss of the operating license.

In both Nevada and in New Jersey the casino operations department is on an equal footing on the organizational chart with many of the other departments. This may be true on paper but in terms of revenue the casino area produces the most gross income for a casino hotel property. Unlike regular hotels where the rooms division earns the majority of gross revenue, the hotel and food and beverage areas in Atlantic City generate about 20% of the total gross revenue. In Nevada the hotel and food and beverage areas produce a little less

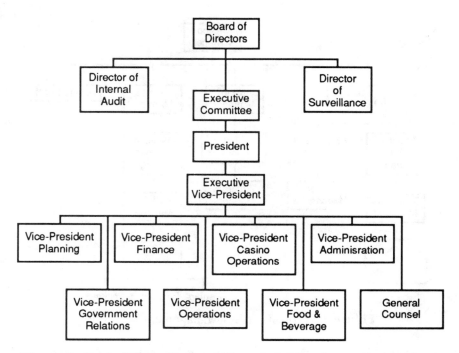

Figure 2. Typical Organizational Chart for a New Jersey Casino Hotel

than 50%. This means that an average Atlantic City casino department brings in 80% gross revenue and a Nevada casino department earns a little over 50% of the gross revenue for their respective hotel casinos properties.[10]

Due to the disproportionate amount of funds generated in the casino area, the other departments such as hotel and food and beverage become secondary to the casino. The needs and demands of the casino and its customers dictate room availability, type of food and beverage offered, banquet space usage, and all the other amenities and services offered by a property.

Casino Management Positions

The management of a casino under the director or vice president of casino operations is performed by the casino manager and her staff. An example of this structure is shown in Figure 3.[9] The organizational charts of casino area management in Nevada and in Atlantic City are identical except that Atlantic City does not have as many different gaming attraction options as Nevada.

The casino manager is responsible for the operation of the casino gaming area. In Nevada that would include the table games, slot machines, keno, poker, bingo, and a race and sports book. Most Nevada casinos have table games and slot machines, or some or all of the other legal gaming options. In Atlantic City only table games, slot machines, and horse-race betting are legal gaming options in the casino.

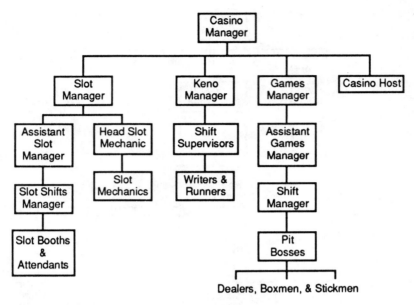

Figure 3. Typical Casino Management Positions

Under the casino manager are shift managers, one for each shift. This person is responsible for the gaming operations on the respective shift. They also do the scheduling for the casino personnel.

Under the shift manager is the games manager, who is responsible for all table games. Table games include black jack, craps, roulette, big 6, red dog, sic boc, and baccarat. A variety of other table games are currently under consideration for legalization both in Nevada and Atlantic City.

The casino is arranged in areas of table groupings called pits. An example of a pit may be six blackjack tables and two roulette tables or eight craps tables. One pit boss is responsible for each area. Floorpersons are supervisors who report to pit bosses. They observe four to two tables in each pit.

Each table game has a required number of dealers. Blackjack and roulette require one dealer per table. Craps requires three dealers. One of the craps dealers, called a stickman, controls the dice and speed of the game. Craps also has a special type of floorperson called a boxman, who sits down at the table and monitors the chips used to pay off the customers' winnings. Baccarat also requires three dealers.

Although to many people a pit boss and floorpersons just look like they stand around watching people, they actually perform many tasks. They ensure that the property's procedures and government regulations are followed by the dealers. They also watch employees and customers to prevent theft and cheating. Floorpersons track customer play and record how much potential high rollers and good customers bet. If a customer gambles enough money in a period of time, the floorperson may request a comp from the pit boss for the customer.

Some customers have credit lines that are agreed to by the casino and customer in advance. A customer planning to use his credit line asks the floorperson for a marker which is a form of IOU. The money is then loaned at the table. The floorperson and pit boss's assistance is needed to check the customer's credit line to complete the transaction. A casino pit clerk is then requested to deliver a form that looks like a check. After the customer signs the check the money is then loaned in the form of gaming chips.

The other casino managers such as keno manager and race and sports book managers are responsible for their respective areas. These areas are also part of the casino operation. Keno and sports books are found in Nevada casinos. Racebooks are legal in both Atlantic City and Nevada.

Slots

The slot manager is responsible for the slot machines. This includes the traditional one-armed bandits, video poker, and other computerized slot games. Slot attendants are employees who aid customers with malfunctioning machines and also pay off the larger jackpots. Slot booth attendants give out change for the dollar, fifty cents, quarter, and nickel machines. Some casinos also have machines that take $5-, $25-, $100-, and $500-tokens too.

The other workers in the slot area are the repair personnel called slot mechanics. Many times the slot machines are repaired right on the casino floor. In places where the casinos never close, the slot mechanics can be seen repairing slot machines in the middle of a customer-filled casino.

Race and Sports Book

The race and sports book mangers operate off track and sports betting. Off track betting involves the taking of bets and broadcasting of live horse and dog races from around the country. Sports betting is where customers may bet on fights, football, baseball, and other national sporting events.

Horse and dog racing is done on a pari-mutuel type of betting. Pari-mutuel gambling is where the participants belong to a betting pool such as one horse race. All those betting on that race bet on first, second, or third place or some combination of the three. These bettors share the total amount of the pool minus a certain percentage for the casino hotel.

In sports betting, handicappers who work for the casino establish a point spread called _the line._ The line is the number that is the point difference required to make an even money bet. Customers can then bet on either team to win. For example, if the Philadelphia Eagles were playing the New Jersey Giants football team and the handicappers predict that the Eagles will "win in seven," a person betting on the Eagles would not win the bet if the Giants or the Eagles won. He would win only if the Eagles won and the difference in the two teams' scores was seven or greater.

Keno

Keno is another game played only in Nevada. This game resembles bingo and uses the numbers 1 through 80. Customers may bet on keno in combinations of one to 15 numbers. A keno manager is responsible for the keno operations in the casino.

Keno may be played in the casino area or in the restaurants. Keno runners will accept tickets from customers and place their bets before each keno game is played. Keno writers actually write the ticket that will be a part of each game.

Poker and Bingo

Many Nevada casinos also have poker rooms. The responsibility of the poker room manager is to oversee the poker dealers. Many of the poker games vary. The casino makes money on this game by taking a percentage of the winnings, called the pot.

Bingo is very popular on Indian reservations and in casinos in Nevada. Bingo in Atlantic City hotels can be played as a marketing gimmick for prizes but not for money.

Gaming Regulations

Both Atlantic City and Nevada casino hotels are subject to strict state government regulations. These rules and laws were implemented for various obvious reasons. Some include keeping the gaming industry legal and out of the hands of organized crime. The regulations and laws were established for the same reasons but vary slightly from state to state.

Nevada

In Nevada, the Nevada Gaming Policy Committee, Nevada Gaming Commission, and the State Gaming Control Board are the agencies that regulate and monitor the casino industry. The Gaming Policy Committee is made up of the governor and eight appointed members. The purpose of the committee is to discuss gaming issues and policy. The committee, then makes recommendations to the commission.

The Casino Gaming Control Commission is made up of five members. They must be U.S. citizens and residents of Nevada but cannot hold any political office or own or be involved with any gaming-related business. The commission has the power to grant licenses, to grant approval to operate gaming establishments, and to investigate and withdraw licensing and gaming approval.

The Gaming Control Board is made up of three members and has six enforcement divisions. The board members have the same restrictions as commission members and therefore cannot be active in Nevada politics and gaming. The board serves two functions: the protector of the casinos and a casino police force. The six enforcement divisions are the audit, corporate securities and economic research, enforcement, investigation, tax and licensing, and administrative divisions.

Employees who work in casino hotels in Nevada must obtain a work permit and be fingerprinted. This work permit allows the government to check an employee's background for criminal convictions. All employees need one of these work permits to legally work in a casino.[2]

Atlantic City

The regulating and enforcement of Atlantic City casino hotels is done by the Casino Control Commission and the Division of Gaming Enforcement. The Casino Control Commission has five members, and no more than three of the members may be from one political party. None of the members are allowed to have any interest in or ownership of any part of the casino hotel business. The purpose of the commission is to adopt casino hotel regulations. The commission oversees licensing and makes certain that casinos adhere to certain policies like affirmative action. The commission also hears appeals from the Administrative Law Office concerning casino-related violations.

The Division of Gaming Enforcement is under the attorney general's office in the State of New Jersey, and it enforces regulations passed by the commission as well as other state laws concerning gaming operations. The purpose of this division is to investigate and prosecute casinos that violate the law. The state police and a team of auditors perform these investigative functions.

The employee licensing requirements for Atlantic City are much different than the work permit process of Nevada. Everyone who works for a casino hotel, or who does a significant amount of business with it, (e.g., a major food purveyor), must be licensed by the state. The fees for the employee licenses vary from a less than $100 to several thousand dollars for a key license.

Anyone who works in an Atlantic City casino hotel whose job does not require them to be on the casino floor in a gaming capacity must have a hotel-only license. This requires an employee to fill out a short personal history form, be fingerprinted and have a promise of employment from one of the casino hotel properties. Front desk clerks, food servers, and room housekeepers are some of the job positions that require this license.[11]

The next license level is the casino gaming license. Any person who works in the casino directly involved with the gaming operation must have this license. This includes dealers, floorpersons, casino accounting employees, and casino and security personnel. This license costs several hundred dollars and is renewable every three years. When filing for this license, the applicant must also fill out the long personal history disclosure form.

The highest level license is the key license. For this license an extensive employee background check is conducted. All pit bosses, casino hosts, casino surveillance, and upper-level management personnel must have this license. This would include the vice presidents of food and beverage, hotel, and casino operations.

The Future of Casino Gaming

The future in gaming operations and in particular in the management of casino hotel properties is excellent. In Atlantic City currently several casino hotels are building hotel rooms, and more probably will be built in the near future. In the early 1990s a multi–million dollar convention center complex and gateway to Atlantic City is being built. It is also possible that "if the state government gets committed to revitalizing Atlantic City as a tourist and convention destination that the number of rooms could even double in ten years."[10]

The outlook for Las Vegas is even more positive. The early 1990s saw a large building boom. An additional 60,000 rooms are projected to be built in this gaming town by the year 2000. This includes expansion of several operating casinos and new development including several 3,000-room hotels, theme parks, and entertainment facilities. The city has added convention space. Soon the aggregate hotel meeting and convention space will exceed 2.2 million square feet, more than twice as much room as the city's convention center. Las Vegas will not only be a gaming giant but a mega-convention site too.

Gaming is also expanding in the United States and around the world. Legislation recently passed riverboat gambling legislation and the rights to open what will be perhaps the largest casino space in the world. The people of Illinois are in the process of considering legalizing gaming in the city of Chicago. More and more states are considering the legalization of gaming as a way of funding the state coffers without raising taxes.

Indian reservations located near population centers similar to the Foxwood Casino in Connecticut have the potential to become large and diverse gaming tourist destinations. Time will tell the impact of these casinos will have on the gaming industry and the country as a whole.

Many former Eastern Bloc countries such as Poland and Czechoslovakia are seriously considering casino gaming as a way to help their depleted economies. Australia also is considered a major growth area for casino gaming. Because this industry is tied to government legislation, it can only grow in limited geographic areas where gaming is legalized. But more and more areas of the world have begun to legalize and develop this industry because it is seen as a useful method to raise money to finance government and supplement taxes.

For a hospitality student who is graduating in the next four years, the casino hotel industry has much to offer. Most of the jobs in the hospitality industry require more than a 40-hour work week and can be quite demanding. However, what the casino hotel industry has to offer is good wages for the hours worked. Most salaries are higher in casino hotels than in standard hotels. This is because gaming is so lucrative and because of the tremendous facility size and large volume of business generated by casino hotels. The work is exciting and challenging. Many casinos offer a unique and ever-changing atmosphere in which to work. There is room for advancement for a professional hospitality graduate who has hospitality experience and people and managerial skills. The opportunity for growth and a great career is there—you can bet on it.

——References——

1. Scarne, John. (1974) *Scarne's New Complete Guide to Gambling.* New York: Simon and Schuster, Inc.
2. Goodwin, John R. (1985) *Gaming Control Law, The Nevada Model. Principles, Statutes and Cases.* Columbus, Ohio: Publishing Horizons, Inc. pp. 13–14, 113–114.
3. Conversations with The Las Vegas Convention and Visitors Bureau, January 1990.
4. *Greater Atlantic City Tourism Marketing Master Plan,* January 1990; p. 8.
5. Bly, Laura. From Deadwood to Dubuque, Gambling is the Bet. *The Atlantic City Press.* February 12, 1990.
6. Clines, Frances X. As States Rush to Gamble, Experts See Risks. *The New York Times.* April 26, 1993.
7. Larrabee, John. Gambling Turns Tribe's Fortunes Around. *USA Today.* May 20, 1993, p. 6A.
8. Pearl, Ralph. (1974) *Las Vegas Is My Beat.* London: Bantam Books.
9. Greenless, E. Malcolm. (1988) *Casino Accounting and Financial Management.* Reno, Nevada: University of Nevada Press, p. 22, 23.
10. Conversations with David Gardner, former Executive Vice President of Government Affairs, The Casino Association of New Jersey. March 1990.
11. Conversations with Walter N. Read, former Chairman of the Casino Control Commission of New Jersey. March 1990.

40

Food Service in Institutions: College, School, Health Care, Military, and Corrections

Thomas E. Walsh
Iowa State University

Introduction

One of the better-kept secrets in hospitality education is the availability of interesting and challenging positions in the various segments of the institutional food service industry. As position vacancies occur, many are filled by food service professionals who seek a change from the sometimes hectic and less secure positions in the commercial section of the food service industry. Iverson reported that many managers find the advantages of institutional food service outweigh the drawbacks and that more and more commercial food service managers are being drawn into institutional food service because of the regular hours, excellent benefits, and comparable pay.[1]

The institutional food service industry includes the following segments: college and university, school (preschool through high school), health care (hospitals and extended care facilities), military, and correctional facility. Industrial food service is occasionally added to the listing. Usually excluded are city and country clubs, although most are also nonprofit organizations.

In a *Restaurants and Institutions* magazine exclusive, Gotschall stated that the line between commercial and institutional food service has almost disappeared. The entrepreneurial spirit is alive and well in institutional food services, which are setting a standard for risk-taking and creativity in their effort not only to break even, but also to make a profit. Examples cited were Notre Dame University's Leprechaun Pizza, which prepares and delivers 400 to 500 pizzas each day; Texas A&M's $4 million-a-year catering service for the campus, stadium, and student center; the New York City School District's expansion to serving dinner, in addition to breakfast and lunch, and to preparing meals for the homeless and senior citizens; and National Medical Enterprises of Santa Monica, California, which offers candlelight dinners, VIP service, guest-room service for overnight visitors, and take-home meals for employees.[2]

Table 1. Top Ten Food Service Management Contractors: 1991

No.	Name	Units	Annual Sales ($MM)
1	ARA Services	2,720	2,830
2	Marriott Management Services	2,400	2,500
3	Gardner Merchant	6,733	2,158
4	Canteen	1,579	1,460
5	Service America	1,100	915
6	Morrison's Custom Management	708	618
7	Ogden Services	82	510
8	Seilers/FDI	477	375
9	ServiceMaster	305	310
10	Restaur Dining Services	320	250

Institutional food services are changing in other ways as well. Marriott Food Services Management provides services from day care to laboratory equipment cleaning for its health care accounts. More institutions own and operate their own vending services, and facilities are being upgraded with cafeteria single-line service making way for station setups with eye-catching signage. Emphasis is being placed on service, with extensive employee training. Marketing efforts have resulted in the development of in-house concepts and tie-ins with well-known commercial food service organizations.[2]

As an example of the commercial tie-in, the student union at Michigan State University converted its cafeteria known as The Grill into a food court renamed One Union Square. Based on a survey of student food preferences, four commercial franchises including Little Caesar's Pizza, Burger King, and two popular local entrepreneurs offering deli and ice cream products respectively, were selected to share the 100-seat dining area. Sales increased by more than 450%. The new arrangement allowed the student union's food service staff to focus its attention on improving its catering services, which have since doubled the number of catered functions and increased sales five-fold.[3]

Many institutional food services are self-operated; however, food service contractors have become major players in the institutional market. The top ten food service management contractors in 1991 were listed by _Restaurants and Institutions_ as shown in Table 1.[4]

The institutional segment of the food service industry offers numerous challenging and exciting career opportunities for graduates of hospitality education programs.Those who successfully complete a food service management curriculum or acquire the registered dietitian credential as administered by The American Dietetic Association have unique advantages in securing some positions.

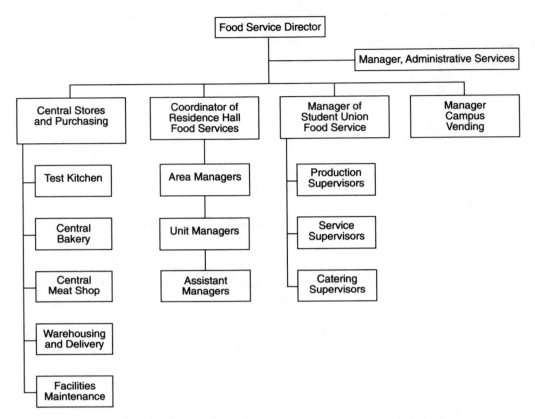

Figure 1. A Typical University Food Service Organization

College and University Food Service

Food service management contractors have made considerable advances in the college food service market since World War II, especially among smaller private colleges. However, many of the larger universities continue to operate their own food service organizations to serve students, faculty, staff, and campus visitors. These organizations are usually complex and offer satisfying career positions at several levels. Figure 1 illustrates a typical university food service organizational structure.

The university food service director will usually report to a person in or supervised by the business office (e.g., auxiliary services officer) or to a person in or supervised by the student affairs office (e.g., residence halls director). Regardless, the food service director is responsible for the satisfactory operation of the food service and the financial success of the organization. Planning and maintaining the food service facilities are included in the director's responsibilities.

The qualifications for a university food service director usually include at least one degree in a hospitality education or related program. Some universities require or give preference to a master's degree. Additionally, some will give consideration to the registered dietitian credential. Management experience in food service is usually required, with a significant portion a university organization specified. Five to ten years of progressive experience frequently is expected to achieve this high-level position.

The unit manager is a key operating position in the organization and is often a prerequisite for advancement. The responsibilities of the unit manager are numerous and include employee staffing, food and supplies ordering, production, service, housekeeping, and customer relations. A staff of 25 or 30 full-time and 75 to 100 part-time student workers is not uncommon. The largest customer group is usually students. Powers recognized that college students are generally pleasant to deal with, but they can be demanding.[5] He suggested that they need to be consulted in planning and to receive patient attention to complaints. Open lines of communication are essential to avoid the "us" versus "them" polarization that leads to trouble.

The food service supervisor or assistant manager is usually the entry position for graduates of hospitality education programs. In addition to performing duties assigned by the unit manager, the supervisor or assistant manager serves as the manager-on-duty on either the early or late shift. As such, she gains considerable knowledge and skills related to food production, service, warewashing and housekeeping, and administrative activities. Following two to four years of success at this level, a person is usually ready to advance to the position of unit manager.

The number of variety of support staff is often based on the size of the food service operation and the organizational philosophy of the school. The functions of purchasing, human resource management, and accounting are necessary to every food service organization. Frequently, these functions are the responsibility of the food service director, whose staff includes appropriate support personnel. Many of the larger university food service organizations centralize some activities, such as meat cutting, bakery, and inventory storage. These specialized operations usually result in greater overall efficiency. To a lesser extent, test kitchens are established to develop large quantity recipes and to evaluate new food products from manufacturers.

Although cafeteria service is the type of service generally associated with college and university food service, other services are common and require versatility of the food service organization. On and off-premises catering, banquet, table service, snack shops, and vending have long been a part of the food service mission. Food courts, deli operations, pizza delivery, and other fast food services have been added in recent years, including agreements with commercial fast food organizations to establish units on campus.

The two professional organizations serving college and university food service personnel are the National Association of College and University Food Services (NACUFS) and the Association of College and University Housing Officers—International (ACUHO-I). They jointly sponsor the eight-week NACUFS–ACUHO-I Food Service Management Training Program, which offers outstanding internship experience for junior students in hospitality education programs.

School Food Service

School food service generally refers to the provision of meals to schoolchildren attending elementary through high school. This may include children participating in preschool programs. As with college and university food service, school food service offers excellent career challenges for hospitality education graduates.

Historically, some schools were serving meals to schoolchildren prior to 1900. According to Powers, school food service gained momentum in the larger U.S. cities before World War I and became established as local agencies by the end of World War II. Concern for the nutrition of poor children, concern for the national interest, the need to stimulate demand for agricultural produced, and the need to accommodate young people too far from home all helped to build support for the school lunch program before World War II.[5]

The National School Lunch Program was established by the federal government after World War II. Only 32% of the U.S. schools participated in the government school lunch program in 1950; however, more than 90% were participating in 1981.[5] Provisions of the law assured a nutritiously balanced, low-cost meal to all children and free or reduced-price meals to low-income students. Free food commodities and government reimbursements enable the reasonable pricing of school meals.

Similar to the college and university food service organization, the school food service director is the highest ranking food service administrator. Most larger school districts require the food service director to have at least a bachelor's degree in a food service–related program, such as food service management, dietetics, hotel and restaurant management, or home economics education. The responsibilities of the school food service director are similar to those of the university food service director.

Larger school districts also employ professionally trained personnel as area coordinators or supervisors. The areas may include a specified geographical locale with several school food service operations or may represent levels of schools (e.g., elementary or secondary schools). The primary responsibility of an area coordinator or supervisor is to work with the mangers of the individual school food service units to ensure that quality, nutritious meals are served efficiently and that established policies and practices are followed.

Most unit managers began their careers as food service workers or cooks and enjoy considerable success and satisfaction. Some school districts will seek professionally educated managers for especially large food service units. Unit managers are often the key to an effective school food service program. They represent the food service program on a daily basis to students, teachers, and parents. They are responsible for meal quality and service and making the system work.

Rieley and Spears defined three school food service systems. The conventional system is one in which food is prepared and served in the same facility. The satellite system is one in which food is prepared in a central kitchen and transported hot to another site for service. The third is a variation of the satellite system which has a finishing kitchen with a small convection oven and food steamer at the service site. Food items that do not retain an acceptable quality standard during transport are prepared at the satellite site.[6]

Although the luncheon meal is the usual activity of school food service organizations, many programs do considerably more. Catering to special school functions such as receptions, snacks, and athletic banquets is common. Breakfast service has become important in some districts. Meal service may also be provided for preschool day care programs, meals-on-wheels to the elderly, and summer recreational activities in certain localities.

The professional organization service school food service personnel is the American School Food Service Association (ASFSA). ASFSA sponsors various services and educational programs for its approximately 65,000 members.

Health Care Food Service

Health care food service usually consists of hospital and nursing home dietary services. Residential retirement centers and other extended care facilities also include food service operations with similar dietary and health care services.

Professional career opportunities in health care food service are numerous and certainly challenging. Because of certain government regulations and other factors, those responsible for the administration of health care organizations are faced with increased financial pressures to become more efficient and more creative in their operations. Greater competition among health care providers has changed management philosophies, resulting in an emphasis on marketing. The patient or resident is also viewed as a consumer requiring special services and amenities. Likewise, visitors and the health care staff are increasingly recognized as consumers who can contribute to the financial success of the dietary operation.

The chief of head of the dietary services usually reports to the administrator of the health care facility. Figure 2 illustrates the functional organization of a typical large dietary department and the potential career path from assistant supervisor to director.

In most hospitals, the chief or head of dietary services is a registered dietitian and may therefore be referred to as an administrative dietitian. Because of the growing concern for financial efficiency, some health care administrators are turning to managers with business training (e.g., hotel and restaurant management or food service management graduates) to head the complex dietary services department.

Opportunities for the registered dietitian are several in health care food service. In addition to food production and service supervisory positions, the registered dietitian may serve as a clinical dietitian working with patients on matters related to special dietary needs or as a consulting dietitian to small hospitals, nursing homes, medical clinics, and other health care organizations. Some dietitians are teaming with physical fitness professionals to offer wellness programs in health clubs, resorts, and as independent entrepreneurs.

Health care organizations continue to offer the traditional patient and public food services, but there are significant changes that may suggest that interesting trends are under way. One is the offering of fine dining experiences for patients and guest, both in the patient's room and in special dining rooms or areas. Menus may include such items as beef Wellington, prime rib, chateaubriand for two, and flambé desserts—all this with a favorite wine.

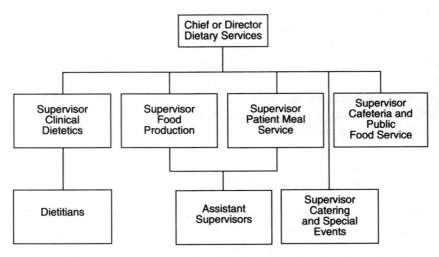

Figure 2. A Typical Large Health Care Food Service Organization

Another trend is the invasion of fast food outlets in hospitals to cater to staff and visitors. Hayes reported in the February 12, 1990 issue of *Nation's Restaurant News* that McDonald's, Pizza Hut, Little Caesars Pizza, Wendy's, and Burger King have established footholds in U.S. hospitals. McDonald's was reported as having 18 units in health care establishments. Many of these fast food operations have expanded their menus or altered aspects of their products to meet certain nutritional standards.[7]

A challenging and enjoyable aspect of health care food service is the varied and frequent caterings and special events. The expertise of many dietary staffs in planning and executing catered events would be envied by many hotel food and beverage executives. Medical board dinners, receptions, retirement parties, awards dinner, patient room service, and other special activities add an important dimension to the careers of health care food service professionals.

Military Food Service

Food service activities in the military are funded by either appropriated government allocations or nonappropriated revenues generated by the activities themselves. Appropriated funds are used to feed soldiers, sailors, marines, and air force personnel where they are assigned for duty, such as at base camps and stations, on field maneuvers, aboard ships and aircraft, and in combat situations.

Most food service personnel in locations using appropriated funds are military personnel, many of whom have the same food service career interests in their civilian counterparts. For example, 15 U.S. Army cooks were selected to participate on the Army's International Culinary Olympic Team in October 1992 in Frankfurt, Germany.[8] The Olympic competition attracts the world's best chefs and culinary professionals.

The nonappropriated funded military food services include exchange services and clubs for officers, noncommissioned officers, and other military personnel. These services range from vending, quick service (fast food), cafeteria and table service dining, fine dining, and catering services. Trends include developing brand-name fast-food concepts including food courts, increased availability of nutrition information while promoting consumption of lower-fat and-calorie foods, and use of computerized systems.[9]

Opportunities for graduates of two-year and four-year hospitality education programs are excellent, both as military and civilian food service professionals. While most appropriated units use military personnel, the exchange and club services are increasingly staffed by civilian personnel.

Correctional Food Service

Possibly the segment of the food service industry least discussed in programs of hospitality administration and dietetics is correctional food service. In fact, the correctional market has the fastest growing population of any institutional food service segment.[10]

While inmate numbers are increasing rapidly, cuts in budgets, staff, and supply of government commodities are among the top challenges to correctional food service administrators. Overcrowding means that some food service facilities are producing two or more times the number of food items and meals when they were designed to prepare, thus causing unanticipated wear and tear on equipment.[10] J. Michael Quinlan, director of the Federal Bureau of Prisons, warned correctional food service personnel to prepare for more budget cuts in the 1990s and challenged them to become as cost effective as possible.[11]

There are some unique features that differentiate correctional food service operations. Although many have key civilian staff members, they also rely heavily on inmates. Such staffing usually requires special security procedures, including accounting for knives and other utensils that might be smuggled as contraband from the kitchen to other areas in the institution. Also, civilian food service workers are frequently trained as correctional officers and prepared to serve at guard posts.[12]

Career opportunities for graduates of hospitality administration programs include serving as food service supervisors and directors at individual institutions, as regional managers and corporate administrators with contract food service management companies, and as food service coordinators for statewide correctional food service systems.

Career Considerations in Institutional Food Service

Institutional food service offers numerous advantages to graduate of hospitality education programs. Wages and benefits are at least competitive with those of commercial food services. Opportunities for advancement are excellent. Working hours are usually relatively normal, with five-day, 40- to 50-hour weeks common, especially among self-operated institutional food services. Vacation time is often more liberal.

Many contract food management companies experience considerable success in the institutional sector and offer outstanding career growth possibilities at the unit, regional, and corporate levels. The ten largest organizations are listed in Table 1. Other excellent contract food management companies are listed in R&I 400.[4]

——References——

1. Iverson, Kathleen M. (1989) *Introduction to Hospitality Management*. New York: Van Nostrand Reinhold. p. 42.
2. Gotschall, Beth. Giants Step Forward. *Restaurants and Institutions*. October 16, 1989; pp. 46–54.
3. Courting Branded Concepts. *Food Management*. July 1992; p. 95.
4. R&I 400: Ranking and Segments. *Restaurants and Institutions*. July 8, 1992; pp. 32–33, 52.
5. Powers, Thomas F. *Introduction to Management in the Hospitality Industry*. Second edition. New York: John Wiley and Sons. p. 87.
6. Rieley, D. M. and M. C. Spears. *Evaluation of Three Alternative School Foodservice Systems*. 1985 Abstracts. The American Dietetic Association, p. 106.
7. Hayes, Jack. Hospital Fast Food: Big Chains Adjust *Nation's Restaurant News*. February 12, 1990; p. 1.
8. Army Selects 15 Olympians. *Food Management*. May 1992, p. 107.
9. R&I 400: Military. *Restaurants and Institutions*. July 8, 1992. p. 131.
10. R&I 400: Institutions. *Restaurants and Institutions*. July 8, 1992. p. 175.
11. Newsline: Government Institutions. *Food Management*. October 1990. p. 128.
12. Florida DOC Locks In Its Future . *Food Management*. August 1990. p. 132.

41

Contract Food Service Management: Business and Industry, Airlines, and Concessions

Polly Buchanan
Eastern Michigan University

Business and Industry Food Service Operations

One of the largest divisions in most contract food service companies is the B&I division, which serves business and industry. This segment of the company operates food service facilities in company executive dining rooms and in company cafeterias feeding factory or plant workers, and company white collar workers such as supervisors, managers, and office personnel.

Such employee feeding operations have been called industrial food service, the company cafeteria, or in-plant feeding. Such facilities often bring to mind an image of a plain room with straight, uncomfortable furniture, and stainless steel food counters displaying assorted casseroles. This was an accurate image years ago, but consider the following description of a modern business and industry food service operation.

> As you enter the dining area, you are greeted with soft music, carpeted floors, relaxing colors on the walls with appropriate artwork, comfortable chairs, and an atmosphere similar to an upscale restaurant. Colorful food counters display assorted homemade soups, made-to-order sandwiches, and a self-select salad and ice cream sundae bar are but a few of the scenes awaiting today's industrial cafeteria customer.

This setting encourages employees to eat on the premises and discourages eating lunch out. While some workers have a noon meal break long enough to allow off-premises eating, others are limited to shorter meal breaks that only allow two choices: eat in the company cafeteria or "brown bag it" and bring lunch from home.

A challenge to increase customer participation is posed to all B&I food service managers today. The manager must try to increase the percentage of employees who eat in the company cafeteria compared to the total number of employees who could eat there. This is called the participation rate or ratio and usually averages from 40% to 60% depending on the competition in the neighborhood and the length of meal breaks allowed by company policy.

Today, B&I food service includes feeding a wide range of customers; blue-collar hourly workers in a factory, white collar supervisors and office personnel, and top corporate executives in elegant dining rooms. With such a wide spectrum of customers, the B&I food service manager is challenged to provide varied food and services for each, often from the same kitchen. Menu design to meet the needs of these diverse groups thus becomes a key planning activity that influences everything from food purchasing and production to food service.

Some employee food service operations are operated by the company itself (self-operated or self-op); in others, the company makes an agreement with a food service contract management company, which provides managers, or managers and employees, to operate the food service. Contract management companies operate many B&I food services in this country today, so they can offer a variety of employment opportunities to graduates of two- and four-year hospitality programs.

Historical Perspective on Employee (or Industrial) Feeding

In-plant feeding was the term first used for food service provided to employees. The practice can be documented as far back as 1815 in Scotland. Robert Owen, the manager of a mill there, is credited as being the father of industrial catering. He established a large eating room for his employees to use for their meal breaks. In the United States, the first in-plant feeding was provided in the cotton mills in Massachusetts around 1820. Besides dining rooms for employees, these mills often provided boardinghouses for female staff members.[1] Such facilities were needed to encourage potential female workers from rural areas to move to emerging urban areas for employment. Such facilities made it possible for more and more young people to consider employment opportunities away from the family farm.

Throughout the 1800s, other employee feeding facilities opened. The Bowery Savings Bank in New York began serving lunch to employees in 1834. By 1890 many factories, department stores, and telephone companies began to serve lunch to their employees either free or below cost.[2] The nation continued to move away from an agricultural economy to an industrial one, in which people moved away from farms, into towns and cities. Lunch eaten away from home became a way of life.

While the field of employee feeding evolved and changed greatly over the decades, the basic philosophy behind this service remained the same. If workers were healthy and not hungry, they would be more productive while at work. Company food service operations also provided *hot* meals with the convenience of being in the same building.

Up until World War II and after, employee feeding could be described as dull, basic, routine, no-frills feeding. Dining rooms were plain, with minimal decoration, and the food was plain. But attitudes were changing among management and employees. Management began to realize that the employee dining area could provide a needed change of environment for workers while on their breaks.[4] Such change encouraged relaxation and provided a mind break from the routine of plant work. When workers returned to their jobs, they were refreshed, more productive, and made fewer errors.

As noted earlier, food was provided to workers free or for low cost in the early years of employee feeding. Management considered this expense to be another employee benefit cost. However, when profits began to drop and the economy became less healthy, free or low-cost meals was often an employee benefit that was eliminated. The psychology of "no one appreciates anything free" may have also played a role in this decision, but the free lunch has all but disappeared today in employee food service operations. While some facilities receive minimal corporate subsidies, most operations today must maintain a break-even financial status, not losing money nor making a profit.

Job Responsibilities of B&I Food Service Managers

The primary job responsibilities of entry-level B&I food service managers include several key functions. They can be summarized as follows:

- Write menus that service the needs of customers.
- Order foods and supplies as needed.
- Hire and train needed employees.
- Supervise food production and service.
- Maintain positive relationships with customers and clients.
- Keep records needed to determine cost-effectiveness of operation.

It should be noted that as a B&I food service manager, job responsibilities may also include more than managing the cafeteria and an executive dining room. Filling vending machines for off-hours, shift feeding, or overseeing a contractor who fills the vending machines may be a part of the job responsibilities. Mobile unit feeding from specially designed trucks may also be the cafeteria manager's responsibility. This requires designing menus with transportable foods such as individually wrapped sandwiches and dessert items, portioned soups and salads, and individual beverages. Each mobile unit has an established route each day, often within an industrial complex or area that has no cafeteria facility. The unit parks for 20 to 30 minutes at each stop, and plant and office workers to come to the truck and purchase foods they want.

Today's B&I Customer

Today's customers, whether eating in the employee cafeteria or at a restaurant, demand their money's worth. They are cost and value conscious and expect the variety of foods and services offered at their workplace to equal what they buy at restaurants. Employee feeding is no longer feasible as a simple employee meal service. Today, employee cafeteria customers want the same quality, variety, service, and convenience they can purchase in any restaurant. To be successful, this requires the B&I food service manager to market available foods and services, track check averages, seek new sources of revenues such as catering within or outside the building, and employ creative merchandising techniques to increase participation.

Nutritional concerns of today's company cafeteria customer have had a great influence on menus and food preparation in recent years. A greater percentage of today's customers are concerned about overall health and wellness. They want to be able to buy healthy foods in the company cafeteria, such as more fresh fruits and vegetables, cooked vegetables without butter and salt, regular or decaffeinated beverages. They want fewer fried foods, fewer red meat entrees, and salt-free preparation, so they can add desired seasonings individually. Cafeteria customers also want low-calorie choices in beverages, salad dressings, gelatin salads, and desserts. While providing additional food varieties for customers may complicate kitchen production, employers support this trend because healthy workers have fewer heart attacks, handle stress on the job better, and often use fewer sick days.

Another factor that has influenced employee feeding operations has occurred because of lifestyle practices and expectations of today's workers. Besides their increased interest in better nutrition as a lifestyle change, workers want their meal break to be a truly relaxing time. They want surroundings similar to the dining room at home with comfortable chairs, relaxing music in the background, a decor that is natural, with plants and sunlight, and acoustics that lower the normal business din of the dining room. The era of stainless steel serving counters, plain white walls, straight wooden chairs, and noise is gone . . .thank heaven!

A sociological trend—the prevalence of the two-income family—has created a new employee need and a new revenue-generating opportunity for B&I food service managers. With both husband and wife working in many families, the demand for carry-out foods from the company cafeteria has increased. For many operations it began with baked products; birthday and anniversary cakes, cookies by the dozen, pies, and muffins. Items such as pizza (whole, unbaked), lasagna, BBQ ribs, fried chicken, and salads were often added to the offerings so that preparing dinner after a long workday became an easy task.

Unique Facets of Business and Industry Food Service Operations

Several unique internal challenges influence the day-to-day operation of B&I food service operations.

1. Open hours of operation vary in each B&I location and may be the result of collective bargaining agreements with local unions. From a minimum of lunch only, Monday through Friday, to a maximum of breakfast, lunch, dinner and midnight feeding seven days a week, are possibilities.

2. Most employees prefer to eat lunch between 12 and 1 P.M., so to avoid customers queuing up, the manager may work with company department heads to stagger lunch breaks every 15 minutes between 11:30 and 1:30.

3. Because some B&I operations are located in unionized organizations, the food service workers may also be unionized and may belong to the same union as the plant workers. This generally causes wage rates of food service workers to be well above the levels paid to workers in regular food service unions in the area.

4. A source of added revenue for an employee food service is to do catering for company events. This can involve complete meals or just beverage breaks, but does put added production pressure on kitchen personnel.
5. Another source of added revenue is to provide carry-out foods such as baked goods, pizza, lasagna, BBQ ribs, fried chicken, and salads. This market has developed with the prevalence of two-income families in which both husband and wife work full-time and a source of ready-prepared, quality food is desired.

What Lies Ahead?

The influence of baby boomers* and DINK[†] may be felt in employee cafeterias and dining rooms to an even greater extent in the coming years. These people receive good salaries and have the money to buy above-average menu items. Cafeterias may find customers demanding more expensive items such as orange roughy, lobster, chicken cordon bleu, and steaks served in attractive, upscale dining rooms. These customers may also request that gourmet foods be available as a carry-out (or take-home) food in single servings or in bulk form.

There is a continuing trend today toward higher service expectations when people eat away from home. Whether in a family restaurant, hotel dining room, or a company cafeteria, customers want friendly, timely, and accurate service. They want interaction with food servers who are concerned about their needs, knowledgeable about the foods they serve, and perform as if they enjoy their jobs. Mediocre service without a smile will not be tolerated. Superior service will be required to keep patrons returning to the employee food service operation.

Customer interest in nutrition and health will continue, but the food service manager may find a greater need to plan healthful food promotions and specials with the help of a registered dietitian. This trained professional can provide nutritional information about specific foods on the menu, especially the fat, cholesterol, calorie, and salt content. Working with the cafeteria chef, the dietitian can recommend ways to reduce the amounts of saturated fats, cholesterol, calories, and salt in recipes and yet have a tasty, acceptable end product.

Computerization will continue to make major inroads in the operation of employee food services. This may take the form of meal payroll-deduction systems in which no money is exchanged in the cafeteria or dining room. The cost of an employee's meals will be automatically deducted from his paycheck through the corporate computer system. Debit card systems are also emerging whereby a sum of money is deposited by an employee into an account, and a credit type card is issued. Each time a food item is purchased, the card is entered into the cash register and the amount of that food is subtracted from the employee's

---

* Well-educated, high-income, young to middle-aged professionals

[†] Families with *Double Income, No Kids*

running account. This card system eliminates the need for any transfer of cash in the dining room or cafeteria. Debit cards can also be programmed for use in vending machines, thus eliminating the need for coin purchases.

An interesting new service is being added for employees in some companies; an on-premises, small C-store (convenience store). These facilities provide assorted amenities and products such as drugstore items, food snacks (even donuts and soft-serve ice cream), and newspapers and magazines. The operation of such facilities often falls under the responsibility of the B&I food service manager.

Summary

The field of B&I or employee food service is a stable but dynamic one that provides managers with a traditional framework within which to work, but allows creativity in customizing services for the company. Employee food service is based on the premise that healthy workers will be happy and productive, and the B&I food service manager plays a key role in accomplishing this goal. As customers demand change and new trends emerge, the cafeteria manager is presented with constant challenges to implement new ideas within traditional settings. Whether run by the company itself or contracted to an outside firm, employee food service will always be a substantial part of the food service industry.

Airline or In-flight Food Service Operation

Providing tasty, appetizing meals to customers thousands of feet in the air is a tremendous challenge. Airline food service, often called in-flight feeding, has expanded and improved as techniques and equipment in food transport, food holding, and end heating have been developed and improved over the years.

Historical Perspective on In-Flight Feeding

The first in-flight meal was served in 1937 by J. Williard Marriott to American and Eastern Airline passengers out of Washington, D.C.[5] The meal served was similar to a box lunch. In those early years, the foods provided were generally cold or room temperature and travelers ate on their laps. Few specific regulations existed then to oversee safety provisions for in-flight food service operations. Years later, however, an incident occurred on a domestic flight where food served contained a foodborne pathogen (bacteria). The passengers *and* the crew who ate it all got very ill. With both pilots *very* sick, landing the plane safely was difficult but accomplished. This unfortunate flight led to the regulation that requires pilots and copilots not to eat the same food 24 hours before flight time, or during the flight. Thus, on every in-flight food delivery, there is one completely different meal for the pilot to eat.

Today's In-Flight Feeding Operation

Today's in-flight food service providers are either airline owned (such as Sky Chef, a subsidiary of American Airlines) or operated by outside food contract companies such as CaterAir who agree to provide food service on flights and in airports. Foods provided on flights are now both hot and cold, attractively plated and nicely garnished—not like the old box lunch. Menus are even coordinated and cycled to avoid a passenger getting the same meal on connecting flights. Special diet meals can also be provided to passengers who order them in advance, including bland, low calorie, diabetic, low cholesterol, low sodium, Kosher, and vegetarian.

A contract company that provides meals for several airlines (often six to ten or more) has several unique operational challenges to face. Each airline provides its own set of menus for the food service manager to produce, which includes different foods and recipes for each flight class served. This puts great pressure on the kitchen production department. In addition, for each flight class, different china, glassware, flatware, and placemats are required by the airline. Storage of these different items for each airline requires a lot of space, and maintaining adequate inventories of each item requires frequent, time-consuming monitoring. Dish and china inventory is a particularly unique challenge in a flight kitchen as thousands of filled dishes leave the kitchen daily and thousands of dirty dishes are received daily off incoming flights. The number and style of dishes sent out never is the same as the number received so maintaining adequate inventories can be a big challenge for the in-flight food service manager.

Communication relevant to time changes of flight departures is closely monitored by the production manager in any flight kitchen. Knowing the exact time to begin plating passenger food is always difficult to determine in order to keep foods fresh and holding times to a minimum. Thus, flight delays are one of the biggest frustrations for in-flight food service managers.

Flights depart at all hours of the day and night, so a flight kitchen must be staffed for round-the-clock service, seven days a week, holidays included. Flight kitchen employees, however, often have the same flight privileges as airline employees, traveling at low cost but on a standby basis.[6]

Summary

The airline industry will always be an active component of our society, particularly as international travel and business increase. While full-service meals on flights have decreased somewhat in a cost-savings effort, management opportunities for employment in kitchens that provide airline and airport food service will always be good. Travelers expect a beverage or snack, even on short flights, and food service in airline terminals will always be needed. Thus, employment opportunities in airline food services will always be good.

Concessions Management

Ever eaten a hot dog at the ball park? Ever bought a cold soda pop at a beach concession stand in the state park? Ever eaten popcorn when you attended a movie? Chances are that these food service operations were run by a concessions management company. These companies specialize in providing food in recreational and leisure settings by contract with government and private facilities.

Americans are active; they use their leisure time to enjoy relaxing activities that often involve some kind of food consumption, be it a full meal or just a snack. Therefore, almost every tourist attraction, park, or recreational facility will provide a food concession for the pleasure and satisfaction of visitors. The National Association of Concessionaires (NAC) identifies the following facilities as typical concession sites.[7]

- Stadiums and arenas
- Zoos
- Amusement and theme parks
- Baseball parks
- Historical sites
- Tourist attractions
- Fairs and expositions

- Movie theaters
- National parks
- State and local parks
- Racetracks
- Convention centers
- Ski resorts
- Auditoriums

"Save the Planet"

One unique aspect of park concessions today is the general public concern about saving our environment and preserving the resources that exist on our planet. Since the beginning of the National Park Service in this country, its mandate has been to encourage visitation while preserving the environment.[8] To encourage visitors to come to parks, concessions management within the park may include the operation of hotels, food service, campgrounds, hostels, marinas, tour operations, rental facilities, and retail stores offering food, general merchandise, apparel, and souvenirs.[9] With the provision of such visitor services and comforts, preserving the natural beauty of the park areas with minimum technical and man-made impact becomes both a challenge and a dilemma. Ecotourism (or responsible tourism) is now a growing trend that implies responsible travel with guest accommodations that conserve the natural environs and also supports the well-being of local communities. Provision of concession facilities as a part of the park system, and the preservation of the natural park, are thus both integral components of these operations and must coexist for a mutually beneficial partnership.

An advantage of concessions management in almost any setting is the often simplified menu offered. Few food items are generally served, so purchasing, preparation, and service also are simplified. However, in some sports arenas there are fine dining facilities provided for special club members and guests.

Job Responsibilities of Concessions Managers

The responsibilities of concessions managers resemble those of B&I food service managers with a few modifications.

- Write menus that service the needs of customers.
- Project food and supplies needed based on estimated attendance figures.
- Hire, train, and schedule workers, usually part-time, temporary, or volunteer.*
- Check operation of all equipment at every location; arrange for replacements as needed.
- Supervise food production and service; monitor back-up storage and restocking of foods and supplies.
- Carefully monitor and control cash flow from every location.
- Maintain positive relationships with customers and clients.
- Keep records needed to determine cost-effectiveness of operations.

Concessions managers may also oversee the operation of vending machines that are located within a facility. These may be filled with foods prepared on-site, from products brought from a centralized food production facility, or purchased from an outside vendor.

Work hours for concessions managers often vary depending on the activities scheduled. Thus, an 8-to-5, Monday-through-Friday schedule is usually rare. In facilities that are seasonal, such as parks or ski resorts, certain months may require the manager to work longer hours due to the high level of business. However, during the off season, managers are able to work shorter hours and fewer days per week. These off season days may be used by managers to rewrite manuals and procedure books, test recipes, and design employee training materials.

Summary

Concessions management is a vast industry, with locations in many different settings and environments. Companies that provide management services for concession operations offer a variety of management positions, both full-time and part-time. With the continued growth in the travel and tourism industry worldwide, opportunities for employment in concessions management will certainly expand.

How to Get In

How can a recent graduate qualify for an entry-level position in a particular segment of the hospitality industry? With dozens of choices available, how can a recent graduate decide which segment of the hospitality industry would be right? Getting a part-time or summer job

---

* Often community groups (i.e., United Way, churches) volunteer to staff concessions stands in exchange for a portion of the profits from the stand they operate, the money going toward their charity. Such arrangements provide needed resources for the community group and they, in turn, provide needed workers for the concession operation. Such relationships, once established, have continued for years in some facilities to the benefit of both parties.

in a particular area would be the best solution, so that first-hand experience is gained. Co-ops or internships required as part of an undergraduate curriculum provide another opportunity to experience a particular segment of the hospitality industry. Discuss your interests with a program advisor.

A successful food service manager in B&I, airline feeding or concessions management needs food production knowledge and experience as well as strong human resource management skills, especially verbal communication.[10] Thus, if you desire a job in one of these areas, seek work experiences in summer jobs, co-ops, or internships that provide opportunities to learn food production standards and procedures, and develop strong human resource skills including verbal communication. Positions that provide such professional experiences will prepare you to successfully enter the hospitality industry as a food service manager.

——References——

1. Stokes, John W. (1973) *Food Service in Industry and Institutions.* Dubuque, Ia.: William C. Brown. p. 2.
2. Villella, Joseph A. (1975) *The Hospitality Industry—The World of Food Service.* New York: McGraw-Hill. p. 26.
3. Anderson, Henry W. (1976) *The Modern Food Service Industry.* Dubuque, Ia.: William C. Brown. p. 52.
4. Lundberg, Donald E. (1989) *The Hotel and Restaurant Business.* New York: Van Nostrand Reinhold. p. 231.
5. McCool, Audrey C. (1991) Contract Foodservice Management. In Robert Brymer's *Hospitality Management—An Introduction to the Industry.* Dubuque, Ia.: Kendall/Hunt. p. 488.
6. O'Halloran, Robert O. Concessions in National Parks: Responsible Tourism. *FIU Hospitality Review.* Spring 1993; Volume 11, Number 1: p. 32.
7. U.S. Department of the Interior. *National Park Service Concessions Management Guidelines.* NPS–48, 1984.

42

Health Club Management

Linsley T. DeVeau
Lynn University

Introduction

The health and fitness industry is experiencing explosive growth. In fact, the annual revenues produced by this segment of the hospitality industry are more than $17 billion. Adults are more concerned than ever with their physical appearance and abilities. This concern has created a tremendous demand for health clubs across the country. Presently there are more than 33,000 health club facilities in the United States, which are found in a variety of settings.

Health Club Locations

Corporate

Many companies are providing their employees with health club services such as exercise and wellness programs. These programs are seen as an investment in the health and welfare of the company's most important assets, its employees. Quite often, companies have an in-house health club, which they own and operate. In other instances companies will pay all or most of its employees' membership fees.

Community

Other opportunities for health club memberships exist in YMCA and Jewish Community Center programs. These organizations offer health club activities to individuals, families, and corporations. These programs are especially popular among families because of the variety of family activities and services that are offered in addition to the diverse health and wellness programs.

Health care in hospitals is seeing an expansion into the health promotion area. Health and wellness is receiving a great deal of attention in the hospital setting. Many hospitals are developing or planning to develop fitness centers as a component of their health promotion activities.

Commercial

The type of health club that is most familiar to most people has been the single-purpose club, such as the racquetball or tennis club. Over the past few years, we have seen a movement away from this single-purpose type of club to the multipurpose health club. Such health clubs bring a change from the earlier indoor-only concept of fitness to an indoor–outdoor, four-season concept. The need for such a system is apparent when one explores the number and variety of health and fitness activities that the average health enthusiast engages in.

Health Club Management Functions

It is simple enough to segregate health clubs according to their location: corporate, community, and commercial. These different health club operations all require their own set of programs based upon the needs and demands of the markets they serve. In addition to location and market demands, health clubs also must design their programs to keep up with changes in the health and fitness industry along with the demands of increased competition. Health club management has three major functional areas: **marketing, program development,** and **administration.** Depending on the location of the health club, these functions will take on a differing degree of importance.

In a community type of health club, which includes hospitals, YMCA, park and recreation departments, and university programs, the three functions of marketing, program development, and administration all play an equal role in the success of the operation. Managers of such operations must remember to balance these functions with the mission of the organization within which they are contained.

In the corporate health club sector, the function of program development receives the most attention. The purpose of corporate clubs is to improve the health and wellness of employees, and to keep employees involved in these programs. Some of the more common programs found in the corporate area are exercise classes, diet planning, quit-smoking programs, and stress management.

Commercial health clubs in the past have placed a great deal of their attention in the marketing area, which has been aimed at selling memberships. Considering that these operations are run on a for-profit basis, this is no surprise. The consequences of this focus, however, in many cases produced negative results. With such a heavy emphasis on selling memberships, the development of programs and staff members was neglected. This led to a new emphasis on the function of administration. By emphasizing administration, commercial health clubs have been able to develop a balance, which has resulted in sufficient numbers of new members, hiring of a talented staff, and creation of appropriate new programs. Members recruited, are retained, assuring the long-term viability of the club.

Marketing

The marketing function includes the areas of promotion, advertising, and research. Marketing works to create a situation in which the consumer wants, and acquires, the services that the club is offering.

Initially, the marketing function focuses on the development of a mission for the health club. In determining the mission of the health club, the organizers must ask themselves the question, what business are we in? For example, is the focus in weight training, racquetball, or stress management? After this initial questioning, the organization will have a main area to focus on.

Next, planners must choose which market area the health club facility will serve. Also, will the health club product be kept in one location, or do the planners intend at some point to expand the concept and offer it on a state, regional, or national level? Following this decision, planners must decide who will make up the customer base of the health club. Possible customers include individuals, families, seniors, and companies. The customer base is an important area, in that it determines the types of programs offered as well as the design of the club and the membership dues.

A competitive analysis of existing health clubs in the area is needed. Planners need to determine what types of programs and services are offered by these other clubs, their strengths and weaknesses, the projected new club's position in the marketplace relative to them. Once the competitive analysis has been prepared, planners can graphically display the data and use it to improve the club's offerings. The marketing staff can use this data for comparison when selling the new club to potential members.

After the competitive analysis has been completed, the information can be used in determining the image the marketing staff chooses to create for the new club. As is the case with the other hospitality industry businesses, the health club business is part of the service industry. Therefore, the new club's physical appearance and the employees' appearance and behavior will be the initial information that potential members and new members will use to formulate their opinions about the club. It is critical that the image that the marketing staff wants to convey to these people is the image that in fact they receive. Remember, the customer's perception of the club is what matters, not what the managers or owners perceive it to be!

In the initial stages of any new business, owners must have enough capital to carry it through the early days of operation. This rule also applies to health clubs. The start-up of a health club requires considerable advertising and promotion. In the beginning of the business's life, owners or managers will need to allocate somewhere between 10% and 15% of revenue to advertising and promotion. Then, once the business is established, up to 10% will still be needed for advertising and promotion.

Program Development

The starting point of program development for a health club is the answers to the following questions: What do my customers want? What is the market demanding? Many businesses start out successfully only to fail later on. The major cause of such business failure is neglect of changes in the marketplace and emerging demand for different products and services. That is to say, once you have developed your programs you must understand that they will need to change as your customer's needs change. If you do not change your programs in line with customer needs, your club will become outdated and you will find your customers shifting over to another club that has responded to the market.

The first step in program development is to conduct a needs assessment. The needs assessment helps determine what programs should be offered to meet the preferences of the health club's customers. A needs assessment will be conducted differently for different types of clubs.

In a corporate location, the first part of the needs assessment will be conducted to learn what corporate management thinks should be offered, followed by employee input, information received from any employee committee established to study the matter, and the results of testing or screening of employees to evaluate health needs. The needs then are compared with the employees' areas of interest, and programs are developed within the financial constraints set forth in the form of a project budget. Corporate health programs are not usually revenue producing, so they must be developed within the boundaries of an employee benefits budget.

The community health club location will begin its needs assessment with a market analysis, which surveys the community to determine its needs as well as surveying current members. Along with these surveys, information can be obtained from various community health–related agencies such as the American Red Cross. Area doctors also will be able to contribute information on the health needs of an areas's population. Other programs that are currently operating can be contacted for their input. One of the largest in most areas is the city's or town's department of recreation.

In program development for the commercial health club location, the starting point is the same as that for the community health clubs. First, planners need to survey the marketplace. The marketplace for a chain operation could be nationwide as well as local. Next, the club's owners and investors will contribute their ideas, for it is these two groups that ultimately are responsible for the financial success of the operation. Another group critical to the long-term success of the operation is the current membership. It is much easier and less expensive to keep current members enrolled than it is to recruit new members to the club.

Administration

Health club administration includes human resources management, financial management, equipment selection and maintenance, food and beverage management, pro shop management, member services management, and safety management.

Safety Management

The one area of administration in the hospitality industry that has received increased attention over past few years is safety management. Health clubs are no exception to this trend. In fact, due to the nature of their business, they not only must focus on the typical safety concerns of the hospitality industry but must also concentrate on their own set of safety issues as well.

One of the most common types of accidents occurring today in hospitality industry businesses is the slip-and-fall accident, and health clubs are no exception to its possible occurrence. Slip-and-fall accidents have many possible causes, some of which include inadequate lighting, poor property maintenance, and design errors. In the case of stairways, poor step design, lack of a handrail or faulty design of one, wrong carpet pattern design choice, lack of warning signs, lack of safety strips, lack of proper step nosing, lack of a nonslip surface, and the failure to use appropriate safety warning color markings are some of the elements that can create a hazardous condition.

In a health club, a safety management program has unique areas to cover. Consideration must be given to the design of facilities such as swimming pools, whirlpools, saunas, steam rooms, locker rooms, exercise rooms, and workout areas. For example, in a swimming pool or whirlpool the access steps' treads and risers should meet design requirements, have handrails extending past the top and bottom treads, have colored tile on the nose of each step, and be nonslip; in the case of a swimming pool, the bottom step should be recessed. One of the best ways to ensure that you have a safe environment in your health club is to hire a safety consultant to evaluate your club and then form a safety committee that will continue to monitor your club's safety program, as well as seeing that all of your employees are trained in safety management.

The Future of Health Club Management

While many trends could be mentioned in a discussion of the future of health clubs, some of the more significant ones will be explored here.

Fitness programs for the older segment of the population are on the increase, especially as the baby boomers move closer to retirement. These people created the demand for health clubs, so it is only natural to assume that they will continue health clubs use to meet their health and fitness needs through new and different programs.

Certification programs will continue to be important. A great many certification programs are available today. More than fifty associations and organizations offer certifications in the health and fitness area. In the future, better regulation of the certification area would be helpful to the industry as well as its consumers.

Technology continues to improve, bringing new and better ways to operate health clubs. Virtual reality will have significant impacts on the settings in which people may exercise. Through virtual reality, health club clients may experience many different simulated environments without ever leaving the health club's exercise room.

43

The Catering Industry

John C. Baker
Indiana University of Pennsylvania

Introduction

The catering and banquet industry is booming and has become the fastest growing segment of the food service industry. Catering has come of age.

Traditionally, the catering business was dominated by social affairs, such as anniversaries, weddings, and bar mitzvahs. Today, however, it has found new markets in the corporate world, the arts, politics, and health care facilities to name a few.

A catered function can range from breakfast in bed for two at a private residence, an executive luncheon for ten in the company's board room, to a fund-raising dinner for a thousand at a private banquet hall or hotel ballroom.

Catering has increased revenues for food and beverage sales for a large number of restaurants and other food service industry businesses, both profit and non-profit oriented. Some of these businesses do so well in the catering business that they close their restaurants to become full-time caterers.

Definition

Catering is an industry in which the preparation and presentation of food and beverages for private and public affairs is the responsibility of one who has been trained in cooking, food purchasing, management, major cuisines, and social etiquette.

Catering requires creativity, efficiency, attention to detail and the ability to organize. It is hard work, requiring long hours, but it is profitable (with 20% gross profit range common). Catering is the only food and beverage service negotiated by a contract and is often prepaid in part (if not in full) with a 48-hour guarantee prior to the function.

Size and Scope

The size and scope of the catering industry is difficult to measure because the business is often incorporated into the normal food and beverage operations of hotels, restaurants, bakeries, delicatessens, grocery stores (with estimates of 18% of all grocery stores offering catering services), and supermarkets.

There are approximately 30,000 caterers in the United States today. (In 1968, the National Restaurant Association noted approximately 2,800 catering and automatic operations in the United States.) Caterers are generally found in the more populated states, such as California, New York, and New Jersey, because these states are more economically able to support them.

The catering business is segmented in size by gross sales. Most caterers (40%) fall into the $100,000 to $150,000 annual sales range. Thirty percent fall into the $150,000 to $340,000 annual sales range, while 20% fall into the $350,000 to $1 million annual sales range. The last 10% fall into the $1 million or more annual sales range category. One category of catering, the social caterer, is estimated to have gross sales that exceed $2.2 billion annually.

Industry Segmentation by Service Type

The catering industry can be segmented into various categories based on the services (or lack of services) that they provide for their clients. However, many of these categories overlap. For the purposes of this chapter, the catering industry is segmented into seven categories: on-premises catering; off-premises catering; accommodator or social catering; mobile catering or vending; retail business with catering services; wholesale caterer (one who prepares and sells food and beverage to a retail caterer); and lastly, event creators, who often are referred to as the artistic people.

On-Premises Caterer

In this type of business, the caterer usually owns, rents, or leases her own facility with an attached kitchen. This caterer offers a complete line of services and staff. This type of business is operated in an atmosphere similar to a restaurant; however, the facility is open only when an event is in progress and does not offer operating hours to the public.

On-premises catering is also referred to as banquet or private catering halls. The word *banquet* is derived from the French word *banc* or "bench," meaning that people sat on benches while partaking in a common meal, rather than haphazardly eating. Banquets can be traced back to the ancient Greeks, Romans, Egyptians, and Assyrians. These banquets lasted for days and the premises were decorated lavishly with silk, gold, and silver tapestries. Guests dressed in special garments and drank precious wines from golden vessels while they ate rare foods served on silver dishes passed by costumed slaves.

The on-premises caterer has several advantages over other caterers. He has a place to store food, food products, beverages, equipment, and supplies. Also, the on-premises caterer generally does not have to go to the client. The client comes to the caterer and uses the facility, which offers the caterer the advantage of working in a familiar location, not afforded when catering at the client's location.

In some parts of the country, liquor licenses are available to on-premises caterers who can realize a profit from the sale of alcoholic beverages.

The on-premise caterer is also faced with many disadvantages, such as overhead costs of operating a large property, taxes, parking, utilities, rent or mortgage, insurance, and upkeep.

Off-Premises Catering

Off-premises caterers usually have commissary or kitchen facilities, but they do not serve food on their premises. This limitation distinguishes them from the full-service caterer. Food prepared by these caterers is served off-site at a location selected by the client, which can be either indoors or out of doors.

Off-premises catering is the fastest-growing segment of the food service community. In addition to the private career caterer, many hotels, restaurants, gourmet food stores, hospitals, schools, department stores, and food contractors are beginning to offer off-premises catering services.

The advantages to operating an off-premises catering service include not having to furnish, equip, or maintain a dining facility. However, because the business is mobile, these caterers must rent or purchase equipment to transport all prepared food safely to the designated site.

The off-premises caterer is responsible for preparing, holding, packing, transporting, serving and cleaning up. She must also set up and take down the function.

The market for the off-premises caterer is unlimited because she can set up and serve almost anywhere. Off-premises work is quite specialized, and is often found in urban areas where the demand for such services is high. Also included in this segment are the concession-type agreements found in amusement parks, highway rest stops, and sports stadiums. However, such enterprises are not to be confused with the larger contract food service organizations.

Accommodator

The accommodator is also referred to as the individual or social caterer. He prepares and cooks the food on the client's premises, with the client supplying the food and equipment for a social function. The accommodator also serves the food and is responsible for cleaning up after the affair is over.

This is usually considered the easiest way of entering the catering business and is often a springboard for people who are interested in establishing a career in catering.

The accommodator does not have to worry about paying any overhead and spends very little on equipment. He does not have to invest in a commissary or food production area.

Also, an accommodator rarely hires staff. If there is a need for assistance, such as a server or bartender, the host will do the hiring. However, the accommodator will generally provide a list of associates who will assist at a function.

The disadvantages are that the accommodator is not provided with insurance plans or employer-generated social security benefits in later years, and he is also responsible for taking care of his federal and state income tax obligations.

Mobile Caterer or Vendor

The mobile caterer, often called the mobile vendor, is often not considered a full-fledged catering operation. However, these organizations are caterers because they operate with a mobile vending license from a commissary. They take their meals semiprepared with them in the vending units and then finish preparing the food on site. They are popular at construction sites and at television and movie production sites, where there is a need to feed a group of people from a mobile unit.

Often, a mobile vendor is part of a larger catering operation. Because equipment costs are high, this type of catering operation requires a sizable investment.

Retail Business with Catering Departments

The catering industry has found its way into many small and large retail food operations as part of another department such as the deli section or hot food take-out department. The catering department generally provides prepackaged cocktail trays or complete meals to take out. Such catering departments can be found in bakeries, convenience stores, supermarkets, and delicatessens.

Wholesale Caterer

The wholesale caterer generally does not become involved with the service of food and beverages, but provides a list of items available in bulk to various organizations and caterers who in turn sell to their clients. An example is the traditional roast beef, vegetable, potato, salad, and dessert often found at a sports banquet. Often, the caterer has an agreement with the wholesale caterer. He places an order with the wholesale caterer, noting the date, time, and place of the event. The advantage to the caterer is a steady supply of product. Also, he has to put little energy into the purchasing and production of meal items, which saves labor and lets the caterer concentrate on the event.

The wholesale caterer often supplies many such meals in one day, allowing for mass production of the items, which lowers the cost. For example, ABC caterer needs 150 portions of an item and XYZ caterer requires 350 portions of the same item, pushing the total to 500 portions of the same item. This increases the production requirement for the wholesale caterer, and decreases the cost to the caterer.

Event Creator, Party Planner, or Artistic Consultant

These specialists, usually work with other caterers for the actual service of food and beverages.

Range of Services Provided by a Caterer

Food

The caterer's services range from arranging and delivering a plate of cold cuts or hors d'oeuvres to preparing and serving an eight-course classical banquet—which includes hot soup, hot appetizer, main course, vegetable, cheese and salad, and dessert served in the correct order. The classical banquet also includes an ice sculpture or tallow center piece. The menu is always planned around the client's budget, and the caterer must consider the color, texture, and flavor of the menu items when menus are planned. Culinary terminology as well as regional cuisine and knowledge are important to the caterer.

Beverage

Caterers serve a wide range of beverages. They may be nonalcoholic, such as coffee, espresso, tea, and punch. Or they may include liquor, as for a bar setup, and use the skills of a professional bartender.

A knowledge of wines is required to properly complement a dinner or hors d'oeuvres. In most states, a license is required if alcohol is served. Laws vary from state to state. If the site has a liquor license, liquor may not be brought in. If this is the situation, liquor can be provided by the licensee. Common bar arrangements include the following:

> **Cash bar,** in which the guest must purchase all beverages. Often a preset price range is agreed to along with operating times

> **Host (client) bar,** commonly known as the open bar. Usually the types of beverages and the time of operation are set by the client and are costed by the caterer by the bottle and the number of drinks consumed (or for the number of people served for a flat fee).

> Clients provide beverages when the caterer does not have a license, and the caterer agrees to provide the mixers, bartender, glasses, and ice for a fixed fee.

Types of Services Offered

Services provided by the caterer include the prepackaged (boxed) lunch; the backyard barbecue; the common American banquet with appetizers, preset tables, preplated courses that are served to the head table, and all guests served at once; the buffet, which requires fewer staff, but makes it more difficult to control costs; or the silver or Russian banquet service—with trained waiters who handle three tables and portion and plate the courses at the tables—a very costly event.

The American banquet is often used at weddings and the buffet at less formal gatherings at which guests are encouraged to circulate. Multiple buffets may be set up that include appetizers, salad bars, main courses, and desserts.

As mentioned above, silver or Russian banquet service is reserved for opulent or formal catering, which can cost as much as $300 per person because of the time, skilled labor, and special service ware required.

Auxiliary Services

Caterers may be called on to provide a clown for a child's birthday party, or a full orchestra for an evening for dining and dancing. They also provide printed invitations for the client to send, as well as flowers, linen, ice sculptures, flags, portable dance floors, and tents, depending on the contractual agreement.

Markets

Caterers serve the social or domestic, business or corporate, and nonprofit markets. These markets can be segmented into three levels: shallow or low-budget, mid-level, and deep level. Low-budget events range from $4 to $10 per person and offer a small profit margin. Mid-level affairs cost around $10 to $20 per person and offer a better profit margin. The deep-level market are image builders and begin as low as $25 per person and escalate, depending on the client's needs. For example, if the event were to be held on a cruise ship, the rental of the ship would be included in the per-person charge and would drive up the cost. The profit margin is higher when catering deep-level affairs.

Catering is a universal market. The concession food vendor at the football game is a caterer; the vending machine operator is also a caterer; and the cafeteria service provider at the local school may also be considered a caterer. Thus catering serves a variety of markets and offers many job opportunities. Today's catering market is very diverse and has tremendous growth potential.

Caterers use various plans to develop markets. However, referrals and repeat business are the most common ways to build market share. Other marketing methods include direct mail, telemarketing, brochures, business ads, and networking with related businesses such as bakers, wedding consultants, and florists.

Job Opportunities and Training

There is a rapid growth in entry-level positions in the catering industry. A recent poll in Pittsburgh revealed that 150 caterers operate in that area.

Entry-level management positions are available in hotels, restaurants, clubs, hospitals, and other food service organizations.

Training opportunities in the industry range from one-day workshops to programs at community colleges, to degree programs in food service and lodging at the university level, which prepares candidates for this diverse field of hospitality management. Recent certification programs for caterers can be found with various industry organizations.

Business Atmosphere

Most businesses require a contract, and the catering business is no different. A contract is a binding agreement between two or more parties. The caterer must provide the food and services agreed on by both parties. The client must pay for the food and services detailed in the agreement. If either party fails to fulfill her obligation, the other party has the right to legal recourse.

Most contracts require a 25% deposit of the anticipated bill, with the balance paid at the completion of the affair.

Consult a lawyer when obtaining information about contracts and insurance requirements, because local and national laws govern contracts and insurance requirements.

The insurance needs of an on-premises or off-premises cater differ from the insurance needs of the restaurant industry as a whole or those of the middle caterer. For example, an off-premises caterer would need general insurance against fire, theft, workmen's compensation covering full- and part-time employees; accident and liability to cover accidents to guests while on the premises; and product insurance for anyone becoming ill from consuming contaminated food. An off-premises caterer would need a floater policy to insure the equipment that goes from job to job. Mobile caterers, on the other hand, need commercial truck accident insurance, liability to cover accidents to persons near the truck or van while being served, and product insurance.

Each locality has its own licensing requirements. Many localities require a license to do business in the city or county; a board of health permit for kitchen and commissary; a board of health permit for preparation of food for public sale consumed on the premises; a permit for preparation of food for public sale not consumed on the premises; a liquor license for liquor consumed on the premises; and a state liquor license issued in conjunction with a regular liquor license for caterers.

Today the catering business is expanding at a phenomenal rate and includes many markets. It parallels the growth of the meetings industry and is providing a wide range of job opportunities. The hours are long but the profits can be high if the business is run properly.

44

The Quick Service (Fast Food) Segment

Gary M. Shingler, *Purdue University*
Jeannine L. Ludwick, *Purdue University*

One can think of the quick service restaurants (QSR) as being the baby boomers of the restaurant industry. Although the first seeds of the industry were sown in the 1930s and the first QSR chains, such as A & W Root Beer, White Castle, and Dairy Queen were in existence by 1940, the impact of World War II on the food service industry enabled the QSR industry to grow quickly following the war's end. Food product shortages brought about portion-controlled packaging and limited menus. Labor shortages led to equipment innovations. Their experience in military service had made returning G.I.'s comfortable with eating on the go. These factors, combined with the increasing postwar population, shorter work-weeks, improved transportation systems that enabled more traveling, and an increased demand for food prepared away from home, all led to the emergence of the QSR industry in the 1950s. During the past four decades, the QSR segment of the food service industry has grown enough that by 1993 it represented more than 50% of the total commercial food service sales of the top 100 chains listed in *Nation's Restaurant News*.

Definition of the QSR Industry

Parsa and Kahn define a Quick Service Restaurant as a "firm with a mission to provide quicker service and core technology geared towards this mission, and commonly more attractive for the customers that demand convenience, speed, and simplicity of service at an affordable price."[2] Presently, 34 of the *Nation's Restaurant News* top 100 chains listing and 91 of *Restaurant and Institutions'* listing of the top 400 food service companies specialize in QSR operations.[1,3] QSR companies tally more than 60% of the *NRN* top 100's $101.8 billion total sales and almost 49% of the 400's $147 billion total.[1,3]

It was a QSR company that developed French fries and milkshakes as we know them today and initiated our industry's ground beef standards, which enable restaurants to receive a consistent product each time it is purchased. It has been reported that one QSR company has employed one out of every seven American citizens. Anyone who wants to work in a segment of the hospitality industry that is at the cutting edge of change and that is leading the food service industry out of its dark ages should give serious consideration to the QSR industry.

Using Parsa and Kahn's definition as a basis for identifying the composition of the QSR industry would cause one to include the following companies:

A & W
A & W Hot Dogs & More
Arby's
Arthur Treacher's
Baskin-Robbins
Bojangles
Boston Chicken
Braum's Ice Cream
Bresler's Ice Cream
Brown's Chicken and Pasta
Burger King
Captain D's
Cargel
Carl's Jr.
Central Park USA
Checkers
Chick-fil-A
Church's
Cinnabon
D'Angelo
Daylight
Del Taco
Dunkin Donuts
El Pollo Loco
Everything Yogurt and
   Salads Cafes
Fosters Freeze
Freshens Premium Yogurt
Grandy's

Great American Chocolate
   Chip Cookie Co.
Haagen-Dazs
Hardee's
Hot'n Now
Hungry Howie's Pizza & Subs
I Can't Believe Its Yogurt
In-N-Out Burgers
Jack in the Box
Jerry's Subs & Pizza
KFC
Krystal
Lee's Famous Recipe
Long John Silver's
Manchu Wok
Mark's Pi's
McDonald's
Miami Subs
Mountain Mike's Pizza
Mr. Doughnut
Mr. Gatti's
Mr. Hero
Mrs. Fields
Mrs. Winner's Chicken
   & Biscuits
Nathan's Famous
Orange Julius
The Original Cookie Co.
Peter Piper

Pizza Hut
Popeye's
Pudgie's Famous Chicken
Rally's
Rax
Round Table Pizza
Roy Rogers
Sbarro
Schlotzsky's
Sir Pizza
Skipper's
Sonic Drive-in
Starbucks Coffee
Taco Bueno
Taco Cabana
Taco John's
Taco Time
Tastee-Freeze
TCBY
Togo's Eatery
Two Pesos Mexican Cafes
Vie de France
Wendy's
Whataburger
White Castle
Winchell's Donut House
Yoshinoya Beef Bowl
   Restaurants

Although the above list is incomplete, it is a good example of the types of restaurants included in the QSR industry.

When classifying QSR restaurants by menu, the segments could be hamburger, sandwich, chicken, snack, seafood, and Mexican. Leaders in these QSR segments are on the next page.

QSR's typically offer a limited number (usually fewer than 20) of menu items per meal period, require customer self-service, have smaller dining rooms than other restaurants, use more high-tech equipment than other restaurants, employ a smaller number of employees per operation than do other types of restaurants, and specialize in selling items that can be prepared in three to five minutes. All of the above assist the QSR in providing quick service to its customers.

Hamburgers

1. McDonald's
2. Burger King
3. Wendy's
4. Hardee's
5. Jack in the Box

Chicken

1. KFC
2. Popeye's
3. Church's
4. Chick-Fil-A
5. Grandy's

Sandwich

1. Subway
2. Arby's
3. Roy Rogers
4. A & W Restaurants
5. Schlotzsky's Deli

Seafood

1. Long John Silver's
2. Captain D's
3. Skipper's
4. Arthur Treacher's

Pizza

1. Pizza Hut
2. Domino's
3. Little Caesar's
4. Round Table Pizza
5. Chuck E. Cheese

Snacks

1. Dairy Queen
2. Dunkin' Donuts
3. Baskin-Robbins
4. TCBY
5. Braum's

Mexican

1. Taco Bell
2. Del Taco
3. Taco John's
4. Taco Time
5. Taco Cabana

What does the future hold for the QSR industry? The trends discussed later in this chapter seem to indicate the following:

1. Menus will be determined by the market niche the QSR is serving. Some QSR's will expand their menu offerings, while others may reduce the number of items.
2. The QSR segment will use more high-tech equipment. Presently, one company has a machine that completely assembles tacos, and another has a robotic soft-drink machine that dispenses everything including a lid. Most of restaurant control will be the responsibility of a computer system.
3. QSR operations that survive the twentieth century will be those that are successful at meeting the needs of particular market niches. Those operations that cannot capture and serve market niches will struggle to survive.

Typical QSR Positions and Career Path

Mone and Umbreit state "At the single unit level, restaurants are examples of consumer service organizations requiring managers to implement a set of standardized operating procedures to achieve predetermined goals," i.e., profit.[4] A recent college graduate joining the management team of a QSR company will spend 30 to 90 days in a training program learning those standardized operating procedures before assuming an assistant manager's position. The graduate will be an assistant manager until he becomes somewhat adept at controlling food, labor, and other costs in addition to meeting company standards of quality, service, cleanliness, and safety. This usually requires a six-month to 1-year tenure in the assistant manager position before promotion to unit manager. A unit manager assumes additional responsibilities for customer relations, controlling semivariable costs, limiting employee turnover, promoting and terminating employees, training employees, and handling company sales promotions. Normally one to two years' work as a unit manager is needed before an individual becomes skilled at all of the responsibilities of the position.

Single-unit management can be a very rewarding position. Busier units require 30 to 70 hourly employees to adequately serve up to 1,500 or more customers daily. Contrary to popular opinion, a study done for the National Institute for Work and Learning indicates that the typical QSR hourly employee is a white female, less than 20 years of age, a high school graduate from a lower- or middle-class family, who lives at home.[5] This "typical" employee works an average 29.5-hour week, has more than 18 months of experience, and while satisfied working at a QSR, aspires to move up within the organization. Most of the QSR's reputation for high employee turnover can be attributed to replacing that 25% of the work force who stay less than six months. Historically, unit managers receive numerous lateral transfers or promotions in order to refine their management skills at higher-volume units and to increase their base salaries and bonuses. Unit managers have been known to earn as much as 25% to 35% of their base salary in bonus pay.

Three to five years of single-unit management can lead to a promotion to a multi-unit management position with responsibility for four to eight units. Doing a good job as a multi-unit manager requires a shift from some of the behaviors required of single-unit managers. To succeed at managing multi-units, one must supervise people rather than stores. Multi-unit managers must learn to motivate and manage managers who are older and have different aspirations from those of hourly employees. A person in this position needs to learn how to recruit, hire, train, and evaluate managers as well as handling management terminations. A multi-unit manager should be an expert at team building and performance orientation and be adept at reading managerial behavior and developing appropriate management training strategies. Mone and Umbreit identified five multi-unit areas of responsibilities.[4] In addition to restaurant operations, multi-unit managers also have responsibility for human resource management, financial management, marketing and promotions management, and facilities and safety management. The multi-unit manager is, in one sense, president and chief operating officer of a four-to-eight-unit company. Her success depends on the ability to delegate responsibility to the single-unit managers under her direction and their ability to achieve company goals. The multi-unit manager holds the most challenging position in the QSR industry.

Annual salaries for degreed QSR management trainees presently start around $22,000 and increase in 5%-to-7% increments as the graduate is promoted through various assistant manager positions. Trainees usually are not eligible for bonus compensation. Unit managers normally earn a salary in the $25,000 to $40,000 range and are eligible for bonus compensation equal to 10% to 35% of their base salary. Multi-unit managers' salaries begin at $30,000, and they are eligible for bonus compensation equal to 20% to 40% of their annual salary in addition to company perks such as a car. Some of the progressive QSR companies have recently advertised partial ownership and profit-sharing plans that give unit managers the opportunity to earn close to $50,000 in annual income. A QSR vice president recently noted that some of his multi-unit managers were earning annual incomes greater than $100,000. He also stated that a few of the multi-unit managers earning such incomes were under 30 years of age. Opportunities for high incomes exist in the QSR industry.

Trends in the QSR Industry

The Parsa and Khan article identifies emerging trends in the QSR industry.[2]

QSR marketing strategies are changing from a reactive follow-the-leader type of marketing to an independent type of marketing strategically targeted toward a company's particular niche markets.

QSR firms are requiring greater flexibility in asset utilization. Periodic upgrading of menus and equipment to meet the needs of changing markets are required. QSR firms will demand that equipment be more sophisticated to save on labor costs. The new equipment must have greater flexibility so it can meet the demands of changing markets, thus minimizing the cost of replacing functional equipment. Inflexible equipment locks a company into a menu that does not satisfy the demands of the marketplace.

Ecological responsibility will become stronger. Though it is well established that QSR's contribute less than 3% of the nation's total solid waste, public opinion is forcing QSR's to reduce their share of solid waste because it is so easily identified by imprinted advertising. Also, QSR firms will begin to work with other industries to develop technology that will reduce automobile idling and the resulting emissions. A failure to do this could result in governmental regulation that would eliminate drive-thru service all together.

QSR's are expanding into nontraditional segments of the industry. QSR companies are already making arrangements with institutions such as high schools, colleges, hospitals, and the U.S. military to open units on the institution's property.

A greater emphasis will be placed on customer service in the 1990s. Customer service will improve through enhancements of service technology and refined training practices.

Decentralized decision making will be forced on the QSR industry to enable a company to respond more quickly to changes in the marketplace. Some companies are presently offering regional menus wherever appropriate.

The QSR manager of the future will definitely need to be an enhanced version of today's manager. As the industry becomes more high-tech oriented and decentralized decision making empowers unit managers to make more basic decisions that affect customers, the QSR manager will need to possess stronger skills in computer usage, human resources, and marketing. The QSR manager will have to be a professional manager in the truest sense.

——References——

Bernstein, Charles. (1981) *Great Restaurant Innovators.* New York: Chain Store Publishing Corp.

Charner, Ivan and Bryna Shore Fraser. (1984) *Fast Food Jobs.* Washington, D.C.: National Institute for Work and Learning.

Foodservice Trends. *Restaurants USA.* August 1991, pp. 36–38.

400 Issue. *Restaurants and Institutions.* July 15, 1993.

Mariani, John. (1991) *America Eats Out.* New York: William Morrow and Company, Inc.

Mone, Mark A. and W. Terry Umbreit. Making The Transition from Single-Unit to Multi-Unit Fast-Service Management: What Are the Requisite Skills and Educational Needs? *Hospitality Education and Research Journal.* Volume 13/3, 1989, pp. 319–331.

Parsa, H. G. and Mahmood A. Khan. Menu Trends in the Quick Service Restaurant Industry During the Various Stages of the Industry Life Cycle (1919–1988). *Hospitality Education and Research Journal.* Volume 15/1, 1991, pp. 93–119.

Parsa, H. G. and Mahmood A. Khan. Trends in the Quick Service Restaurant Industry. *FIU Hospitality Review.* Spring 1992, pp. 19–26.

Pillsbury, Richard. (1990) *From Boarding House to Bistro.* Boston,: Unwin Hyman.

Top 100 Issue. *Nation's Restaurant News.* August 2, 1993.

Umbreit, W. Terry. Multi-Unit Management: Managing at a Distance. *Cornell HRA Quarterly.* May 1989, pp. 53–59.

45

The Commercial Cafeteria Industry

Clayton W. Barrows
University of New Orleans

Introduction

Commercial cafeterias represent a significant segment of the restaurant industry, yet one that is often overlooked by graduates of hospitality management programs. Even during difficult economic times, cafeteria companies offer promising careers for graduates interested in working for high-volume food service operations.

Commercial cafeterias should not be confused with institutional or noncommercial cafeterias, which serve primarily as support operations. Commercial cafeterias, by themselves, represent a $4 billion segment of the food service industry. They are found predominantly in the southern region of the United States. For those graduates choosing to live around the Sun Belt, they offer a particularly attractive opportunity.

While many cafeterias are operated independently, the industry is dominated by a few large chains, which have grown steadily in recent years. Additionally, relatively new concepts, such as the all-you-can-eat format, are becoming increasingly popular. With the continued solid performance of the larger chains, cafeteria companies are in need of qualified college graduates to manage their restaurants. Each year, the largest chains recruit and hire graduates of hospitality management programs for their management training programs. While this segment has experienced steady growth in the past decade, many industry observers view cafeterias as a concept that has yet to reach its full potential, meaning even more management opportunities for hospitality graduates. Recruiters from the larger chains have indicted that they would like to attract an even higher percentage of students from hospitality programs. A recruiter from Piccadilly Cafeterias, one of the largest national chains, indicated that fewer than 25% of recently hired college graduates had majored in hospitality management. A singular reason for this may be a general lack of awareness on the part of graduates.

Commercial cafeterias are founded on the concept of offering the customer a varied selection of prepared foods. Cafeterias serve a broad segment of consumers who desire high quality, low prices, and a casual atmosphere. The best companies combine all of these qualities, which results in high consumer satisfaction ratings and intense customer loyalty. In

423

fact, in a recent survey by *Restaurants and Institutions* (February 1992), Luby's Cafeterias, the largest cafeteria company, was ranked first in a survey of customers' overall satisfaction levels with all types of restaurant chains.[1] Morrison's was third overall in the same survey.

Cafeterias vary in size and scope but are similar, by definition, in that they offer a wide variety of foods all visible to the customer before purchase. Customers proceed down the cafeteria line and indicate the items that they wish to purchase. Most cafeterias price their food by the item, although some offer specially priced complete meals. Some cafeterias have even begun offering an all-you-can-eat format. Newer companies, such as Old Country Buffets, specialize in the all-you-can-eat buffet-style format.

History

Gerald Lattin has cited the development of the cafeteria concept as being a landmark in the history of food service.[2] The concept is said to have developed from the Swedish smorgasbord. Cafeterias first appeared during the latter part of the last century and began to gain prominence in the early part of this century. Though few cafeterias are to be found there anymore, the concept of cafeterias actually originated in the West. Until about the 1950s, cafeterias were also quite popular in several northern cities and particularly New York City. The reason for their loss of popularity in these markets is subject to debate, but now cafeterias continue to expand their territories, re-entering areas in which they were once popular.

The original purpose of cafeterias, and that which remains trademark today, was to save customers' money. The cafeteria concept began as a profitable way to feed large numbers of people, and continues to be.

Cafeteria Operations

Operationally, cafeterias combine the speed of fast food with the environment of a sit-down restaurant. Typically, cafeterias have lower food and labor costs than dinner houses and other segments of the food service industry. Because of this, they are able to pass the savings along to the customer. While they require more labor than fast food restaurants to serve customers, they require much less labor than similarly sized full-service operations. Most of the staffing is required in the areas of food production and on the service line. Much less is required in the dining room.

Food costs are also lower than most full-service restaurants, with costs usually falling well below 30% of sales. One reason for this is the chains' ability to bulk purchase, their use of standardized recipes, and their total use of food products.

Menus are usually cyclical in nature, with certain items, such as salads and breads, appearing every day. The total number of items that cafeteria chains are able to offer is immense. For example, Piccadilly Cafeterias has an inventory of 1,300 standardized recipes from which managers can choose. A typical Piccadilly restaurant will offer 130 different items each day, and the items will vary from location to location.

Nature of the Work

Cafeterias tend to be high-volume, busy places to work. A cafeteria that makes between $2 million and $3 million in annual revenues is not uncommon. Some of the larger companies include their managers in incentive plans, which entitle managers to a percentage of the restaurant profits. Cafeterias are often located in high-traffic areas such as suburban malls, although free-standing cafeterias are becoming more popular.

Needless to say, managers must be skilled in menu planning, purchasing, production, and staffing and must be able to control food and labor costs. Additionally, in a recent survey of company recruiters, recruiters indicated that a successful manager must be competent in a variety of areas including human resource management, public relations, communication, and customer relations.

Organizational Structure

The organizational structure of a typical corporately owned cafeteria is depicted in Figure 1. In this particular chain, a college graduate would begin as a management trainee. After completing a management training program, graduates work their way up through the company, progressing to the position of district supervisor and even beyond. Typical management training programs range from 13 to 28 weeks. For most, training continues even in the lower-level management positions. While some cafeteria companies may have additional levels of management and perhaps different titles, the positions described here represent one possible structure.

Once a graduate has completed the training program, the next step generally is to that of assistant manager or production manager. The production manager typically oversees all food production activities and assists with forecasting, ordering, receiving, and storage and inventory control. An assistant manager position involves many of the same activities while also dealing with front-of-the-house functions such as customer relations as well as scheduling and cash control.

Promotion to the position of associate manager may take several years but is usually the last step before the general manager position. The associate cafeteria manager assumes many of the duties of the cafeteria manager and is responsible for the store in the absence of the unit manager. Much of this person's responsibility is in the area of staff development.

The general manager is the person ultimately responsible for the overall operation of the cafeteria. Most cafeteria companies reward their general managers with a percentage of unit profits above a designated performance level. The general manager must deal with all phases of the operation including the training and development of other managers.

Only after years of experience and service will individuals generally rise to the ranks of district supervisor or above. These are essentially executive positions requiring dedication and commitment to both the company and the industry.

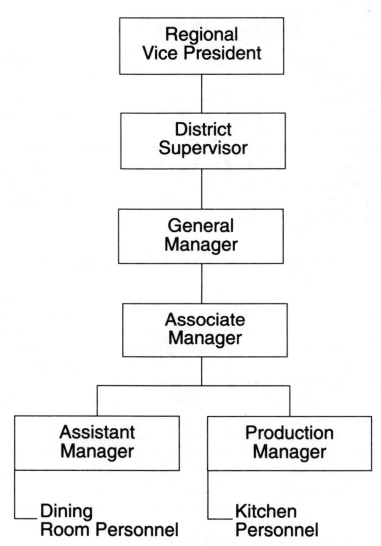

Figure 1. Organizational Chart

Table 1. Cafeteria Chains

Company	Year Founded	Number of Units	1991 Sales ($ millions)
Luby's	1947	162	$330.4
Morrison's	1920	165	306.4
Piccadilly	1944	128	275.0
Furr's/Bishop's	1947	142	216.0
Old Country Buffet	1984	120	207.0
Wyatt	1931	96	166.0

The Cafeteria Industry

Commercial cafeterias can be divided into two major categories. The first type is the traditional cafeteria in which the customer proceeds down the service line, choosing the food items desired and paying on a per-item basis. A more recent addition to the cafeteria segment are all-you-can-eat style buffet restaurants. In addition, some cafeterias combine the two styles. The six largest cafeteria companies in the United States include Luby's, Morrison's (family dining division), Piccadilly, Furr's/Bishop's, Old Country Buffet, and Wyatt Cafeterias. All of these companies continually rank among the top food service chains overall, based upon systemwide sales (Table 1). Together, these chains operate just less than 20% of all commercial cafeteria units in the United States and generate about one-third of all sales.

Between 1988 and 1989, cafeterias experienced a 6% increase in sales.[3] With consumers trading down to less expensive restaurant concepts during recessionary times, cafeterias may prove to be somewhat recession-proof with their low check averages. Industry sales are expected to reach $4.8 billion in 1992, and according to NPD/CREST (1987), cafeteria sales are highest in the South Atlantic and the Southwest regions of the United States.[4]

How to Prepare

How should a student begin to prepare for a career in commercial cafeterias? A four-year hospitality management degree can certainly give you the required edge in obtaining a job, but that edge is greatly enhanced by restaurant experience. Obtaining a part-time job in a cafeteria while attending school is a good place to start. Also, focusing on courses in restaurant operations, food production, food cost control, and hands-on management skills clearly would help. Finally, learning about the companies in the industry is critical. Many of them advertise for managers in trade journals. Write to them and ask for additional information. No matter which field you choose, you cannot know to much about the companies doing business in it.

Summary

The cafeteria industry is a unique segment of the food service industry and is one of the better environments in which to learn about managing restaurants. Like other segments, it has advantages and disadvantages. Cafeterias offer the chance to see high-volume operations in action, to learn about control systems, and to learn how to manage large quantities of food. The cafeteria companies mentioned offer stability, advancement opportunities, and competitive salary and benefits. Cafeterias are a proven concept with significant growth potential. They differ from traditional full-service restaurants in several ways. They are open seven days a week but usually only for lunch and dinner. They rarely serve alcoholic beverages, which eliminates the complications associated with beverage service. Most of the cooking is done from scratch, which obviously increases the expertise required of both managers and employees. And operations tend to be rather sophisticated, with sometimes complicated service systems and many employees. For students interested in learning the ins and outs of the food service industry, cafeterias can provide the basis for a rewarding career.

——References——

America's Choice in Chains. *Restaurant and Institutions.* February 1992; pp. 76–96.

Lattin, G. (1989) *The Lodging and Food Service Industry.* Educational Institute of the American Hotel and Motel Association.

Top 100 Chains. *Restaurant Hospitality.* August 1989; pp. 99–132.

NPD/CREST. *Annual Household Report.* 1987.

46

Hospitality Real Estate Opportunities

John M. Stefanelli
University of Nevada, Las Vegas

One of the advantages of working in the hospitality industry is the wide array of career options available. While most of the jobs are in operations, i.e., production and service positions, several staff positions are available for persons who want to be in the hospitality industry but are not interested in operations. For example, staff positions exist in hospitality accounting, purchasing, inventory control, human resources, data processing, and real estate.

There are many avenues to staff positions. Some people enter these careers while going to school. Some move into them on graduation. Others move into them after working in several operations positions. And a few find themselves thrust into these jobs through a combination of circumstances.

Hospitality real estate offers interesting and rewarding career opportunities. Several hospitality firms employ real estate specialists such as market analysts, location analysts, and lease negotiators. However, you do not have to be employed by a hospitality company in order to work in this field. You could be an independent appraiser or work for a lender, private investor, or real estate brokerage firm.

Typical Hospitality Real Estate Positions

Several career options relate directly or indirectly to the hospitality industry. Persons wishing to work in this area may find employment with real estate departments in multi-unit hospitality corporations, appraisal firms, real estate brokerages, business brokerages, site selection firms, time-share operations, and lending entities.

Company Real Estate Representatives

Many large multi-unit hospitality corporations employ a real estate director and one or more real estate representatives. These persons are usually responsible for the following activities:

1. Performing location analyses, i.e., evaluating real estate sites to determine whether the company should construct new businesses in these locations

2. Negotiating lease agreements
3. Interfacing with the company's legal, construction, operations, and financial personnel.

Company real estate representatives usually travel a great deal. It is usual for them to be on the road four days a week. Such extended travel, though, is necessary in order to evaluate a site properly. If you do not spend enough time researching a location, the company may make a rash decision.

Appraisers

Real estate appraisers are employed to render estimates of value. They are trained to value the real estate (i.e., land and buildings); furniture, fixtures, and equipment (FFE); collectibles and artifacts; and going-concern businesses.

Appraisers are engaged by commercial lenders, investors, sellers, insurance companies, contractors, attorneys, accountants, pension funds, and other entities having a financial stake in a project. For example, before a commercial lender, such as a bank or savings and loan, can lend money, it must have the collateral appraised by an independent appraiser it selects. A hospitality firm that needs to borrow money to build a new property must pay the cost of the appraisal needed to satisfy this regulatory requirement.

Some appraisers specialize exclusively in the hospitality industry. The major one, Hospitality Valuation Services, has offices in New York, California, and London and appraises only lodging properties. It is unusual, though, for individual appraisers to specialize in hospitality appraisal because there may be insufficient work available to make it a full-time job. Generally speaking, appraisers tend to specialize in a particular category and not in a particular industry. For instance, a business valuation specialist who appraises restaurants will typically appraise related businesses, such as taverns, liquor stores, bakeries, and food marts.

In addition to appraisal assignments, appraisers usually counsel clients. For example, a motel owner may hire an appraiser to estimate the most likely sales price for the property. He may also ask the appraiser to suggest things the owner could do to make the motel more attractive to potential buyers.

In addition to appraising and counseling, some appraisers get involved with real estate sales, property management (overseeing a shopping center complex), and loan brokerage (helping clients search for and secure the most favorable debt financing available).

Real Estate Sales

While property owners are free to sell their properties without help from other professionals, most prefer using a third party to represent their interests. The same is true for potential buyers.

Several brokerages specialize in the sale of lodging properties. For instance, member offices of the Hotel and Motel Brokers of America (HMBA) account for approximately one-fourth of all lodging properties sold in the United States.

Several offices also specialize in the sale of restaurants, taverns, liquor stores, and other similar hospitality businesses. In large cities, it is not unusual to find offices that deal exclusively with the sale and purchase of restaurants. There are also specialists in large cities that work exclusively with tavern operations.

Persons working in a sales office generally are in business for themselves, i.e., they are independent contractors. Their livelihood depends on the amount of property sold, in that their main (and most often, only) source of income is sales commissions generated when deals are concluded.

Some sales associates represent sellers and some represent buyers. Few represent both parties because doing so may be a conflict of interest.

While sales commissions are the primary source of income, some sales associates prefer to operate as independent consultants. In the typical sales transaction, the seller pays the commission, which is then divided among the relevant sales offices that helped consummate the deal. However, some salespersons work strictly for hourly fees and are paid regardless of the outcome of a particular transaction. In effect, they sell their time and advice and are compensated accordingly.

A day in the life of the typical real estate sales associate finds her showing property to potential buyers, gathering pertinent data, suggesting appropriate sales and purchase strategies, recommending alternative financing arrangements, estimating the most likely sales prices, organizing and completing the paperwork, negotiating contract terms and conditions, and shepherding the deal to ensure that it stays on track and is finalized.

Business Opportunity Sales

A business opportunity is an ongoing business located in leased real estate facilities. The owner typically sells the furniture, fixtures, and equipment (FFE); leasehold improvements (i.e., interior finishing of the leased premises); the business's name and reputation; and perhaps some other types of assets, such as inventory or a valuable liquor license. The business opportunity purchase usually includes everything but the real estate.

A business opportunity brokerage is very similar to the typical real estate brokerage. While business brokers do not normally sell real estate, they do sell businesses that usually have assumable leasehold interests that must be transferred to buyers. In effect, the work performed by business sales associates parallels almost exactly that performed by most real estate sales associates.

Site Analysts

Some research firms, real estate brokerages, and business brokerages provide location analysis for persons or firms unable or unwilling to do the work themselves. These companies typically maintain computerized databases that can be adapted to suit any need or answer any question. Their reports help clients make sound real estate and business investment decisions.

Some hospitality firms prefer to contract out this type of work to independent firms because it is more economical than maintaining their own real estate divisions. However, even those large hospitality companies that have real estate divisions are apt to use an outside firm once in a while because it is not always feasible for them to study every potential site.

Time-share Sales

A time-share operation is in business to sell long-term vacation packages to guests. They sell "slices of time," in that they normally sell a guest the right to use a vacation apartment, hotel room, or condominium for a specified time period per year (usually two weeks) for several years (usually seven to twenty years).

Guests who prepay for these vacations usually have the option of swapping their time at one location for comparable time at other vacation locations that are part of a time-share exchange network.

In most cases, the prepaid vacation is an economical alternative to paying for vacations every year. Usually the guest needs to pay only a relatively modest maintenance fee each year in order to defray the cost of routine repairs, remodeling, and so forth.

At one time time-share operations had a seedy reputation. Most of them were high-pressure sales operations that generated numerous consumer complaints. However, while a few of these boiler-room operations probably still exist, generally speaking the industry is considered quite aboveboard today. This is due primarily to major lodging firms such as Disney and Marriott entering the field. Their participation has legitimized the time-share industry.

Lenders

Many lenders are active in hospitality finance. The major players include the following organizations:

1. Life insurance companies that specialize in financing lodging properties
2. Pension funds that invest in lodging properties or lend to them
3. Banks and savings and loans that make real estate and business loans to qualified hospitality buyers

4. Government agencies (such as the Small Business Administration) that make direct loans or guarantee loans made by a third party
5. Leasing companies that will construct a property and/or provide all necessary equipment and lease these assets to a hospitality operator on a rent-to-own plan.

Lenders must qualify borrowers: before recommending a loan, the lender must ensure that there is a high probability that the money will be repaid. Lenders must perform "due diligence"—they must evaluate a borrower's creditworthiness, character, reputation, capacity to repay, business skill, and collateral.

Desirable Background for Hospitality Real Estate Positions

If these career opportunities seem exciting, you should begin to prepare for them now. It is never to early to select the right college courses and work experiences most likely to give you an edge when applying for this type of work.

These positions are very academically oriented, in that a great deal of research, writing, and computer skills are needed to succeed. You should take college courses designed to develop and enhance these skills.

You also should take a basic real estate course, real estate investments course, and real estate appraisal course. These classes will give you the best perspective of the industry as well as highlight the various career opportunities that may exist in your local area.

Accounting and finance courses are also necessary. At the very least you should take the basic accounting and financial principles classes. Generally, though, additional finance courses are necessary to acquire the techniques needed to quantify the types of research projects you will encounter.

Computer literacy is a must. You should be very familiar with word processing, database, and spreadsheet software. In addition to working with your own computer files, you must be able to use the computerized databases most offices subscribe to. For instance, a real estate sales office usually subscribes to a computerized multiple listing service (MLS). Sales offices also typically use services that provide demographic data and updated lists of lenders and their current loan terms and conditions.

Many real estate positions require licensing or certification, or both. For instance, if you want to be an appraiser, you will likely need a state license as well as certification from a nationally recognized appraisal association.

Finally, you should have a reasonable amount of operations experience before tackling one of these staff positions. If you want to work in a hospitality company's real estate division, you should have a basic understanding of how the company's food or lodging units are operated and managed. This provides the perspective needed when wrestling with decisions that can make or break your employer's bottom line.

Your Future in Hospitality Real Estate

Research and experience have shown that for every four people graduating with a degree in hospitality administration, one of them leaves operations within one year, or leaves the industry entirely. Interestingly enough, for every four who leave operations or the hospitality industry, one of them ends up in some type of financial management career. In a nutshell, then, the odds are one in eight that you will end up working for, or owning, one of the operations discussed here.

Hospitality is a people industry, and so is real estate. The education and work experience you have earned and will earn will qualify you for many types of careers. Take the time to explore the many options available. Hospitality can accommodate many career interests.

47

Hospitality Education

Stevenson W. Fletcher, III
University of Massachusetts

Educating people for careers in the field of hospitality is not a new undertaking, but a relatively young one in comparison to other professions such as medicine, engineering, or business. Professional development in most other fields—the growth of a viable formal educational activity to support the preparation of individuals for positions in the field—has followed the industry's growth and maturity. As the size, complexity, and diversity of the hospitality industry has grown, so has the need for better-educated individuals.

The increase in the number of educational institutions involved in hospitality education and training has paralleled the growth of the industry, the increased knowledge available to the field, the complexity of individual units and corporate organizations, and the increased use of advanced technology and operating systems. Early inns and restaurants were small, independently owned and operated, and had relatively simple management systems. The information base and skills needed for success in operating these units was basic and limited. Thus, there was little need for employees with advanced education. Education responded to what limited need existed.

However, as a result of customer demand, property system development, larger properties, and the growth of chains and multi-unit operations, the need has emerged for individuals with the basic skill, knowledge, and business foundation necessary to operate and manage large companies and properties. Likewise, the tremendous growth of the industry has demanded an increased number of such trained individuals.

Thus the educational effort has grown and changed to parallel the industry. Initial efforts in education were designed to meet industry needs centered on skills training (mainly at the postsecondary level), apprenticeships, and position-specific training. Later, in the 1950s and 1960s as the industry developed, the need for better-educated individuals increased, and the educational effort focused on the associate degree, which provided students with business skills as well as knowledge in operations. In the 1970s and 1980s in the United States, the industry developed a level of sophistication that called for still further preparation. Thus the rapid growth in baccalaureate degree programs began. The 1990s continue with the burgeoning demand for broadly educated, highly skilled graduates who are prepared to manage in a highly technical hospitality industry. We see an increasing need for an expansion of graduate studies. A similar parallel development is occurring in other parts of the world, as the international component of the industry rapidly expands and develops.

For these reasons, a large and diverse educational community has developed to meet the needs of the industry. Numerous high schools have specialized programs that serve to train and prepare students for entry-level positions in the industry. The industry depends heavily on these programs to provide the large number of individuals needed to staff the expanding industry. Many of these individuals have already moved into supervisory and management responsibilities throughout the industry. In order to advance, supervisors and managers need increasingly more knowledge, more information, and more education. Thus the need for and expansion of the second level of education: junior or community colleges, trade schools, and industry educational programs.

We now have a large and important group of programs that meet the requirements of those who need and want the further education required to qualify them for advanced positions in the industry. In the United States, this need has been primarily met by community college and junior colleges that offer programs or options in either hospitality management or culinary arts. Such programs generally offer a field of knowledge specific to the various components of the industry as well as some business background. Most prepare students well for careers in the industry, for other operating areas starting at the skilled level, and for supervisory and management positions of smaller units. Some programs are general in preparation, and others, such as culinary arts programs and schools, move graduates into specific careers. Demand for these graduates developed early and has increased as the industry has grown. Many leading industry managers, owners, and corporation officers have had this educational foundation on which to build.

Through its professional organizations, the industry has often been involved in this level of educational effort. The American Hotel/Motel Association, through its Educational Institute, has developed a series of courses, diplomas, and programs to train and educate individuals for the industry and give them the further foundation needed to advance their careers. The Educational Foundation of the National Restaurant Association has similar programs directed toward the food service industry, especially in sanitation and alcohol serving certification. Other associations have strong educational components designed to support those segments of the industry that they represent.

More recently, the educational needs of the hospitality industry have been met by the baccalaureate programs at various institutions of higher education in the United States. These programs, which combine general education with a strong business foundation and industry-specific knowledge, are designed to prepare students for management careers in the hospitality industry. Graduates of these programs are in high demand by major chains and are hired into a management training program or a direct placement position. The call for these graduates has paralleled the development and maturity of the industry, in a manner like that seen in professions such as in engineering, medicine, and public health. These four-year programs, increasingly offered by major universities in the United States, have become recognized as professional educational disciplines in their own right. Some of the brightest and most capable students entering our universities are entering these fields and, on graduation, are providing highly innovative and capable leaders to the industry for the future.

Finally, graduate programs are developing rapidly at the masters and doctoral levels. Here the students are exposed to advanced concepts, more information, decision making experiences, and research procedures that can be used in complex organizations in the industry. Again, like any industry that has matured and become more complex, the hospitality industry is finding a need, especially at the corporate level, for individuals with advanced degrees. This demand is expected to increase through the 1990s and beyond.

At each level, the education programs described above have recognized the importance and interdependence of education and work experience. All in some way require a work experience component, in which students gain experience, learn about operating practices, develop their supervisory and management skills, and obtain a framework of skills to apply to their formal coursework. The hospitality industry, like other professional fields, realizes that good education requires both formal and hands-on exposure and learning. The industry further recognizes this combination through the fast-growing industry certification programs, which require both education and work experience.

The Development of Formal Education

In the 1920s hospitality education in the United States, especially for those trained in the European tradition, was provided primarily through work experience. The first formal educational program to be established at a college level was at Cornell University under the leadership of Howard B. Meek, the father of hospitality education. The program, started in 1922, was supported by Ellsworth Statler and the American Hotel Association (AHA), thus establishing productive traditions of cooperative effort between colleges, industry, and professional associations that continue into the present. Soon thereafter, programs were started at Michigan State University, Pennsylvania State University, The University of Massachusetts at Amherst, The University of New Hampshire, and Washington State University. After World War II, programs were established at Florida State University and the University of Denver. Later, many major universities started hospitality programs to meet student demands and educational opportunities. Now, more than 160 four-year programs exist to meet this segment of educational need. At the two-year level, such programs are now more than 400 in number. Programs such as those at Paul Smith, City College of San Francisco, Miami Dade, Sullivan County Community College, and others, have long histories of success. The Culinary Institute of America and Johnson and Wales are two of the many schools specializing in the preparation of students for careers in culinary arts. In addition, numerous high school and similar programs provide foundation in hospitality education.

Internationally, educational program support for the industry is also undergoing significant change and growth. Historically, the primary thrust has been to provide diplomas and certificates that emphasize skill training. These schools, however, are moving into advanced education, sometimes in cooperation with established baccalaureate programs in the United

States, and are being recognized for the quality of their programs. England and Canada have educational programs that parallel those found in the United States. In Switzerland, schools have developed that support the development of professionals throughout the world. India, Sweden, France, Singapore, and Thailand have long-established, quality programs training professionals for their countries' hospitality industry needs.

Hospitality educators have long recognized the need for a forum in which professional educators might share ideas, communicate information, and speak for their areas of endeavor. In the United States the Council of Hotel, Restaurant and Institutional Education (CHRIE) is such a forum. An international association, based in Washington, D.C., it is the focal point for educational activities, placement, and professional development. Individuals, programs, and companies work together to continue the quality development of the industry's educational thrust.

Educational Concerns

For those in hospitality education, the past 20 years have been exciting, challenging, and changing years. We have seen the size and number of programs increase. New activities and directions have developed, highly able and committed students have been graduated, and the quality of the educational effort significantly improved. A more highly qualified and able group of graduates has entered the industry. Hospitality-related programs have gained wider respect as educational disciplines in their own right at the various institutions in which they are located. In spite of their continued growth, the demand for graduates from programs at every level still exceeds the total number graduated each year from all programs, thus creating an excellent job climate. The industry has benefitted greatly, both professionally and operationally.

However, with this growth and development have come serious problems that the educational community continues to face. Among them are the need for more qualified faculty with background in both industry and academia. These faculty must not only be capable in the classroom and be able to demonstrate scholarship and research ability and public service—traditional obligations for respected faculty in any discipline—but also have first-hand knowledge and experience of industry. Increasingly the need exists for information, practices, principles, and new concepts to be developed, advanced, and communicated to and throughout the industry to meet the numerous challenges of the coming years. Faculty and programs involved in hospitality education must take the lead in this effort, just as their counterparts in other developed professional fields have done.

Other areas of concern and challenge faced by educational programs include a need to move away from the high student/faculty ratios that exist in many programs, and a need to focus on the basic framework of knowledge that students must obtain during their educational experience, although not to the detriment of the continued need for uniqueness, specialization, and diverse thrusts by individual programs. A major step that addresses questions of educational standards and direction has been taken with the creation of an accreditation process for hospitality programs.

Extended Education

While the public thrust for education tends to focus on formal classroom education, leading to a degree or diploma, this is only a part of the educational opportunity available to personnel in the field. Extended or continuing education plays a significant role as it enables qualified individuals to meet the challenges found in today's dynamic hospitality industry. Education is a lifelong pursuit and obligation in any profession. Being exposed to new concepts and facts, expanding the knowledge base for new opportunities, and bringing important new developments to current practice are constant needs. This holds true for all practicing professionals in the industry and in education.

Thus, in addition to the formal education found in the various institutions of education, there exist significant educational efforts outside the classroom. Most hotel and food service companies provide in-house seminars, training programs, and other forums for professional development. Increasingly, these organizations support educational opportunities (even degree work) in related fields of study. Numerous professional associations such as AH&MA, NRA, CMAA, IHSMA, and CFA have strong educational programs for their members both at the national and local level. Many colleges take their traditional courses or topic expertise into the field on a part-time basis. Also significant is the individual development that can be acquired through home study programs, trade journals, topic-specific books, and research journals.

Education as a Career

In addition to the large number of career opportunities that exist now and that will continue to exist for graduates in the industry, and increasing number of career opportunities can be found in the formal educational programs that support the industry. As mentioned previously, there currently exists a large unmet demand for faculty and instructors at every level of formal education. Careers in this growth industry are frequently overlooked and misunderstood.

Careers and positions at any level of teaching require a strong educational background, a knowledge of industry practice, and an ability and commitment to encourage, assist, and support student's learning. The educational background required for available positions varies according to the position. To teach at the high school level, a four-year degree is minimal and a graduate degree is preferred, along with basic general knowledge of the industry. A master's degree is a common requirement for teaching at the two-year (junior college) level. In addition, candidates must show an interest in and ability to engage in public service efforts and activities, including extended education at the local or national level. University faculty requirements, relative to tenure and promotion, require a master's degree at the very least. In most institutions, a doctorate in a related field is needed. At this level, ability, interest, and commitment to public service, scholarship, and research along with the formal classroom and advising obligations are expected of all faculty.

A career in education offers unique opportunities in the field. Foremost is the opportunity to share knowledge, work with students, and develop the potential of the future leaders of our industry. Furthermore, the diversity of activity that occurs in the educational environment, the flexibility, and the opportunity to explore individual interests for the benefit of the program and industry also exist. Often, during the summer and at other periods of the year, opportunities exist to build on regular faculty activities: research, giving seminars at the university or elsewhere, writing articles and books, or other activities of personal interest or professional development. These opportunities provide continuous growth, challenge, and change for faculty and their students. The University is an environment in which individual efforts and ability are recognized and rewarded: the workload is heavy but flexible, and the pressures that exist are assumed by the individual rather than placed on him by external forces.

More people with demonstrated academic skills, experience in the industry, communication skills, and a commitment to learning are needed in hospitality education. It is another career option available to college graduates.

The Future

As the industry continues to expand and mature, it will face a significant need for more- and better-educated individuals. During the 1990s and beyond, the hospitality industry must develop its human resources. The quality of the work force will affect the quality of the guest's experiences, the productivity of operations, the industry's ability to adapt to change, and thus its profit level. The industry will continue to expand and change, but it will also become more complex and sophisticated in its operational methods. A better-educated work force is the foundation for the future of any profession.

Today's educational community is educating and training the work force for the next century. These educators also must prepare them for the future and continue the quest for quality, academic recognition, and relevancy through traditional educational efforts and innovative activities and concepts. Educational leadership and success will, more than ever, depend on the quality of faculty, levels of program support, quality of students attracted to the field, and the courses of study offered. If education is to meet the challenges of the future, it must attract and retain talented, able, and educated people in its educational programs as well as in the industry that hospitality education serves.

48

Senior Services Management

Robert H. Bosselman, *University of Massachusetts*
Richard A. Wentzel, *Johnson and Wales University*

The field of health care management, and in particular, long-term health care management (also referred to as senior services management), is one on which most hospitality and tourism students do not focus their attention. This field, however, offers exciting opportunities for the future hospitality manager. In this chapter, the reader will be introduced to this field: its history, terms of importance, complexities of management, skills needed for successful management, and potential career paths in the field.

The dramatic change in demographics is the main reason for the increasing concern with senior services management. People are living longer, and more people are entering the category of what we call old age. For our purposes, we are concerned with individuals beyond the age of 65. Currently, about 12% of the population falls into this range. However, over the next 40 years (the reader's working lifetime) the over-65 group will increase markedly as the baby boom generation ages. Advances in medicine and technology now make it possible for the average American to live beyond 80 years, and many experts predict that those born in the latter half of this century could live until 90. Despite the marvels that science and technology yield, they have yet to slow the aging process. One thing is certain: as people age, the body slowly breaks down until eventually we die. How people age, of course, is influenced by many factors including family history, health, nutrition, and environment.

History of Senior Services Management

The field of senior services management is not a new one. Early predecessors of today's operations were associated with religious groups in the latter half of the nineteenth century. These not-for-profit operations still operate, although for-profit establishments are emerging at a rapid pace. During the early history of long-term health care, the elderly and chronically ill person had no federal government laws to ensure their care. There were, however, different individual state regulations dealing with institutionalization.

The modern era of senior services management began in 1935 with passage of the Social Security Act. This bill provided federal funds to pay for nursing home care for the elderly.

About the same time, small private nursing homes were started and operated for profit. The Hill-Burton Act of 1946 provided grants and loans for construction and equipment for long-term care facilities. In 1960, the Kerr-Mills Program increased federal funds to states using medical vendor payments. These states had established satisfactory licensing and inspection programs. The Medicare and Medicaid amendments to the Social Security Act, passed in 1965 and titled The Conditions of Participation, established minimum standards of inspection and staffing needs for health care organizations. External government funding introduced the need to comply with rules and regulations for licensure, quality of care, and staffing. Government programs and the health care system in general are currently under review. It is not yet clear what changes are likely to occur, but the manager's role in long-term health care will be a continuing one.

Terms of Insurance

Long-term health care involves several types of facilities, and this has led to numerous terms that describe the process. The word *long-term* is quite broad, and the field of long-term health care includes different classifications of care.

Extended care facilities or skilled nursing care facilities provide 24-hour nursing care under physician supervision. This nursing care includes registered nurses, licensed practical nurses, nurse's aides and orderlies, all of whom provide service prescribed by a physician. This type of facility can receive Medicare and Medicaid payments if the facility meets criteria for program participation. The level of care found in these operations is the most intensive of all long-term care facilities.

Intermediate care facilities, or basic nursing care facilities, provide basic medical, nursing, social, and lodging services for persons not capable of living on their own. The level of care in these operations is not as intensive as that found in skilled nursing facilities. These facilities are eligible for participation in the Medicaid program only.

Resident care facilities provide regular care and service to patients of any age. Medical and nursing care does not approach either of the aforementioned types of facilities. These establishments often care for mentally ill or mentally retarded patients. Resident care facilities do not participate in these specific government programs.

Assisted living and continuing care retirement communities are the newest entry into the senior services system. These provide an array of medical, nursing, social, and lodging services to older adults capable of independent living as well as those requiring assisted living environments. Nursing service is available 24 hours a day in these operations.

Patient Care and Service

In some ways, senior services management resembles other institutional operations, such as military or college and university operations. The significant difference, however, is in the level of nursing and medical care provided to the patron. Until the development of continuing care retirement communities, it was rare for food service and lodging companies to become involved in the total operation of senior services facilities. Primary emphasis for hospitality managers associated with long-term health care in the past was in the area of food service. This translates to three meals (breakfast, lunch, and dinner) and nourishments or snacks provided to patients.

In most operations, a dietitian assists in the food service operation. Most dietitians work as consultants, usually associating with several senior services facilities. The amount of time they spend in each facility is regulated by state law, although federal regulations are on the horizon. The food service manager in senior service facilities must meet the requirements set forth in "The Conditions of Participation for Nursing Homes." Together, the dietitian and food service manager develop menus for the patients. The function of menu planning is perhaps the most critical task facing management. The reader will recall the many types of senior services facilities, and the variety of people served by each. Numerous challenges face those responsible for menu planning. Some patrons will be able to eat regular meals, while others will require various modifications to their diet. In addition to medical requirements, one must also consider chewing ability and reduced appetite. Older adults need fewer calories because their physical activity usually is decreased and their body processes have slowed.

Just as in commercial food service and lodging operations, we must identify the consumer of our services. Information on each person's food habits should be obtained as soon as she enters a senior services facility. When someone enters such a facility after living independently, he probably will experience a psychological reaction to his new surroundings. Because food is an integral part of daily life, it often becomes the focus of an individual's attention, i.e., refusing to eat, complaining about food, or wanting only familiar food items. Mealtime is perhaps the highlight of the patron's day, and food should stimulate her appetite and interest. Menus should consist of a variety of food textures and colors. Certain foods may be avoided, while adjustments can be made in preparation of others. For example, apple slices may be needed instead of whole apples, or toast instead of bread. Quite often, the main meal of the day will be served at mid-day because many patrons do not want to eat heavily before going to bed.

Menus also have a key role to play from a nutritional perspective. The purpose of the senior services facility is to provide care service, so the menu should provide the necessary nutrients to help maintain the individual patient in a healthy condition. A good example of this concern is the inclusion of whole-grain items (such as bran) in meals. This helps elderly patrons with elimination, reduces medical costs, and makes the individual feel better. Dining areas need to be comfortable and attractive, with space for wheelchairs and service aides to move freely. Usually table service is provided because patrons may have difficulty managing a tray. There will also be tray service for persons confined to their rooms. Trays should be prepared attractively as well as functionally. Persons responsible for feeding patients need to be familiar with food items so they can answer questions posed by patrons. Nourishments and snacks can supplement diets and have been noted to reduce the amount of medication needed. Facilities that provide patients with a glass of wine (only if sanctioned by physician) also report a reduction in medication required.

Management Concerns

The complexity of menu planning involved in senior services operations also affects other areas of the food service operation—purchasing, receiving, storage, production, and service. Also of paramount importance is the labor crisis in our industry. Shortages in the area of senior services are primarily in the general worker category and among dietitians. Lack of available workers may force some operations to use increased quantities of convenience food products in menus. While convenience products have improved in quality, they are not always the best choice for the senior services patron. Another factor to consider is the cost parameter. Many long-term health care operations are under tight budget constraints, and this will significantly affect food service functions. Convenience products often cost more than items prepared on-premises. The use of convenience products will depend on increased funding. Food service budgets often are expressed n terms of cost per patient day, and these figures vary from one senior services facility to another. Budgets usually are set every six months to stay current with ever-changing food and labor costs.

The shortage of dietitians is also a concern for senior services operations. Most dietitians prefer to work in acute care settings where there may be more responsibilities (clinical dietitian, administrative dietitian). Also, fewer students are seeking careers in dietetics. In addition, recent decisions by The American Dietetic Association now make it more difficult for individuals to become dietitians. One result of these actions may be increased responsibilities for food service managers and possible for medical and nursing professionals. Much will depend on future government regulations on staffing requirements.

Toward Life Care Systems

As previously noted, assisted living or continuing care retirement communities are rapidly increasing. Today nearly 230,000-people, most of them over 75, live in 800 such settings in the United States. By the turn of the century, the number of these communities is likely to double. We have already noted some of the factors behind the growth in senior services facilities. In the case of continuing care retirement communities, we also see the impact of divided families, such that the elderly can't go home to live with a child. Independence, however, is the critical factor of success in the growth of the life care systems. Individuals can continue to live on their own as long as they are capable. This independent living arrangement may be a private home, a townhouse, a cottage, a luxury high-rise, or a small apartment. From this setting, a participant would move to a congregate, assisted-living area when her health mandated such a move. Finally, when health concerns are critical, she would move to a skilled nursing facility. All of these environments are under the direction of one management concern. Participants pay an entry fee (usually large) and a monthly rental or maintenance fee. In some cases, meals, housekeeping, and other services are included in monthly fees; sometimes additional fees are charged.

Because these operations involve lodging and food service functions, major corporations have become involved. Living in these communities has often been described as similar to a hotel or country club. As the reader can see, in these communities the line between commercial and institutional hospitality management has all but disappeared. Hyatt Hotels, Marriott Corporation, Food Dimensions, Inc., Morrison Custom Management, and ARA are some of the companies involved in developing, or contracting for management in, the continuing care retirement communities. Initial ventures in this field were in the South and West, but growth is now in the Midwest and Northeast as well. Currently, ARA Living Centers represent the largest hospitality venture into the continuing care retirement community system. ARA has been active in this area for more than ten years and offers numerous employment opportunities. Marriott Senior Living Services is a rapidly expanding division of the company. It has been estimated that Marriott will have more than 150 such communities by 1995 with a total investment in excess of $1 billion. If that projected rate of growth is realized, Marriott will have the largest group of these communities. Hyatt Hotels, a recent entrant into the field, has introduced its Classic Residence in six locations across the United States. Anticipated growth is four to five new facilities annually. Patrons contract for breakfast each day and an additional 25 to 30 main meals each month. Additional food may be purchased à la carte. To meet nutritional demands, Hyatt has introduced Classically Caring Cuisine—low-cholesterol, low-fat, and low-sodium food items prepared with a gourmet touch.

The influx of large corporations into the senior services field will significantly affect independent, free-standing operations. This has already occurred in hospals, with corporate facilities (chains) buying independents or taking over former independent facilities when the latter go out of business. The large chains take advantage of economies of scale in operating and managing their senior services facilities. In addition, because the chains often are involved in other hospitality-related establishments in the area, they can spread their costs over different operations. For example, one central kitchen can serve a continuing care retirement community, a meals-on-wheels program for independently living elders, a school lunch program, or the latest food service ventures—day care programs. These large companies can usually operate more efficiently and effectively than independent operations. For example, better purchasing contracts can be negotiated, which could lead to lower food costs. There is likely to be a management information system (computer network) available to reduce operating costs and maintain control in the operation. Labor costs will likely be reduced because most work can be performed in one operation with minimal preparation and production in auxiliary facilities. Large companies also have better training programs, offer more career growth, and probably provide better wages and benefits than independents. In the competition for scarce labor resources, these factors could mean less turnover, less absenteeism, and increased productivity. The bottom line is lower costs and increased profits. There is, however, opportunity for independent, free-standing senior services facilities. The key will be to specialize in a specific area of care and service rather than offer a myriad of programs. An example of this would be a facility that specializes in care for patients with

Alzheimer's disease. This concept of specialization should not be entered into without first analyzing the need for such services and designing an operation to meet that need. Still other modes of care are developing at the community level that offer new opportunities.

Community-Based Health Services

Home health care is generally considered to include the provision of skilled nursing and other allied health professional services based on patient care needs. The care given and who gives the care will depend on a number of factors including restrictions on what is covered by a given funding source. Care can be given exclusively by health care professionals or may be offered by a durable medical equipment company, temporary nurse or medical employee organization, or community group either in combination or individually.

Generally, five types of agencies administer home care programs:

1. Public agencies
2. Nonprofit agencies such as Visiting Nurses Association or other voluntary community-based agencies
3. Agencies located in or operated by hospitals, skilled nursing facilities, or rehabilitation facilities
4. Proprietary organizations
5. Combination agencies, operated by organizations with dual sponsorships such as a governmental unit and a VNA.

Noninstitutional Home Care Services

Homemaker and chore services are general housekeeping services needed to keep someone in his home (e.g., house cleaning, shopping, meal preparation, minor repairs, laundry, and errands). Wide variation exists in both the types and quality of food services provided, and the amount of public funding is rather limited. The major resource is Title XX of the Social Security Act; at 19% of all Title XX expenditures goes for homemaker and chore services.

Hospice care is the provision of services intended to improve the quality of life for terminally ill patients. Some hospice care is delivered in the institutional setting with all the same implications as discussed under long-term care facilities. There is, however, a growing emphasis on home care with the intentional inclusion of family in both settings. There is strong support for an interdisciplinary team approach to the care delivered. The overall goal of hospice care is to avoid suffering and "heroic" intervention, while offering supportive care to patients and their families during the dying process.

Title III-B of the Federal Older Americans Act provides funding to Area Agencies of Aging. These funds are used for as wide variety of community-based programs including in-home services. In-home services for older persons not paid for by Medicare vary greatly and may include homemaker services, home health services, shopping assistance, escort services, reader and letter-writing services, and other services designed to assist the maximum number of older persons in continuing to live independently in a home environment.

Funding for home-delivered meals has been available since 1972 under Title III-C, Nutrition Program for the Elderly, of the Older Americans Act. These meals are usually provided at least five days a week, and special diets are usually available depending on the resources of the county that administers the program. Congregate meal programs, supported in great part by funding under the Older Americans Act, serve hot meals to an estimated 2.85 million elderly. Such meals are considered important not only for providing the elderly with one-third of the daily nutritional requirement five times a week, but also because they provide the opportunity for social contact and recreation. The meal program sites also are used to conduct health screening, education, and outreach programs.

The Senior Services Manager

Students considering careers in the field of senior services management will have numerous opportunities. Most students in hospitality and tourism programs choose a career with a lodging or restaurant company. The area of institutional management (including contract management) is the unsung hero of career opportunities. There will be less competition for available jobs, and pay and benefits will equal or surpass those of lodging or restaurant positions. In order to take advantage of these opportunities, students need to be prepared. Recall that senior services involve not just the hospitality field. Managers in this field will deal with medical, nursing, social services, and government personnel. Students should develop strong interpersonal skills such as listening and oral and written communication. Courses in human relations and communication, as well as a foreign language (e.g. Spanish), should prove helpful. The student should go beyond basic courses in these areas. In upper-level classes, students are often exposed to situational analysis, case studies, or role playing, which can serve as excellent examples for realistic situations. Other courses to consider in association with these human skills may be found in psychology, sociology, and anthropology. Many universities now have courses focusing on terminally ill or gerontological patients. One such university, Johnson and Wales, recently developed a multidisciplinary hospitality and health services administration program. Courses on the sociology of aging, the psychology of aging, or gerontology are suggested electives.

Basic technical hospitality skills are important in senior services management. Traditional courses in food service and lodging provide the foundation for the hospitality student. Recommended electives in the hospitality program include purchasing, institutional management, contract food service management, and any hands-on food service courses. The student is also encouraged to develop a strong business background, particularly in accounting and finance. With the rapid growth of continued care retirement communities, students should have a strong foundation in lodging-related courses. This would include courses in hotel operations, housekeeping, and property management. The latter area is one often overlooked by students, yet opportunities in this area will be particularly strong in future years.

Students planning a career in this field should try to gain some work experience in this area before graduation. This work experience will likely tell the student whether or not the field is appropriate for them.

In the past, many food service operations in senior services facilities were managed by dietitians. The same was true for hospitals. Today, however, the dietitian is primarily a staff or consultant position under the direction of the food service manager. Dietitians, while undergoing a rigorous academic plan, nonetheless usually lack training in human relations and finance. This is not to say that dietetic students should not consider careers in management. They should consider them, but only if they get training in these cited areas. Until they do, the managerial jobs in the field of senior services management will continue to be the domain of students from hospitality and tourism programs.

Future Concerns and Opportunities

Throughout this chapter we have drawn the reader's attention to the complexity of the senior services field. The complexity is likely to continue, with greater regulation from government as well as expanded types of senior services facilities. There will be continued growth; from fiscal year 1987 to fiscal year 1990, the entire field of nursing home and elder care increased from $3.94 billion in sales to $4.73 billion (20% growth). With the population aging, this growth level seems likely to continue and could even increase. The question of more government regulation is a moot point; the real question is when it will occur. Note that most people needing long-term health care cannot afford it. It is estimated that one year of care in a nursing home averages $20,000; 90% of single patients are bankrupted in that time. There are numerous proposals as to resolving this situation, but none are ready for implementation. Those corporations specializing in continuing retirement communities will likely develop different segments much like the current lodging industry. They will also develop flexible financing programs to gain a larger share of the senior services market. We will likely see new concerns for patient rights, which may affect areas of interest to the hospitality manager. And finally, pervading all areas of senior services will be the emphasis on cost containment. For the student seeking a challenging career in a growth industry, the field of senior services management is a wise selection.

49

International Hospitality Management

Michael Kaile, *Canadian Pacific Hotels & Resorts*
William F. Lougheed, *Ryerson Polytechnic Institute*

A Letter of Introduction

Dear potential international manager:

This chapter on international hotel management will give you an overview of the requirements of this career goal in relation to objectives of students enrolled in hospitality programs across the country. Prospective international hotel managers should become skilled in human resource management, marketing management, and financial management. These will complement essential practical and operational experience. We will provide some insight into the professional and personal decisions that may affect your choice of an international career. Michael Kaile has had a varied and successful career in the international hotel field. Bill Lougheed has participated in the selection of international management. Together, they discuss the personal and professional qualifications needed to meet the demands of an international assignment.

Should you include broader worldwide opportunities in your career ambitions?

National Versus International Management

A common question posed to an internationally experienced general manager by one who is looking into an international assignment is, what is the difference in managing people in other countries?

The key word is *flexibility*. The following outlines some of the topics to consider:

Management Style

Typical and appropriate management styles for domestic operations are well defined in textbooks and periodicals. Most companies have clearly defined management styles. An individual going from the national to the international scene, however, will generally encounter a less rigid approach and will have to demonstrate greater flexibility with regard to their own personal management style.

The manager at home in the modern and highly structured company should seriously consider whether an international position is a feasible alternative. The ability to adapt one's style to the circumstances and environment is key to the success and acceptability of the international manager.

Culture and Religion

One of the greatest differences is that of understanding and coming to terms with the culture and religion of the country of assignment. Extensive research concerning these areas is vital before undertaking an international position. Sources within our own country vary from the library to embassies or consulates of the country involved. Most countries have tourist boards that provide the potential manager with valuable information. This research is highly recommended and is an essential ingredient in preparation for an international posting.

Language

Time spent learning a new language will of course depend on the location. It is clearly an advantage to have at least two languages and sometimes is it necessary to learn a third. While foreign language fluency ordinarily is essential for work in European countries, in the Middle or Far East the second language is usually English. While enrolled in an educational institution it would be an advantage to select a language elective to complement your objectives.

Climate

Research the climate of the area. Consider the temperature and seasons as well as the prevailing dress code for the work environment. Manager's must conform to the standards and social mores of the selected country.

Technology

Your research into the sociological elements of an international appointment is important, but so is research into the technological aspects of the assigned property. Whether your new responsibilities involve handling computers, safety and security systems, or other major operating equipment, the more information on local technology and practices you can gain before your arrival the better prepared you will be for the assignment.

Experts, manuals (in English), and training on procedures may be more readily available to you in your present location than they will be in the country of assignment. Use these resources and maintain these contacts.

Hotel Positions Available in the International Market

Within chain, government, or independently owned companies, some positions are more commonly in demand internationally. Where special training and experience are specifically required for the country, such positions usually are offered for a specific period of time; i.e. a fixed-term contact. There are also positions where local nationals will predominate at a senior level. Most hotels run by large international companies are on management contracts. Therefore the management will be responsible to both head office and the owners of the property. The positions available will vary with the contract and the availability of local management. Since titles are often deceiving, additional information is necessary in the job description and job specifications. Details regarding experience, personal characteristics, and qualifications must be of a more specific nature in order to meet the criteria of the country and company involved.

General Management

Although this title in itself denotes a generalist, specific experience with achievements in food and beverage, finance, or marketing is usually required depending on location.

Executive Assistant Manager

This position requires on the average three to five years experience in the areas of food and beverage management, marketing and sales, and some accounting management in at least a middle management level. Where high-volume accommodation and computerization exist, those candidates with a strong rooms division experience will have greater opportunities.

Food and Beverage Management

This specialist, with three to five years of related experience, is in high demand internationally. Those with a cross-section of types of operations often have the advantage because many hotels have a variety of food and beverage offerings.

Executive Chef

The demand is for the chef with a quality and high-volume background. Those with business management skills have often moved into the area of general management or gone into business for themselves.

Engineers

Because the international hotel industry abounds with openings, renovations, and ongoing operations of international properties, engineers with strong relevant experience have been key managers for many years. Preventative maintenance programs are a major thrust in operations due to limited technical resources and high cost, so this individual has many opportunities to advance into upper management positions.

Positions such as executive housekeeper, restaurant manager, and comptroller also must be filled by many international operations. Often many countries seek executives who can train and develop management potential domestically to eventually take over in some of the management areas. This process provides employment opportunities for these countries' nationals and enables the nations to become more self-sufficient.

The International Hotel Manager—Profile

When examining the profile of the international manager, it becomes apparent that there are no absolute criteria with regard to the qualifications and suitability of the potential candidate. Success in the international market depends on a number of factors and conditions. Outlined below are some of the key elements.

Academic Background

Generally, the better educated the graduate, the more broadly prepared and mature she is. In our industry the emphasis has been and will continue to be on the practical, results-oriented manager. This person is far more a generalist than a specialist, showing both versatility and understanding of all aspects of the hotel operation and demonstrating sound practical knowledge, integrity, and personality. Many successful operators have excellent practical knowledge but have a limited academic background. The combination of hotel school and practical working knowledge also generates excellent international managers. Academic qualifications must be accompanied by hands-on experience in order to meet the demands of the international marketplace.

Personal Characteristics

The reader should imagine himself in a room of international managers. A certain thread runs through the room, noticeably one generating an aura of self-confidence and maturity. Among those present will be patient and decisive managers who have proven successful while developing their international career portfolio. Certain management skills will predominate, for example, human resource skills, a real command of the industry, and a flexibility of attitude which permit achievement of desired results with the means at hand. Leadership and motivation are necessary to become a successful international operator.

Previous Experience

Experience in all operational areas makes the candidate more attractive for any international position. Again, the generalist with varied areas of expertise will gain the acceptance of supervisors, peers, and subordinates because this individual has a better overall concept of the operation.

Management of domestic properties now recognizes the need for engineering awareness as a necessity. Internationally, this area has always been a requisite for the safety, security, and cost control of the operation. Opening and renovation experience, including design and layout and maintenance of older properties, is a definite asset to the international manager.

Special Emphasis Should Be Placed on Training Experience

At the general manager level the individual probably will not be involved directly in training. There will be ongoing training within the operation at all levels, so failure to grasp the area fundamentals and recognizing their importance will inevitably result in serious operational difficulties. Such experience will improve results in service and productivity as well as establishing good employee relations.

With good education and real practical experience, the individual can be more successful in problem solving. Internationally, textbook solutions often are impractical. Solutions generally are found in good human resource management combined with sound decision making.

Personal

Relationships

The international job marketplace makes specific demands on an individual's personal status. For example, in some countries a spouse is an invaluable asset. In other situations, the manager might find it advantageous to be single. Let us make the assumption that the position you are considering is suitable for a family situation. In respect to children, it is hard to see how they could avoid becoming mature as a result of this experience. Your partner must be committed to the move and should be aware of the limitations that may be placed on the family unit. In some countries, these can be severe. For the international manager with or without family, the adjustment to the change from domestic family support and a familiar social system to a new environment without any support must be considered before embarking on this career.

Health

A key to handling the effects of change and business stress is to follow a disciplined health and fitness program. The whole area of health and fitness is one that the successful executive takes seriously irrespective of location. It is not advisable to work internationally if your health requires specialized treatment. Every individual should question themselves very seriously about his state of health before taking on any foreign assignment.

Regulations—International and Local

Medical and Health

Immunization regulations and associated health matters can be accessed through the embassy or consulate of the country of destination. It is important to comply with all these regulations to be allowed into the country.

Visa and Work Permit

Scrupulous attention to detail will avoid any problems or pitfalls. This area can prove to be one of frustration and help from the following sources is invaluable:

The Company's Executive Offices

Consult immigration officials of the country of destination and legal counsel specializing in the areas of visa and work permits.

The country to which you are going may have an office staffed by an international corporation representative or by a representative of the company owning the hotel. Normally, such an office will also have available a local who is familiar with government regulations and the local labor market. Such assistance is invaluable, and it is helpful to establish a good relationship with this individual.

Passports

The passport should be current and valid for a period of at least two years.

Local Currency

Any information you can gather with respect to local currency regulations is to your advantage. You should be aware of any restrictions applicable to removing money from the country and also of the historical fluctuation of the currency in question.

Compensation Package

An international posting requires a package in the form of a letter of agreement or a contract that guarantees meeting the standard of living appropriate to the position and location. Such a package would generally include the following:

Term of contract
Base salary (with built-in inflation factor)
Bonus clauses
Medical and health costs
Educational costs
Accommodation allowance
Travel expenses
Automobile (with or without driver)
Vacation (including terms and conditions of home leave)
Entertainment and business allowances
Disability and life insurance
Cost of relocation

The level and nature of the position would dictate the items that would be included and the degree and amount of the benefits provided.

The Manager as Diplomat

This role varies according to the location. However, the following lists some of the factors that the general manager may find herself representing and possibly defending:

1. Your own country of origin
2. The country that your organization represents
3. Your host country
4. Your hotel
5. Your company, especially if a multinational organization
6. Your owner's interest if the hotel is operated on a management contract basis
7. Yourself

How you respond to the above subjects will be seen as a direct reflection on your company, your country, and yourself.

Conclusion

In our introduction we asked whether you should include broader worldwide opportunities in your career objectives. No attempt has been made to write a definitive article on international hotel management. However, we are providing an insight which is intended to be thought provoking yet practical for anyone considering an international assignment in hotel management.